EDNOS: Eating Disorders Not Otherwise Specified

Eating Disorders Not Otherwise Specified covers all eating disorders that do not fall into either of the two main diagnostic groups: Anorexia Nervosa and Bulimia Nervosa. Although these less well known conditions are common and can be very severe, they are often neglected.

This book brings together contributions from many of the leading researchers and practitioners in the field of eating disorders and presents the topic of EDNOS from a range of perspectives including the clinical, the epidemiological, the nosological, the biological and the transcultural. Subjects covered include:

- History of the classification of eating disorders
- Clarifying the nature of EDNOS: cluster analysis, diagnosis and comorbidity
- How family and twin studies inform the developing nosology of eating disorders
- EDNOS: a neurodevelopmental perspective

This comprehensive summary of the subject of EDNOS demonstrates that by investigating the nature, cause and treatment of these disorders, we can throw light on the classification and nature of eating disorders as a whole. It will be of great interest to all professionals in the field of eating disorders.

Claes Norring is the director of the National Resource Centre of Eating Disorders in Sweden and Associate Professor of Psychology at Örebro University.

Bob Palmer is Senior Lecturer in Psychiatry at the University of Leicester and Hon. Consultant Psychiatrist at the Leicestershire Partnership NHS Trust.

EDNOS: Eating Disorders Not Otherwise Specified

Scientific and clinical perspectives on the other eating disorders

Edited by
Claes Norring and Bob Palmer

Routledge
Taylor & Francis Group

LONDON AND NEW YORK

First published 2005 by Routledge
27 Church Road, Hove, East Sussex, BN3 2FA

Simultaneously published in the USA and Canada
by Routledge
270 Madison Avenue, New York, NY 10016

Routledge is an imprint of the Taylor & Francis Group

Typeset in Times by RefineCatch Ltd, Bungay, Suffolk
Printed and bound in Great Britain by MPG Books Ltd,
Bodmin, Cornwall
Cover design by Sandra Heath

British Library Cataloguing in Publication Data
A catalogue record for this book is available from the British Library

Library of Congress Cataloging in Publication Data
EDNOS, eating disorders not otherwise specified : scientific and
clinical perspectives on the other eating disorders / editors,
Claes Norring & Bob Palmer.
   p. cm.
  Includes bibliographical references and index.
  1. Eating disorders.   2. Eating disorders—Classification.   I. Title:
Eating disorders not otherwise specified.   II. Norring, Claes.
III. Palmer, Robert L.   IV. Title.
  RC552.E18E34 2005
  616.85′26–dc22   2004021432

ISBN 1-58391-163-4 hbk

Contents

Figures

Contributors

Charles B. Anderson, PhD, Post-doctoral Fellow, Department of Psychiatry, University of North Carolina, Chapel Hill, NC, USA.

Stephanie Bauer, Dipl Psych, Research Assistant, Center for Psychotherapy Research, Stuttgart, Germany.

Katarzyna Bisaga, MD, Assistant Professor of Clinical Psychiatry, Department of Child Psychiatry, Columbia University, New York, USA.

Cynthia M. Bulik, PhD, William R. and Jeanne H. Jordan Distinguished Professor of Eating Disorders, Departments of Psychiatry and Nutrition, University of North Carolina, Chapel Hill, NC, USA.

Eric Button, PhD, Consultant Clinical Psychologist, Leicestershire Partnership NHS Trust and the University of Leicester, UK.

David Clinton, PhD, Clinical Psychologist, Research Fellow, Member Swedish Psychoanalytic Society, Karolinska Institutet, Neurotec Department, Division for Psychiatry, Stockholm, Sweden.

David Collier, PhD, Professor, Institute of Psychiatry, London, UK.

Alexandra E. Dingemans, MA, National Center for Eating Disorders, Robert-Fleury Stichting, Leidschendam, The Netherlands.

Eric F. van Furth, PhD, National Center for Eating Disorders, Robert-Fleury Stichting, Leidschendam, The Netherlands.

Patricia van Hanswijck de Jonge, PhD, Research Associate, MEDTAP International Inc., London, UK.

Melissa Hart, Bachelor of Health Sciences (Nutrition and Dietetics), Accredited Practicing Dietitian, Child and Adolescent Mental Health Nutrition Consultant, Child and Adolescent Mental Health Statewide Network (CAMHSNET), John Hunter Hospital, NSW, Australia.

Hans Kordy, DrPhil, Dipl-Math, Co-Director, Center for Psychotherapy Research, Stuttgart, Germany.

Kathleen Kwok, MSSc, Clinical Psychologist, Hong Kong Eating Disorders Center, The Chinese University of Hong Kong, Hong Kong, China.

Sing Lee, MBBS FRC Psych, Professor, Department of Psychiatry, Faculty of Medicine, The Chinese University of Hong Kong, Hong Kong, China.

Rebecca Murphy, MA(Oxon), Psychologist in Clinical Training, Section of Eating Disorders, Institute of Psychiatry, London, UK.

Dasha Nicholls, MBBS MD, Consultant Child and Adolescent Psychiatrist and Honorary Senior Lecturer, Great Ormond Street Hospital and the Institute of Child Health, London, UK.

Claes Norring, DMSc, Associate Professor, Director, National Resource Centre for Eating Disorders (NÄT), Psychiatric Research Centre, Örebro County Council and Department of Behavioral, Social, and Legal Sciences (Psychology), Örebro University, Örebro, Sweden.

Kenneth Nunn, MBBS (Hons) FRANZCP FRCPsych PhD, Professor, Director of Nexus, Director of CAMHSNET, Nexus Child and Adolescent Inpatient Psychiatric Unit, CAMHSNET, John Hunter Hospital, NSW, Australia.

Bob Palmer, MD, Senior Lecturer in Psychiatry, Hon. Consultant Psychiatrist, University Department of Health Sciences (Psychiatry), University of Leicester, UK.

Sarah Perkins, BSc, Research Psychologist, Section of Eating Disorders, Institute of Psychiatry, London, UK.

Robert Peveler, MA, DPhil, BM, BCh, Professor of Psychiatry, University of Southampton Mental Health Group, Community Clinical Sciences Division, Southampton, UK.

Matthias Richard, DrPhil, Dipl-Psych, Institut für Psychotherapie und Medizinische Psychologie, Universität Würzburg, Würzburg, Germany.

Ulrike Schmidt, MD, Reader in Eating Disorders, Section of Eating Disorders, Institute of Psychiatry and Maudsley Hospital, Eating Disorders Outpatients, London, UK.

Jorunn Sundgot-Borgen, MS, PhD, Professor, Department of Sports Medicine, Norwegian University of Sport and Physical Education (NUSPE) and Olympic Training Center, Oslo, Norway.

Janet Treasure, MD, Professor, Institute of Psychiatry, London, UK.

Hannah Turner, DClinPsych, Clinical Psychologist, University of Southampton Mental Health Group, Community Clinical Sciences Division, Southampton, UK.

Glenn Waller, DPhil, Consultant Clinical Psychologist, Professor, South West London and St George's Mental Health NHS Trust and St George's Hospital Medical School, London, UK.

B. Timothy Walsh, MD, Ruane Professor of Psychiatry, Department of Psychiatry, College of Physicians & Surgeons, Columbia University and New York State Psychiatric Institute, New York, USA.

Martina de Zwaan, MD, Professor, Department of Psychosomatics and Psychotherapy, University Hospital Erlangen, Erlangen, Germany.

Acknowledgements

We would like to thank all those who have contributed to this book; the authors who have been cooperative and patient throughout the too long process of compiling the book; our editorial contacts at Routledge, Joanne Forshaw, Dawn Harris and Claire Lipscomb, who have given us invaluable support and advice and also extended the deadline for the manuscript longer than they really wanted to; and, last but not least, our secretaries, Debra Bugler and Annika Karlsson, without whose assistance the completion of the book would not have come about.

Abbreviations

AA	Anorexia Athletica
AN	Anorexia Nervosa
APA	American Psychiatric Association
BED	Binge Eating Disorder
BMI	Body Mass Index
BN	Bulimia Nervosa
BN-NP	Bulimia Nervosa Non-Purging type
BN-P	Bulimia Nervosa Purging type
CBT	Cognitive Behavioural Therapy
CEDRI	Clinical Eating Disorders Rating Instrument
CF	Cystic Fibrosis
CGI	Clinical Global Impression
CNS	Central Nervous System
CSF	Cerebrospinal Fluid
DSM-III-R	*Diagnostic and Statistical Manual of Mental Disorders* – third edition revised
DSM-IV	*Diagnostic and Statistical Manual of Mental Disorders* – fourth edition
DZ	Dizygotic
EAT	Eating Attitudes Test
ED	Eating Disorder
EDE	Eating Disorder Examination
EDI	Eating Disorder Inventory
EDNOS	Eating Disorder Not Otherwise Specified
FAED	Food Avoidance Emotional Disorder
GAD	Generalized Anxiety Disorder
IBW	Ideal Body Weight
ICD-10	International Classification of Disease – tenth version
IPT	Interpersonal Psychotherapy
MD	Major Depression
MZ	Monozygotic
NES	Night Eating Syndrome

OCD	Obsessive-Compulsive Disorder
OCPD	Obsessive-Compulsive Personality Disorder
RAB	Rating of Anorexia and Bulimia
RDC	Research Diagnostic Criteria
SASB	Structural Analysis of Social Behaviour
SCL	Symptom Check List
SSRI	Selective Serotonin Reuptake Inhibitor
T1DM	Type 1 Diabetes Mellitus
TFEQ	Three-Factor Eating Questionnaire
VLCD	Very Low Calorie Diets
WHO	World Health Organization

Chapter 1

EDNOS – the other eating disorders

Bob Palmer and Claes Norring

Introduction

Eating Disorders Not Otherwise Specified (EDNOS) is a category in the classification of mental disorders in the fourth edition of the *Diagnostic and Statistical Manual of Mental Disorders* (DSM-IV) of the American Psychiatric Association (APA 1994). It is the category to which eating disorders are assigned if they fail to fulfil diagnostic criteria for one of the major eating disorders, Anorexia Nervosa (AN) and Bulimia Nervosa (BN). On the face of it, this would seem to be an unpromising, even an eccentric topic for a whole book. Surely, it is an esoteric subject. Indeed, something like that was the first reaction of publishers when we proposed this book. However, the reactions of many of our colleagues – clinicians and researchers in the field of the eating disorders – were quite different. They recognized both the importance of the subject and its relative neglect hitherto. But why is a minor category in the classification of the eating disorders worthy of such interest and attention?

First, EDNOS is a minor category only in the sense that it is the residual category in the classification dominated by the two major disorders. It lacks formal criteria except that a state thus categorized must be an eating disorder of clinical significance that does not match the criteria for the two main disorders. Thus it is defined mainly by what it is not. It is a "rag-bag" or "catch-all" category without clearly specified positive criteria. So why is it inappropriate to think of this as a minor category? The simple answer is that EDNOS is often the commonest diagnosis in clinical practice. Far from being a minor category, EDNOS is a major issue. Indeed, sometimes patients thus diagnosed not only form the biggest single category but also may even comprise the overall majority of people with significant eating disorders presenting for help (Fairburn *et al.* 2003; Turner and Bryant-Waugh 2004).

Second, the fact that the residual category in a classificatory system proves to be so large and important raises questions about the validity and utility of that system and the categories that it contains. It is these questions that this book will address.

Classification

Classification is essential for thought. We can get to grips with the world only by the use of words and categories. Ambiguity may be a source of delight and insight in poetry and literature but language needs some precision for empirical and scientific work. For such purposes, a classification should provide a set of categories that are mutually exclusive and collectively exhaustive. In other words the categories should not overlap but together they should cover the ground. Our classificatory systems for eating disorders meet these criteria poorly and do so at all only by means of the use of the residual EDNOS category (Palmer 2003). This is not especially unusual. Many classifications of diseases and disorders have recourse to the use of a residual category to catch those cases that do not fit any of the closely defined states. However, it is unusual for such a residual category to be the largest group as is the case with the clinical eating disorders. What does this say about our classificatory systems? Surely the conclusion must be that they are unsatisfactory (Nielsen and Palmer 2003).

The two main classificatory systems relevant to the eating disorders are the *Diagnostic and Statistical Manual* of the American Psychiatric Association, for which the present version is the fourth edition (DSM-IV), and the International Classification of Disease (ICD) by the World Health Organization (WHO), for which the present version is the tenth version (ICD-10: WHO 1992). (For the full diagnostic criteria sets for eating disorders in DSM-IV and ICD-10, see the Appendix.) The two systems are similar but not identical. Both contain criteria for the two main disorders – AN and BN. However, they deal differently with the issue of potential overlap between the two diagnoses. Thus, ICD-10 would categorize a disorder with binge eating at very low weight as BN whereas in DSM-IV such a case would be assigned to a subdivision of AN, namely the binge-purging type. This issue of overlap has been dealt with differently in the revisions of the systems over the years. Thus for instance, the DSM revision before the present version, DSM-III-R (APA 1987), would have given such a case the dual diagnoses of both AN and BN. The details of these changes are interesting and may be illuminating. The history and development of our present systems are described and discussed by Bisaga and Walsh in Chapter 2.

It is not only the classificatory criteria that change over time. So do individual people and their disorders. People who suffer from an eating disorder of clinical severity but which fulfils criteria for neither AN nor BN are to be diagnosed at the point of study as suffering from EDNOS. However, some may well have fulfilled such criteria in the past and may do so again in the future. There is much variation over time. This change is the focus of Chapter 6 by Bauer, Richard, Kordy and the COST Action B6 Project. Their work, together with that of others, provides evidence that people who have had one of the two main syndromes may move into a position where they no longer fulfil the relevant criteria but nevertheless remain clinically eating disordered. Thus, AN or BN may change into EDNOS and indeed vice versa. Furthermore, it is certainly possible that this state of EDNOS is not at all trivial, either in respect of severity or duration. EDNOS is not necessarily or even usually a transient state or one of partial recovery although it sometimes may be. Our naming of syndromes and disorders needs to take account of this. Thus, a young woman who has had inpatient treatment for AN restricting subtype may no longer fulfil all of the criteria for the disorder when she leaves hospital with some continuing attitudinal and behavioural symptoms but at a normal weight; for most purposes it would not be useful to have to rediagnose her as suffering from EDNOS. She is better described as having AN in partial – and perhaps temporary – remission (Kordy *et al.* 2002). However, what if she remains stuck in that position – significantly eating disordered but not fulfilling criteria for AN or indeed BN – for the next five years? How should that state be described? And if someone had been in an identical state for a similar length of time but had never fulfilled criteria for AN, is she to be thought of as having the same disorder or a different one?

There is another perspective involving time and indeed geography. The eating disorder syndromes that form the basis of our nosology are the products of twentieth-century "Western" thought. Are they applicable to historical cases from earlier centuries or to present-day sufferers in other cultures? Will they remain useful as the twenty-first century progresses or will different patterns of disorder emerge? Presumably many disorders and diseases remain essentially the same over time. Malaria, sarcoma or phobic anxiety may have been thought about differently over the years but are unlikely to have changed in themselves. However, there has been speculation that the eating disorders may have changed over time in respect of some of their features that have often been thought of as essential (Russell 2004). For instance, the early accounts of AN in the nineteenth century did not include any emphasis upon body weight concern (Palmer 1993; Russell 1995). Furthermore, Lee and colleagues from China have reported that many contemporary cases of "AN" lack the weight-related psychopathology specified and indeed required by the usual criteria (Lee *et al.* 1993). Strictly, Lee's cases should be described as EDNOS rather than AN. Lee and Kwok discuss some of the issues arising from these and other observations in Chapter 10.

Our classificatory systems are also less than satisfactory when used to consider the youngest sufferers from eating disorders. The eating disorders as they are seen in children and early adolescents commonly fail to fit easily the diagnostic categories developed for adults. Nicolls discusses this perspective in Chapter 12. The disorders arising in other more particular populations also challenge the adequacy of our usual concepts. Thus, eating disorders may be different when they occur in athletes, discussed in Chapter 13 by Sundgot-Borgen, or in people with diabetes mellitus, discussed in Chapter 14 Peveler and Turner. In Chapter 15 Nunn and Hart discuss the many varied eating disturbances that may occur with a variety of mainly neuropsychiatric disorders, many of which are not usually thought of as eating disorders.

But what is an eating disorder? EDNOS is defined as any eating disorder of clinical significance that is not either AN or BN. However, this begs the question of what is an eating disorder and, of course, what is clinical significance. The latter problem is shared with many other disorders where the defining characteristics occur in a continuous spectrum from the unequivocally normal to the unequivocally morbid. For instance, just how anxious do you have to be to have an anxiety disorder? Ideas of personal or social impairment would seem to be relevant. However, with the eating disorders there is some uncertainty about what kind of features are necessary or sufficient for a state to be described as an eating disorder. Certainly, some disorders with notable impairment of weight and eating are usually left out. Thus, most clinicians would wish to exclude from being diagnosed as having an eating disorder someone who is eating little and losing weight as a consequence of a severe depressive illness. However, someone with AN may have comorbid depression, so is it their ideas that allow them into the diagnosis? But what if the sufferer is from China and does not have the typical psychopathology? What is *essential* to the diagnosis of an eating disorder? It is tempting to fall back on statements such as "we all know one when we see one" but such a stand is hardly rigorous. However, definitions too have their problems and there have been rather few attempts to produce a definition of eating disorders as such. One has been produced by Fairburn and Walsh (2002), who suggest that:

> an eating disorder be defined as a persistent disturbance of eating or eating-related behaviour that results in the altered consumption or absorption of food and that significantly impairs physical health or psychosocial functioning. This disturbance should not be secondary to any recognized general medical disorder or any other psychiatric disorder.
>
> (Fairburn and Walsh 2002: 171)

We suggest that readers keep this definition in mind and test it out against the issues and observations discussed in this volume. How well does it serve? Can we do better?

Thus, the classification of the eating disorders is unsatisfactory in many ways. Clearly, the concepts of AN and BN have value and cannot be dismissed. However, it may be that these two main disorders are better thought of as archetypes rather than as clear categories. The third category EDNOS therefore becomes a reservoir that contains what is left over once cases that match these archetypes have been siphoned off. The study of all of the cases that fall into the EDNOS category should pay dividends. It could tell us something about the main disorders and about the nature of eating disorders as a whole.

There are those who are radical in the face of such issues. They suggest that we may be being led astray by our use of categories rather than dimensions to describe the eating disorders. Indeed, there is much to be said for a dimensional approach. For instance, body weight – or indeed body mass index (BMI) – is clearly a continuous variable and a key issue in our field. However, medical tradition and thinking have always favoured categories and with some good reasons. A clinician finds it very useful to be able to assign a categorical diagnosis to the disorder of an individual if in doing so there is a clear implication that a particular treatment and prognosis are likely to apply. Diagnosis needs to be useful. In broad terms the two main diagnoses do live up to this standard, even if their usefulness is more contingent on the symptoms they are defined by than on the syndromes per se. Certainly for better or worse their use dominates the discourse in both clinical practice and research. However, many would argue for a greater emphasis upon dimensions or symptoms rather than upon categorical diagnoses or syndromes.

One theoretical perspective that has never put very much emphasis on traditional diagnostic categories is the psychoanalytic. In this tradition focus is most often on functional aspects of symptoms, and a diagnosis is seen as a continuously evolving hypothesis – a hypothesis that is constantly re-evaluated as treatment proceeds and new facts emerge. An example of a psychoanalytic diagnostic hypothesis encompassing all eating disorders is developed and elaborated upon by Clinton in Chapter 11.

However, most of what we claim to know about eating disorders is expressed in terms of the two main diagnoses. But what can be said about people with disorders that can be described only as EDNOS? At present the answer is rather little.

Another radical response to the problems of classification has been to accept the category of "Eating Disorders" but to eschew or at least treat as highly provisional any subdivisions within it. Fairburn et al. (2003) have put forward their so-called "transdiagnostic approach". Earlier contributions in the same spirit were provided by Waller (1993) and Beumont et al. (1994), maintaining that eating disorders should be defined as one large group based on the single feature that really differentiates them from other disorders, the preoccupation with control of eating. Within this large group, symptom dimensions rather than subcategories should be used to describe patients. In Chapter 16, Waller elaborates on this theme and on the psychological grounds for diagnosis.

Hidden beneath these discussions is an uncertainty as how to best view our diagnostic categories or indeed our dimensions. What is their status? Are they to be thought of as real entities in the real world or are they better considered as conceptual tools? Is AN something that is more than just a syndrome? Is it something whose nature can be discovered? Or is it an idea which should be judged on its utility in clarifying discourse and guiding practice. Is AN more like gout or multiple sclerosis or syphilis (disease concepts with multidimensional implications and great explanatory powers) or is it more like suicidality or backache or Munchausen's syndrome by proxy (concepts that may be important but that offer much less). We can and perhaps should duck this issue by emphasizing the provisional nature of almost all diagnoses in the field of mental health. And it is perhaps one message of this book that our diagnoses in the field of eating disorders are even more questionable and provisional than is the case with many other mental disorders.

It is possible to emerge from consideration of these issues imbued with a sense of their importance or alternatively with a view that they are mainly the preoccupations of those who have become so engrossed in the minutiae of academic study of the eating disorders that they have become detached from the real world. However, before we tell them – ourselves? – to "get a life", we should perhaps consider whether these issues and especially the neglect of EDNOS do or do not have real effects in the real world. It seems to us that they can have important influence in the real world of research and arguably also in the even more real world of clinical practice.

Research

The widespread use of operationally defined diagnostic criteria has played an important part in facilitating research into the eating disorders. Subjects for research are nearly always selected for research using criteria from the classificatory systems. Cases that do not strictly fulfil diagnostic criteria – that is, cases of EDNOS – tend to be excluded. Such strict diagnostic purity has been an important feature of research. It has been seen as a virtue. Indeed, it has had benefits. However, the cost of this practice is that there has been little study of the biggest category, EDNOS. The widespread exclusion from research of many potential subjects who have eating disorders that differ either subtly or importantly from the main diagnoses is only just being recognized as a major disadvantage for the generalization of the results of research and thus for their utility in clinical practice (Fairburn and Harrison 2003).

Furthermore, undue reliance upon a flawed classificatory system and the exclusion of cases of EDNOS may distort the range and conclusions of aetiological research. Thus, the search for genetic markers and predispositions and the attempts to define endophenotypes are likely to be impeded if only people with "typical" eating disorders are studied. Biological aspects of the eating disorder nosology are discussed in Chapter 8 by Treasure and Collier, and family/genetic aspects in Chapter 9 by Bulik and Anderson.

Clinical practice

What goes for research can also go for clinical practice. Sometimes hard-pressed services are tempted to ration treatment and one way of doing so is to limit access to people deemed to be suffering from what are thought of as "real" eating disorders. The archetypal disorders are used to define who should get services and who should not. This excludes people with EDNOS even though the one positive criterion for such a diagnosis is that the person should have a disorder *of clinical severity*. And, of course, some cases of EDNOS may be very severe indeed. However, the evidence that might support the treatment of people with EDNOS is largely absent because of the parallel exclusion of such cases from research mentioned above.

The nature of EDNOS

We consider that there is a strong case for more attention being paid to eating disorders other than AN and BN. In future our services and our research efforts should include rather than exclude the problems of people presenting with EDNOS. So what is currently known about the nature of EDNOS? As a residual category, it is to be expected that EDNOS may contain people with a variety of problems and symptoms. Some may closely resemble cases of AN or BN. Others may be quite different. Major questions arise about whether we can be confident that the borders of the two main syndromes, AN and BN, are currently drawn in the correct place. And how might we judge what is the "correct" place? What are the criteria for making that judgement? Chapter 3 by Murphy, Perkins and Schmidt describes such issues and reviews what evidence there is about how our systems work out in practice.

There is also an upsurge of research trying to establish what is the "correct" place for the borders around eating disorder categories. Since the early 1990s there has been an increasing use of old and new statistical approaches in the search for naturally occurring subgroups of eating disorders (e.g. Bulik *et al.* 2000; Crow *et al.* 2002; Gleaves *et al.* 2000; Williamson *et al.* 2002), with varying results. In Chapter 7, Clinton, Button, Norring and Palmer make their contribution to this accumulating vein of research, indicating that the main diagnoses are too narrowly defined and that the relocation of a substantial proportion of EDNOS patients into these broader categories would make sense from a clinical point of view.

It could be that in the large residual category that is EDNOS, there are additional syndromes that could and should be defined and take their place alongside AN and BN. Probably, many clinicians have their own private ideas about what such syndromes might be. However, only one has emerged into public prominence and use, namely Binge Eating Disorder (BED). DSM-IV contains the category of BED as a provisional diagnosis. It is strictly a variety of EDNOS. It was included to promote "further study". Indeed, for a variety of reasons, BED has been studied a good deal and furthermore it has been widely used as a clinical diagnosis. Even before the publication of DSM-IV there had been an enthusiastic lobby for the category and a body of research supporting its adoption. Now a decade or so on, it would seem that BED is set fair to join the canon as the third archetypal eating disorder. However, there remains controversy as to whether it is a robust and useful category (Russell 2004). The status of BED will be discussed by Dingemans, van Hanswijck de Jonge and van Furth in Chapter 4. Many of those diagnosed with BED are overweight and the eating problems of the obese are discussed by de Zwaan in Chapter 5. Indeed the relationship between obesity – a state typically excluded from consideration as an eating disorder – and the eating disorders as usually defined is itself an important issue.

Conclusion

This book is designed to promote attention to a too frequently neglected topic, EDNOS. We believe that the consideration of EDNOS is necessary because so many of our patients present with problems and disorders that can be described only in terms of that diagnosis. Furthermore, we believe that such consideration may bring benefits to the field of eating disorders in general. However, these benefits are potential and uncertain. It seems appropriate that we end this introductory chapter with a flurry of clichés. Thus, we would certainly say that "this book provides more questions than answers" and that "more research is needed". More research and more thought.

References

American Psychiatric Association (1987) *Diagnostic and Statistical Manual of Mental Disorders*, 3rd edn revised (DSM-III-R), Washington, DC: APA.

American Psychiatric Association (1994) *Diagnostic and Statistical Manual of Mental Disorders*, 4th edn (DSM-IV), Washington, DC: APA.

Beumont, P.J.V., Garner, D.M. and Tuoyz, S.W. (1994) "Diagnoses of eating or dieting disorders: what may we learn from past mistakes?", *International Journal of Eating Disorders* 16, 349–62.

Bulik, C.M., Sullivan, P.F. and Kendler, K.S. (2000) "An empirical study of the classification of eating disorders", *American Journal of Psychiatry* 157, 886–95.

Crow, S.J., Agras, W.S., Halmi, K., Mitchell, J.E. and Kraemer, H.C. (2002) "Full syndromal versus sub-threshold anorexia nervosa, bulimia nervosa, and binge eating disorder: a multicenter study", *International Journal of Eating Disorders* 32, 309–18.

Fairburn, C.G. and Harrison, P.J. (2003) "Eating disorders", *Lancet* 361, 407–16.

Fairburn, C.G. and Walsh, B.T. (2002) "Atypical eating disorders (eating disorder not otherwise specified)", in C.G. Fairburn and K.D. Brownell (eds) *Eating Disorders and Obesity: A Comprehensive Handbook*, 2nd edn, New York: Guilford Press.

Fairburn, C.G., Cooper, Z. and Shafran, R. (2003) "Cognitive behaviour therapy for eating disorders: a 'transdiagnostic' theory and treatment", *Behaviour Research and Therapy* 41, 509–28.

Gleaves, D.H., Lowe, M.R., Green, B.A., Cororve, M.B. and Williams, T.L. (2000) "Do anorexia and bulimia nervosa occur on a continuum? A taxometric analysis", *Behavior Therapy* 31, 195–219.

Kordy, H., Kramer, B., Palmer, R.L., Papezova, H., Pellet, J., Richard, M. and Treasure, J. (2002) "Remission, recovery, relapse and recurrence in eating disorders: conceptualisation and illustration of a validation strategy", *Journal of Clinical Psychology* 58, 833–46.

Lee, S., Ho, T.P. and Hsu, L.K.G. (1993) "Fat phobic and non-fat phobic anorexia nervosa: a comparative study of 70 Chinese patients in Hong Kong", *Psychological Medicine* 23, 999–1017.

Nielsen, S. and Palmer, R.L. (2003) "Diagnosing eating disorders: AN, BN and the others", *Acta Psychiatrica Scandinavica* 108, 161–2.

Palmer, R.L. (1993) "Weight concern should not be a necessary criterion for the eating disorders: a polemic", *International Journal of Eating Disorders* 14, 459–65.

Palmer, R.L. (2003) "Concepts of eating disorders", in J. Treasure, U. Schmidt and E. Van Furth (eds) *Handbook of Eating Disorders*, 2nd edn, Chichester: Wiley.

Russell, G.F.M. (1995) "Anorexia nervosa through time", in G. Szmukler, C. Dare and J. Treasure (eds) *Handbook of Eating Disorders: Theory, Treatment and Research*, New York: Wiley.

Russell, G.F.M. (2004) "Thoughts on the 25th anniversary of bulimia nervosa", *European Eating Disorders Review* 12, 139–52.

Turner, H. and Bryant-Waugh, R. (2004) "Eating disorder not otherwise specified (EDNOS): profiles of clients presenting at a community eating disorders service", *European Eating Disorders Review* 12, 18–26.

Waller, G. (1993) "Why do we diagnose different types of eating disorder? Arguments for a change in research and clinical practice", *European Eating Disorders Review* 1, 74–89.

Williamson, D.A., Womble, L.G., Smeets, M., Netemeyer, R.G., Thaw, J.M., Kutlesic, V. and Gleaves, D.H. (2002) "Latent structure of eating disorder symptoms: a factor analytic and taxometric investigation", *American Journal of Psychiatry* 159, 412–18.

World Health Organization (1992) *ICD-10 Classification of Mental and Behavioural Disorders: Clinical Descriptions and Diagnostic Guidelines*, Geneva: WHO.

Chapter 2

History of the classification of eating disorders

Katarzyna Bisaga and B. Timothy Walsh

Introduction

As described in DSM-IV, the group of eating disorders consists of Anorexia Nervosa (AN), Bulimia Nervosa (BN) and a category of Eating Disorder Not Otherwise Specified (EDNOS). The cardinal behavioural feature of AN is dietary restriction. The cardinal behavioural features of BN are binge eating and recurrent inappropriate compensatory behaviours, such as self-induced vomiting, laxative use, diuretic or diet pill use, dietary restriction and exercise to prevent weight gain. Concern about body weight is a shared psychological feature of AN and BN. EDNOS represents a heterogeneous group which includes partial syndromes of AN and BN, atypical eating disorder presentations and Binge Eating Disorder.

Epidemiological studies have found that eating disorders and eating disorder symptoms are frequent among young females in many countries. Prevalence rates of 0.5 per cent to 1 per cent for AN (Hoek 1991), of 1–3 per cent for BN (Fairburn and Beglin 1990) and of 2–3 per cent for BED (Yanovski 1998) have been reported in the United States and in Europe. However, component behaviours of eating disorders, such as dieting, binge eating and self-induced vomiting, are more frequent (Button and Whitehouse 1981; King 1989). Given these epidemiological data, the nosology and classification of eating disorders remain an important area of research with implications for detection and treatment. While current DSM-IV diagnostic criteria represent significant progress in classification of eating disorders, the nosology of these disorders remains a subject of considerable debate among researchers and clinicians. Not only epidemiological findings, but also emerging genetic and psychobiological data are likely to lead to future revisions of the diagnostic criteria.

In this chapter we first focus on AN and BN; both are considered "typical" eating disorders. Most of the research effort to improve classification has focused on these disorders. However, the history of classification of typical eating disorders is closely connected with the history of classification of EDNOS, also called "atypical" eating disorders. This is because any changes in the diagnostic criteria for typical eating disorders lead to a change in what is considered to be an atypical eating disorder. Development of refined diagnostic criteria for these "atypical" presentations of eating disorders is of great importance as these disorders are common and a substantial source of morbidity.

History of classification of Anorexia Nervosa

The descriptive period

Historically AN was certainly the first eating disorder to be recognized as a separate diagnostic entity. During the past few centuries, historians and other writers have documented food abstinence of a kind that is a cardinal feature of AN. They described this phenomenon in several contrasting ways. One was in the context of religious ascetic ideals as exemplified by miraculous maidens and fasting saints such as Saint Catherine of Sienna. Another was as the result of diabolic possession at a time when any ill health was explained by the influence of the devil. A third was as the supernatural capacity for starvation among so-called "hunger artists" who were displayed in public for monetary gains (Vandereyken and van Deth 1994). Regardless of the particular context in which self-inflicted starvation occurred, food abstinence seems to have received universal attention and awe. As AN is associated with food refusal, a behaviour which opposes a basic physical need, the lay public, media and researchers alike remain intrigued by it.

The recognition that certain types of food abstinence represent a medical problem became evident in the seventeenth century, when the English physician Richard Morton (1694) described an adolescent girl with "nervous consumption" caused by "sadness and anxious cares". Morton ruled out physical causes and underscored "nervous" causes for the observed weight loss. Two centuries later, Lasegue (1873) reported the loss of appetite as a form of "hysteria linked to hypochondriasis" and emphasized an array of emotional problems. The next year, Gull (1874) offered another detailed description of AN, which included physical symptoms such as amenorrhoea, constipation, loss of appetite, decreased vital signs and emaciation. Gull did not express any interest in emotional problems associated with disease but recommended refeeding in a highly structured setting away from familiar figures.

At the turn of the nineteenth century, both Charcot and Gille de la Tourette wrote about AN and connected this particular type of weight loss to hysteria (Lucas 1986). In 1920, Janet viewed AN as psychologically determined and distinguished primary and secondary AN. Janet considered hyperactivity as a core feature of the disease and noted "physical and moral activity" and "euphoria" which ameliorated fatigue and the need to eat (Yates 1989).

While AN was gaining recognition in Europe, a report in 1859 by an American, William Stout Chipley (Di Nicola 1990), of "sitomania" characterized by "an intense dread of food" encountered among emaciated adolescent girls in "high born families" attracted little attention by his contemporaries.

The pituitary period

A major shift in the classification of AN followed Simmonds' description of a fatal case of emaciation due to atrophy of the anterior pituitary lobe (Simmonds 1914). For the next two decades, cases of AN were considered secondary to dysfunction of anterior pituitary lobe regardless of the actual presence of pituitary dysfunction. The previously accepted view relating aetiology of the disorder to emotional problems was abandoned. Pituitary grafts and extracts became the treatment of choice. Twenty years later, in 1937, another endocrinologist, Sheehan noted that post-partum pituitary necrosis (Sheehan's syndrome) was not accompanied by weight loss (Lucas 1986). This finding challenged the assumption that weight loss is universally associated with pituitary destruction and led to the rediscovery of AN as a mental disorder.

The modern era

Once AN was rediscovered as a mental disorder, psychoanalytic writers elaborated on the previously postulated relation of food refusal to hysteria and other emotional problems. According to traditional psychoanalytic views, intra-psychic conflict results in symptom formation. Thus, food refusal was connected to unconscious fantasies and fears related to sexual wishes, in particular, wishes of oral impregnation (Waller et al. 1940).

By 1960, outside the psychoanalytic field, psychiatrists tended to use the term AN in a non-specific manner to refer to weight loss in the course of any psychological disorder (Bliss and Branch 1960). Thus, weight loss encountered in schizophrenia, depression or substance abuse disorder was called AN, even though the actual weight loss was related to symptoms as different as delusional thinking in schizophrenia, behavioural inhibition in depression, hyperactivity in mania or withdrawal symptoms in substance abuse. Clearly, these conditions should be distinguished from AN, and from each other, based on their different clinical features, course, and response to treatment and prognosis. In 1973, Hilde Bruch described primary AN in a manner consistent with current usage, namely as a mental disorder with its own characteristic psychopathology. She emphasized that food refusal and/or weight loss in the course of another psychiatric disorder, such as in schizophrenia, mania or depression, was unrelated to AN (Bruch 1973).

Bruch advanced our clinical understanding of AN by identifying three areas of concern frequently present in individuals with AN (Bruch 1973). She noted:

a disturbance of delusional proportions in the body image and body concept ... The true anorexic is identified with his [*sic*] skeleton-like appearance, denies its abnormality and actively maintains it.

(Bruch 1973: 251–2)

She also described:

a disturbance in the accuracy of the perception or cognitive interpretation of stimuli arising in the body, with failure to recognize signs of nutritional need as the most pronounced deficiency ... Awareness of hunger and appetite in the ordinary sense seems to be absent.

(Bruch 1973: 252)

Last, she added:

a paralyzing sense of ineffectiveness which pervades all thinking and activities. They experience themselves as acting only in response to demands coming from other people in situations, and not as doing things because they want to.

(Bruch 1973: 254)

Bruch was trained as a psychoanalyst, but gradually modified her treatment approach away from psychoanalysis. She moved beyond the traditional approach when she recognized that it could not adequately address the core psychopathology of AN. Bruch's recognition of the perceptual and conceptual disturbance in AN not only inspired and educated clinicians working with eating disordered individuals but also generated new lines of research. Body image disturbance was soon recognized as a core psychological symptom; subsequently, it was incorporated in accepted diagnostic criteria. Further, the recognition of a conceptual disturbance, which leads to development of faulty cognitive structures, informed psychotherapies developed specifically to treat individuals with AN.

Bruch's novel approach to the psychopathology characteristic of AN ushered in novel hypotheses related to the aetiology of the disorder. In particular, Selvini-Palazzoli (1978) in Italy and Minuchin *et al.* (1978) in the United States developed a family therapy approach. Their views were rooted in observations of dysfunctional family interactions thought to generate symptoms of AN. However, while developments in the family therapy field have offered potential therapeutic benefits, this particular approach has not altered the classification of AN.

During the 1970s, a host of studies investigating the hormonal and neuroendocrine mechanisms – including hypothalamic–pituitary relationships – were published. Katz and Weiner (1975) suggested that the origin of AN was hypothalamic immaturity. This hypothesis generated substantial research efforts, which clarified many biological abnormalities. Multiple disturbances of hypothalamic function in individuals with AN were identified, but for the most part these disturbances were found to be related simply to weight loss. A psychosocial perspective was offered by Crisp (1980), who proposed that the weight gain associated with puberty in the context of societal expectations for thinness leads to development of AN.

Gradually, a notion that a single causative mechanism led to the development of AN become obsolete and in 1982 Garfinkel and Garner proposed a multidimensional aetiological model. Their multidimensional model proposed that an array of factors interacted and contributed to the development of disorder, including individual psychological and biological vulnerability, familial factors and sociocultural influences. This multifactorial model was empirically driven and it offered a useful framework within which to integrate a vast body of research investigating different mechanisms contributing to AN (e.g. genetic, individual vulnerabilities, psychological factors, sociocultural values). This model was also clinically relevant, as patients' individual characteristics could be linked to various elements of the model. While the search for the underlying causes of AN continues to be an area of great importance, the classification of AN, as of other psychiatric disorders, has remained descriptively based and is not rooted in any aetiologic model.

Russell's diagnostic criteria for Anorexia Nervosa (1970)

In 1970, Russell made a major advance in the classification of AN when he proposed a set of diagnostic criteria for AN:

1   The patient's behaviour leads to a marked loss of body weight.
2   There is an endocrine disorder which manifests itself clinically by cessation of menstruation in females. (In males the equivalent symptom is loss of sexual appetite.)
3   There is a psychopathology characterized by a morbid fear of becoming fat.

Three aspects of the disorder were deemed diagnostically significant: self-inflicted weight loss, cessation of menses in females and decrease in libido in males, and a morbid fear of becoming fat. Russell's (1970) requirement that this constellation of symptoms be present ensured that self-inflicted weight loss related to fear of becoming fat was clearly differentiated from weight loss associated with other psychiatric disorders. Later diagnostic criteria followed Russell's recommendation by incorporating his assertion that a morbid fear of fatness be coupled with self-inflicted weight loss. Menstrual abnormality remained a more controversial issue given the variable relationship between weight loss and cessation of menses. In a majority of cases, substantial weight loss precedes the onset of menstrual abnormality, but for a group of individuals with AN the reverse is true.

Feighner's diagnostic criteria for Anorexia Nervosa (1976)

The earliest editions of the classification of mental disorders in the United States, namely DSM-I in 1952 and DSM-II in 1968, did not list criteria for eating disorders (APA 1952, 1968). In 1972, however, the growing interest in development of uniform diagnostic research criteria led to publication of research diagnostic criteria for several psychiatric disorders, including AN (Feighner *et al.* 1976).

For a diagnosis of Anorexia Nervosa, A through E were required:

A   Age of onset prior to 25.
B   Anorexia with accompanying weight loss of at least 25 per cent of original body weight.
C   A distorted, implacable attitude towards eating, food or weight that over-rides hunger, admonitions, reassurance and threats; e.g. (1) denial of illness with a failure to recognize nutritional needs, (2) apparent enjoy-ment in losing weight with overt manifestation that food refusal is a pleasurable indulgence, (3) a desired body image of extreme thinness with overt evidence that it is rewarding to the patient to achieve and maintain this state, and (4) unusual hoarding or handling of food.
D   No known medical illness that could account for the anorexia and weight loss.
E   No other known psychiatric disorder with particular reference to pri-mary affective disorders, schizophrenia, obsessive-compulsive and pho-bic neurosis. (The assumption is made that even though it may appear phobic or obsessional, food refusal alone is not sufficient to qualify for obsessive-compulsive or phobic disease.)
F   At least two of the following manifestations: (1) amenorrhoea; (2) lanugo; (3) bradycardia (persistent resting pulse of 60 or less); (4) periods of overactivity; (5) episodes of bulimia; (6) vomiting (may be self-induced).

These criteria reflected a comprehensive conceptualization of AN as a disorder characterized by the co-occurrence of physical symptoms (weight loss, amenorrhoea, lanugo, bradycardia), psychological features (distorted attitudes toward eating, food and weight) and behavioural symptoms (over-activity, bulimia and vomiting). Feighner's criteria provided examples of distorted attitudes toward eating, and also food and weight, defined the degree of weight loss required (25 per cent of original body weight) and added the exclusion criterion of weight loss due to medical illness, and following up on Russell's work incorporated amenorrhoea.

While Feighner's criteria represented a significant achievement in the classification of AN, several elements were problematic. For example, the age of onset prior to 25 is controversial; even though AN typically begins in adolescence, new onset later in life is widely recognized. Similarly, the requirement of a 25 per cent weight loss was quite severe, and excluded individuals who failed to gain weight when developmentally expected.

DSM-III criteria for Anorexia Nervosa (1980)

In 1980, AN finally made its way into the DSM (DSM-III: APA 1980). Given its typical onset during adolescence, AN appeared in the section on "Disorders usually first evident in infancy, childhood, or adolescence" along with Bulimia, Pica and Rumination Disorder of Infancy. The following criteria were required:

A   Intense fear of becoming obese, which does not diminish as weight loss progresses.
B   Disturbance of body image, e.g. claiming to "feel fat" even when emaciated.
C   Weight loss of at least 25 per cent of original body weight or, if under 18 years of age, weight loss from original body weight plus projected weight gain expected from growth charts may be combined to make the 25 per cent.
D   Refusal to maintain body weight over a minimal normal weight for age and height.
E   No known physical illness that would account for the weight loss.

The DSM-III relied on previously published diagnostic criteria but with a degree of refinement. For example, the DSM-III appeared to follow the required weight loss criterion of Feighner *et al.* (1976) of 25 per cent, but developmental aspects of weight loss were now added as listed in Criterion C. The age of onset was no longer included as it had no diagnostic specificity. While fear of becoming fat was not included in Feighner's criteria, the DSM-III followed Russell's diagnosis of AN and included this symptom in Criterion A. The DSM-III also followed Feighner *et al.*'s (1976) requirement that "distorted attitudes toward weight" be present and this item was included in Criterion B ("disturbance of body image"). "Refusal to maintain body weight over a minimal normal weight for age and height" was added (Criterion D). Out of the five criteria required by the DSM-III for the diagnosis, the first two symptoms listed cover the psychological symptoms of AN, namely fear of becoming fat and disturbance of body image. These were followed by the weight-related criteria namely weight loss, refusal to maintain the body weight over a minimum normal weight and the exclusion criterion of weight loss due to medical illness. Unlike Russell (1970) and Feighner *et al.* (1976), the DSM-III did not include amenorrhoea.

DSM-III-R criteria for Anorexia Nervosa (1987)

In 1987, the DSM-III-R (APA 1987) provided a major refinement of previous criteria:

A   Refusal to maintain body weight over a minimal normal weight for age and height, e.g. weight loss leading to maintenance of body weight 15 per cent below that expected; or failure to make expected weight gain during period of growth, leading to body weight 15 per cent below that expected.

B   Intense fear of gaining weight or becoming fat, even though underweight.

C   Disturbance in the way in which one's body weight, size or shape is experienced, e.g. the person claims to "feel fat" even when emaciated, believes that one area of the body is "too fat" even when obviously underweight.

D   In females, absence of at least three consecutive menstrual cycles when otherwise expected to occur (primary or secondary amenorrhoea). (A woman is considered to have amenorrhoea if her periods occur only following hormone administration, e.g. oestrogen.)

AN was moved out of the section "Disorders usually first evident in infancy, childhood, or adolescence" and placed in a separate section called "Eating disorders". In the DSM-III-R several changes were introduced. First, the weight loss criterion was revised to include "refusal to maintain body weight over a minimal normal weight for age and height, e.g. weight loss leading to maintenance of body weight 15 per cent below that expected". This criterion was given more emphasis as it appeared at the top of the list (Criterion A). Second, two psychological symptoms, namely fear of becoming fat (Criterion B) and disturbance related to weight, size and shape (Criterion C), followed the weight loss criterion. Third, the exclusion criterion of weight loss related to medical illness was removed. Fourth, following Russell's (1970) recommendation, a requirement that three consecutive menstrual cycles be absent, when otherwise expected to occur, was added. The development of secondary amenorrhoea related to disordered eating patterns and abnormal body attitudes had been well recognized, but the inclusion of both primary and secondary amenorrhoea was more controversial. Indeed, some individuals with AN may experience delayed puberty and primary amenorrhoea, but other medical causes of primary amenorrhoea unrelated to AN or weight loss must be considered.

DSM-IV criteria for Anorexia Nervosa (1994)

In 1994, the DSM-IV (APA 1994) followed to a large extent the previous edition of the DSM in defining the criteria for AN:

A   Refusal to maintain body weight at or above a minimally normal weight for age and height (e.g. weight loss leading to maintenance of body weight less than 85 per cent of that expected; or failure to make expected weight gain during period of growth, leading to body weight less than 85 per cent of that expected).

B   Intense fear of gaining weight or becoming fat, even though underweight.

C   Disturbance in the way in which one's body weight or shape is experienced, undue influence of body weight or shape on self-evaluation, denial of the seriousness of the current low body weight.

D   In postmenarcheal females, amenorrhoea, i.e. the absence of at least three consecutive menstrual cycles. (A woman is considered to have amenorrhoea if her periods occur only following hormone administration, e.g. oestrogen.)

Specify type:

*   Restricting type: during the current episode of Anorexia Nervosa, the person has not regularly engaged in binge eating or purging behaviour (i.e. self-induced vomiting or the misuse of laxatives, diuretics or enemas).
*   Binge eating/purging type: during the current episode of Anorexia Nervosa, the person has regularly engaged in binge eating or purging behaviour (i.e. self-induced vomiting or misuse of laxatives, diuretics or enemas).

It did, however, utilize a novel diagnostic concept of subtyping individuals with AN. This change reflected a growing body of clinical and research evidence that individuals with AN tend to dichotomize based on their clinical presentation and that this, in turn, has impact on response to treatment and prognosis (Beumont 1977; Casper *et al.* 1980). Two subtypes were included: the restricting type without any binge eating or purging and the binge eating/purging type with binge eating and/or purging behaviour. This new classification replaced an earlier practice of giving a dual diagnosis of AN and BN to individuals with AN who engage in binge eating.

In addition, two criteria were reworded. Criterion C was broadened to include more comprehensive descriptions of body image disturbance. Previously this criterion emphasized only one aspect of body image disturbance, e.g. "feeling fat" and "believing that one area of the body is too fat". Now other manifestations, such as "undue influence of body weight or shape on self-evaluation" and "denial of the seriousness of current low body weight" were added. Also Criterion D, a menstrual item, was clarified to include only secondary amenorrhoea.

ICD-10 diagnostic criteria for Anorexia Nervosa (1992)

The International Classification of Diseases published by the WHO offered diagnostic criteria for mental and behavioural disorders in parallel to DSM:
For a definite diagnosis, all the following are required:

(a) Body weight is maintained at least 15 per cent below that expected (either lost or never achieved), or Quetelet's body mass index is 17.5 or less. Pre-pubertal patients may show failure to make the expected weight gain during the period of growth.

(b) The weight loss is self-induced by avoidance of "fattening foods" and one or more of the following: self-induced vomiting; self-induced purging; excessive exercise; use of appetite suppressants and/or diuretics.

(c) There is body image distortion in the form of a specific psychopathology whereby a dread of fatness persists as an intrusive, overvalued idea and the patient imposes a low weight threshold on himself or herself.

(d) A widespread endocrine disorder involving the hypothalamic–pituitary–gonadal axis is manifest in women as amenorrhoea and in men as a loss of sexual interest and potency. (An apparent exception is the persistence of vaginal bleeds in anorectic women who are receiving replacement hormonal therapy, most commonly taken as a contraceptive pill.) There may also be elevated levels of growth hormone, raised levels of cortisol, changes in the peripheral metabolism of the thyroid hormone, and abnormalities of insulin secretion.

(e) If onset is pre-pubertal, the sequence of pubertal event is delayed or even arrested (growth ceases; in girls the breasts do not develop and there is a primary amenorrhoea; in boys the genitals remain juvenile). With recovery, puberty is often completed normally, but the menarche is late.

However, comparisons between the DSM and ICD are complicated (First and Pincus 1999). The ICD has multiple versions developed for different purposes, including the Clinical Descriptions and Diagnostic Guidelines version intended for "general clinical educational and service use" and the research diagnostic criteria (RDC) version intended for "research use only".

The most current version, the ICD-10 (WHO 1992), listed AN along with other eating disorders in the section "Behavioural syndromes associated with physiological disturbances and physical factors". The Clinical Description and Diagnostic Guidelines version offered diagnostic guidelines comparable to the DSM-III-R and the DSM-IV criteria for AN. Similarly to the DSM-III-R criterion, ICD-10 stipulated in Criterion (a) body weight 15 per cent below that expected but an alternative of a body mass index of 17.5 kg/m^2 or less was added. Weight control behaviours driven by the fear of fatness listed in Criterion (b) had no equivalent in the DSM. Compared with the DSM-III-R and the DSM-IV, Criterion (c) describing body image distortion emphasized "dread of fatness" as opposed to the more general self-evaluative aspects of body image distortion (Criterion D). Criterion (d) mentioned endocrine disorder of hypothalamic–pituitary–gonadal axis manifest as amenorrhoea, corresponding to Criterion D in the DSM-III-R and DSM-IV. Unlike the DSM, a separate provision for males recognized the endocrine disorder as "loss of sexual interest and potency". Also unlike the DSM, Criterion (e) addresses the issue of pre-pubertal onset in both genders.

ICD-10 research diagnostic criteria for Anorexia Nervosa (1993)

The RDC version (WHO 1993) offered diagnostic criteria for AN similar to the Clinical Descriptions and Diagnostic Guidelines version:

A   There is weight loss or, in children, a lack of weight gain, leading to a body weight at least 15 per cent below the normal or expected weight for age and height.

B   The weight loss is self-induced by avoidance of "fattening foods".

C   There is self-perception of being too fat, with an intrusive dread of fatness, which leads to a self-imposed low weight threshold.

D   A widespread endocrine disorder involving the hypothalamic–pituitary–gonadal axis is manifest in women as amenorrhoea and in men as a loss of sexual interest and potency. (An apparent exception is the persistence of vaginal bleeds in anorexic women who are on replacement hormonal therapy, most commonly taken as a contraceptive pill.)

E   The disorder does not meet criteria A and B for Bulimia Nervosa.

Comments

The following features support the diagnosis, but are not essential elements: self-induced vomiting, self-induced purging, excessive exercise, and use of appetite suppressants and/or diuretics.

If onset is pre-pubertal, the sequence of pubertal events is delayed or even arrested (growth ceases; in girls the breasts do not develop and there is a primary amenorrhoea; in boys the genitals remain juvenile). With recovery, puberty is often completed normally, but the menarche is late.

The two versions differ only with respect to the exclusion criterion E which required that Criterion A (recurrent episodes of overeating at least twice a week over a period of three months) and B (persistent preoccupation with eating, and a strong desire to eat) for BN should not be met. This requirement runs contrary to the DSM-IV recognition of subtypes of AN with restricting and binge eating/purging types. The RCD of ICD-10 thus precludes a diagnosis of AN in an individual with required weight loss of 15 per cent below the norm who would have met all the other criteria of AN, but also engaged in binge-eating episodes. In DSM-IV such an individual would receive a diagnosis of AN, binge/purge type.

Future directions

While the diagnostic criteria for AN are largely agreed upon, several points continue to generate discussion. The requirement that amenorrhoea be present remains controversial, given the variable relation of weight loss to secondary amenorrhoea (Devlin et al. 1989) and reports of patients with regular menses who appear to otherwise closely resemble patients with the full syndrome of AN (Garfinkel et al. 1996). On the other hand, the resumption of menses, regardless of the weight stabilization, has been suggested as a marker of psychological recovery (Falk and Halmi 1982). Additionally, Andersen (1995) has argued that an equivalent criterion should be provided for males, such as lowered testosterone level with loss of libido. This would be a significant change for the DSM system, as the results of laboratory testing are not generally employed as criteria. The subtyping scheme introduced in DSM-IV appears useful, but a thorough evaluation of its utility and of possible alternatives would be worthwhile.

A persistent challenge in the definition of AN is what degree of underweight should be the minimum required for the diagnosis, and whether a substantial weight loss, even in the absence of becoming underweight (for example, from 100 kg to 50 kg), should suffice. There may be no ideal solution to this challenge, given the variation among individuals in what constitutes normal body weight and the impressive changes in weight and body composition typically present in adolescence. Although not widely appreciated, the DSM-IV attempts to deal with the inherent difficulty in judging the normality of weight by suggesting ("e.g. weight loss leading to maintenance of body weight less than 85 per cent of that expected") rather than mandating an absolute amount. In any case, it would be useful for the DSM to move to a metric guideline (i.e. a body mass index).

Finally, more effort may be required in clearly articulating the psychological characteristics required for the diagnosis. The history of the definition of AN clearly indicates that a specific psychopathology is an important diagnostic criterion. However, as the illness persists, the nature of the psychopathology and patients' ability to acknowledge it vary. Some patients, while clearly exhibiting stereotypic features of AN for years, vehemently deny that they are afraid of gaining weight. DSM-IV's decision to incorporate three related but distinct expressions of psychological disturbance related to weight loss as listed in Criterion C reflects an inherent difficulty of capturing the psychopathology in a few words. It is noteworthy that, after several centuries of effort, a simple, concise and universally accepted articulation of the core psychopathology of AN has not been developed.

History of classification of Bulimia Nervosa

Historical background

Based on the Greek words *bous* and *limos*, "bulimia" implies either an appetite as large as an ox or the ability to consume an ox. Since ancient times, historical sources have mentioned bulimia as a state of a ravenous hunger associated with prolonged food deprivation. In addition, bulimia was used to describe Roman patricians practising induced emesis between banquet courses. During medieval times with insecure food supplies, uncontrolled eating known as gluttony occurred when food availability increased. Miraculous maidens and fasting girls practised self-induced vomiting in the context of prolonged food abstinence. In the nineteenth century, clinicians described cases of voracious appetite among individuals with organic central nervous system (CNS) pathology and among individuals with diabetes mellitus. At the beginning of the twentieth century, bulimia as an anomaly of satiation was attributed to hysteria and neurasthenia, or alternatively to emotional deprivation and psychosocial maladjustment. Periodic loss of control over eating and self-induced vomiting were described as associated features of AN, as for example in a well-known case of Ellen West in 1944 (Jackson *et al.* 1990). In 1959, interest in eating patterns associated with obesity led Stunkard (1959) to describe two syndromes of episodic overeating: "Night Eating Syndrome" and "Binge Eating Syndrome". The first was observed mostly in women and was characterized by morning anorexia followed by evening hyperphagia and insomnia. The syndrome seemed to be precipitated by stressful life situations. Overeating occurred daily until the stress was relieved and was not usually associated with self-condemnation. The second, "Binge Eating Syndrome", was characterized by the sudden, compulsive ingestion of very large amounts of food in a short time, usually with subsequent discomfort and self-condemnation. Bouts of overeating were linked to specific stressful precipitating circumstances and had a dissociated-like quality. Ingestion of food usually had personalized, symbolic meaning.

The modern era

Hilde Bruch described bulimic symptoms among her cases of AN (Bruch 1973). She also identified binge eating in a number of obese individuals. While many of her patients fitted Stunkard's (1959) description of Binge Eating Syndrome, she felt that the Night Eating Syndrome was very rare (Bruch 1973). Following Bruch's observations, others reported bulimic symptoms to be present in clinical samples of AN (e.g. Beumont 1977; Casper *et al.* 1980).

Russell's diagnostic criteria for Bulimia Nervosa (1979)

In 1979, Russell generated a more systematic approach to classification of bulimia with his publication of a case series of 30 individuals showing a syndrome which he named Bulimia Nevosa (BN). In this seminal contribution, he provided a detailed clinical description of psychological symptoms, abnormal behaviours and physical symptoms associated with this disorder. Russell (1979) noted that a number of patients had histories of AN. He compared individuals with BN to individuals with AN to delineate the relation of these disorders. If present in individuals with BN, the degree of weight loss was significantly less pronounced than seen in AN. Interestingly, Russell felt that BN represented an ominous variant of AN and carried a worse prognosis than uncomplicated AN. Based on this case series, Russell (1979) proposed diagnostic criteria:

1   The patients suffer from powerful and intractable urges to overeat.
2   They seek to avoid the "fattening" effects of food by inducing vomiting or abusing purgatives or both.
3   They have a morbid fear of becoming fat.

The last criterion was shared with AN. The proposed combination of symptoms became accepted as a diagnostic standard.

DSM-III criteria for Bulimia (1980)

As mentioned earlier, early editions of the DSM did not list eating disorders. Bulimia made its way into the DSM in 1980 (DSM-III: APA 1980). Given its typical onset during the adolescence and early adulthood, Bulimia appeared in the section on "Disorders usually first evident in infancy, childhood, or adolescence" along with AN, Pica and Rumination Disorder of Infancy:

A   Recurrent episodes of binge eating (rapid consumption of a large amount of food in a discrete period of time, usual less than two hours).
B   At least three of the following:
  1   consumption of high-calorie, easily ingested food during a binge
  2   inconspicuous eating during a binge
  3   termination of such eating episodes by abdominal pain, sleep, social interruption or self-induced vomiting
  4   repeated attempts to lose weight by severely restrictive diets, self-induced vomiting, or use of cathartics or diuretics
  5   frequent weight fluctuations greater than ten pounds due to alternating binges and fasts.

C   Awareness that the eating pattern is abnormal and fear of not being able to stop eating voluntarily.
D   Depressed mood and self-depreciating thoughts following eating binges.
E   The bulimic episodes are not due to Anorexia Nervosa or any known physical disorder.

The DSM-III deviated somewhat from Russell's criteria by emphasizing the importance of binge eating as a core symptom of the disorder, hence the name Bulimia and not Bulimia Nervosa. Out of five criteria, four provided a detailed description of binge-eating episodes and their associated features that were deemed to be diagnostically significant. Awareness that the eating pattern was abnormal accompanied by the fear of not been able to stop eating voluntarily (Criterion C) and depressed mood and self-depreciating thoughts associated with eating binges were required (Criterion D). While many patients described depressed mood following a binge-eating episode and a sense that eating pattern was abnormal, the diagnostic significance of these symptoms remained unclear. Weight control behaviours were included as one of five symptoms listed in Criterion B, but the DSM-III required any three of these five symptoms for the diagnosis. Thus weight control behaviours were not a necessary requirement. Likewise a core psychological feature, namely, fear of fatness was not required. "Undue concerns with body image" were mentioned as an associated feature in the text, but were not considered to be of diagnostic significance. Thus, this set of criteria identified individuals with bulimic symptoms who presented with binge eating and possibly purging behaviours, but not necessarily with morbid fear of fatness and/ or body image disturbance. For example, an individual who overate in the context of a depressive disorder but experienced no body image concerns would have met the DSM-III criteria for Bulimia. Because a heterogeneous group of individuals could be included, this set of diagnostic criteria posed questions regarding both treatment and research applications. In epidemiological research, these broad diagnostic criteria yielded high prevalence rates (Halmi *et al.* 1981). Similar limitations applied to treatment trials. Some of the conflicting findings regarding the effectiveness of antidepressants might have been due to diagnostic confusion created by criteria, which allowed the inclusion of individuals with bulimic symptoms but not BN as we would now define it.

DSM-III-R criteria for Bulimia Nervosa (1987)

The DSM-III-R (APA 1987) represented major progress in the classification of the disorder:

A   Recurrent episodes of binge eating (rapid consumption of a large amount of food in a discrete period of time).

B   A feeling of lack of control over eating behaviour during the eating binges.
C   The person regularly engages in either self-induced vomiting, use of laxatives or diuretics, strict dieting or fasting, or vigorous exercise in order to prevent weight gain.
D   A minimum average of two binge-eating episodes a week for at least three months.
E   Persistent overconcern with body shape and weight.

First, the disorder was renamed as Bulimia Nervosa. BN followed AN into a separate section called "Eating disorders". The emphasis on binge eating was lessened and other symptoms of the disorder were incorporated. The first two criteria referred to recurrent episodes of binge eating (Criterion A) and a feeling of lack of control during those episodes (Criterion B). The DSM-III-R required that weight control behaviours be present and included self-induced vomiting, laxative and diuretic use, strict dieting or fasting, and vigorous exercise (Criterion C). This was an improvement over the DSM-III, which did not require weight control behaviours for the diagnosis. The DSM-III-R also defined the frequency and duration of binge-eating episodes as twice a week for at least three months (Criterion D). Persistent concern with body weight and shape became diagnostically significant and was listed as Criterion E. The exclusion criterion of bulimic symptoms due to AN was no longer included, so in the DSM-III-R nomenclature an individual could receive the diagnosis of AN and BN simultaneously.

Although the DSM-III-R criteria represented major progress in the classification of BN, it still needed further refinement. For example, the definition of binge eating was the source of considerable debate as research failed to establish firm guidelines regarding characteristics of binge eating, such as "rapidity" and "large amount of food" (Wilson 1997). The "discrete period of time" remained unspecified for the episode of binge eating. Also, the frequency and duration criteria for weight control behaviours were unspecified.

DSM-IV criteria for Bulimia Nervosa (1994)

In 1994, the DSM-IV (APA 1994) revised the diagnostic criteria in an attempt to address controversies regarding the definition of binge eating:

A   Recurrent episodes of binge eating. An episode of binge eating is characterized by both of the following:

1   eating, in a discrete period of time (e.g. within any two-hour period), an amount of food that is definitely larger than most people would eat during a similar period of time and under similar circumstances

2   a sense of lack of control over eating during the episode (e.g. a feeling that one cannot stop eating or control what or how much one is eating).

B   Recurrent inappropriate compensatory behaviour in order to prevent weight gain, such as self-induced vomiting; misuse of laxatives, diuretics, enemas, or other medications; fasting; or excessive exercise.
C   The binge eating and inappropriate compensatory behaviours both occur, on average, at least twice a week for three months.
D   Self-evaluation is unduly influenced by body shape and weight.
E   The disturbance does not occur exclusively during episodes of Anorexia Nervosa.

Specify type:

*   Purging type: during the current episode of Bulimia Nervosa, the person has regularly engaged in self-induced vomiting or the misuse of laxatives, diuretics or enemas.
*   Non-purging type: during the current episode of Bulimia Nervosa, the person has used other inappropriate compensatory behaviours, such as fasting or excessive exercise, but has not engaged in self-induced vomiting or the misuse of laxatives, diuretics or enemas.

Several changes were notable. An example for the "discrete period of time" for the episode of binge eating of two hours was provided (Criterion A1). "Amount of food" was defined as "definitely larger than most people would eat during a similar period of time and under similar circumstances" (Criterion A1). This last revision provided a needed social background against which individual eating pattern could be evaluated. The diagnosis of a binge episode continued to require a sense of lack control over eating (Criterion A2). The definition of compensatory behaviours was elaborated in Criterion B to emphasize the recurrent nature of these behaviours. Examples of compensatory behaviours were broadened to include the use of enemas or other medications. Previously defined frequency and duration criteria for binge eating were retained (as twice a week for at least three months), but were referred to both binge eating and to compensatory behaviours (Criterion C). Persistent concern with body weight and shape continued to be included (Criterion D). Exclusion criterion of bulimic symptoms due to AN was now included (Criterion E) to reflect the clinical practice of giving the precedence to the diagnosis of AN over BN.

The DSM-IV required subtyping of BN in parallel to the subtyping of individuals with AN. The purging type referred to individuals who regularly engaged in self-induced vomiting or the misuse of laxatives, diuretics or enemas. The non-purging type referred to individuals who used other inappropriate compensatory behaviours, such as fasting or excessive exercise, but did not engage in self-induced vomiting or the misuse of laxatives, diuretics or enemas. This distinction was based on observations that non-purging bulimic women tended to be older, of higher weight, have less associated psychopathology and binge eat less often than purging bulimic women (Mitchell 1998). It should be noted that non-purging individuals represented a minority among women with BN so treatment studies tended to include individuals with a purging subtype of BN. Thus, their results may have not been applicable to non-purging individuals.

ICD-10 diagnostic criteria for Bulimia Nervosa (1992)

As mentioned earlier, the ICD-10 (WHO 1992) listed eating disorders in the section "Behavioural syndromes associated with physiological disturbances and physical factors". The Clinical Descriptions and Diagnostic Guidelines version offered three guidelines for BN, which incorporated Russell's (1970) criteria:

(a) There is a persistent preoccupation with eating, and an irresistible craving for food; the patient succumbs to episodes of overeating in which large amounts of food are consumed in short periods of time.
(b) The patient attempts to counteract the "fattening" effects of food by one or more of the following: self-induced vomiting; purgative abuse, alternating periods of starvation; use of drugs such as appetite suppressants, thyroid preparations or diuretics. When bulimia occurs in diabetic patients, they may choose to neglect their insulin treatment.
(c) The psychopathology consists of morbid fear of fatness and the patient sets himself or herself a sharply defined weight threshold, well below the premorbid weight that constitutes the optimum or healthy weight in the opinion of the physician. There is often, but not always, a history of an earlier episode of Anorexia Nervosa, the interval ranging from a few months to several years. This earlier episode may have been fully expressed, or may have assumed a minor cryptic form with a moderate weight loss and/or a transient phase of amenorrhoea.

Includes: bulimia NOS
            hyperorexia nervosa.

Episodes of overeating were defined by "large amounts of food consumed in short periods of time" (Criterion (a)). Weight control behaviours were included in Criterion (b). Morbid fear of fatness combined with a wish for "a sharply defined weight threshold below healthy weight" was required in Criterion (c). In a comprehensive way, this set of criteria captured clinical features of the disorder and offered more diagnostic specificity than the DSM-III category of Bulimia. However, the frequency and duration criteria for overeating and weight control behaviours were not included. Also the definition of overeating continued to lag behind the DSM-III-R and DSM-IV.

ICD-10 research diagnostic criteria for Bulimia Nervosa (1993)

The RDC version (WHO 1993) for BN overcame some of the shortcomings of the Clinical Descriptions and Diagnostic Guidelines:

A   There are recurrent episodes of overeating (at least twice a week over a period of three months) in which large amounts of food are consumed in short periods of time.
B   There is persistent preoccupation with eating, and a strong desire or sense of compulsion to eat (craving).
C   The patient attempts to counteract the "fattening" effects of food by one or more of the following:

   1   self-induced vomiting
   2   self-induced purging
   3   alternating periods of starvation
   4   use of drugs such as appetite suppressants, thyroid preparations, or diuretics; when bulimia occurs in diabetic patients they may choose to neglect their insulin treatments.

D   There is self-perception of being too fat, with an intrusive dread of fatness (usually leading to underweight).

Similar to the DSM-III-R and the DSM-IV, it specified frequency and duration criteria for bouts of overeating (Criterion A). However, the definition of overeating in Criterion A continued to lag behind the DSM-IV as no specific guidelines regarding amount of food and timing of food ingestion were offered. A sense of loss of control over eating was not required. Instead Criterion B called for "persistent preoccupation with eating, and a strong desire or sense of compulsion to eat (craving)". Criterion C listed a number of weight control behaviours but included no frequency and duration stipulations. Finally, Criterion D included "a self-perception of being too fat, with an intrusive dread of fatness (usually leading to underweight)." This broadly corresponded to the DSM-IV Criterion D but emphasized one aspect of self-perception, namely, self-perception of being "too fat and fear of fatness", as opposed to more general self-evaluation influenced by body weight and shape as stated in the DSM-IV. ICD-10 followed Russell's terminology by referring to bouts of overeating instead of episodes of binge eating.

Future directions

There appears to be general agreement on the defining characteristics of BN: recurrent binge eating, recurrent inappropriate efforts to avoid weight gain, and an overconcern with weight. However, a number of important issues are unresolved. One is the status of "non-purging" BN. Virtually all of the clinical data on BN focus on patients who binge and purge; the limited information on non-purging BN suggests both similarities and differences from purging BN. It is not clear whether these two entities are best viewed as variations of the same syndrome or as distinct syndromes.

The definition of binge eating remains problematic, and without an obvious resolution. The limited data available do not suggest that there is a sharp dividing line between "normal" and "definitively large" amounts of food consumed by patients with BN. When thinking about the characteristics of binge eating, non-professionals appear to focus more on a sense of loss of control rather than the amount of food consumed (Beglin and Fairburn 1992). One way to escape these dilemmas is to redefine the core behavioural phenomenon not as binge eating but as purging (Garfinkel 1995). This would eliminate the problem of how to define binge eating, but exclude non-purging BN and allow those individuals who purge after consuming normal or small amounts of food to receive a specific diagnosis. More data are needed to evaluate the utility of this notion.

It is clear that virtually all patients who meet the behavioural criteria for BN are more concerned about body shape and weight than the average person (Goldfein *et al.* 2000). However, it is unclear how critical overconcern with shape and weight is as a diagnostic criterion. How frequently are individuals excluded from the BN category because they fail to meet the overconcern criterion, and are their characteristics substantially different from those of individuals meeting full criteria?

An additional incompletely resolved issue relates to the "twice a week for three months" criterion of DSM-IV. While there appears to be broad agreement regarding the need for some minimal frequency of disturbed behaviour, concerns have been raised that twice a week may be too high, and that once a week might be more useful (Fairburn and Cooper 1984; Wilson and Eldredge 1991).

History of classification of EDNOS

EDNOS, also called "atypical" eating disorder, represents a heterogeneous category of eating disorders used to describe individuals with eating disorders symptoms which do not meet criteria for the two "typical" eating disorders, AN and BN. As our understanding of diagnostic criteria for typical eating disorders has evolved considerably since the early 1980s, so has our understanding of "atypical" eating disorders. The history of the classification of

EDNOS is thus tightly connected to the changing classification of AN and of BN.

In clinical practice the term EDNOS is used in several ways. First, the EDNOS category describes individuals who present with symptoms characteristic of either AN or BN, but who do not meet all of the diagnostic criteria either because one of the diagnostic essential features is missing (sometimes the term "partial syndrome" is used) or because one or more feature is not sufficiently severe to reach the specified threshold (a "sub-threshold" or "subclinical" disorder). Second, the EDNOS category also includes eating disorders clinically distinct from typical presentations in that cardinal features of AN and BN are absent but other symptoms indicative of abnormal eating are present. For example, a regular use of inappropriate compensatory behaviour by an individual of normal body weight after eating small amounts of food (e.g. self-induced vomiting after the consumption of two cookies). Another atypical presentation consists of repeatedly chewing and spitting out, but not swallowing, large amounts of food. What follows is a historical review of developments, which led to the current classification of EDNOS.

In 1973, Bruch described atypical forms of eating disorder among her patients. In her case series of 60 females with AN, 25 per cent were diagnosed with atypical AN (Bruch 1973). As opposed to individuals with "genuine" AN, atypical presentations were characterized by a lack of "relentless pursuit of thinness" and there was no denial of weight loss. Individuals with atypical AN actually complained about the weight loss and valued it as a source of influence over others. "Inability to eat, due to symbolic misinterpretation of the eating function, was the leading symptom in the atypical group", said Bruch. She distinguished the atypical group from individuals affected by malnutrition secondary to psychotic disorder, depression or psychiatric disorders. Other clinicians also commented that atypical eating disorders are common among individuals presenting for treatment in eating disorders centres.

Diagnostic criteria

DSM-III criteria for Atypical Eating Disorder (1980)

Systematic classification of atypical eating disorders was initiated in 1980 when a category of Atypical Eating Disorder made its way into the DSM-III (APA 1980). A general statement described a "residual category for eating disorders that could not be adequately classified in any of the previous categories". Subsequently, growing interest in the epidemiology of typical eating disorders generated data that validated the clinical significance of atypical eating disorders. For example, Button and Whitehouse (1981) found that only 1 per cent of their college sample met criteria for AN, but as many as 5 per cent reported symptoms of AN: abnormal preoccupation with weight and food intake, self-induced vomiting and/or purging and significant weight loss. Because this group did not meet full criteria for AN, it was called "subclinical AN". Others have also argued that AN and BN are not all-or-none phenomena but rather a spectrum of eating disorders symptoms that can be identified in the community (Schleimer 1983). Several epidemiological studies have confirmed the clinical significance of partial and subclinical eating disorders, but researchers varied widely in their definitions. For example, prior to the publication of the DSM-III-R, Johnson-Sabine *et al.* (1988) described partial syndrome as "major preoccupation with weight which has become invested with abnormal significance so that morbid fears of weight gain develop, weight remains within limits and menstruation persists although it may be irregular." Similarly, King (1989) considered "anorexic"- and "bulimic"-like symptoms (e.g. dietary restrictions, binge eating, self-induced vomiting) to warrant a diagnosis of partial syndrome among female attendees of a general clinic in London.

DSM-III-R criteria for Eating Disorders Not Otherwise Specified (1987)

In 1987, the DSM-III-R advanced the classification of atypical eating disorders by introducing a new term, Eating Disorder Not Otherwise Specified. It listed three specific examples of EDNOS: an atypical presentation called "purging disorder," partial syndrome of AN and partial syndrome of BN.

> Disorders of eating that do not meet the criteria for a specific eating disorder
>
> *Examples:*
>
> 1 a person of average weight who does not have binge-eating episodes, but frequently engages in self-induced vomiting for fear of gaining weight
> 2 all of the features of Anorexia Nervosa in a female except absence of menses
> 3 all of the features of Bulimia Nervosa except the frequency of binge-eating episodes.

This refinement of diagnostic criteria advanced epidemiological studies of EDNOS. For example, in the early 1990s, Rathner and Messner (1993) evaluated a spectrum of eating disorders among adolescent girls in a rural area in Italy. They broadly followed the DSM-III-R guidelines for EDNOS in their definition of subclinical syndromes of AN and BN. Dancyger and Garfinkel (1995) also assessed partial syndromes among adolescent and young adult females. Partial syndrome AN diagnosis required that all of the DSM-III-R criteria for AN were met except for the degree of weight loss and the requirement of amenorrhoea. Partial syndrome BN diagnosis followed the DSM-III-R criteria for BN except for the duration and frequency stipulations.

DSM-IV criteria for Eating Disorders Not Otherwise Specified (1994)

In 1994, the DSM-IV further evolved the diagnostic criteria and included an expanded list of six specific presentations.

> The Eating Disorder Not Otherwise Specified category is for disorders of eating that do not meet the criteria for any specific eating disorder. Examples include:
>
> 1   For females, all of the criteria for Anorexia Nervosa are met except that the individual has regular menses.
> 2   All of the criteria for Anorexia Nervosa are met except that, despite significant weight loss, the individual's current weight is in the normal range.
> 3   All of the criteria for Bulimia Nervosa are met except that the binge eating and inappropriate compensatory mechanisms occur at a frequency of less than twice a week or for a duration of less than three months.
> 4   The regular use of inappropriate compensatory behaviour by an individual of normal body weight after eating small amounts of food (e.g. self-induced vomiting after the consumption of two cookies).
> 5   Repeatedly chewing and spitting out, but not swallowing, large amounts of food.
> 6   Binge Eating Disorder: recurrent episodes of binge eating in the absence of the regular use of inappropriate compensatory behaviours characteristic of Bulimia Nervosa.

Three were referred to individuals with partial or subclinical AN or BN (examples 1, 2 and 3). Three other examples referred to "proper" atypical eating disorders: "purging" disorder (regular use of inappropriate compensatory behaviour by an individual of normal body weight after eating small amounts of food), repeated chewing and spitting out, but not swallowing large amounts of food, and BED. With the exception of BED, these atypical presentations remain poorly understood. For example, it is only recently that the syndrome of repeated chewing and spitting out food has been described in more detail. One study reported that a significant proportion of individuals with restrictive eating behaviours, self-induced vomiting and excessive exercise engaged in chewing and spitting up food at least several times a week (Heinberg *et al.* 2002). These behaviours may indicate a more severe eating disorder as this group reported greater sense of personal ineffectiveness and poorer physical functioning but further research into the classification and epidemiology of this syndrome is needed.

DSM-IV research criteria for Binge Eating Disorder (1994)

BED has been a focus of research since 1990 and has become an established entity. Interest in BED began in the early 1990s when American investigators described a syndrome of pathological overeating without compensatory weight control behaviours observed among individuals with BN. Accumulating evidence from clinical studies indicated that a significant proportion of individuals presenting for treatment of obesity reported episodes of over-eating, but did not meet other DSM criteria for BN (Brody et al. 1994). A multi-site study drawing on samples from weight loss programmes and eating disorder clinics validated a diagnostic construct of BED. Diagnosis of BED was associated with impairment in work and social functioning, over-concern with body/shape and weight, general psychopathology, significant amount of time in adult life on diets, history of depression, alcohol/drug abuse and treatment for emotional problems (Spitzer et al. 1993). Another comparison of obese individuals, with and without binge eating, revealed that the presence of binge eating was associated with higher distress and poorer treatment outcomes (Ferguson and Spitzer 1995). To account for this group of individuals, a provisional diagnosis of BED was introduced in the DSM-IV (APA 1994) Appendix B, "Criteria and Axes Provided for Further Study":

A   Recurrent episodes of binge eating. An episode of binge eating is characterized by both of the following:

1   eating, in a discrete period of time (e.g. within any two-hour period), an amount of food that is definitely larger than most people would eat in a similar period of time under similar circumstances
2   a sense of lack of control over eating during the episode (e.g. a feeling that one cannot stop eating or control what or how much one is eating).

B   The binge-eating episodes are associated with three (or more) of the following:

1   eating much more rapidly than normal
2   eating until feeling uncomfortably full
3   eating large amounts of food when not feeling physically hungry
4   eating alone because of being embarrassed by how much one is eating
5   feeling disgusted with oneself, depressed, or very guilty after overeating.

C   Marked distress regarding binge eating is present.
D   The binge eating occurs, on average, at least two days a week for six months.
     Note: the method of determining frequency differs from that used for Bulimia Nervosa; future research should address whether the preferred method of setting a frequency threshold is counting the number of days on which binges occur or counting the number of episodes of binge eating.
E   The binge eating is not associated with the regular use of inappropriate compensatory behaviours (e.g. purging, fasting, excessive exercise) and does not occur exclusively during the course of Anorexia Nervosa or Bulimia Nervosa.

While recurrent episodes of binge eating are shared by individuals with both BN and BED, some differences have been noted. Individuals with BED tend to have longer episodes and have a less clear beginning and end. Individuals with BED have a general tendency to overeat and do not attempt strict diets characteristic of individuals with BN (Goldfein *et al.* 1993). In an attempt to address these potential problems, the proposed DSM criteria for BED suggest that "binge days" rather than binge episodes be enumerated. Minimum frequency of two binge days per week over six months was considered diagnostically significant rather than over three months as required for BN.

Individuals with BED do not engage in compensatory behaviours characteristic of individuals with BN. Overconcern with body weight and size is not deemed diagnostically significant; individuals with BED tend to be older and the gender ratio is less uneven. It is not clear if this provisional diagnosis will be incorporated into future revisions of the DSM criteria for eating disorders as a considerable controversy continues to surround its status. However, development of BED as a new diagnostic construct represents a model for future research into other atypical eating disorders and EDNOS.

ICD-10 criteria for Atypical Eating Disorders (1992)

In parallel to DSM, ICD-10 (WHO 1992) provides criteria for eating disorders. The Clinical Descriptions and Diagnostic Guidelines version provided diagnostic guidelines for atypical eating disorders in the Eating Disorders section and included six categories:

• **Atypical Anorexia Nervosa**
  This term should be used for those individuals in whom one or more of the key features of Anorexia Nervosa, such as amenorrhoea or significant weight loss, is absent, but who otherwise present a fairly typical clinical picture. Such people are usually encountered in psychiatric liaison services in general hospitals or in primary care. Patients who have

all the key symptoms but to only a mild degree may also be best described by this term. This term should not be used for eating disorders that resemble Anorexia Nervosa but that are due to known physical illness.

- **Atypical Bulimia Nervosa**
  This term should be used for those individuals in whom one or more of the key features listed for Bulimia Nervosa is absent, but who otherwise present a fairly typical picture. Most commonly this applies to people with normal or even excessive weight but with typical periods of over-eating followed by vomiting or purging. Partial syndromes together with depressive symptoms are not uncommon, but if the depressive symptoms justify a separate diagnosis of a depressive disorder two separate diagnoses should be made.
  Includes: normal weight bulimia.
- **Overeating associated with other psychological disturbances**
  Overeating that has led to obesity as a reaction to distressing events should be noted here. Bereavements, accidents, surgical operations and emotionally distressing events may be followed by a "reactive obesity", especially in individuals predisposed to weight gain.
  Includes: psychogenic overeating.
- **Vomiting associated with other psychological disturbances**
  Apart from the self-induced vomiting of Bulimia Nervosa, repeated vomiting may occur in dissociative disorders, hypochondriacal disorder when vomiting may be one of several bodily symptoms, and in pregnancy when emotional factors may contribute to recurrent nausea and vomiting.
  Includes: psychogenic hyperemesis gravidarum
  psychogenic vomiting.
- **Other eating disorders**
  Includes: pica of non-organic origin in adults
  psychogenic loss of appetite.
- **Eating disorder, unspecified**

Atypical AN and atypical BN categories are similar to the DSM-III-R and the DSM-IV categories of partial AN and BN syndromes. However, contrary to the DSM-IV, ICD-10 made an additional provision for eating disturbances associated with other disorders. It included overeating associated with other psychological disturbances such as bereavement, accident and childbirth and called it "reactive obesity in individuals predisposed to weight gain". An additional category included vomiting associated with other psychological disturbances such as dissociative and somatoform disorders or recurrent nausea and vomiting in pregnancy with contributing emotional factors. These two categories would not be classified as eating disorders according to current DSM criteria as they occur secondary to other psychological conditions. The two last categories were "Other eating disorders", which listed pica of non-organic origin in adults and psychogenic loss of appetite, and finally "Eating disorders, unspecified" category, which did not include any examples.

ICD-10 research diagnostic criteria for Atypical Eating Disorders (1993)

The RDC version (WHO 1993) covers the same categories as the Clinical Descriptions and Diagnostic Guidelines version. However, the RDC version makes a recommendation that researchers studying each category design their own criteria. ICD does not list a diagnostic category equivalent to BED. The following categories were included:

- **Atypical Anorexia Nervosa**
  Researchers studying atypical forms of Anorexia Nervosa are recommended to make their own decisions about the number and type of criteria to be fulfilled.
- **Atypical Bulimia Nervosa**
  Researchers studying atypical forms of Bulimia Nervosa, such as those involving normal or excessive body weight, are recommended to make their own decisions about the number and type of criteria to be fulfilled.
- **Overeating associated with other psychological disturbances**
  Researchers wishing to use this category are recommended to design their own criteria.
- **Vomiting associated with other psychological disturbances**
  Researchers wishing to use this category are recommended to design their own criteria.
- **Other eating disorders**
- **Eating disorder, unspecified**

Future directions

EDNOS represent the largest diagnostic category within the eating disorders group but has received the least attention. While diagnostic criteria for partial and sub-threshold/subclinical syndromes have become more clearly defined, other "atypical" presentations of eating disorders need to be further delineated. For example, recent epidemiological and genetic studies included broader definitions of typical eating disorders (Bulik *et al.* 2000; Strober *et al.* 2000). These studies indicate that transdiagnostic aetiological mechanisms may be operating within eating disorders as group. However, epidemiology and genetic liability for atypical eating disorders (other than partial and subclinical syndromes) remain poorly understood. Moreover, treatment studies have focused exclusively on typical presentations, thus response to treatment and prognosis of atypical eating disorders is currently unknown.

Conclusion

Clinical focus on eating disorders since the early eighteenth century has produced acceptable and useful diagnostic criteria for AN and BN. However, important details about the specific diagnostic criteria for these "typical" eating disorders require additional study and clarification. Of greater importance is how best to deal with the large number of individuals with obvious disturbances of eating behaviour who do not meet current criteria for AN and BN. The status and future of the most studied atypical eating disorder, BED, remain unresolved, and there has been little effort to construct criteria for other syndromes of disturbed eating. The dramatic surge in knowledge about clinical characteristics and treatment options which followed the definition of BN in the late 1970s suggests that efforts to develop diagnostic criteria for other eating disorders should be of high priority for the field.

References

American Psychiatric Association (1952) *Diagnostic and Statistical Manual of Mental Disorders*, Washington, DC: APA.

American Psychiatric Association (1968) *Diagnostic and Statistical Manual of Mental Disorders*, 2nd edn (DSM-II), Washington, DC: APA.

American Psychiatric Association (1980) *Diagnostic and Statistical Manual of Mental Disorders*, 3rd edn (DSM-III), Washington, DC: APA.

American Psychiatric Association (1987) *Diagnostic and Statistical Manual of Mental Disorders*, 3rd edn revised (DSM-III-R), Washington, DC: APA.

American Psychiatric Association (1994) *Diagnostic and Statistical Manual of Mental Disorders*, 4th edn (DSM-IV), Washington, DC: APA.

Andersen, A.E (1995) "Eating disorders in males", in K.F.C. Brownell (ed.) *Eating Disorders and Obesity: A Comprehensive Handbook*, New York: Guilford Press.

Beglin, S.J. and Fairburn, C.G. (1992) "What is meant by the term 'binge'?", *American Journal of Psychiatry* 149, 123–4.

Beumont, P.J.V. (1977) "Further categorization of patients with anorexia nervosa", *Australian and New Zealand Journal of Psychiatry* 11, 223–6.

Bliss, E. and Branch, C. (1960) *Anorexia Nervosa: Its History, Psychology and Biology*, New York: Hoeber.

Brody, M.L., Walsh, B.T. and Devlin, M.J. (1994) "Binge eating disorder: reliability and validity of a new diagnostic category", *Journal of Consulting and Clinical Psychology* 62, 381–6.

Bruch, H. (1973) *Eating Disorders: Obesity, Anorexia Nervosa and the Person Within*, New York: Basic Books.

Bulik, C.M., Sullivan, P.F., Wade, T.D. and Kendler, K.S. (2000) "Twin studies of eating disorders: a review", *International Journal of Eating Disorders* 27, 1–20.

Button, E.J. and Whitehouse, A. (1981) "Subclinical anorexia nervosa", *Psychological Medicine* 11, 509–16.

Casper, R.C., Eckert, E. and Halmi, K.A. (1980) "Bulimia: its incidence and clinical importance in patients with anorexia nervosa", *Archives of General Psychiatry* 37, 1030–5

Crisp, A.H. (1980) *Anorexia Nervosa: Let Me Be*, London: Academic Press.

Dancyger, I.F. and Garfinkel, P.E. (1995) "The relationship of partial syndrome eating disorders to anorexia nervosa and bulimia nervosa", *Psychological Medicine* 25, 1019–35.

Devlin, M., Walsh, B., Katz, J., Roose, S., Linkie, D., Wright, L., Vande, W. and Glassman, A. (1989) "Hypothalamic-pituitary-gonadal function in anorexia nervosa and bulimia", *Psychiatry Research* 28, 11–24.

Di Nicola, V.F. (1990) "Anorexia multiforma: self-starvation in historical and cultural context. Part I: self-starvation as a historical chameleon", *Transcultural Psychiatry Research Review* 27, 165–96.

Fairburn, C.G. and Beglin, S. (1990) "Studies of the epidemiology of bulimia nervosa", *American Journal of Psychiatry* 147, 401–8.

Fairburn, C.G. and Cooper, P.J. (1984) "Binge eating, self-induced vomiting and laxative abuse: a community study", *Psychological Medicine* 14, 401–10.

Falk, J.R. and Halmi, K.A. (1982) "Amenorrhea in anorexia nervosa: examination of the critical body weight hypothesis", *Biological Psychiatry* 17, 799–806.

Feighner, J.P., Robin, E., Guze, S.B., Woodruff, R.A., Winokur, G. and Monoz, R. (1976) "Diagnostic criteria for use in psychiatric research", *Archives of General Psychiatry* 26, 57–63.

Ferguson, K.J. and Spitzer, R.L. (1995) "Binge eating disorder in a community-based sample of successful and unsuccessful dieters", *International Journal of Eating Disorders* 18, 167–72.

First, M. and Pincus, H.A. (1999) "Classification in psychiatry: ICD-10 v. DSM-IV", *British Journal of Psychiatry* 175, 205–9.

Garfinkel, P.E. (1995) "Classification and diagnosis of eating disorders", in K. Brownell and C.G. Fairburn (eds) *Eating Disorders and Obesity: A Comprehensive Handbook*, New York: Guilford Press.

Garfinkel, P. and Garner, D. (1982) "The multidetermined nature of Anorexia Nervosa", in P. Garfinkel and D. Garner, *Anorexia Nervosa: A multidimensional perspective*, New York: Brunner/Mazel.

Garfinkel, P.E., Lin, E., Goering, P., Spegg, C., Goldbloom, D., Kennedy, S., Kaplan, A.S. and Woodside, D.B. (1996) "Should amenorrhoea be necessary for the diagnosis of anorexia nervosa? Evidence from a Canadian community sample", *British Journal of Psychiatry* 168, 500–6.

Goldfein, J.A., Walsh, B.T., LaChaussee, J.L., Kissileff, H.R. and Devlin, M.J. (1993) "Eating behavior in binge eating disorder", *International Journal of Eating Disorders* 14, 427–31.

Goldfein, J.A., Walsh, B.T. and Midlarsky, E. (2000) "Influence of shape and weight on self-evaluation in bulimia nervosa", *International Journal of Eating Disorders* 27, 435–45.

Gull, W.W. (1874) "Anorexia nervosa (apepsia hysterica, anorexia hysterica)", *Transactions of the Clinical Society of London* 7, 22–8.

Halmi, K.A., Falk, J.R. and Schwartz, E. (1981) "Binge eating and vomiting: a survey of a college population", *Psychological Medicine* 11, 697–706.

Heinberg, L., Guarda, A., Cummings, M. and Haug, N. (2002) "Chewing and spitting behavior among hospitalized eating disordered patients", abstract presented at the International Conference on Eating Disorders in Boston, MA, April.

Hoek, H.W. (1991) "The incidence and prevalence of anorexia nervosa and bulimia nervosa in primary care", *Psychological Medicine* 21, 455–60.

Jackson, C., Davidson, G., Russell, J. and Vandereycken, W. (1990) "Ellen West revisited: the theme of death in eating disorders", *International Journal of Eating Disorders* 9, 529–36.

Johnson-Sabine, E., Wood, K., Patton, G., Mann, A. and Wakeling, A. (1988) "Abnormal eating attitudes in London schoolgirls – a prospective epidemiological study: factors associated with abnormal response on screening questionnaires", *Psychological Medicine* 18, 615–22.

Katz, J.L. and Weiner, H. (1975) "A functional, anterior hypothalamic defect in primary anorexia nervosa?", *Psychosomatic Medicine* 37, 103–5.

King, M.B. (1989) "Eating disorders in a general practice population: prevalence, characteristics and follow-up at 12 to 18 months", *Psychological Medicine – Monograph Supplement* 14, 1–34.

Lasegue, C. (1873) "On hysterical anorexia", *Medical Times and Gazette* 6, 265–6.

Lucas, A.R. (1986) "Anorexia nervosa: historical background and biopsychological determinants", *Seminars in Adolescent Medicine* 2, 1–9.

Minuchin, S., Rosman, B. and Baker, L. (1978) *Psychosomatic Families: Anorexia Nervosa in Context*, New York: Harvard University Press.

Mitchell, J.E. (1998) "Subtyping of Bulimia Nervosa", in T.A Widiger, A.J. Frances, H.A Pincus, R. Ross, M.B. First, W. Davis and M. Kline (eds) *DSM-IV Sourcebook* (volume IV), Washington, DC: American Psychiatric Association.

Morton, R. (1694) *Phthisiologia – or a Treatise of Consumptions*, London: Smith & Walford.

Rathner, G. and Messner, K. (1993) "Detection of eating disorders in a small rural town: an epidemiological study", *Psychological Medicine* 23, 175–84.

Russell, G.F.M. (1970) "Anorexia Nervosa: its identity as an illness and its treatment", in J.H. Prince (ed.) *Modern Trends in Psychological Medicine*, London: Butterworths.

Russell, G.F.M. (1979) "Bulimia nervosa: an ominous variant of anorexia nervosa", *Psychological Medicine* 9, 429–48.

Schleimer, K. (1983) "Dieting in teenage schoolgirls: a longitudinal prospective study", *Acta Paediatrica Scandinavica Supplement* 312, 1–54.

Selvini-Palazzoli, M. (1978) *Self-starvation: From Individual to Family Therapy in the Treatment of Anorexia Nervosa*, New York: Jason Aronson.

Simmonds, M. (1914) "Ueber Hypophysisschwund mit todlichem Ausgang", *Deutsche Medizinische Wochenschrift* 40, 322–3.

Spitzer, R.L., Yanovski, S., Wadden, T., Wing, R., Marcus, M.D., Stunkard, A., Devlin, M., Mitchell, J., Hasin, D. and Horne, R.L. (1993) "Binge eating disorder: its further validation in a multi-site study", *International Journal of Eating Disorders* 13, 137–53.

Strober, M., Freeman, R., Lampert, C., Diamond, J. and Kaye, W. (2000) "Controlled family study of anorexia nervosa and bulimia nervosa: evidence of shared liability and transmission of partial syndromes", *American Journal of Psychiatry* 157, 393–401.

Stunkard, A. (1959) "Eating patterns and obesity", *Psychiatric Quarterly* 33, 248–95.

Vandereyken, W. and van Deth, R. (1994) *From Fasting Saints to Anorexic Girls: The History of Self-Starvation*, New York: University Press.

Waller, J.V., Kaufman, M.R. and Deutsch, F. (1940) "Anorexia nervosa: a psycho-somatic entity", *Psychosomatic Medicine* 2, 3–16.

Wilson, G. (1997) "Diagnostic criteria for bulimia nervosa", in T. Widiger, A.J. Frances, H.A. Pincus, R. Ross, M.B. First and W. Davis (eds) *DSM-IV Sourcebook* (volume III), Washington, DC: American Psychiatric Association.

Wilson, G.T. and Eldredge, K. (1991) "Frequency of binge eating in bulimic patients: diagnostic validity", *International Journal of Eating Disorders* 10, 557–61.

World Health Organization (1992) *ICD-10 Classification of Mental and Behavioural Disorders: Clinical Descriptions and Diagnostic Guidelines*, Geneva: WHO.

World Health Organization (1993) *ICD-10 Classification of Mental and Behavioural Disorders: Diagnostic Criteria for Research*, Geneva: WHO.

Yanovski, S.Z. (1998) "Obesity and eating disorders", in G.A. Bray, C. Bouchard and W.P.T. James (eds) *Handbook of Obesity*, New York: Marcel Dekker.

Yates, A. (1989) "Current perspectives on the eating disorders: I. History, psychological and biological aspects", *Journal of the American Academy of Child Psychiatry* 28, 813–28.

Chapter 3

The empirical status of atypical eating disorders and the present EDNOS diagnosis

Rebecca Murphy, Sarah Perkins and Ulrike Schmidt

Current classification of eating disorders

Eating disorders have been defined as disorders where there is

> a persistent disturbance of eating behaviour or behaviour intended to control weight, which significantly impairs physical health or psycho-social functioning. This disturbance should not be secondary to any recognized general medical disorder (e.g. a hypothalamic tumour) or any other psychiatric disorder (e.g. an anxiety disorder).
>
> (Fairburn and Walsh 2002: 171)

Those eating problems which do not fulfil the criteria for Anorexia Nervosa or Bulimia Nervosa, but which are considered to be of clinical severity, are classified by DSM-IV as Eating Disorder Not Otherwise Specified (APA 1994: see p. 32) or by ICD-10 as atypical eating disorder (WHO 1992: see pp. 34–5). As DSM-IV states:

> No classification of mental disorders can have a sufficient number of specific categories to encompass every conceivable clinical presentation. The Not Otherwise Specified categories are provided to cover the not frequent presentations that are at the boundary of specific categorical definitions.
>
> (APA 1994)

Binge Eating Disorder is a form of EDNOS and although it has not been officially recognized as constituting a diagnosis in its own right, it seems to have been granted this status by researchers and practitioners alike. DSM-IV provides a set of diagnostic criteria for aiding further study of this disorder (see Appendix). There is no comparable disorder in ICD-10.

Aims of the chapter

Fairburn and Walsh (1995: 139) comment that "attempts to define and characterize the atypical eating disorders are likely to clarify and improve the classification of the typical eating disorders." Hence, the aims of this chapter are to present empirical evidence concerning the classification of atypical eating disorders and to discuss the diagnostic states currently defined as EDNOS and the present classification of eating disorders in general. We will also present evidence concerning the problems of such classification and consider the purpose of classification and its alternatives.

What is a syndrome?

In order for the atypical eating disorders or EDNOS to be a valid subgroup of eating disorders, they should fulfil certain criteria. The following are based on Robins and Guze's (1970) six phases of syndrome identification.

Descriptive validity

Individuals with EDNOS/atypical eating disorders should differ significantly from those with other eating disorders in terms of eating disorder features and symptomatology. There should be adequate identification and description of the syndrome, either by clinical intuition or cluster analysis. As Spitzer et al. (1993a) write:

> new diagnoses have always arisen from clinicians noting certain commonalities among the patients who they are trying to help. These commonalities, or distinctive clinical features, distinguish these patients with the new disorder from other patients who do not have the disorder. The validity of the disorder is the extent to which the defining features of the disorder provide useful information.
>
> (Spitzer et al. 1993a: 167)

Cluster analysis is a "well established and appropriate statistical technique for suggesting possible diagnostic categories since it attempts to divide individuals into clusters of those with similar features" (Hay et al. 1996: 809); however, it has been more useful in validating existing syndromes than generating new ones.

Construct validity

A diagnosis has good construct validity if most of the people who meet the criteria are alike in ways unrelated to the diagnostic criteria, e.g. in terms of aetiology, general psychopathology and prognosis. Such boundaries or points of rarity between related syndromes can be demonstrated by discriminant function analysis or latent class analysis. If there is a genuine point of rarity between related syndromes then patients with mixed symptomatology should be less common than typical members of the syndromes.

Predictive validity

Valid diagnostic categories should follow unique courses or outcomes. Kendell (1989) argues that the concept of a syndrome has always been inherently linked to a more or less distinctive outcome, whereby differences in outcome over perhaps a few days or across many years, may distinguish between two syndromes. However, just demonstrating a difference in outcome is not enough. This difference must be attributable to a diagnostic difference and not to some other factor such as age.

Distinct treatment response

Individuals with EDNOS or atypical eating disorders should show a distinct response to treatments in comparison to individuals with other eating disorders. This phase could be viewed as an extension of predictive validity as treatment response could be considered a form of manipulated condition before follow-up. This is particularly tricky to use as in general there are few treatments specific to one syndrome.

Family studies

Family studies are used to establish if a syndrome breeds true, i.e. if first degree relatives of people with EDNOS or atypical eating disorders have a raised risk for that syndrome alone, this is evidence that it is a syndrome in its own right. A "syndrome will only breed true if it is fairly stable and well delineated" (Kendell 1989: 50).

Fundamental abnormality

Other evidence for a distinct syndrome would be an association with some more fundamental abnormality, e.g. histological, psychological, biochemical or molecular.

Problems in using the classifications

In addition to these methods of validating a syndrome the current classificatory system should be evaluated in terms of current problems in using the classifications. For example, diagnoses should be reliable, i.e. the same patient should ideally be given the same diagnosis independently of who diagnoses them and where this diagnosis takes place and this diagnosis should be relatively stable over time. If certain classificatory criteria do not apply well to all patients then this could lead to different diagnoses.

We shall now examine atypical eating disorders/EDNOS as compared to the more clearly delineated AN and BN in the light of the above validity criteria.

The EDNOS diagnosis

EDNOS (or atypical/subclinical/sub-threshold/partial eating disorders; see p. 32 for DSM-IV examples) is a large and heterogeneous group. This is due to the fact that it is defined essentially by exclusion, i.e. any clinical eating disorder that does not fulfil AN or BN criteria and therefore contains all the "leftover" cases. This negative criterion appears dubious for those cases which come just short of the AN or BN diagnoses either qualitatively (e.g. lack of amenorrhoea for AN) or quantitatively (e.g. failure to meet the specified binge frequency for BN). Should someone who meets all but one of the AN or BN criteria really be diagnosed with a separate unspecified disorder? "Subclinical" has been used to refer to EDNOS cases, but this term belies the fact that such cases must by definition be of clinical severity and indeed are commonly as severe as cases meeting full criteria. For example, an underweight individual, vomiting ten times a day and meeting all other AN criteria except amenorrhoea, would be classified as EDNOS, despite having such serious difficulties. In a study of 189 female outpatients, no significant differences between EDNOS and AN/BN patients were found in terms of general and psychopathological features (Ricca *et al.* 2001). However, significant differences were found between patients with bulimic-like (similar to BN) and anorectic-like (similar to AN) EDNOS, and also between those with AN and BN. Therefore, on the basis of the similarities in psychopathological features between EDNOS and typical eating disorders, EDNOS patients should be divided into anorectic-like and bulimic-like patients. ICD-10 is consistent with such findings as it provides "atypical AN" and "atypical BN" diagnoses for those people who closely miss meeting complete criteria, but "the manner in which subjects may deviate from the full diagnosis and attract this label is not specified" (Palmer 1993: 460).

In addition to difficulties with the "negative" criteria for EDNOS, Palmer (2003) argues that the "positive" criterion of EDNOS, i.e. clinical significance, is not clearly defined in DSM-IV. The judgement may be dependent on other factors such as comorbidity. A judgement of clinical significance may also be influenced by the types of cases (severity and number) that a diagnosing clinician is exposed to, and perhaps even by available resources.

It has been argued that the term "atypical" is a misnomer given that from 25 per cent to 60 per cent of cases treated fall in the EDNOS category (Carlat *et al.* 1997; Mizes and Sloan 1998; Williamson *et al.* 1992). Differences in these estimates are likely to result from both differences in the samples and in clinical decisions regarding what constitutes an atypical eating disorder. However, it appears that given the large proportion of eating disorder patients presenting to services as atypical/EDNOS, the AN and BN diagnoses are too restrictive or the EDNOS category should be subdivided.

EDNOS versus Anorexia Nervosa and Bulimia Nervosa

Descriptive validity

Andersen *et al.* (2001) hypothesized that most EDNOS cases would fall within the current AN or BN categories. They were able to group the majority of the EDNOS patients into one of two sub-threshold groups: an AN sub-threshold group (i.e. meeting all criteria for AN except for having less than three months amenorrhoea and/or weight loss greater than 85 per cent of norms, but more than 20 per cent reduction of body weight) or a BN sub-threshold group (i.e. meeting all criteria except for less than the required frequency or duration of symptoms). Only 18 per cent appeared to be "true" EDNOS. They argue that the category of EDNOS is unhelpfully inclusive and contains many cases which could be included in a broader AN or BN, while retaining the core characteristics of these typologies.

Williamson *et al.* (1992) used cluster analysis in a study of 46 EDNOS patients, finding three distinct subgroups within this diagnostic category which were similar in their symptom profile to sub-threshold AN and BN, as well as BED. These findings are consistent with the cluster analysis of Mizes and Sloan (1998) to the extent that within EDNOS there appears to be an atypical AN and BN subtype. This suggests that the categories of atypical AN and atypical BN have good descriptive validity as subgroups of EDNOS.

Construct validity

In common with patients meeting DSM-IV criteria for AN and BN, high rates of psychiatric comorbidity have been found in EDNOS patients (Carlat *et al.* 1997). For example, in this sample, the percentage of patients with major depression were 55 per cent, 59 per cent and 46 per cent for AN, BN and EDNOS respectively, suggesting that EDNOS does not have a pattern of comorbidity distinct from AN and BN. In contrast, in a sample of hospitalized male veterans, distinct patterns of psychiatric comorbidity in men with different eating disorders were found (Striegel-Moore *et al.* 1999). Men with AN were at risk for schizophrenia/psychotic disorder, while men with BN were at risk for comorbid personality disorder and men with EDNOS were at risk for comorbid organic mental disorder and schizophrenia/psychotic disorder. In addition, support for distinct comorbidities for EDNOS comes from Marino and Zanarini (2001), who found that EDNOS was more prevalent than the more well-defined eating disorders among criteria-defined female borderline patients. They also found that 75 per cent of borderline women with EDNOS had never met the diagnostic criteria for AN or BN and suggested that these cases represent a cluster of separate disorders rather than residual forms of AN or BN.

Predictive validity

A prospective, naturalistic cohort study of AN, BN and EDNOS patients found support for distinct identities for AN and BN, with obvious differences in overall outcome (Ben-Tovim et al. 2001). At five-year follow-up almost three-quarters of the BN group had no diagnosable eating disorder, some were still BN and over 10 per cent had remaining symptoms and were diagnosed as EDNOS. Over half of those in the AN group no longer met criteria for AN, although they continued to have some symptoms of AN. In the EDNOS patient group, over three-quarters of survivors had no clinical diagnosis of an eating disorder and only a few were diagnosed with AN or BN at follow-up. It seems that EDNOS does have some predictive validity, with EDNOS individuals more likely than AN/BN groups to recover from their eating disorder. However, for those who continue to experience clinically severe eating problems it is unclear whether they will go on to develop AN or BN. The authors suggest that the EDNOS group may be better split into atypical AN and atypical BN.

In a number of one- to two-year longitudinal studies, around 15 per cent of individuals with a partial syndrome have gone on to develop a full syndrome eating disorder (King 1989, 1991; Patton 1988; Patton et al. 1990; Schleimer 1983). In addition, in a number of one- to four-year studies, 30–45 per cent of those with a partial syndrome had developed a full syndrome eating disorder by the end of the study (Herzog et al. 1993; Striegel-Moore et al. 1989; Yager et al. 1987). This evidence suggests that a proportion of those diagnosed with a partial syndrome or EDNOS eventually go on to develop "full-syndrome" eating disorders such as AN or BN. Therefore an EDNOS diagnosis appears to be a risk factor for AN or BN. Again, EDNOS has some predictive validity in that it may predict the development of AN or BN in the future but it does not tell us which one an individual might develop and thus does not predict an evidently unique outcome.

Alternatively, EDNOS may simply be a different stage of the same illness. Herzog et al. (1993) found that in a sample of sub-diagnostic DSM-III-R females, 46 per cent went on to develop an eating disorder that met full criteria after initial screening and 82 per cent had had an eating disorder meeting full diagnostic criteria at least once during the course of their illness. Herzog et al. (1993) therefore suggested that these sub-diagnoses may be an artefact of the timing of the intake interview and that these women may have been in an improved state or may have been progressing towards a full disorder. One might thus conclude that given the dynamic nature of eating disorders, EDNOS or atypical eating disorder may not be a useful subtype.

Family studies

In order to establish whether the syndrome of EDNOS breeds true, i.e. if first-degree relatives of people with EDNOS or atypical eating disorders have a raised risk for that syndrome alone, research would need to be conducted with relatives of EDNOS sufferers and their risks would need to be compared to those of AN and BN sufferers. However, there appear to be no current studies addressing this.

Studies have however shed light on the relationship between EDNOS, or atypical AN and BN, and AN and BN. Family studies have found a raised rate of atypical eating disorders among the female family members of probands with AN or BN. For example, Halmi *et al.* (1991) found that of the 57 AN probands studied, the diagnosis and rate of EDNOS in their mothers was 1 per cent, compared to 0 per cent for the mothers of controls. In addition, it was found that the relatives of AN and BN probands have similar lifetime rates of EDNOS and other eating disorders and these rates were significantly higher than in relatives of controls (Lilenfeld *et al.* 1998). This suggests a common familial vulnerability for AN and BN, which may range from sub-threshold forms to full-blown eating disorders.

One study examined the lifetime rates of full and partial AN and BN in first-degree relatives of proband groups which were diagnostically pure (Strober *et al.* 2000). AN was found to be rare in comparison subjects' families, whereas full and partial AN syndromes aggregated in female relatives of AN and BN probands. For the full AN syndrome, the female relatives of AN and BN probands had risks of 11.3 and 12.3 respectively. BN was found to be more common than AN in female relatives of comparison subjects. However, BN also aggregated in ill probands' families. The risk for BN for female relatives of AN and BN probands was 4.2 and 4.4 respectively. The risk of a partial AN syndrome was 5.7 times higher in a relative of an AN proband while the risk of a partial BN syndrome was 2.8 times higher in a relative of a BN proband, compared to control subjects. Strober *et al.* (2000) concluded that AN and BN were both familial and suggested that the milder phenotypes should be included in a continuum of familial liability due to their observed cross-transmission and familial aggregation.

A study of eating disorders in the first-degree relatives of males with AN found for the full AN syndrome that the risk for female relatives of ill probands was 20.3, whereas it was 3.3 for the partial AN syndrome, while BN was found to be comparably uncommon among relatives of ill probands (Strober *et al.* 2001). It was concluded that there is a pattern of familial aggregation, which is similar to that found in studies of affected females, despite the rarity of AN in males.

This evidence may suggest that there is not a separate familial transmission for EDNOS but rather a considerable overlap in the familial liability for EDNOS, AN and BN.

Atypical Anorexia Nervosa versus Anorexia Nervosa

Descriptive and construct validity

Amenorrhoea

Currently, an individual who meets all the criteria for AN except amenorrhoea falls into the category of Atypical AN (ICD-10) or EDNOS (DSM-IV). Previously, DSM-III (APA 1980) did not include amenorrhoea as a diagnostic criterion, and it was not until DSM-III-R and DSM-IV (APA 1987, 1994) that this was required for a diagnosis of AN (Garfinkel 1995). The inclusion of amenorrhoea is problematic for a number of reasons. For example, some eating disorder patients continue to menstruate at low weight. This may be due to a biological adaptation to low weight, as occurs in populations where famine is widespread. In addition, amenorrhoea can occur in a minority of women before there is any significant weight loss (Theander 1970). This may reflect dietary changes leading to altered neurotransmitter function, or may be a result of psychological distress experienced at an early stage in the illness (Garfinkel et al. 1996). Indeed, the view that amenorrhoea is secondary to starvation has led some to claim that this cannot be an essential criterion for AN. Malnutrition can perpetuate amenorrhoea, but it is not primarily responsible for the endocrine disorder (Halmi 2000).

Additional problems in classifying individuals based on this criterion include: problems with accurate recall of menses, masking of amenorrhoea by the contraceptive pill (particularly relevant given the gender and age distribution of AN) and difficulties diagnosing pre-pubescent subjects. Also, there is the issue of this criterion not being applicable to males.

Several studies have questioned the validity of amenorrhoea as a diagnostic criterion (e.g. Watson and Andersen 2003). For example, women with anorexic features, but with no amenorrhoea, show the same levels of eating disorder symptoms, body-image disturbance, and eating disorder psychopathology as anorexic women with amenorrhoea (Cachelin and Maher 1998). Another study found that 30 per cent of patients who met all the other criteria for a diagnosis of AN, did not have amenorrhoea (Kruger et al. 1998). It therefore seems questionable whether one can or should distinguish full-blown AN from atypical AN or EDNOS on the basis of amenorrhoea. Garfinkel et al. (1995b) argue that all this criterion does is emphasize the hypothalamic disturbance and alert clinicians to potential problems related to the disorder (e.g. osteoporosis) and therefore consider that it may be appropriate to remove this criterion.

Degree of weight loss

The degree of weight loss necessary for a diagnosis of AN remains a "fuzzy" issue (Halmi 1985), and it has been argued that:

> The requirement of achieving less than 85 per cent of normal weight for diagnosis is arbitrary. It is, in fact, the decrement of weight from any stable set point to a substantially lower weight that produces the starvation symptoms that are typical of AN.
>
> (Andersen 2001: 517)

The fact that the previous diagnostic classification in DSM-III required a 25 per cent weight loss, further demonstrates the arbitrary nature of this criterion (Garfinkel *et al.* 1996). This brings up the issue of what does constitute a "normal" weight. The loss or gain of a few kilograms could mean the difference between a diagnosis of AN or EDNOS. The criterion of 15 per cent or more below expected weight is argued to be useful as it allows definite cases to be diagnosed early in their course and takes into account younger patients who are still growing (Garfinkel *et al.* 1995b). However, it has also been suggested that AN criteria should not require a specific lowest weight but rather illness driven weight loss which has led to functional impairment (Andersen *et al.* 2001).

Comorbidity

Patients with subclinical AN have been found to have comparable psychological distress to those who meet full criteria (Bunnell *et al.* 1990), while AN subjects have been found to score almost identically to those with restrictive EDNOS on self-report measures (e.g. Eating Disorder Inventory II and Brief Symptom Inventory) with AN subjects scoring significantly higher only on the EDI body dissatisfaction scale (Geist *et al.* 1998). In addition, Garfinkel *et al.* (1996) found that those meeting the full criteria for AN, and those only lacking amenorrhoea, had similar rates of comorbidity. These studies suggest poor descriptive and construct validity for EDNOS/atypical AN based on the current criteria of AN.

Body weight and shape concern

Definitions of AN have always included concern about body weight and shape, yet clinical experience suggests there are patients who present with what otherwise seem to be classic eating disorders, but who do not have weight or shape concern. These patients may be denying a "true" weight concern or may provide other reasons for their anorexic behaviour, e.g. religious fasting, food allergies. In particular, the absence of these features in underweight individuals in some non-Western countries (e.g. Hsu and Lee 1993) have led authors to argue against the notion that weight and shape concern are critical in the diagnosis of AN (Hsu and Lee 1993; Hsu and Sobkiewicz 1991; Palmer 1993).

Instead of the current criterion of weight and shape concern, another psychological criterion may be more appropriate. However, any revised criterion must serve to exclude those cases in which the eating problem is best classified elsewhere, for example a loss of appetite due to other physical or psychological conditions. Palmer (1993) suggests that an over-investment in the importance of eating restraint may be a more suitable criterion. This would include all current cases, would not count secondary loss of appetite cases, and would be broad enough to include those cases where restraint is not only motivated by weight or shape concern. If this revised criterion was applied then those individuals without weight or shape concern, who meet all other criteria of AN/BN, would no longer fall into atypical or EDNOS categories.

Predictive validity

Research on the course of eating disorders has highlighted the natural association between typical and atypical eating disorders, as reflected in ICD-10 current diagnoses. This fluidity is less apparent in cross-sectional studies. A substantial number of those people with AN who do not recover tend to evolve into atypical AN. Some research also suggests that a significant number of participants with sub-threshold AN will advance into typical AN (Fairburn and Walsh 2002). However, these subtypes still seem to have some predictive validity as separate classifications. A prospective longitudinal follow-up study, comparing 95 patients meeting typical AN criteria and 20 atypical AN patients over 10 to 15 years, found that atypical ANs had only 19 per cent the chance of ANs of progressing to chronic morbidity, a quicker rate of full clinical recovery and a lower risk of developing onset of binge eating (Strober et al. 1999). It therefore seems that AN and atypical AN may have different outcomes, at least in terms of these factors.

Atypical Bulimia Nervosa versus Bulimia Nervosa

Descriptive and construct validity

Two studies (Stice et al. 1998; Vanderheyden and Boland 1987) used discriminant function analysis to investigate whether BN is at the endpoint of an eating disorder continuum (continuity hypothesis) or forms an eating disorder group clearly separated from sub-threshold BN or no eating disorder (discontinuity hypothesis). The results of both studies supported the continuity hypothesis on measures of weight concern and psychopathology.

In DSM-III-R, the frequency of binge eating that was required to warrant a diagnosis of BN was arbitrarily set at two episodes a week over a three-month period (APA 1987). Studies comparing individuals with full syndrome BN and those who only lack the frequency criterion have had mixed findings. Bunnell *et al.* (1990) found that patients with subclinical BN did not strongly resemble those with clear-cut BN on measures of general psychopathology. However, other research (Garfinkel *et al.* 1995b; Wilson and Eldridge 1991) has found that individuals who binge once a week are similar to those who binge more often on most significant dimensions, e.g. comorbidity, psychosocial impairment and risk of earlier sexual abuse.

There is also mixed evidence as to whether binge frequency itself is meaningful in predicting associated psychopathology, which has been found to increase as binge eating frequency increases (Williamson *et al.* 1987). However, others have not found such a relationship (Fairburn and Cooper 1984).

Predictive validity

There are no studies assessing the predictive validity of atypical BN.

Problems in classification

The definition of Atypical BN in ICD-10 is deliberately vague. It states: "Researchers studying atypical forms of bulimia nervosa, such as those involving normal or excessive body weight, are recommended to make their own decisions about the number and type of criteria to be fulfilled." The aim of this vagueness presumably is to give researchers the freedom to elucidate the diagnostic uncertainty further. However, it also poses problems for the comparability of research findings.

Binge Eating Disorder versus Bulimia Nervosa

In Chapter 4 Dingemans and her colleagues present evidence on the empirical status of BED. This following section examines the validity of BED as a diagnostic entity distinct from EDNOS and BN.

Descriptive and construct validity

Perhaps because this disorder is relatively new, there has been much research into the validity of BED, relative to the amount of research into the validity of other subtypes of eating disorders.

Research supporting the notion that BN and BED are distinct diagnostic entities

One characteristic that differentiates BED from BN in field studies is the male to female ratio, which is 1:1 in community samples (e.g. Spitzer *et al.* 1992, 1993b). However, as Garfinkel *et al.* (1995b) argue, this is not enough to grant a separate diagnosis to BED and "it is not possible to support the inclusion of 2 separate groups of non-purging BN and BED. They may represent the same people during different phases of their disorder" (Garfinkel *et al.* 1995a: 451). BN and BED are further differentiated in that BN patients are generally of a normal weight, whereas the majority of individuals with BED are overweight (APA 1994). Moreover, there are differences in BN and BED in the order in which their symptoms typically develop. In BN, dieting usually starts before bingeing (Polivy *et al.* 1984), whereas the reverse is true in a significant proportion of individuals with BED (Abbott *et al.* 1994; Mussell *et al.* 1995; Spitzer *et al.* 1993b; Spurrell *et al.* 1997; Wilson *et al.* 1993). In addition, people with BED clearly differ from those with BN purging type (BN-P) in eating disorder symptomatology and more general psychopathology (Fichter *et al.* 1993; Raymond *et al.* 1995).

More recent research has specifically focused on differences between BN non-purging type (BN-NP) and BED. These two groups have been found to differ in age and weight, in binge eating and dieting behaviour, previous AN episodes, body mass index and comorbidity (Santonastaso *et al.* 1999; Tobin *et al.* 1997; Williamson *et al.* 1992). In addition, the BED patients appear to form a heterogeneous group, whereas BN-NP appear to be a homogeneous group sharing a number of clinical characteristics with BN-P (e.g. similar age, gender, determination to compensate for bingeing and a similar pathway to binge eating). Such differences between BED and BN-NP patients, lends support to the distinction made by DSM-IV.

Mizes and Sloan (1998) conducted a cluster analysis of 53 EDNOS patients divided into clinically derived subgroups. They found a heterogeneous EDNOS group and an overweight binge eating group. The two groups differed in terms of their history of high weight, current weight, binge eating, and unrealistic ideas about ideal weight and body dissatisfaction. However, the two groups did not differ in terms of purging or restricting behaviours, as current diagnostic criteria require. This study therefore supports the need for a subgroup of binge eating patients who are distinct from other EDNOS patients but does not support the current criterion of "without compensatory behaviours" for BED.

Research which does not support the notion of BED as a separate diagnostic entity

Cluster analysis on a community sample of recurrent binge eaters revealed four separate clusters (Hay *et al.* 1996). Their findings failed to support the category of BED, since none of the clusters resembled this condition. A study by the same group found no significant differences between women with either BED or BN-NP in self-reported self-esteem, psychopathology or social adjustment (Hay and Fairburn 1998).

A comparison of women with BED, BN-P and BN-NP recruited from the community found that BED women had significantly higher BMIs than BN-P women but did not differ from BN-NP women in this respect (Striegel-Moore *et al.* 2001). This similarity in BMI between BN-NP and BED subjects has been previously noted (Spitzer *et al.* 1993b). Striegel-Moore *et al.* (2001) found no differences between the groups in rates of current or lifetime psychiatric comorbidity and scores on the Eating Disorders Examination-Questionnaire (EDE-Q: Fairburn and Beglin 1994) Weight Concern or Shape Concern subscales. They also found that 20 per cent of women with BN-P and 13 per cent with BN-NP met lifetime criteria for AN, while only 10 per cent of BED women did. They conclude that there is only tentative evidence to support BED as a clinical disorder distinct from BN-NP.

A different line of research examined binge quality. Although BED and BN patients have not been found to differ in terms of binge quantity, differences have been found in binge quality (e.g. Fitzgibbon and Blackman 2000), with BED individuals bearing more resemblance to non-BED obese subjects than BN subjects in terms of temporal patterns of eating (Cooke *et al.* 1997).

Predictive validity

A community-based sample of 250 young women with recurrent binge eating found that although BN-NP and BED subjects did not differ on any current eating disorder symptomatology measure, they had high predictive validity (Hay and Fairburn 1998). Those with BN had more severe eating disorder symptomatology at a one-year follow-up than those with BED. Also, both BN-P and BN-NP had similar predictive validity. These groups were similar in temporal stability whereas BED patients showed less temporal stability. If, as Kendell (1989) argues, predictive validity is a key criterion for evaluating psychiatric diagnoses, then these findings support the notion of both sub-types of BN being conceptualized as part of a single disorder that is separate from BED.

Other research lends some support to retaining a distinction in terms of diagnostic categories, between BED and BN. A prospective study of a community sample of 102 BN patients and 48 BED patients over five years found a distinct outcome for BN compared to BED (Fairburn *et al.* 2000). BNs were found to have a relatively poor prognosis, whereas the majority of those with BED recovered. In addition, the BN sample experienced a highly fluctuating course of outcome, whereas in the BED group there was a steady trend towards improvement from bingeing, however, the rate of obesity in this group had doubled by the five-year follow-up. The findings suggest a difference in course and outcome between BN and BED.

Distinctive treatment response

There is very little work on the treatment of atypical eating disorders, other than that for BED, and even this is limited. At this stage, it is unclear whether BED has a distinctive treatment response compared to other eating disorders. See Chapter 4 for a review of BED treatment.

Family studies

Lee *et al.* (1999) examined 32 obese BED females and 23 non-BED obese females for a potential familial tendency for BED among the obese. It was found that the frequencies of all eating disorders, BED included, and the risk of other psychiatric disturbances, did not differ significantly between the relatives of those with and without BED. Hence, the study failed to find a familial propensity for BED or a familial relationship between other eating disorders and BED.

Problems in classification

Difficulties with classification may arise from the precise definition of binge eating. Individuals with BN often overestimate the size of binges (Hadigan *et al.* 1992) and the majority of binge episodes described by women with BN have been found to involve an intake of less than 1000 kcal (Rossiter and Agras 1990).

The difficulties women with BN have in objectifying the size of a binge led Fairburn and Cooper (1993) to differentiate between objective binge episodes (which coincides with the DSM-IV definition) and subjective binge episodes, on the basis of the amount of food consumed and the subjective loss of control. This latter perception of loss of control may be of more importance than the actual amount of food in defining binge-eating episodes (Fairburn 1983). In a sample of obese women with BED asked to define the term binge, the majority defined it by loss of control (Telch *et al.* 1998), which supports the DSM-IV criterion of loss of control as central to binge eating. However, less than a half reported a large amount of food as central to binge eating. Telch *et al.* (1998) concluded that it is the subjective experience of binge eating rather than the quantity eaten that is the critical issue. They suggested two new features be considered for inclusion in proposed DSM criteria: "(1) eating as an attempt to cope with or regulate negative affect and (2) eating that involves the consumption of a certain type of food usually designated as forbidden by the individual" (Telch *et al.* 1998: 316).

BED versus sub-threshold BED

A study of four groups of obese women and men (individuals with BED, sub-threshold BED, individuals who had reported recurrent overeating and normal controls) selected from a large community-based sample, was conducted in order to examine the utility of the BED diagnosis (Striegel-Moore *et al.* 1998). Individuals with BED could be distinguished from overeaters and controls on a number of psychological and behavioural variables. However, few differences between BED and sub-threshold BED were found, prompting Striegel-Moore and colleagues to question the diagnostic validity of the frequency threshold. In addition, women and men with BED did not differ from each other above and beyond the gender-related differences observed across all four groups. They concluded that their findings support the notion of BED as a distinct syndrome.

Summary and conclusion

The evidence on the validity of the EDNOS diagnosis described earlier is limited and uneven. Many studies are based on small numbers, highly selected patient populations and self-report measures of eating disorder symptoms or diagnoses. Any conclusions from the evidence have to be drawn with some degree of caution. Nonetheless, the following summary can be made.

Atypical AN seems to lack descriptive and construct validity. It cannot be clearly distinguished from AN in terms of eating disorder features or other psychopathology, and it has been thought that typical and atypical AN may simply be different stages of the same illness. Only one study found atypical AN to have predictive validity. Taken together research in this area suggests that AN, as currently defined, may be too narrow a diagnosis, resulting in an overly broad EDNOS/atypical AN category. Similarly, atypical BN appears to lack descriptive and construct validity. It seems that distinguishing typical from atypical cases on the basis of the frequency criterion may not be useful due to its arbitrary nature. There does, however, seem to be some evidence to warrant the consideration of BED as a distinct diagnostic entity. BED does appear to have predictive validity, but there is mixed evidence for descriptive and construct validity. As yet, cluster analytic studies have not found conclusive evidence for this disorder and it is unclear how BED differs from BN-NP. Therefore, further research is necessary before any conclusive decisions can be reached.

These tentative conclusions need to be put into a wider context.

The bigger picture: findings from a population-based study

Latent class analysis "attempts to determine the number and composition of the unobserved latent classes that give rise to the observed data" (Bulik *et al.*

2000: 887). Bulik *et al.* (2000) used this method with nine lifetime symptoms of DSM-III-R AN and BN to determine the naturally occurring empirical typology of eating disorders in a large cohort of female twins from a population-based registry. The findings were consistent with three general classes of eating disorders similar to the current AN, BN and BED diagnoses. A further three atypical classes which did not seem to reflect clinical eating disorders were found which may however reflect those at risk for the development of clinical eating disorders. For example, there was a shape/weight preoccupied class which had no significant weight loss yet displayed the psychological features of AN and may therefore reflect a subclinical group who are greatly concerned with shape/weight but do not engage in clinically significant disordered eating. However, as Bulik *et al.* (2000) argue themselves, the data used to create diagnostic categories come mainly from clinical samples, which may not reflect the true nosology of the population of people with eating disorders – many of whom do not present for treatment. Within the group resembling AN, only half of the women endorsed body image distortion and a number did not report amenorrhoea at the time of low weight. In addition, the criterion of lack of control added little towards defining this group. Hence, Bulik *et al.* (2000) cite the need for continued evaluation of these diagnostic criteria, in terms of the amenorrhoea and body image distortion for AN and the sense of loss of control occurring with bingeing for BN and BED.

The clinical utility of classification of eating disorders

Waller (1993) questions whether the current diagnostic criteria have adequate clinical utility for eating disorders and suggests that a general eating disorder category may be more useful than the current subgroups. He argues that identified eating disorder syndromes have so far failed to meet the three important criteria for clinical utility of a diagnosis, i.e. adequate differentiation, standardization of communication, and indication of treatment. Fairburn *et al.* (2003) propound a transdiagnostic view of eating disorders, stating that "anorexia nervosa, bulimia nervosa and the atypical eating disorders share the same distinctive psychopathology, and patients move between these diagnostic states over time" (Fairburn *et al.* 2003: 520) and "common mechanisms are involved in the persistence of bulimia nervosa, anorexia nervosa and atypical eating disorders." This movement of patients between the diagnoses has been little researched. Fairburn *et al.* (2003) state the relevance of age and/or duration of disorder in this process, and the difficulty of disentangling these two factors. They propose that in their new transdiagnostic treatment, a patient's specific eating disorder diagnosis is not of relevance to treatment and that it is the psychopathological features present and the apparent maintaining processes which should dictate treatment content.

Categories or continuum?

As discussed, some of the evidence seems to suggest a continuum of eating disorders, especially regarding typical and atypical forms of the same disorder. Although many researchers have theorized eating disorders around an anorexic–bulimic dichotomy (Pope and Hudson 1989), others have argued for a continuum between AN and BN (e.g. Fairburn and Cooper 1984). Indeed, consistent with the finding that a significant proportion of AN sufferers go on to experience BN, a sequential model has also been proposed (Clinton and Glant 1992). It is beyond the scope of this chapter to fully discuss the relative merits of a category or continuum model of eating disorders, but it seems to us that at present the jury is still out.

References

Abbott, D., de Zwaan, M., Mussell, M., Raymond, N., Seim, H., Crow, S., Crosby, R. and Mitchell, J. (1994) "A comparison of binge eaters who begin to binge before and after dieting", paper presented at the Sixth International Conference on Eating Disorders, New York.

American Psychiatric Association (1980) *Diagnostic and Statistical Manual of Mental Disorders*, 3rd edn (DSM-III), Washington, DC: APA.

American Psychiatric Association (1987) *Diagnostic and Statistical Manual of Mental Disorders*, 3rd edn revised (DSM-III-R), Washington, DC: APA.

American Psychiatric Association (1994) *Diagnostic and Statistical Manual of Mental Disorders*, 4th edn (DSM-IV), Washington, DC: APA.

Andersen, A.E. (2001) "Progress in eating disorders research", *American Journal of Psychiatry* 158, 515–17.

Andersen, A.E., Bowers, W.A. and Watson, T. (2001) "A slimming program for eating disorders not otherwise specified: reconceptualizing a confusing, residual diagnostic category", *Psychiatric Clinics of North America* 24, 271–81.

Ben-Tovim, D.I., Walker, K., Gilchrist, P., Freeman, R., Kalucy, R. and Esterman, A. (2001) "Outcome in patients with eating disorders: a 5 year study", *Lancet* 357, 1254–7.

Bulik, C.M., Sullivan, P.F. and Kendler, K.S. (2000) "An empirical study of the classification of eating disorders", *American Journal of Psychiatry* 157, 886–95.

Bunnell, D.W., Shenker, I.R., Nussbaum, M.P., Jacobson, M.S. and Cooper, P. (1990) "Subclinical versus formal eating disorders: differentiating psychological features", *International Journal of Eating Disorders* 9, 357–62.

Cachelin, F.M. and Maher, B.A. (1998) "Is amenorrhea a critical criterion for anorexia nervosa?", *Journal of Psychosomatic Research* 44, 435–40.

Carlat, D.J., Camargo, C.A. and Herzog, D.B. (1997) "Eating disorders in males: a report on 135 patients", *American Journal of Psychiatry* 154, 1127–32.

Clinton, D.N. and Glant, R. (1992) "The eating disorders spectrum of DSM-III-R: clinical features and psychosocial concomitants of 86 consecutive cases from a Swedish urban catchment area", *Journal of Nervous and Mental Disease* 180, 244–50.

Cooke, E.A., Guss, J.L., Kissileff, H.R., Devlin, M.J. and Walsh, B.T. (1997)

"Patterns of food selection during binges in women with binge eating disorder", *International Journal of Eating Disorders* 22, 187–93.

Fairburn, C.G. (1983) "Bulimia nervosa", *British Journal of Hospital Medicine* 29, 537–42.

Fairburn, C.G. and Beglin, S.J. (1994) "Assessment of eating disorders: interview or self-report questionnaire?", *International Journal of Eating Disorders* 16, 363–70.

Fairburn, C.G. and Cooper, P.J. (1984) "Binge eating, self-induced vomiting, and laxative abuse: a community study", *Psychological Medicine* 14, 401–10.

Fairburn, C.G. and Cooper, Z. (1993) "The eating disorder examination (12.0D)", in C.G. Fairburn and G.T. Wilson (eds) *Binge Eating: Nature, Assessment and Treatment*, New York: Guilford Press.

Fairburn, C.G. and Walsh, B.T. (1995) "Atypical eating disorders", in K.D. Brownell and C.G. Fairburn (eds) *Eating Disorders and Obesity: A Comprehensive Handbook*, New York: Guilford Press.

Fairburn, C.G. and Walsh, B.T. (2002) "Atypical eating disorders (eating disorders not otherwise specified)", in C.G. Fairburn and K.D. Brownell (eds) *Eating Disorders and Obesity: A Comprehensive Handbook*, 2nd edn, New York: Guilford Press.

Fairburn, C.G., Cooper, Z., Doll, H.A., Norman, P. and O'Connor, M. (2000) "The natural course of bulimia nervosa and binge eating disorder in young women", *Archives of General Psychiatry* 57, 659–65.

Fairburn, C.G., Cooper, Z. and Shafran, R. (2003) "Cognitive behaviour therapy for eating disorders: a 'transdiagnostic' theory and treatment", *Behaviour Research and Therapy* 41, 509–28.

Fichter, M.M., Quadflieg, N. and Brandl, B. (1993) "Recurrent overeating: an empirical comparison of binge eating disorder, bulimia nervosa, and obesity", *International Journal of Eating Disorders* 14, 1–16.

Fitzgibbon, M.L. and Blackman, L.R. (2000) "Binge eating disorder and bulimia nervosa: differences in the quality and quantity of binge-eating episodes", *International Journal of Eating Disorders* 27, 238–43.

Garfinkel, P.E. (1995) "Classsification and diagnosis of eating disorders", in K.D. Brownell and C.G. Fairburn (eds) *Eating Disorders and Obesity: A Comprehensive Handbook*, New York: Guilford Press.

Garfinkel, P.E., Kennedy, S.H., Kaplan, A.S. (1995a) "Views on classification and diagnosis of eating disorders", *Canadian Journal of Psychiatry* 40, 435–6.

Garfinkel, P.E., Lin, B., Goering, P., Spegg, C., Goldbloom, D., Kennedy, S., Kaplan, A. and Woodside, B. (1995b) "Bulimia nervosa in a Canadian community sample: prevalence, comorbidity, early experiences and psychosocial functioning", *American Journal of Psychiatry* 152, 1052–8.

Garfinkel, P.E., Goering, L.P., Spegg, C., Goldbloom, D., Kennedy, S., Kaplan, A.S. and Woodside, D.B. (1996) "Should amenorrhoea be necessary for the diagnosis of anorexia nervosa", *British Journal of Psychiatry* 168, 500–6.

Geist, R., Davis, R. and Heinmaa, M. (1998) "Binge/purge symptoms and comorbidity in adolescents with eating disorders", *Canadian Journal of Psychiatry* 43, 507–12.

Hadigan, C.M., LaChaussee, J.L., Walsh, B.T. and Kissileff, H.R. (1992) "24-hour dietary recall in patients with bulimia nervosa", *International Journal of Eating Disorders* 12, 107–11.

Halmi, K.A. (1985) "Classification of the eating disorders", *Journal of Psychiatric Research* 19, 113–19.

Halmi, K.A. (2000) "Eating disorders", in B.J. Sadock and V.A. Sadock (eds) *Kaplan and Sadock's Comprehensive Textbook of Psychiatry, Volume II*, 7th edn, London: Lippincott Williams & Wilkins.

Halmi, K.A., Eckert, E., Marchi, P., Sampugnaro, V., Apple, K. and Cohen, J. (1991) "Comorbidity of psychiatric diagnoses in anorexia nervosa", *Archives of General Psychiatry* 48, 712–18.

Hay, P. and Fairburn, C.G. (1998) "The validity of the DSM-IV scheme for classifying bulimic eating disorders", *International Journal of Eating Disorders* 23, 7–15.

Hay, P.J., Fairburn, C.G. and Doll, H.A. (1996) "The classification of bulimic eating disorders: a community-based cluster analysis study", *Psychological Medicine* 26, 801–12.

Herzog, D.B., Hopkins, J.D. and Burns, C.D. (1993) "A follow-up study of 33 subdiagnostic eating disordered women", *International Journal of Eating Disorders* 14, 261–7.

Hsu, L.K.G. and Lee, S. (1993) "Is weight phobia always necessary for a diagnosis of anorexia nervosa?", *American Journal of Psychiatry* 150, 1466–71.

Hsu, L.K.G. and Sobkiewicz, T.A. (1991) "Body image disturbance: time to abandon concept for eating disorders?", *International Journal of Eating Disorders* 10, 15–30.

Kendell, R.E. (1989) "Clinical validity", *Psychological Medicine* 19, 45–55.

King, M.B. (1989) "Eating disorders in a general practice population: prevalence, characteristics and follow-up at 12 to 18 months", *Psychological Medicine – Monograph supplement* 14, 1–34.

King, M.B. (1991) "Update: eating disorders", *Comprehensive Therapy* 17, 35–40.

Kruger, S., McVey, G. and Kennedy, S.H. (1998) "The changing profile of anorexia nervosa at the Toronto programme for eating disorders", *Journal of Psychosomatic Research* 45, 533–47.

Lee, Y.H., Abbott, D.W., Seim, H., Crosby, R.D., Monson, N., Burgard, M. and Mitchell, J.E. (1999) "Eating disorders and psychiatric disorders in first-degree relatives of obese probands with binge eating disorders and obese non-binge eating disorder controls", *International Journal of Eating Disorders* 26, 322–32.

Lilenfeld, L.R., Walter, H.K., Greeno, C.G., Merikangas, K.R., Plotnicov, K., Pollice, C., Rao, R., Strober, M., Bulik, C.M. and Nagy, L. (1998) "A controlled family study of anorexia nervosa and bulimia nervosa", *Archives of General Psychiatry* 55, 603–10.

Marino, M.F. and Zanarini, M.C. (2001) "Relationship between EDNOS and its subtypes and borderline personality disorder", *International Journal of Eating Disorders* 29, 349–53.

Mizes, J.S. and Sloan, D.M. (1998) "An empirical analysis of eating disorder, not otherwise specified: preliminary support for a distinct subgroup", *International Journal of Eating Disorders* 23, 233–42.

Mussell, M.P., Mitchell, J.E., Weller, C.L., Raymond, N.C., Crow, S.J. and Crosby, R.D. (1995) "Onset of binge eating, dieting, obesity, and mood disorders among subjects seeking treatment for binge eating disorders", *International Journal of Eating Disorders* 17, 395–401.

Palmer, R.L. (1993) "Weight concern should not be a necessary criterion for the eating disorders: a polemic", *International Journal of Eating Disorders* 14, 459–65.

Palmer, R.L. (2003) "Concepts of eating disorders", in J. Treasure, U. Schmidt and E. van Furth (eds) *Handbook of Eating Disorders: Theory Treatment and Research*, 2nd edn, Chichester: Wiley.

Patton, G.C. (1988) "The spectrum of eating disorder in adolescence", *Journal of Psychosomatic Research* 32, 579–84.

Patton, G.C., Johnson-Sabine, E., Wood, K., Mann, A.H. and Wakeling, A. (1990) "Abnormal eating attitudes in London schoolgirls – a prospective epidemiological study: outcome at twelve month follow-up", *Psychological Medicine* 20, 383–94.

Polivy, J., Herman, C., Olmsted, M. and Jazwinski, C. (1984) "Restraint and binge eating", in R.C. Hawkins, W.J. Fremouv and P.F. Clement (eds) *The Binge–purge Syndrome: Diagnosis, Treatment and Research*, New York: Springer.

Pope, H.G. and Hudson, J.I. (1989) "Are eating disorders associated with borderline personality disorder? A critical review", *International Journal of Eating Disorders* 8, 1–11.

Raymond, N.C., Mussell, M.P., Mitchell, J.E., de Zwann, M. and Crosby, R.D. (1995) "An age-matched comparison of subjects with binge eating disorder and bulimia nervosa", *International Journal of Eating Disorders* 18, 135–43.

Ricca, V., Mannucci, E., Mezzani, B., Di Bernardo, M., Zucchi, T., Paionni, A., Placidi, G.P., Rotella, C.M. and Faravelli, C. (2001) "Psychopathological and clinical features of outpatients with an eating disorder not otherwise specified", *Eating and Weight Disorders* 6, 157–65.

Robins, E. and Guze, S.B. (1970) "Establishment of diagnostic validity in psychiatric illness: its application to schizophrenia", *American Journal of Psychiatry* 126, 107–11.

Rossiter, E. and Agras, W.S. (1990) "An empirical test of the DSM-III-R definition of binge", *International Journal of Eating Disorders* 9, 513–8.

Santonastaso, P., Ferrara, S. and Favaro, A. (1999) "Differences between binge eating disorder and nonpurging bulimia nervosa", *International Journal of Eating Disorders* 25, 215–18.

Schleimer, K. (1983) "Dieting in teenage schoolgirls: a longitudinal prospective study", *Acta Paediatrica Scandinavica, Supplement* 312, 1–54.

Spitzer, R.L., Devlin, M., Walsh, B.T., Hasin, D., Wing, R., Marcus, M., Stunkard, A., Wadden, T., Yanovski, S., Agras, S., Mitchell, J. and Nonas, C. (1992) "Binge eating disorder: a multi-site field trial of the diagnostic criteria", *International Journal of Eating Disorders* 11, 191–203.

Spitzer, R.L., Stunkard, A., Yanovski, S., Marcus, M.D., Wadden, T., Wing, R., Mitchell, J. and Hasin, D. (1993a) "Binge eating disorder should be included in DSM-IV: a reply to Fairburn et al.'s 'The classification of recurrent overeating: the binge eating disorder proposal' ", *International Journal of Eating Disorders* 13, 161–9.

Spitzer, R.L., Yanovski, S., Wadden, T., Wing, R., Marcus, M.D., Stunkard, A., Devlin, M., Mitchell, J., Hasin, D. and Horne, R.L. (1993b) "Binge eating disorder: its further validation in a multi-site study", *International Journal of Eating Disorders* 13, 137–53.

Spurrell, E.B., Wilfley, D.E., Tanofsky, M.B. and Brownell, K.D. (1997) "Age of onset for binge eating: are there different pathways to binge eating?", *International Journal of Eating Disorders* 21, 55–65.

Stice, E., Killen, J.D., Hayward, C. and Taylor, C.B. (1998) "Support for the continuity hypothesis of bulimic pathology", *Journal of Consulting and Clinical Psychology* 66, 784–90.

Striegel-Moore, R.H., Silberstein, L.R., Frensch, P. and Rodin, J. (1989) "A prospective study of disordered eating among college students", *International Journal of Eating Disorders* 8, 499–509.

Striegel-Moore, R.H., Wilson, G.T., Wilfley, D.E., Elder, K.A. and Brownell, K.D. (1998) "Binge eating in an obese community sample", *International Journal of Eating Disorders* 23, 27–37.

Striegel-Moore, R.H., Garvin, V., Dohm, F.A. and Rosenheck, R.A. (1999) "Psychiatric comorbidity of eating disorders in men: a national study of hospitalized veterans", *International Journal of Eating Disorders* 25, 399–404.

Striegel-Moore, R.H., Cachelin, F.M., Dohm, F., Pike, K.M., Wilfley, D.E. and Fairburn, C.G. (2001) "Comparison of binge eating disorder and bulimia nervosa in a community sample", *International Journal of Eating Disorders* 29, 157–65.

Strober, M., Freeman, R. and Morrell, W. (1999) "Atypical anorexia nervosa: separation from typical cases in course and outcome in a long-term prospective study", *International Journal of Eating Disorders* 25, 135–42.

Strober, M., Freeman, R., Lampert, C., Diamond, J. and Kaye, W. (2000) "Controlled family study of anorexia nervosa and bulimia nervosa: evidence of shared liability and transmission of partial syndromes", *American Journal of Psychiatry* 157, 393–401.

Strober, M., Freeman, R., Lampert, C., Diamond, J. and Kaye, W. (2001) "Males with anorexia nervosa: a controlled study of eating disorders in first-degree relatives", *International Journal of Eating Disorders* 29, 263–9.

Telch, C.F., Pratt, E.M. and Niego, S.H. (1998) "Obese women with binge eating disorder define the term binge", *International Journal of Eating Disorders* 24, 313–17.

Theander, S. (1970) "Anorexia Nervosa: a psychiatric investigation of 94 female patients", *Acta Psychiatrica Scandinavica, Supplementum* 214.

Tobin, D.L., Griffing, A. and Griffing, S. (1997) "An examination of subtype criteria for bulimia nervosa", *International Journal of Eating Disorders* 22, 179–86.

Vanderheyden, D.A. and Boland, F.J. (1987) "A comparison of normals, mild, moderate, and severe binge eaters, and binge vomiters using discriminant function analysis", *International Journal of Eating Disorders* 6, 331–7.

Waller, G. (1993) "Why do we diagnose different types of eating disorder? Arguments for a change in research and clinical practice", *European Eating Disorders Review* 1, 174–89.

Watson, T.L. and Andersen, A.E. (2003) "A critical examination of the amenorrhea and weight criteria for diagnosing anorexia nervosa", *Acta Psychiatrica Scandinavica* 108, 175–82.

Williamson, D.A., Prather, R.C., Upton, L., Davis, C.J., Ruggiero, L. and Van Buren, D. (1987) "Severity of bulimia: relationship with depression and other psychopathology", *International Journal of Eating Disorders* 7, 825–35.

Williamson, D.A., Gleaves, D.H. and Savin, S.S. (1992) "Empirical classification of eating disorders not otherwise specified: support for DSM-IV changes", *Journal of Psychopathology and Behavioural Assessment* 14, 210–16.

Wilson, G.T. and Eldredge, K. (1991) "Frequency of binge eating in bulimia nervosa: diagnostic validity", *International Journal of Eating Disorders* 10, 557–61.

Wilson, G.T., Nonas, C.A. and Rosenblum, G.D. (1993) "Assessment of binge eating in obese patients", *International Journal of Eating Disorders* 13, 25–33.

World Health Organization (1992) *ICD-10 Classification of Mental and Behavioural Disorders: Clinical Descriptions and Diagnostic Guidelines*, Geneva: WHO.

Yager, J., Landsverk, J. and Edelstein, C.K. (1987) "A 20-month follow-up study of 628 women with eating disorders, I: Course and severity", *American Journal of Psychiatry* 144, 1172–7.

Chapter 4

The empirical status of Binge Eating Disorder

Alexandra E. Dingemans, Patricia van Hanswijck de Jonge and Eric F. van Furth

Introduction

In the fourth edition of the *Diagnostic and Statistical Manual of Mental Disorders* of the American Psychiatric Association, Binge Eating Disorder is proposed as a new diagnostic category requiring further study and as an example of EDNOS (APA 1994) (see Appendix for diagnostic criteria). The criteria are described in an appendix, indicating that BED requires further research before it can be incorporated as a fully accepted category in the DSM. No comparable diagnostic category exists in ICD-10 (WHO 1992).

BED was introduced as a new eating disorder in the early 1990s. The aim of this chapter is to give an overview of the results and to discuss the empirical status of BED after a decade of research. What is the empirical evidence for and against the state currently defined as BED in the DSM-IV? In this chapter we will focus on the present status of BED as an eating disorder. The issue of the relationship between BED and obesity will be discussed elsewhere in the book (see Chapter 5).

The *Diagnostic and Statistical Manual of Mental Disorders*

Classifying mental disorders by means of the DSM is one of the many methods of classification. Since the publication of the third edition of the DSM the taxonomy proposed by the American Psychiatric Association has become more dominant than anyone would have believed possible in the light of the limited impact of the first and second editions (APA 1952, 1968; Follette and Houts 1996). In its proposal for the DSM-III the APA (1980) considered mental disorders as medical disorders. Although there is not yet an agreement about the diagnosis and the criteria, in actual practice BED is already accepted as an eating disorder. However, there is considerable debate about how much effort should be made to treat these patients in an eating disorder clinic. If patients with a BED are treated within an eating disorder clinic there is also discussion about the kind of therapy which is suited for these patients (Dingemans *et al.* 2002).

Objections to this viewpoint came from the American Psychological Association. The DSM reflects the underlying model of traditional medicine. In order to gain wide acceptance of the system the task force of the DSM decided to abandon the theoretical (medical) view and to cease referring to mental disorders as a subset of medical disorders. This decision largely explains the syndrome-based and non-theoretical nature of the DSM (Follette and Houts 1996).

According to the DSM-IV a mental disorder is defined as:

> a clinically significant behavioural or psychological syndrome or pattern that occurs in an individual and that is associated with present distress (e.g. a painful symptom) or disability (i.e. impairment in one or more important areas of functioning) or with a significant increased risk of suffering death, pain, disability, or an important loss of freedom. In addition, this syndrome or pattern must not be merely an expectable and culturally sanctioned response to a particular event, for example, the death of a loved one. Whatever its original cause, it must currently be considered a manifestation of a behavioural, psychological, or biological dysfunction in the individual.
>
> (APA 1994: xxi)

The definition of dysfunction is crucial to the definition because something is not a disorder unless something has gone amiss in the person concerned (Follette and Houts 1996).

The proposal of Spitzer and others

Spitzer *et al.* (1991) suggested that BED should be included in the DSM-IV. The rationale for their proposal was that many individuals with marked distress about binge eating could not be diagnosed as having Bulimia Nervosa. People with the BED syndrome have episodes of binge eating as do patients with BN, but unlike the latter they do not engage in compensatory behaviours such as self-induced vomiting, the misuse of laxatives, diuretics or diet pills, fasting and excessive exercise. The authors indicated that such patients are common among the obese involved in weight control programmes and/or belonging to overeaters anonymous (Spitzer *et al.* 1992, 1993). Although the diagnosis BED was formulated with the obese in mind, obesity is not a criterion for BED.

For inclusion in a new version of the DSM, the "new" diagnostic is required to describe a pattern of symptoms not captured in the existing categories (Pincus *et al.* 1992). Pincus *et al.* (1992: 113), who served on the DSM-IV task force, stated that for a new category to be considered for inclusion in the DSM-IV, "there must be solid evidence that the diagnosis is useful in predicting prognosis, treatment selection or outcome."

Fairburn *et al.* (1993) considered whether Pincus *et al.*'s arguments would apply to the proposed addition of BED to the DSM. One argument against new diagnoses is that if they are rare, they may add unnecessary complexity to the already cumbersome system of classification and be irrelevant for clinical use. Furthermore, incorporation of new categories is likely to increase the overall prevalence of mental disorders. The addition of new and unproven diagnoses carries the risk of trivializing the construct mental disorder and/or its misuse. This is relevant for BED since we would not wish normal gluttony to be classed as a psychiatric disorder (Fairburn *et al.* 1993). The criteria proposed by Spitzer *et al.* (1992) have been designed to minimize this risk. However, Fairburn *et al.* (1993) argued that adding BED to the section of eating disorders does not make it very complex because the present scheme is relatively simple.

A second argument against adding new diagnostic categories is that new diagnoses are generally proposed by experts in the field concerned and are subsequently used by less expert assessors who may identify more false positives. These inaccurate diagnoses may lead to faulty treatments.

A third argument put forward by Fairburn and others is that "adding unproven diagnostic categories may confer upon such categories an approval that they do not merit yet." They argue that there is no evidence to suggest that delineating BED from EDNOS is a useful or valid approach. This delineation "may impede efforts to devise better classificatory schemes since investigators will inevitably tend to define their samples along the new lines" (Fairburn *et al.* 1993: 158).

A fourth argument concerns the risk of definitional overlap across related categories. Fairburn *et al.* (1993) argue that the delineation of BED could cause definitional overlap between the non-purging type of BN and BED. BN non-purging type is distinguished from BED by the presence of compensatory behaviours (fasting and excessive exercise) and/or undue emphasis on self-evaluation of body shape or body weight. Although the existence of substantial differences between BN non-purging type and BED has been confirmed (Santonastaso *et al.* 1999), it is difficult to draw clear boundaries between these two categories. It is unclear when these distinguishing behaviours are severe enough to warrant the diagnosis of BN non-purging type rather than BED.

Another reason for adding a new diagnosis to the DSM is to initiate research in the field. The DSM-III (APA 1980) and DSM-III-R (APA 1987) have been facilitators of research in areas that would have remained unresearched if they had not been included in an official nomenclature. Some see this as one of the most important goals of the DSM. Others, however, think that research should drive DSM and not the other way around. It makes no sense to include a category for which there is no empirical support

(Pincus *et al.* 1992). Once categories are included in the DSM they are not easily deleted (Blashfield *et al.* 1990). The insertion of BED in the DSM-IV has led to a considerable increase in the amount of research into BED since the early 1990s. The term BED was first used in a paper that appeared in 1991. The number of papers in which BED has been investigated has grown immensely since 1994 (Figure 4.1).

Classification criteria

The Eating Disorders Work Group of the DSM-IV task force in conjunction with Spitzer *et al.* (1992) developed preliminary criteria for the new eating disorder diagnosis designed to identify "the many people who have problems with recurrent binge eating, but who do not engage in compensatory behaviours of BN, vomiting or the abuse of laxatives." The criteria for the diagnosis of BED were adapted from those for BN, extra criteria being added to define the differences between the two disorders.

The definition of binge eating (Criterion A) is identical for BN and BED. However, in practice, binge eating among BED patients does not always conform to the requirement of the consumption of "a large amount" of food during a "discrete period of time", such as two hours. Rossiter *et al.* (1992) reported that many obese patients who overeat with a sense of loss of control consume quantities of food that would not be described as "large" during any "discrete period of time" but would be considered excessive over the course of the day. This pattern of overeating has been termed "grazing" and is a frequent occurrence within the obese binge-eating population (Marcus *et al.* 1992).

Binge-eating episodes are required to be associated with behavioural symptoms of loss of control (Criterion B). Spitzer *et al.* (1992, 1993) felt that

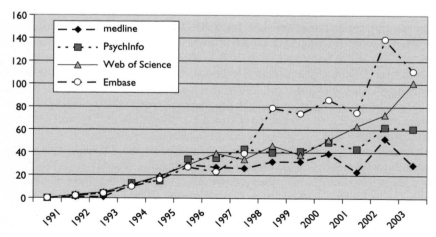

Figure 4.1 Overview of papers with "Binge Eating Disorder" as keyword.

Criterion B (symptoms of loss of control) should be included so as to set a high threshold for the diagnosis of BED and to ensure that normal gluttony would not be classed as BED. However, this criterion does not seem to be fully distinct from Criterion A2 (a sense of loss of control) or Criterion C (feelings of distress regarding binge eating). Criteria B1, B2 and B3 refer to aspects of loss of control while eating a large amount of food in a discrete period of time (Criterion A). Criteria B4 and B5 are related to characteristics of distress described in Criterion C.

The distress criterion was included in the DSM-IV proposed criteria for BED in order to minimize false positives. Removal of this criterion would have increased the number of individuals meeting criteria for the disorder by 10 per cent in a weight control sample and by more than 100 per cent in a community sample in Spitzer's field trail (Spitzer et al. 1992). However, it is not clear what is meant by "marked distress". Distress may refer to emotional distress or impaired social or occupational functioning as a consequence of binge-eating behaviour. Does distress reflect the patient's self-report of his/her emotional state or does it also require social and/or occupational impairment due to binge eating? Furthermore, de Zwaan (1997) stated that by including the distress criterion one may identify individuals with high levels of general distress which is not directly related to binge eating.

For a diagnosis of BED, binge eating is required to occur on two days a week (Criterion D) whereas patients with BN are required to have two episodes per week. This definition is based on the rationale that BED patients may have more difficulty in recalling and labelling binge-eating episodes than BN patients (Rossiter et al. 1992). The end of a binge-eating episode in BN is often characterized by purging behaviour, whereas in BED the termination of a binge episode is not punctuated by such behaviour. However, defining the frequency of binge eating in terms of the number of days on which the binge occurs seems to allow binges to be non-episodic, lasting as long as an entire day.

The twice-weekly frequency criterion for binge-eating episodes is arbitrary and has no empirical support in cases of BN or BED. Various authors have found that raising the frequency criteria of binge-eating episodes from once or twice a week did not change the pattern on measures of psychopathology or treatment outcome in binge eaters (Garfinkel et al. 1995; Striegel-Moore et al. 1998, 2000; Wilson et al. 1993).

Two binge eating days per week are required to occur during a six-month period in BED whereas a three-month period is specified for BN. The minimum duration of six months is required in order to ensure that transitory episodes of binge eating are not diagnosed as BED. Nevertheless, BED has been found to have a natural course that has a tendency to remit (Cachelin et al. 1999; Fairburn et al. 2000; Hay et al. 1996).

DSM-IV proposed diagnostic criterion E, which states that the diagnosis of BED should not be made if the patient engages in regular inappropriate compensatory behaviours also seen in BN (self-induced vomiting, laxative abuse, fasting, excessive exercise) or if he/she suffers from Anorexia Nervosa. However, there is no clear definition of what is meant by "inappropriate" compensatory behaviours. Some compensatory behaviour in the obese is not necessarily inappropriate. Moreover, there is no definition for the term regular. The term regular implies that some compensatory behaviour could be compatible with the diagnosis of BED.

Unlike BN, the DSM-IV research diagnostic criteria for BED do not include "unduly influenced self-evaluation by body weight and body shape." It is not clear why this criterion has been excluded from the proposed diagnostic criteria. However, Eldredge and Agras (1996) suggest that it may be due to uncertainty regarding the impact of the level of obesity on such concerns. Although obesity is not among the diagnostic criteria for either disorder, fewer BN patients are overweight than BED patients. The strong association between BED and obesity may be related to a patient's failure to compensate for the increased calories consumed during the binge-eating episodes. Despite omission of this criterion various authors have observed a significant association between BED and an overconcern about body weight and body shape (Cachelin et al. 1999; Marcus et al. 1992; Masheb and Grilo 2000; Striegel-Moore et al. 2000; van Hanswijck de Jonge et al. 2003; Wilfley et al. 2000; Wilson et al. 1993).

A comparison of characteristics of Binge Eating Disorder and Bulimia Nervosa

Most studies that compared BED and BN used the criteria for BN in the DSM-III-R, which made no distinction between the purging and non-purging subtypes of BN. The DSM-IV does make such a distinction between these subtypes. Purging bulimics engage in self-induced vomiting, misuse of laxatives, diuretics or enemas. Non-purging bulimics do not purge but do use other inappropriate compensatory behaviours (i.e. fasting or excessive exercise). Several studies have compared BED patients with bulimics (with no distinction between purging and non-purging subtype) (Goldfein et al. 1993; Kirkley et al. 1992; LaChaussee et al. 1992; Marcus et al. 1992; Mussell et al. 1995; Raymond et al. 1995; Tobin et al. 1997), and a few studies have compared BED patients to purging (Fichter et al. 1993; Masheb and Grilo 2000; Mitchell et al. 1999) and non-purging BN patients (Hay and Fairburn 1998; Santonastaso et al. 1999; Tobin et al. 1997). In order to interpret the results of these studies correctly it is important to know which version of the DSM was used.

In a study in which normal weight subjects with BN (DSM-III-R) were compared to obese subjects with BED, the latter seemed less anxious about their eating patterns and body weight, felt less guilty about being overweight, were less preoccupied with their eating behaviour, had a better overall opinion of themselves, were able to perceive internal states more accurately, were more socially adjusted, and were more comfortable in maintaining inter-personal relationships (Raymond *et al.* 1995). Both obese and non-obese BED subjects have lower levels of dietary restraint than subjects with BN purging type (Masheb and Grilo 2000). However, Marcus and others (1992) found that obese women seeking treatment for binge eating reported levels of eating disorder psychopathology that were comparable to those of normal weight BN patients (DSM-III-R). Similarly, a cross-sectional study (van Hanswijck de Jonge 2002) comparing BED to BN and obesity reported no significant difference between the two eating disorders on overall restraint psychopathology, eating concern psychopathology, body weight and body shape psychopathology. In all instances both BED and BN patients scored significantly higher in eating disorder psychopathology than the non-binge eating obese population.

Energy intake during an episode of binge eating seems to be different in BN (DSM-III-R) and BED. In a laboratory subjects were asked to binge on ice cream. Subjects with BN (DSM-III-R) consumed four times as much as normal weight healthy controls (LaChaussee *et al.* 1992). The same research group reported that subjects with BED ate only half the amount of ice cream eaten by subjects with BN (Goldfein *et al.* 1993). One study compared the quality and quantity of binges reported in individuals with BED and BN (Fitzgibbon and Blackman 2000). Binges of subjects with BN included food that was higher in carbohydrates and sugar content than the binges of sub-jects with BED. No difference was observed in the mean number of calories consumed.

BED patients seem to show fewer comorbid psychiatric symptoms than BN patients with either purging or non-purging subtype (Tobin *et al.* 1997). Schmidt and Telch (1990) have documented higher levels of depression, impulsivity, self-defeating tendencies and lower levels of self-esteem in BN than in BED. Similarly, Raymond *et al.* (1995) report higher levels of depres-sion and anxiety in BN patients than in BED patients. Another study (Tobin *et al.* 1997) compares purging BN to non-purging BN, BED and EDNOS on the Hopkins Symptom checklist and a measure of borderline syndrome and depression. The BED patients were reported to display significantly less anx-iety, paranoia and psychoticism than the other three groups. No other differ-ences were found between the groups on general psychopathology on the remaining measures. Unlike previous studies, no significant differences were found between BED and the two BN subtypes. Another study (van Hanswijck de Jonge 2002) could not distinguish between BN and BED on general psychopathology as measured by the Symptom Checklist-90-Revised (SCL-90-R). Furthermore, no distinction was reported between the two disorders on total levels of impulsivity. However, both BN and BED patients scored significantly higher on both general psychopathology and levels of impulsivity than did a group of non-binge eating obese patients. A study by Santonastaso and others (1999) showed no difference between non-purging bulimics and BED subjects on clinical and psychological characteristics, such as psychiatric symptoms, frequency of bingeing and impulsiveness traits. However, on many of the variables, the BED group showed a significantly greater variance. Webber (1994) does not document any significant differences between BN and BED.

Aetiology

In a community-based, retrospective case-control study, Fairburn and others (1998) aimed to identify specific risk factors for BED. They compared subjects with BED with healthy controls, subjects with other psychiatric disorders and subjects with BN. Their findings support the prediction that BED is associated with exposure to risk factors that increase the risk of psychiatric disorder in general and that increase the risk of obesity.

Little is known about the family characteristics of BED patients. One study found that BED subjects rated their family environment as less supportive and cohesive, and less engendering of direct and open expression of feelings than healthy controls. The BED group scored worse than other eating disorder groups (Hodges et al. 1998). One study investigated familial tendency for BED and the risk of other psychiatric disorders, but failed to show this (Lee et al. 1999).

In BN most individuals start dieting prior to the onset of binge eating (Haiman and Devlin 1999; Marcus et al. 1995; Mussell et al. 1997). However, a fairly large subgroup (35–54 per cent) of the individuals with BED start binge eating prior to the onset of dieting (Abbott et al. 1998; Grilo and Masheb 2000; Mussell et al. 1995; Spurrell et al. 1997). Dieting seems to play a role in the aetiology of BED, but research does not indicate that dieting is always a key factor in BED, as it seems to do in BN (Howard and Porzelius 1999). The binge-first group seem to diet because they binge, not binge because they diet (Abbott et al. 1998). For subjects who start binge eating before dieting, binge eating seems to be the primary symptom that leads to weight gain. Obesity is found to develop several years after the onset of binge eating (Haiman and Devlin 1999; Mussell et al. 1995).

Course of Binge Eating Disorder

Two studies have investigated the natural course of BED in the general population. Fairburn et al. (2000) followed 102 subjects with BED for five years. After five years only 10 per cent of these subjects still fulfilled the criteria for BED (1 subject fulfilled the criteria for BN and 2 subjects for EDNOS). In total 18 per cent had an eating disorder of clinical severity. At the five-year follow-up 77 per cent of the group was abstinent (i.e. no objective bulimic episodes). However, the group as a whole became heavier during the five years and a large proportion tended to have a BMI over 30 (obesity) (22 per cent at recruitment compared to 39 per cent at follow-up). It was striking that only 8 per cent had been treated for an eating disorder during these five years.

Cachelin *et al.* (1999) examined women with BED in the general population for a period of six months. At the six-month follow-up 52 per cent of these women suffered from full-syndrome BED, whereas 48 per cent appeared to be in partial remission. Treatment seeking in general did not appear to be associated with improvement in BED over a relatively short time period.

Fichter *et al.* (1998) assessed the course and outcome of 68 women with BED over a period of six years after intense inpatient treatment. In general, the majority of these patients showed substantial improvement during treatment, a slight (in most cases non-significant) decline during the first three years after treatment ended and further improvement and stabilization in the four, five and six years following treatment. At the six-year follow-up only 6 per cent fulfilled the criteria for BED. In total 20 per cent met the criteria for some eating disorder according to the DSM-IV.

The studies mentioned above could be taken to indicate that treatment worsens the course of BED, since a higher percentage of subjects improved without treatment. However, subjects seeking help for BED seem to have more severe problems than subjects with BED in the general population (Fairburn *et al.* 1996; Wilfley *et al.* 2001). Furthermore, it is unclear from these studies whether objective binge-eating behaviour is replaced by overeating or subjective binge-eating behaviour (explaining weight increase) in those patients reporting abstinence from bingeing behaviour at follow-up.

Treatment

The treatment of BN has been researched extensively and there have also been numerous controlled treatment studies (Schmidt 1998); however, far less attention has been paid to BED (Wilfley and Cohen 1997). Because BED is more similar to BN than to obesity without binge eating, the first generation of BED treatment research focused on examining the efficacy of those treatments that had been shown to be effective for BN: cognitive behavioural therapy (CBT), interpersonal psychotherapy (IPT) and antidepressant medication. Many individuals with BED however seek help for overweight. Treatment of obesity focuses on the reduction of caloric intake, encourages a shift to a low fat diet, addresses any medical contribution to the condition and initiates exercise. The underlying behavioural disturbances or the social and psychological consequences of obesity are often neglected. If the treatment of obese subjects with BED focuses only on the reduction of body weight and does not address binge eating or underlying problems, binge eating continues or even worsens (Howard and Porzelius 1999; Romano and

Quinn 1995). Weight-loss programmes seem to have little effect on the reduction of binge eating in obese subjects with BED (Kirkley *et al.* 1992).

The studies that will be discussed here are those in which BED is classified by means of the DSM-IV. To date there have been seven randomized controlled clinical trials conducted in which the psychological treatment of BED has been evaluated (Agras *et al.* 1994, 1995; Carter and Fairburn 1998; Eldredge *et al.* 1997; Peterson *et al.* 1998, 2001; Wilfley *et al.* 2002).

CBT seems to cause a statistically significant reduction in binge eating compared to no treatment (reduction in number of episodes after treatment: 68–90 per cent; abstinence from binge eating after treatment: 40–87 per cent; reduction in number of episodes after waiting list: 8–22 per cent).

Two studies combined CBT with weight loss treatment (Agras *et al.* 1995; Eldredge *et al.* 1997). Treatment of obese subjects with BED seems to be more successful if binge eating is treated before any attempts are made to lose weight.

Two studies compared the efficacy of CBT versus IPT. Agras *et al.* (1995) investigated the efficacy of IPT in treating overweight patients with BED who did not stop binge eating after 12 weeks of CBT. Subjects who were successful after 12 weeks of CBT received weight loss treatment. IPT did not lead to further improvement in those who did not improve with CBT. Wilfley and others (2002) randomized 162 overweight patients with BED to either CBT or IPT. The frequency of binge eating dropped significantly in both groups after 20 weeks of treatment (abstinence: CBT = 79 per cent versus IPT = 73 per cent) and at one-year follow-up (abstinence: CBT = 59 per cent versus IPT = 62 per cent). No differences were found between the two groups.

Nauta *et al.* (2001) investigated the effectiveness of cognitive therapy and behavioural therapy in a group of obese subjects with and without BED, who were recruited from an obese community sample. Cognitive therapy appeared to be more effective than behavioural therapy with regard to abstinence from binge eating at six-months follow-up (86 per cent and 44 per cent respectively). At the end of treatment no differences were found in the abstinence rates (67 per cent and 44 per cent respectively).

Two studies (Carter and Fairburn 1998; Peterson *et al.* 1998, 2001) examined the efficacy of a self-help format (CBT) in the treatment of BED. Self-help formats seem to be effective (abstinence varied between 50 per cent and 87 per cent). However, some caution is needed with the interpretation of the high abstinence rates, because the participants in these "self-help" studies were probably less severely ill than those in the other studies (for example, subjects in the study by Carter and Fairburn (1998) and others had not received any prior treatment).

Also a few double-blind placebo-controlled pharmacological trials have been conducted in patients with BED. Drugs which have been examined are selective serotonin reuptake inhibitors (SSRIs: fluoxetine, fluvoxamine, sertraline) (Arnold *et al.* 2002; Greeno and Wing 1996; Hudson *et al.* 1998;

McElroy *et al.* 2000), appetite suppressants – d-fenfluramine (Stunkard *et al.* 1996) and sibutramine (Appolinario *et al.* 2003) – and an anticonvulsant (topiramate: McElroy *et al.* 2003). Fluoxetine seemed to reduce dietary intake but did not affect the frequency of binge episodes. This finding suggests that fluoxetine affects satiety, not hunger (Greeno and Wing 1996). In another study (Arnold *et al.* 2002) fluoxetine reduced binge frequency significantly compared to placebo. Fluvoxamine was found to be effective in reducing the frequency of binge episodes and in lowering Clinical Global Impression (CGI) severity scores (Hudson *et al.* 1998). Sertraline seemed to be effective and well tolerated, although the number of participants in that study was low (McElroy *et al.* 2000). D-fenfluramine reduced the frequency of binge eating in obese women with BED, but failed to reduce their body weight (Stunkard *et al.* 1996). A significant reduction of binge eating and weight was found in the sibutramine group compared to the placebo group (Appolinario *et al.* 2003). Topiramate was associated with significantly greater reductions in binge frequency compared to placebo after 14 weeks (94 per cent versus 46 per cent respectively).

A striking finding in these pharmacological studies is a high placebo-effect. All studies had a single-blind lead-in period from 1 to 4 weeks. After this lead-in period 42 to 44 per cent of the participants no longer met the DSM-IV criteria for BED.

In all studies the drugs under investigation seemed to be more effective than placebo with regard to the primary outcome measures. However, no long-term effects were found. Further, drugs did not seem to bring about a reduction in body weight. Disadvantages of these studies were the small number of participants and the short duration of the trials.

Cognitive behavioural psychotherapy is currently the most investigated treatment for BED and consequently the treatment of choice for BED.

Category or continuum?

The main question treated in this chapter is whether BED can be distinguished as a separate mental disorder. In order to define a distinct eating disorder, the disorder must have well-described characteristics. Is BED distinct from obesity? Another important question is whether bulimic disorders are dimensional or categorical in nature?

In a few cross-sectional studies (Fichter *et al.* 1993; Howard and Porzelius 1999; Kirkley *et al.* 1992) patients with BED were compared to matched samples of patients with BN purging type and of patients with obesity (BMI > 30). The scores of patients with BED had an intermediate position between BN and obesity but were closer to BN than to obesity. In a series of cross-sectional studies (van Hanswijck de Jonge 2002) patients with BED were compared to patients with BN and non-binge eating obesity on eating disorder psychopathology, general psychopathology and personality pathology (categorical and dimensional). The study revealed a dichotomy between binge eaters (BN and BED) and non-binge eaters (obesity) rather than a continuum of severity between the groups on all measures of psychopathology.

Williamson *et al.* (1992) identified three relatively homogeneous subgroups of subjects who had been diagnosed with EDNOS using two cluster analytic procedures. The three atypical subgroups were contrasted with two groups of subjects with AN and BN. These groups were very similar to the descriptions of sub-threshold AN, non-purging BN and BED. Subjects in the "BED" group were morbidly obese but did not report extreme motivation for thinness. They reported significant problems with binge eating, including significant concern about loss of control over eating. These subjects did not resort to extreme weight control methods such as purging or extremely restrictive eating. Estimations of current body size were closer to norms and ideal body weight preferences were larger than those predicted from norms. Members of the group also were less biased in their assessment of actual and ideal weight than those of the other clinical groups. They expressed a more realistic dissatisfaction with obesity.

In another study, Williamson *et al.* (2002) found further empirical support for conceptualizing BN and BED as discrete syndromes. Three factors were found to account for 66 per cent of the variance in eating disorder symptoms: binge eating, fear of fatness/compensatory behaviours and drive for extreme thinness. The BN group scored high on the features of binge eating and fear of fatness/compensatory behaviours but not on drive for thinness. The BED group scored high on binge eating but not on the other two features. Furthermore, persons with a diagnosis of an eating disorder appeared to differ (at least partly) from persons with non-pathological eating behaviours in kind rather than simply in degree.

Hay *et al.* (1996) investigated the presence of clinically meaningful subgroups among subjects with recurrent binge eating recruited from the general population. They identified four subgroups by means of a cluster analysis. The results supported the concept of BN and its division into purging and non-purging subtypes. The study failed to provide evidence to support the construct "BED". A possible explanation is that the population under investigation was too young (16–35 years). Patients with BED seem to present themselves for therapy in a later stage, when they are in their thirties and forties, whereas subjects with the other eating disorders seek help when they are generally much younger. The same population was reanalysed by classifying the subjects according to the DSM-IV (Hay and Fairburn 1998). A number of subjects were excluded from the analysis because they did not meet the DSM-IV criteria for any eating disorder. It was found that subjects with BN purging type did not differ from those with BN non-purging type and the latter did not differ from those with BED. There was a significant difference between subjects with BN purging type and BED.

There seems to be some evidence that subjects who binge without purging are different from subjects who binge and purge. Much research has focused on binge eating as the core psychopathological feature of bulimic disorders. Some state that compensatory behaviour ought to be the focal clinical feature of BN rather than binge eating (Tobin *et al.* 1997). Few studies (Garfinkel *et al.* 1996; McCann *et al.* 1991; O'Kearney *et al.* 1998; Walters *et al.* 1993) have investigated the differences between BN purging type and BN non-purging type. The overall evidence is that there is a difference between these two subtypes. So far, no study has found evidence for the division of bulimic eating disorders into the three distinct DSM categories such as BN purging type, BN non-purging type and BED. Others assume that bulimic disorders differ in degree rather than in kind. There is some support for the notion that bulimic eating disorders exist on a continuum of clinical severity, which starts with BN purging type (most severe), passes through BN non-purging type (intermediate severity) and finishes with BED (least severe).

Discussion

The aim of this chapter has been to evaluate the empirical status of BED as defined by the DSM-IV. In the early 1990s Spitzer *et al.* (1991) reported that there was no classification taxonomy in the DSM for the many individuals who engage in binge eating but do not engage in inappropriate compensatory behaviours. The present discussion considers Pincus *et al.*'s arguments for and against the inclusion of a new diagnostic category in the DSM following a decade of research in the field of BED.

First, Pincus *et al.* (1992) argued that rare diagnostic categories may add unnecessary complexity to the already cumbersome system of classification. However, epidemiological studies have shown that 1 to 3 per cent (Hay 1998; Spitzer *et al.* 1992, 1993) of the general population has binge-eating episodes but does not engage in inappropriate behaviours. The prevalence is higher in obese populations (1.3–70 per cent). Furthermore, BED seems to be more prevalent as the degree of obesity increases (Basdevant *et al.* 1995; Ramacciotti *et al.* 2000; Ricca *et al.* 2000; Spitzer *et al.* 1992, 1993; Varnado *et al.* 1997). Therefore, BED does not rank as a rare diagnostic disorder.

Second, Pincus *et al.* (1992) argued that new diagnoses are generally proposed by experts and are subsequently used by less expert assessors who may identify more false positives. Clinical practice has indeed shown difficulties can arise in attempting to differentiate between binge eating and emotional overeating in obese patients; such difficulties can lead to high false positive diagnoses. A clear operationalization of the criteria of a binge-eating episode is needed.

Third, Pincus *et al.* (1992: 114) argued that "adding unproven diagnostic categories may confer upon such categories an approval that they do not merit yet." Many studies have indicated that BED does represent a distinct diagnostic entity. The characteristics of subjects with BED differ significantly from those of subjects with BN and from those of obese subjects without binge eating. Furthermore, taxonomic studies have shown that there is a distinct category of BED, which differs from other clinical eating disorder categories. In day-to-day clinical practice BED is a generally accepted category and various eating disorder clinics have developed programmes for the treatment of BED.

Pincus et al.'s fourth and last argument concerned the definitional overlap across related categories. To date it has been difficult to distinguish BED from non-purging BN. Various studies have shown that there is a significant difference between the BN purging subtype and BED. Non-purging BN seems to occupy an intermediate position between these two categories, not differing significantly from either of them (Hay and Fairburn 1998). It is not yet clear whether non-purging BN bears a closer resemblance to purging BN (supporting continued classification under BN) or a closer resemblance to BED (supporting a merger of BED and non-purging BN) (Striegel-Moore et al. 2000). Research is needed to clarify this issue.

Conclusion

Although there is evidence to suggest that BED represents a distinct eating disorder category, the criteria as currently described would benefit from some major revision.

Criterion A as currently defined should be maintained. Binge-eating episodes should be characterized by the consumption of a large amount of food within a discrete period with a sense of lack of control over eating. Criterion B seems to be superfluous. Criterion B measures binge-eating characteristics, which overlaps with Criterion A (binge-eating characteristics) and Criterion C (feelings of distress regarding binge eating). It is not clear what is meant by the term distress (Criterion C) as currently described. Distress may refer to an emotional state with regard to binge eating or it may describe impairment in social or occupational functioning due to binge eating. We suggest that both types of distress should be operationalized in the revised version of Criterion C. The DSM guidelines state that impairment in functioning is crucial in the definition of any mental disorder. For a diagnosis of BED, binge eating is required to occur on two days a week (Criterion D) rather than in the form of two episodes per week. This is based on the rationale that BED patients may have more difficulties in recalling and labelling binge-eating episodes due to the absence of purging behaviours punctuating the termination of an episode. However, counting the number of days allows binges to last an entire day (in theory). In a population characterized by a high percentage of compulsive overeaters (without loss of control), this may complicate the separation of the diagnoses of binge-eating episodes and compulsive overeating. Therefore, we suggest counting the number of binge-eating episodes rather than counting the number of days.

We suggest eliminating the term "regular" as mentioned in Criterion E. The elimination of this term ensures clearer boundaries between BN and BED.

Existing studies support the need for cognitive criteria in addition to the existing behavioural diagnostic criteria for BED. Hitherto, various existing studies have argued for the inclusion of overconcern with body weight and body shape in self-evaluation (Eldredge and Agras 1996; Wilfley *et al.* 2000; Wilson *et al.* 1993).

Furthermore, future research needs to clarify the impact of obesity on the psychopathology of BED and vice versa. Although obesity is not a criterion for the diagnosis of BED, the classification for BED was created with the obese in mind (Spitzer *et al.* 1991). Future research will show whether obesity should be admitted as a criterion for BED in the same way as underweight was included as a criterion for AN.

In summary, we believe that BED represents a distinct eating disorder category and suggest that it be admitted into the next version of the DSM.

References

Abbott, D.W., de Zwaan, M., Mussell, M.P., Raymond, N.C., Seim, H.C., Crow, S.J., Crosby, R.D. and Mitchell, J.E. (1998) "Onset of binge eating and dieting in overweight women: implications for etiology, associated features and treatment", *Journal of Psychosomatic Research* 44, 367–74.

Agras, W.S., Telch, C.F., Arnow, B., Eldredge, K., Wilfley, D.E., Raeburn, S.D., Henderson, J. and Marnell, M. (1994) "Weight loss, cognitive-behavioral, and desipramine treatments in binge eating disorder: an additive design", *Behavior Therapy* 25, 225–38.

Agras, W.S., Telch, C.F., Arnow, B., Eldredge, K., Detzer, M.J., Henderson, J. and Marnell, M. (1995) "Does interpersonal therapy help patients with binge eating disorder who fail to respond to cognitive behavioural therapy?", *Journal of Consulting and Clinical Psychology* 63, 356–60.

American Psychiatric Association (1952) *Diagnostic and Statistical Manual of Mental Disorders*, Washington, DC: APA.

American Psychiatric Association (1968) *Diagnostic and Statistical Manual of Mental Disorders*, 2nd edn (DSM-II), Washington, DC: APA.

American Psychiatric Association (1980) *Diagnostic and Statistical Manual of Mental Disorders*, 3rd edn (DSM-III), Washington, DC: APA.

American Psychiatric Association (1987) *Diagnostic and Statistical Manual of Mental Disorders*, 3rd edn revised (DSM-III-R), Washington, DC: APA.

American Psychiatric Association (1994) *Diagnostic and Statistical Manual of Mental Disorders*, 4th edn (DSM-IV), Washington, DC: APA.

Appolinario, J.C., Bacaltchuk, J., Sichieri, R., Claudino, A.M., Godoy-Matos, A., Morgan, C., Zanella, M.T. and Coutinho, W. (2003) "A randomized, double-blind, placebo-controlled study of sibutramine in the treatment of binge eating disorder", *Archives of General Psychiatry* 60, 1109–16.

Arnold, L.M., McElroy, S.L., Hudson, J.I., Welge, J.A., Bennett, A.J. and Keck, P.E.

(2002) "A placebo-controlled, randomized trial of fluoxetine in the treatment of binge eating disorder", *Journal of Clinical Psychiatry* 63, 1028–33.

Basdevant, A., Pouillon, M., Lahlou, N., Le Barzic, M., Brillant, M. and Guy-Grand, B. (1995) "Prevalence of binge eating disorder in different populations of French women", *International Journal of Eating Disorders* 18, 309–15.

Blashfield, R.K., Sprock, J. and Fuller, A.K. (1990) "Suggested guidelines for including or excluding categories in the DSM-IV", *Comprehensive Psychiatry* 31, 15–19.

Cachelin, F.M., Striegel-Moore, R.H., Elder, K.A., Pike, K.M., Wilfley, D.E. and Fairburn, C.G. (1999) "Natural course of a community sample of women with binge eating disorder", *International Journal of Eating Disorders* 25, 45–54.

Carter, J.C. and Fairburn, C.G. (1998) "Cognitive-behavioral self-help for binge eating disorder: a controlled effectiveness study", *Journal of Consulting and Clinical Psychology* 66, 616–23.

de Zwaan, M. (1997) "Status and utility of a new diagnostic category: binge eating disorder", *European Eating Disorders Review* 5, 226–40.

Dingemans, A.E., Bruna, M.J. and van Furth, E.F. (2002) "Binge eating disorder: a review", *International Journal of Obesity* 29, 299–307.

Eldredge, K.L. and Agras, W.S. (1996) "Weight and shape overconcern and emotional eating in binge eating disorder", *International Journal of Eating Disorders* 19, 73–82.

Eldredge, K.L., Agras, W.S., Arnow, B., Telch, C.F., Bell, S., Castonguay, L. and Marnell, M. (1997) "The effects of extending cognitive behavioural therapy for binge eating disorder among initial treatment nonresponders", *International Journal of Eating Disorders* 21, 347–52.

Fairburn, C.G., Welch, S.L. and Hay, P.J. (1993) "The classification of recurrent overeating: the 'binge eating disorder' proposal", *International Journal of Eating Disorders* 13, 155–9.

Fairburn, C.G., Welch, S.L., Norman, P.A., O'Connor, M.E. and Doll, H.A. (1996) "Bias and bulimia nervosa: how typical are clinic cases?", *American Journal of Psychiatry* 153, 386–91.

Fairburn, C.G., Doll, H.A., Welch, S.L., Hay, P.J., Davies, B.A. and O'Connor, M.E. (1998) "Risk factors for binge eating disorder", *Archives of General Psychiatry* 55, 425–32.

Fairburn, C.G., Cooper, Z., Doll, H.A., Norman, P.A. and O'Connor, M.E. (2000) "The natural course of bulimia nervosa and binge eating disorder in young women", *Archives of General Psychiatry* 57, 659–65.

Fichter, M.M., Quadflieg, N. and Brandl, B. (1993) "Recurrent overeating: an empirical comparison of binge eating disorder, bulimia nervosa, and obesity", *International Journal of Eating Disorders* 14, 1–16.

Fichter, M.M., Quadflieg, N. and Gnutzmann, A. (1998) "Binge eating disorder: treatment outcome over a 6-year course", *Journal of Psychosomatic Research* 44, 385–405.

Fitzgibbon, M.L. and Blackman, L.R. (2000) "Binge eating disorder and bulimia nervosa: differences in the quality and quantity of binge eating episodes", *International Journal of Eating Disorders* 27, 238–43.

Follette, W.C. and Houts, A.C. (1996) "Models of scientific progress and the role of theory in taxonomy development: a case study of the DSM", *Journal of Consulting and Clinical Psychology* 64, 1120–32.

Garfinkel, P.E., Lin, E., Goering, P., Spegg, C., Goldbloom, D.S., Kennedy, S., Kaplan, A.S. and Woodside, D.B. (1995) "Bulimia nervosa in a Canadian community sample: prevalence and comparison of subgroups", *American Journal of Psychiatry* 152, 1052–8.

Garfinkel, P.E., Lin, E., Goering, P., Spegg, C., Goldbloom, D.S., Kennedy, S., Kaplan, A.S. and Woodside, D.B. (1996) "Purging and nonpurging forms of bulimia nervosa in a community sample", *International Journal of Eating Disorders* 20, 231–8.

Goldfein, J.A., Walsh, B.T., LaChaussee, J.L. and Kissileff, H.R. (1993) "Eating behavior in binge eating disorder", *International Journal of Eating Disorders* 14, 427–31.

Greeno, C.G. and Wing, R. (1996) "A double-blind, placebo-controlled trial of the effect of fluoxetine on dietary intake in overweight women with and without binge eating disorder", *American Journal of Clinical Nutrition* 64, 267–73.

Grilo, C.M. and Masheb, R.M. (2000) "Onset of dieting vs binge eating in outpatients with binge eating disorder", *International Journal of Obesity* 24, 404–9.

Haiman, C. and Devlin, M.J. (1999) "Binge eating before the onset of dieting: a distinct subgroup of bulimia nervosa?", *International Journal of Eating Disorders* 25, 151–7.

Hay, P. (1998) "The epidemiology of eating disorder behaviors: an Australian community-based survey", *International Journal of Eating Disorders* 23, 371–82.

Hay, P. and Fairburn, C. (1998) "The validity of the DSM-IV scheme for classifying bulimic eating disorders", *International Journal of Eating Disorders* 23, 7–15.

Hay, P.J., Fairburn, C.G. and Doll, H.A. (1996) "The classification of bulimic eating disorders: a community-based cluster analysis study", *Psychological Medicine* 26, 801–12.

Hodges, E.L., Cochrane, C.E. and Brewerton, T.D. (1998) "Family characteristics of binge eating disorder patients", *International Journal of Eating Disorders* 23, 145–51.

Howard, C.E. and Porzelius, L.K. (1999) "The role of dieting in binge eating disorder: etiology and treatment implications", *Clinical Psychology Review* 19, 25–44.

Hudson, J.I., McElroy, S.L., Raymond, N.C., Crow, S., Keck, P.E.J., Carter, J., Mitchell, J., Strakowski, S.M., Pope, H.G.J., Coleman, B.S. and Jonas, J.M. (1998) "Fluvoxamine in the treatment of binge eating disorder: a multicenter placebo-controlled, double-blind trial", *American Journal of Psychiatry* 155, 1756–62.

Kirkley, B.G., Kolotkin, R.L., Hernandez, J.T. and Gallagher, P.N. (1992) "A comparison of binge-purgers, obese binge eaters and obese nonbinge eaters on the MMPI", *International Journal of Eating Disorders* 12, 221–8.

LaChaussee, J.L., Kissileff, H.R., Walsh, B.T. and Hadigan, C.M. (1992) "The single-item meal as a measure of binge eating behavior in patients with bulimia nervosa", *Physiology and Behavior* 38, 563–70.

Lee, Y.H., Abbott, D.W., Seim, H.C., Crosby, R.D., Monson, N., Burgard, M. and Mitchell, J.E. (1999) "Eating disorders and psychiatric disorders in the first-degree relatives of obese probands with binge eating disorder and obese non-binge eating disorder controls", *International Journal of Eating Disorders* 26, 322–32.

McCann, U.D., Rossiter, E.M., King, R.J. and Agras, W.S. (1991) "Nonpurging bulimia: a distinct subtype of bulimia nervosa", *International Journal of Eating Disorders* 10, 679–87.

McElroy, S.L., Casuto, L.S., Nelson, E.B., Lake, K.A., Soutullo, C.A., Keck, P.E. and Hudson, J.I. (2000) "Placebo-controlled trial of sertraline in the treatment of binge eating disorder", *American Journal of Psychiatry* 157, 1004–6.

McElroy, S.L., Arnold, L.M., Shapira, N.A., Keck, P.E.J., Rosenthal, N.R., Karim, M.R., Kamin, M. and Hudson, J.I. (2003) "Topiramate in the treatment of binge eating disorder associated with obesity: a randomized, placebo-controlled trial", *American Journal of Psychiatry* 160, 255–61.

Marcus, M.D., Smith, D.E., Santelli, R. and Kaye, W. (1992) "Characterization of eating disordered behavior in obese binge eaters", *International Journal of Eating Disorders* 12, 249–55.

Marcus, M.D., Moulton, M.M. and Greeno, C.G. (1995) "Binge eating onset in obese patients with binge eating disorder", *Addictive Behaviors* 20, 747–55.

Masheb, R.M. and Grilo, C.M. (2000) "Binge eating disorder: a need for additional diagnostic criteria", *Comprehensive Psychiatry* 41, 159–62.

Mitchell, J.E., Mussell, M.P., Peterson, C.B., Crow, S., Wonderlich, S., Crosby, R.D., Davis, T. and Weller, C.L. (1999) "Hedonics of binge eating in women with bulimia nervosa and binge eating disorder", *International Journal of Eating Disorders* 26, 165–70.

Mussell, M.P., Mitchell, J.E., Weller, C.L., Raymond, N.C., Crow, S.J. and Crosby, R.D. (1995) "Onset of binge eating, dieting, obesity, and mood disorders among subjects seeking treatment for binge eating disorder", *International Journal of Eating Disorders* 17, 395–401.

Mussell, M.P., Mitchell, J.E., Fenna, C.J., Crosby, R.D., Miller, J.P. and Hoberman, H.M. (1997) "A comparison of onset of binge eating versus dieting in the development of bulimia nervosa", *International Journal of Eating Disorders* 21, 353–60.

Nauta, H., Hospers, H., Kok, G. and Jansen, A. (2001) "A comparison between a cognitive and a behavioral treatment for obese binge eaters and obese non-binge eaters", *Behavior Therapy* 31, 441–61.

O'Kearney, R., Gertler, R., Conti, J. and Duff, M. (1998) "A comparison of purging and nonpurging eating disordered outpatients: mediating effects of weight and general psychopathology", *International Journal of Eating Disorders* 23, 261–6.

Peterson, C.B., Mitchell, J.E., Engbloom, S., Nugent, S., Mussell, M.P. and Miller, J.P. (1998) "Group cognitive-behavioral treatment of binge eating disorder: a comparison of therapist-led versus self-help formats", *International Journal of Eating Disorders* 24, 125–36.

Peterson, C.B., Mitchell, J.E., Engbloom, S., Nugent, S., Mussell, M.P., Crow, S.J. and Thuras, P. (2001) "Self-help versus therapist-led group cognitive-behavioral treatment of binge eating disorder at follow-up", *International Journal of Eating Disorders* 30, 363–74.

Pincus, H.A., Frances, A., Davis, W.W., First, M.B. and Widiger, T.A. (1992) "DSM-IV and new diagnostic categories: holding the line on proliferation", *American Journal of Psychiatry* 149, 112–17.

Ramacciotti, C.E., Coli, E., Passaglia, C., Lacorte, M., Pea, E. and Dell'Osso, L. (2000) "Binge eating disorder: prevalence and psychopathological features in a clinical sample of obese people in Italy", *Psychiatry Research* 94, 131–8.

Raymond, N.C., Mussell, M.P., Mitchell, J.E. and de Zwaan, M. (1995) "An age-matched comparison of subjects with binge eating disorder and bulimia nervosa", *International Journal of Eating Disorders* 18, 135–43.

Ricca, V., Mannucci, E., Moretti, S., Di Bernardo, M., Zucchi, T., Cabras, P.L. and Rotella, C.M. (2000) "Screening for binge eating disorder in obese outpatients", *Comprehensive Psychiatry* 41, 111–15.

Romano, S.J. and Quinn, L. (1995) "Binge eating disorder: description and proposed treatment", *European Eating Disorders Review* 3, 67–79.

Rossiter, E.M., Agras, W.S., Telch, C.F. and Bruce, B. (1992) "The eating patterns of non-purging bulimic subjects", *International Journal of Eating Disorders* 11, 111–20.

Santonastaso, P., Ferrara, S. and Favaro, A. (1999) "Differences between binge eating disorder and nonpurging bulimia nervosa", *International Journal of Eating Disorders* 25, 215–18.

Schmidt, N.B. and Telch, M.J. (1990) "Prevalence of personality disorders among bulimics, nonbulimic binge eaters, and normal controls", *Journal of Psychopathology and Behavioral Assessment* 12, 169–85.

Schmidt, U. (1998) "The treatment of bulimia nervosa", in H.W. Hoek, J.L. Treasure and M.A. Katzman (eds) *Neurobiology in the Treatment of Eating Disorders*, Chichester: Wiley.

Spitzer, R.L., Devlin, M., Walsh, B.T., Hasin, D., Wing, R., Marcus, M.D., Stunkard, A., Wadden, T., Yanovski, S., Agras, W.S., Mitchell, J. and Nonas, C. (1991) "Binge eating disorder: to be or not to be in DSM-IV", *International Journal of Eating Disorders* 10, 627–9.

Spitzer, R.L., Devlin, M., Walsh, B.T., Hasin, D., Wing, R., Marcus, M.D., Stunkard, A., Wadden, T., Yanovski, S., Agras, W.S., Mitchell, J. and Nonas, C. (1992) "Binge eating disorder: a multisite field trial of the diagnostic criteria", *International Journal of Eating Disorders* 11, 191–203.

Spitzer, R.L., Yanovski, S.Z., Wadden, T. and Wing, R. (1993) "Binge eating disorder: its further validation in a multisite study", *International Journal of Eating Disorders* 13, 137–53.

Spurrell, E.B., Wilfley, D.E., Tanofsky, M.B. and Brownell, K.D. (1997) "Age of onset for binge eating: are there different pathways to binge eating?", *International Journal of Eating Disorders* 21, 55–65.

Striegel-Moore, R.H., Wilson, G.T., Wilfley, D.E., Elder, K.A. and Brownell, K.D. (1998) "Binge eating in an obese community sample", *International Journal of Eating Disorders* 23, 27–37.

Striegel-Moore, R.H., Dohm, F.A., Solomon, R.A., Fairburn, C.G., Pike, K.M. and Wilfley, D.E. (2000) "Subthreshold binge eating disorder", *International Journal of Eating Disorders* 27, 270–8.

Stunkard, A., Berkowitz, R., Tanrikut, C., Reiss, E. and Young, L. (1996) "d-Fenfluramine treatment of binge eating disorder", *American Journal of Psychiatry* 153, 1455–9.

Tobin, D.L., Griffing, A. and Griffing, S. (1997) "An examination of subtype criteria for bulimia nervosa", *International Journal of Eating Disorders* 22, 179–86.

van Hanswijck de Jonge, P. (2002) "Personality characteristics in binge eating disorder: a comparison study with bulimia nervosa and obesity", Phd thesis, St George's Hospital Medical School, University of London.

van Hanswijck de Jonge, P., van Furth, E.F., Lacey, J.H. and Waller, G. (2003) "The prevalence of DSM-IV personality pathology among individuals with bulimia nervosa, binge eating disorder and obesity", *Psychological Medicine* 33, 1311–17.

Varnado, P.J., Williamson, D.A., Bentz, B.G., Ryan, D.H., Rhodes, S.K., O'Neil, P.M. and Sebastian, S.B. (1997) "Prevalence of binge eating disorder in obese adults seeking weight loss treatment", *Eating Weight Disorders* 2, 117–24.

Walters, E.E., Neale, M.C., Eaves, L.J., Heath, A.C., Kessler, R.C. and Kendler, K.S. (1993) "Bulimia nervosa: a population-based study of purgers versus nonpurgers", *International Journal of Eating Disorders* 13, 265–72.

Webber, E.M. (1994) "Psychological characteristics of bingeing and nonbingeing obese women", *Journal of Psychology* 128, 339–51.

Wilfley, D.E. and Cohen, L.R. (1997) "Psychological treatment of bulimia nervosa and binge eating disorder", *Psychopharmacology Bulletin* 33, 437–54.

Wilfley, D.E., Schwartz, M.B., Spurrell, E.B. and Fairburn, C.G. (2000) "Using the eating disorder examination to identify the specific psychopathology of binge eating disorder", *International Journal of Eating Disorders* 27, 259–69.

Wilfley, D.E., Pike, K.M., Dohm, F.A., Striegel-Moore, R.H. and Fairburn, C.G. (2001) "Bias in binge eating disorder: how representative are recruited clinic samples?", *Journal of Consulting and Clinical Psychology* 69, 383–8.

Wilfley, D.E., Welch, R.R., Stein, R.I., Spurrell, E.B., Cohen, L.R., Saelens, B.E., Dounchis, J.Z., Frank, M.A., Wiseman, C.V. and Matt, G.E. (2002) "A randomized comparison of group cognitive behavioural therapy and group interpersonal psychotherapy for the treatment of overweight individuals with binge eating disorder", *Archives of General Psychiatry* 59, 713–21.

Williamson, D.A., Gleaves, D.H. and Savin, S.S. (1992) "Empirical classification of eating disorder not otherwise specified: support for DSM-IV changes", *Journal of Psychopathology and Behavioral Assessment* 14, 201–16.

Williamson, D.A., Womble, L.G., Smeets, M.A.M., Netemeyer, R.G., Thaw, J.M., Kutlesic, V. and Gleaves, D.H. (2002) "Latent structure of eating disorder symptoms: a factor analytic and taxometric investigation", *American Journal of Psychiatry* 159, 412–18.

Wilson, G.T., Nonas, C. and Rosenblum, G.D. (1993) "Assessment of binge eating in obese patients", *International Journal of Eating Disorders* 13, 25–33.

World Health Organization (1992) *ICD-10 Classification of Mental and Behavioural Disorders: Clinical Descriptions and Diagnostic Guidelines*, Geneva: WHO.

Chapter 5

Binge eating, EDNOS and obesity

Martina de Zwaan

Introduction

Many abnormal eating patterns have been described among obese populations, mostly in clinical weight loss samples and, more recently, also in bariatric surgery patients. Many terms have been used to describe problematic eating behaviour among the obese which have been more or less well defined such as "binge eating", "hyperphagia", "stuffing syndrome", "craving for food", "nibbling", "picking", "grazing", "frequent snacking", "sweet eating", and "night eating". According to DSM-IV or ICD-10 criteria most eating disorders among obese populations fall within the category of Eating Disorders Not Otherwise Specified (APA 1994) and "Atypical or other eating disorders" (ICD-10: WHO 1992).

This chapter will focus primarily on Binge Eating Disorder in the obese but will also include preliminary information on Night Eating Syndrome (NES). In some places, bariatric surgery will be highlighted separately. Most of what is known about BED and the NES derives from obese patients in clinical settings even though the diagnoses are not limited to overweight individuals (Rand *et al.* 1997; Spitzer *et al.* 1993).

Historical evidence

Abnormal eating patterns among the obese have been recognized in the obesity literature since the early 1950s. Hamburger (1951) described a type of hyperphagia in eight obese patients characterized by "compulsive craving for food, especially candy, ice cream, and other sweets, which is frequently uncontrollable." The author compared this "most malignant" type of hyperphagia with an addiction to alcohol. In 1959, Stunkard's frequently cited paper on "Eating patterns and obesity" was published, describing binge eating as a distinct eating pattern among some obese individuals. Stunkard (1959) characterized an eating binge as "having an orgiastic quality" and noted that "enormous amounts of food are consumed in relatively short periods." He noticed that the eating binge is "frequently related to a specific precipitating event, and is regularly followed by severe discomfort and self-condemnation." In 1970, Kornhaber identified the "stuffing syndrome" as a distinct clinical entity among the obese, and thought it characterized by three symptoms: hyperphagia, emotional withdrawal and clinical depression.

In 1955 Stunkard *et al.* described a syndrome characterized by nocturnal hyperphagia, insomnia and morning anorexia in a group of 25 treatment refractory obese patients. This NES was associated with failure of or even untoward reactions to weight reduction programmes.

Diagnostic criteria

BED has been given provisional status by being included in the Appendix of the DSM-IV for diagnostic categories meriting further study, and is also included as an example of EDNOS (see Appendix for diagnostic criteria).

It is important to keep in mind that there are many obese subjects with binge eating problems who do not meet full BED criteria but, nevertheless, view themselves as having an eating problem and indicate that they would like to receive help. They frequently do not meet the frequency criterion of two binge days per week. There is evidence that sub-threshold BED subjects do not differ significantly from subjects meeting all criteria. They frequently have the same risk for psychiatric distress and overconcern with shape and weight (Striegel-Moore *et al.* 1998, 2000).

Criteria for NES are still evolving. They have been revised and modified several times by different authors (Birketvedt *et al.* 1999; Gluck *et al.* 2001; Napolitano *et al.* 2001; Rand *et al.* 1997; Stunkard *et al.* 1996b). None of the modifications seems to have been formally validated and NES is not an official diagnostic category in the DSM-IV (APA 1994) or ICD-10 (WHO 1992). The most recent provisional criteria of the NES criteria are summarized here:

- Morning anorexia, even if the subject eats breakfast.
- Evening hyperphagia, in which more than 50 per cent of the daily energy intake is consumed after the last evening meal.
- Awakenings at least once a night.
- Consumption of snacks during the awakenings.
- Repetition of the provisional criteria for more than three months.
- Subjects do not meet criteria for Bulimia Nervosa or Binge Eating Disorder.

Birketvedt *et al.* (1999)

Originally, "awakening with eating" was not part of the diagnostic criteria. This symptom is called "nocturnal eating" and has been included in the revised International Classification of Sleep Disorders (ICSD-R) by the American Academy of Sleep Medicine (2000). Nocturnal eating is defined as "frequent and recurrent awakenings to eat and normal sleep onset following ingestion of the desired food". The individual maintains full awareness during the episode and has no subsequent amnesia for the nocturnal eating episode. Birketvedt *et al.* (1999) reported that nocturnal eating is common among patients with NES and Ceru-Björk *et al.* (2001) described similarities between patients with NES and patients with "simple nocturnal eating". Both studies were carried out in obese treatment-seeking samples. Nocturnal eating needs to be distinguished from eating during awakenings that is associated with reduced level of awareness (state of alertness) and reduced level of recall (partial or total amnesia). This phenomenon has been described mainly by sleep researchers and has been labelled as a unique variant of complex sleepwalking (Schenck *et al.* 1993; Winkelman *et al.* 1999).

There has been some debate concerning whether NES represents a distinct entity among overweight individuals or whether it is a variant of BED in which the bingeing occurs in the evening. Results indicate that NES appears to be somewhat correlated with BED with a clear overlap between BED and NES, although this is less strong than might be expected. The percentage of patients exhibiting both diagnoses ranges from 0 to 26.5 per cent in the obese samples investigated. Hence, the majority of subjects report only one of the disorders (Table 5.1).

BED and NES share several characteristics. As with BED, it appears that the frequency of NES is higher in obese samples compared to normal weight community samples. Obese patients with NES exhibit more psychopathology compared to obese patients without NES and they are younger when they present for treatment. However, NES appears to be independent of pre-occupation with food (Adami *et al.* 1999) and is not associated with self-condemnation related to overeating in BED (Stunkard *et al.* 1955). In addition, the amount of food ingested by night eaters is usually far smaller than that

Table 5.1 Comorbidity between NES and BED in obese patients

Authors	% NES in BED pts	% NES in non-BED pts	% ED pts with both BED and NES
Stunkard *et al.* 1996b (TV sample)	30	9.8	21
Stunkard *et al.* 1996b (weight loss sample)	0.0	9.6	0.0
Stunkard *et al.* 1996b (BED sample)	15	—	15
Adami *et al.* 1999	18.5	0.0	15.6
Powers *et al.* 1999	15.8	9.3	10.7
Napolitano *et al.* 2001	50	40.4	26.5

Notes: ED = eating disorder, BED = Binge Eating Disorder, NES = Night Eating Syndrome, pts = patients, TV = television.

reported in patients with BED. They would not represent "objective binges" (Birketvedt *et al.* 1999). BED on the other hand typically is not associated with morning anorexia.

Prevalence

BED appears to be quite common among subjects attending hospital-affiliated weight loss programmes with an overall frequency of DSM-IV criteria of approximately 30 per cent (Grissett and Fitzgibbon 1996; Kuehnel and Wadden 1994; Spitzer *et al.* 1992, 1993; Yanovski and Sebring 1994), ranging from 7.5 per cent to 47.4 per cent (Ho *et al.* 1995). However, estimates based on interviews rather than self-reports vary between 9 per cent (Stunkard *et al.* 1996b) and 19 per cent (Brody *et al.* 1994). BED is relatively rare in the general population of different countries with only approximately 2 per cent (ranging from 0.7 per cent to 4.6 per cent) meeting full criteria for BED (French *et al.* 1999; Kinzl *et al.* 1999; Spitzer *et al.* 1992, 1993). In Spitzer *et al.*'s (1992) first multi-site study, interestingly, only 19 per cent of the BED subjects in the community were obese (BMI > 27.5 kg/m^2) and only 4.4 per cent of the obese subjects in the community met BED criteria. Consequently, the relationship between BED and obesity is less pronounced in community samples. Given the apparent relationship between obesity and BED, routine screening for BED in obese patients seems indicated.

Despite renewed interest in NES prevalence, data are still limited. In only one study (Rand *et al.* 1997) a random sample of the general population was interviewed finding a prevalence of NES of 1.5 per cent. This is comparable with the prevalence rates found for BED in population samples. As with BED, NES appears to be more common among obese persons, especially those seeking weight loss treatment (de Zwaan *et al.* 2003a). However, since there are no generally accepted criteria available for NES, a wide range of prevalence estimates has been reported, ranging from 6 per cent to 64 per cent (Ceru-Björk *et al.* 2001; Stunkard 1959; Stunkard *et al.* 1955, 1996b). Greeno *et al.* (1995) focused on nocturnal eating and found a prevalence of 7.6 per cent in 79 weight loss patients.

Bariatric surgery

Conventional approaches to the management of obesity generally have proven unsuccessful for the morbidly obese, leading to the development of surgical alternatives. BED appears to be common among the morbidly obese presenting for bariatric surgery, with prevalence rates ranging from 1.4 per cent to 49 per cent (Adami *et al.* 1995; de Zwaan *et al.* 2003b; Dymek *et al.* 2001; Herpertz *et al.* 2001; Hsu *et al.* 1996, 1997; Mitchell *et al.* 2001; Powers *et al.* 1999; Wadden *et al.* 2001). Those studies assessing the prevalence of pre-surgery BED retrospectively (Mitchell *et al.* 2001), often many years after surgery (Hsu *et al.* 1996, 1997) have found the highest prevalence rates of 40 per cent or more.

Also NES has been assessed in bariatric surgery patients. Again, the frequency seems to be quite high, ranging from 7.9 per cent to 26 per cent (Adami *et al.* 1999; Powers *et al.* 1999; Rand and Kuldau 1993). In retrospective studies, nocturnal eating was reported in 33.3 per cent and 42 per cent of bariatric surgery patients preoperatively (Hsu *et al.* 1996, 1997).

Ethnicity and gender

Data indicate that BED is as common among black women as it is among white women, a relationship that appears to hold both within the community (Bruce and Agras 1992; Striegel-Moore and Franko 2003) and among those presenting for treatment (Yanovski *et al.* 1993, 1994). Race seems to play a role in the clinical presentation of BED. A study in community samples of black and white women with BED found significant differences between the two groups. Black women with BED were heavier and reported more frequent binge eating; however, they reported less concern about body weight, shape and eating and were less likely to have a history of Bulimia Nervosa than white women with BED. Cultural differences in the acceptance of larger body sizes might account for these findings (Pike *et al.* 2001).

Available estimates are that women are roughly 1.5 times more likely to have BED than men (Spitzer *et al.* 1992, 1993; Wilson *et al.* 1993). Thus, men comprise a substantial proportion of the BED population. Few studies have focused on gender differences in patients with BED (Barry *et al.* 2002; Striegel-Moore *et al.* 1998; Tanofsky *et al.* 1997). Males are more similar to females in their developmental history or in current eating disorder features, depression and self-esteem. However, studies found significantly higher substance abuse problems in men. There is also evidence that women struggle with more body image dissatisfaction and drive for thinness, and are more likely to eat in response to negative emotions than men.

Most studies that investigated gender issues did not find differences in the prevalence of NES between women and men, neither in community samples (Rand and Kuldau 1986) nor in obese samples (Ceru-Björk *et al.* 2001; Gluck *et al.* 2001; Napolitano *et al.* 2001; Rand and Kuldau 1993). The preponderance of the female gender that can be found in most eating disorders seems less pronounced in BED and even less so in NES.

Dieting and restraint

Results in the bulimia literature suggest that binge eating develops in the context of dieting or restraint eating (Polivy and Herman 1985). Restraint theory postulates that overeating results from the disruption of restraint in vulnerable individuals. In BN restrictive dieting is almost viewed as a "precondition" for the development of binge eating, is central to most aetiologic and risk models, and plays an important role in treatment approaches. Patients with BN consistently display elevated scores on restraint scales (Three-Factor Eating Questionnaire (TFEQ): Stunkard and Messik 1985; Eating Disorder Examination (EDE): Fairburn and Cooper 1993; see also Brody *et al.* 1994; Fichter *et al.* 1993; McCann *et al.* 1991; Marcus *et al.* 1992; Masheb and Grilo 2000a; Molinari *et al.* 1997; Wilfley *et al.* 2000b). However, the association between dieting/restraint and binge eating does not apply to a substantial number of individuals with BED. There are several lines of evidence supporting the lack of a relationship between dieting/restraint and binge eating in obese subjects with BED.

First, measures of restraint of eating (TFEQ, EDE) are usually significantly lower in obese BED subjects compared to patients with BN and have consistently shown either no correlation or even a negative correlation with binge eating among obese subjects (Brody *et al.* 1994; de Zwaan *et al.* 1994; Fichter *et al.* 1993; Kuehnel and Wadden 1994; Lowe and Caputo 1991; Marcus *et al.* 1985, 1992; Masheb and Grilo 2000b, 2002; Molinari *et al.* 1997; Wadden *et al.* 1993; Wilfley *et al.* 2000a; Wilson *et al.* 1993).

Second, in BED, in contrast to BN, there is evidence that the onset of binge eating precedes the onset of self-reported dieting in many cases with 35–65 per cent of patients developing binge eating in the absence of prior dieting (Table 5.2).

As can be seen in Table 5.3, the "binge-first" groups in all studies were significantly younger at onset of binge eating, when first overweight, and at onset of BED diagnosis compared to the "diet-first" groups. The studies found surprisingly similar mean ages. In accordance with these results, women with BED with early onset of binge eating (<18 years) were more likely than those with later onset to binge eat before dieting and to have early onset of obesity (Marcus *et al.* 1995). They also exhibited more eating disorder psychopathology and were more likely to report a lifetime history of BN and mood disorder. Early onset binge eaters or "binge-first" subjects might have a more severe variant of BED (Marcus *et al.* 1995).

Table 5.2 Sequence of onset of dieting and binge eating

Authors	DIET-first	BINGE-first	N, sample
Spitzer *et al.* 1993	37%	48.6%	387, weight control programmes
Wilson *et al.* 1993	8.7%	64%	
Mussell *et al.* 1995	25%	54.2%	30, clinical trial
Spurrell *et al.* 1997	45%	55% (men 58%)	87, clinical trial
Abbott *et al.* 1998	48.1%	38.7%	clinical trial
Grilo and Masheb 2000	65%	35%	98, clinical trial

Table 5.3 Differences between "diet-first" and "binge-first" groups

	Authors	DIET-first	BINGE-first
Age first overweight (years)	Grilo and Masheb 2000	15.8	12.4
	Marcus 1993	18.0	13.0
	Marcus et al. 1995*	19.6	12.2
Age at onset of binge eating (years)	Grilo and Masheb 2000	24.9	11.6
	Spurrell et al. 1997	24.9	12.6
	Abbott et al. 1998	25.7	11.8
	Marcus 1993	24.0	13.0
	Marcus et al. 1995*	28.8	12.8
Age at onset of BED diagnosis (years)	Grilo and Masheb 2000	25.8	17.8
	Spurrell et al. 1997	33.2	18.8
Comorbidity	Spurrell et al. 1997	—	more psychiatric problems, more Axis II
	Marcus 1993	—	more depression

Note: * Early onset versus late onset group: onset of dieting 14.4 versus 20.4 years.

In addition, there is evidence that early onset of binge eating may predict poor outcome from psychological treatments (Agras et al. 1995). In this trial, patients reporting that their binge eating began prior to age 16 had a 0 per cent success rate while patients reporting that binge eating began after age 16 had a 75 per cent success rate in a 24-week treatment programme for binge eating. The findings suggest the importance of early interventions for binge eating.

Weight loss treatments have not been shown to worsen binge eating among BED patients, or to result in binge eating among obese individuals who previously reported little difficulty in this area, even though they usually increase restraint (Yanovski and Sebring 1994; Yanovski et al. 1994). On the contrary, treatment studies for weight loss have generally reported significant reductions in binge eating and BED subjects are equally likely to report total adherence to weight loss programmes such as Very Low Calorie Diets (VLCD), as non-binge eaters (de Zwaan et al. in press; LaPorte 1992; Yanovski and Sebring 1994).

Analyses of food records showed that, unlike patients with BN, obese BED subjects report greater energy intake than obese controls not only on days during which they report binge eating, but also on days during which they feel their eating is under control (Yanovski and Sebring 1994).

Finally, findings from laboratory studies indicate (Yanovski 1995) that obese BED subjects consumed significantly more energy than obese controls, regardless if they were asked to eat normally or to binge eat. BED subjects usually show no relationship between feeling hungry and bingeing.

In summary, about half of obese patients with BED start binge eating first in the absence of dieting. The "binge-first" groups consistently begin bingeing around the onset of puberty while the "diet-first" groups usually begin in young adulthood (Table 5.3). Since an early age of onset of binge eating has shown to be related to poor outcome of psychological treatments, this finding is of significant clinical importance. These findings also have implications for aetiologic models of binge eating and there is a need to consider alternative factors in the maintenance of binge eating in BED. It has been hypothesized that binge eating might be a behavioural mechanism involved in the expression of obesity in genetically vulnerable individuals (Drewnowski 1995). In other words, the propensity to binge eat might be among the behavioural manifestations of the obese phenotype. Alternatively, it has been suggested that negative emotional states could play a major role in the pathogenesis of binge-eating episodes in patients without any previous attempt at dietary restriction (Agras and Telch 1998). Binge eating in obese BED patients seems to be more closely linked to disinhibition and negative emotional states (Ardovini et al. 1999).

Course

Data on the natural course of BED are mixed. Crow (2002) reported that only about 7 per cent of subjects diagnosed with BED were recovered at the end of one year. However, there is also evidence that BED might have a high spontaneous remission rate or may be an unstable state with a tendency for symptoms to wax and wane. Fairburn et al. (2000) reported that only 18 per cent had an eating disorder of clinical severity five years after an initial BED diagnosis. However, the sample investigated was relatively young (24.7 years) with a low rate of obesity (53 per cent). Subjects with BED gained on average 4.2 kg over the five years and the percentage of subjects with a BMI of more than 30 increased from 22 to 39 per cent. In line with this result, treatment studies with a no-treatment control group found that BED, if left untreated, will lead to continued weight gain (Agras et al. 1995). In another community sample of subjects with BED (Cachelin et al. 1999) half of those reassessed after six months no longer met criteria for BED.

As opposed to natural course studies, there is evidence from treatment-seeking samples that BED is a stable and persistent disorder (Wilfley et al. 2003). However, the treatment literature indicates that most of the proposed treatments for BED result in significant improvement in binge eating symptoms or remission of the disorder. This may also be consistent with a high spontaneous remission rate or a response to non-specific treatment modalities.

Metabolic characteristics

Even though obese patients with BED are more prone to weight cycling (de Zwaan *et al.* 1994), there is no evidence that they are more at risk for medical consequences of obesity than obese subjects without BED if one controls for weight and age. There have been no significant differences observed in blood pressure, resting metabolic rate, body fat distribution (waist/hip ratio), percentage body fat, and routine blood serum measures such as glucose, lipid levels and thyroid hormones (Brody *et al.* 1994; Wadden *et al.* 1993).

Newer research, however, suggests that BED may be associated with substantial physical morbidity independent of the effects of obesity or comorbid psychopathology (for review, see Bulik and Reichborn-Kjennerud 2003).

Eating behaviour

The binge episodes of overweight individuals are generally not as large, and may differ in other important ways from the bingeing described by patients with BN (Brody *et al.* 1994). If so, the single definition of a binge episode for both disorders, as currently proposed in DSM-IV, may not fit clinical reality (Gladis *et al.* 1998). During a binge meal, binge eaters consume a greater percentage of energy as fat and a lesser percentage as protein than in a normal meal. In line with data on BN subjects, obese binge eaters appear to increase their intake of fat rather than carbohydrates (Goldfein *et al.* 1993; Yanovski *et al.* 1992).

Aronoff *et al.* (2001) reported that according to self-report, patients with NES consumed more than 70 per cent of their daily energy intake after 7 p.m. with food preferences tending toward foods high in fat, sugar and salt, items generally not preferentially consumed earlier in the day.

The eating behaviour during nocturnal eating episodes (awakenings to eat) has been described in great detail by many authors (for a review, see de Zwaan *et al.* 2003a). Taken together the results suggest a great variability in caloric intake during nocturnal eating episodes; however, most patients seem to ingest only small amounts of food in a single episode, report more than one eating episode per night, and a relatively short duration of the episodes. Eating occurs throughout the night sleep cycle and the behaviour is usually present across weekdays, weekends, vacations and sleeping away from home. Foods chosen are usually high in calorie content. Nocturnal eating episodes do not appear to be associated with hunger but the perceived control over eating is low. Patients at times eat inedible substances or eat in a sloppy manner sometimes resulting in injuries, e.g. from careless cutting of food. However, in these patients the level of consciousness might be reduced suggesting sleepwalking.

Clinical characteristics

Eating-related psychopathology

Reviews of the literature suggest that obese individuals with BED differ significantly from non-BED obese individuals in several important ways including an early onset of obesity, a higher percentage time on diet, and more frequent body weight fluctuations (Brody *et al.* 1994; de Zwaan *et al.* 1994; Yanovski and Sebring 1994). BED patients are very similar to patients with BN in terms of their level of dysfunctional attitudes regarding eating, and overvalued ideas regarding weight and shape. This has been found in clinical as well as community samples (Striegel-Moore *et al.* 2001). The results suggest that one should consider dysfunctional attitudes regarding eating, shape and weight as diagnostic features of BED (Eldredge and Agras 1996; Masheb and Grilo 2000a; Striegel-Moore *et al.* 1998, 2001; Wilfley *et al.* 2000a). This undue influence of weight and shape on self-evaluation might also have implications for treatment. The tendency towards disinhibition of control over eating caused by affective, cognitive or pharmacological factors, and the susceptibility to hunger (TFEQ: Stunkard and Messik 1985) have consistently been demonstrated in patients with BED.

Napolitano *et al.* (2001) compared four groups in 83 self-selected obese patients enrolled in a university-based weight loss programme: NES only, BED only, NES and BED, and no eating disorder diagnosis. NES patients scored lower on disinhibition than BED patients but higher than individuals without an eating disorder diagnosis. Individuals who met criteria for both NES and BED scored highest.

Interestingly, the hedonic properties of binge eating may differ between BN and BED patients. BED patients are more likely to report that they have enjoyed the food, taste, smell and texture while binge eating (Mitchell *et al.* 1999). This finding might have implications for the treatment of BED, where the more positive valence associated with binge eating might make it harder for patients to focus on this as a problem behaviour.

General psychopathology

Most investigations found significantly higher levels of general psychiatric symptomatology in obese patients with BED than those without binge eating in clinical samples as well as in community samples (Antony *et al.* 1994; Fichter *et al.* 1993; Marcus *et al.* 1988; Schlundt *et al.* 1991; Spitzer *et al.* 1993; Striegel-Moore *et al.* 1998), but significantly lower values compared with bulimic patients (Brody *et al.* 1994; Fichter *et al.* 1993; Raymond *et al.* 1995, Spitzer *et al.* 1993). Obese BED patients also report significantly lower self-esteem (de Zwaan *et al.* 1994; Hawkins and Clement 1980; Lowe and

Caputo 1991; Striegel-Moore *et al.* 1998) and lower self-efficacy (Miller *et al.* 1999) than non-binge eaters do.

NES and nocturnal eating also appear to be associated with other clinical problems, especially mood disturbances, at least in the clinical samples investigated. This cannot be attributed solely to an overlap with BED. This suggests that NES might represent a distinct entity. However, the nature of this relationship remains unclear and there are not enough data available to draw any firm conclusions. The sample sizes investigated have been small and the studies did not include control groups (de Zwaan *et al.* 2003a).

Comorbidity

Individuals with BED have significantly higher rates of lifetime Axis I comorbidity compared with non-BED obese individuals. Prevalence rates range from 42 to 81 per cent for any diagnosis in various treatment-seeking and non-treatment-seeking BED samples. In particular, affective disorders are by far the most common diagnoses with a lifetime prevalence ranging from 32 to 91 per cent (Hudson *et al.* 1988; LaPorte 1992; Marcus *et al.* 1988, 1990a; Mussell *et al.* 1996; Specker *et al.* 1994; Spitzer *et al.* 1993; Telch and Stice 1998; Wilfley *et al.* 2000a, 2000b; Wing *et al.* 1989; Yanovski *et al.* 1993). The results of controlled studies are listed in Tables 5.4 and 5.5.

Depressive symptomatology may render individuals more vulnerable to binge eating relapse; binge eating might even be used as a means to regulate affect (Mussell *et al.* 1995; Telch and Stice 1998). There is some evidence that BED frequently predates the development of affective symptoms (Mussell *et al.* 1995), suggesting that depression might be a consequence of the eating disorder. Since comorbid depression is more the norm than the exception in BED patients, this comorbidity has implications for treatment. However, Wilfley *et al.* (2000a) did not find an influence of any specific area of Axis I on treatment outcome in BED patients participating in group cognitive behaviour therapy or interpersonal psychotherapy.

The results on anxiety disorders and substance abuse are controversial. One study found higher rates of panic disorder (Yanovski *et al.* 1993) in obese subjects with BED compared to those without BED. Wilfley *et al.* (2000c) reported that community BED cases were over nine times more likely to have a current anxiety disorder than treatment-seeking cases, suggesting that comorbid anxiety problems may inhibit treatment seeking among individuals with BED. Only one study found higher rates of substance abuse (Mussell *et al.* 1996) in obese BED subjects compared with non-BED subjects.

A history of DSM-III-R AN seems to be very rare (McCann *et al.* 1991; Specker *et al.* 1994); a history of BN, on the other hand, seems to be more common in BED patients than non-BED patients (Mussell *et al.* 1996; Specker *et al.* 1994; Yanovski *et al.* 1993). A history of BN in BED subjects does not appear to be associated with increased rates of comorbid

Table 5.4 Lifetime prevalence rates in percent of Axis I disorders using structured clinical interviews in treatment samples of obese binge eaters; comparisons to obese non-binge eaters

Authors	Sample size	Diagnostic criteria	Any Axis I diagnosis	Any affective disorder	Major depression	Substance use disorder	Anxiety disorder	Bulimia Nervosa
Hudson et al. 1988	23	obese Bulimia (DSM III)	—	91*	87*	21	17	—
Marcus et al. 1990b	25	BES ≥ 29	60*	32*	24	12	20	—
Yanovski et al. 1993	43	DSM-IV	60*	—	51*	12	9* (panic)	7*
Brody et al. 1994	13	DSM-IV	41.7	33.3	—	8.3	—	—
Specker et al. 1994	43	DSM-IV	72.1*	48.8*	47*	27.9	11.6	18.6*
Mussell et al. 1996	80	DSM-IV	70*	50*	46.3*	22.5*	18.8	12.5*

Note: * Significantly higher values compared to control group.

Table 5.5 Lifetime prevalence rates in percent of Axis I disorders using structured clinical interviews in treatment samples of obese binge eaters; comparisons to community samples or psychiatric samples

Authors	Sample size	Diagnostic criteria	Any Axis I diagnosis	Any affective disorder	Major depression	Substance use disorder	Anxiety disorder	Bulimia Nervosa
Telch and Stice 1998[a]	61	DSM-IV	59[b]	—	49[b]	15 (alcohol)	12 (panic)	2
Wilfley et al. 2000a[c]	162	DSM-IV	77	61	58	33	29	—
Wilfley et al. 2000a[d]	37	DSM-IV	81	68	—	50	22	—

Notes:
a Comparison with obese non-BED community sample.
b Significantly higher values compared to control group.
c Comparison with psychiatric sample.
d Comparison with BED community sample.

psychopathology, severity of eating problems, dietary restraint or attitudinal disturbance (Peterson *et al.* 1998).

It is well known that people with more than one problem are more likely to seek treatment than those with only one problem (Berkson's bias), resulting in an overestimation of comorbidity in clinical samples. However, Telch and Stice (1998) found few differences in rates of current and lifetime comorbid psychiatric disorders between treatment-seeking women with BED and similarly obese community cases. The only difference was a significantly higher lifetime prevalence rate of major depression in the clinical sample of BED women. Wilfley *et al.* (2000c) did not find any differences in current and lifetime prevalence rates of psychiatric diagnoses between a clinic sample of 37 BED patients as compared to 108 BED community cases. These results suggest that previous studies using recruited treatment-seeking samples have not overestimated the rate of comorbid psychiatric disorders. They found, however, a more severe eating disorder and a higher level of social impairment in the clinic sample. The clinic sample was older, exclusively white, and better educated than the community sample.

Comparisons with patients with BN present a somewhat mixed picture. Significantly higher current and lifetime prevalence rates of affective disorders in patients with BN when compared with non-purging BN patients and obese binge eaters have been reported (McCann *et al.* 1991; Raymond *et al.* 1995; Spitzer *et al.* 1993). However, others found similar prevalence rates of affective disorders in BED and BN subjects (Alger *et al.* 1991; Fichter *et al.* 1993; Hudson *et al.* 1988; Schwalberg *et al.* 1992). Also in community samples of women with BED and BN, comorbidity rates did not differ between groups (Striegel-Moore *et al.* 2001).

Although fewer studies have examined the pattern of Axis II diagnoses associated with BED, they have consistently found higher prevalence rates of these disorders among BED than non-BED obese samples (Specker *et al.* 1994; Telch and Stice 1998; Wilfley *et al.* 2000a; Yanovski *et al.* 1993), with rates ranging from 20 to 37 per cent. Axis II psychopathology was significantly related to more severe binge eating at baseline and specifically Cluster B personality disorder was related to outcome predicting significantly higher levels of binge eating at one-year follow-up after group CBT or IPT (Wilfley *et al.* 2000a). This is in accordance with findings in patients with BN.

Treatment

The treatment of BED poses a special problem since obesity is a major comorbidity in BED patients (Striegel-Moore *et al.* 2001; Wilfley and Cohen 1997). Clinicians are faced with the importance of weight loss or at least prevention of additional weight gain. In treating obese patients with BED there are several potential goals of treatment, including cessation of binge eating, weight loss or prevention of further weight gain, improvement of physical health, and reduction of psychological disturbances. Goals must be prioritized, preferably without influencing negatively on other goals. A major question to be resolved is whether it is best to treat the patient's binge eating first and then the obesity or to reverse this order.

Weight loss treatment

Treatment studies comparing patients with and without BED in weight reduction programmes do not find a significant differential outcome in weight loss, regardless of the approach employed: (cognitive) behaviour therapy for weight loss and diet treatment (Brody *et al.* 1994; Gladis *et al.* 1998; Marcus *et al.* 1988; Reeves *et al.* 2001), VLCD (de Zwaan *et al.* in press; LaPorte 1992; Telch and Agras 1993; Wadden *et al.* 1992; Yanovski *et al.* 1994), pharmacotherapy (Alger *et al.* 1991) and combined behaviour therapy for weight loss and pharmacotherapy (de Zwaan *et al.* 1992; Marcus *et al.* 1990b). Gladis *et al.* (1998) even found BED subjects to lose significantly more weight during a liquid meal programme compared to non-BED subjects. It is now clear that weight loss programmes are even effective in reducing binge eating frequency, at least in the short term (Goodrick *et al.* 1998; LaPorte 1992; Marcus *et al.* 1990b, 1995; Porzelius *et al.* 1995).

Some studies provide evidence that obese binge eaters might be at higher risk for dropping out of weight loss treatment, and might relapse – in terms of weight regain – more rapidly than non-binge eaters (Gormally *et al.* 1982; LaPorte 1992; Marcus *et al.* 1988; Porzelius *et al.* 1995; Yanovski *et al.* 1994). Subsequent studies reported that binge eating did not affect adherence to a diet, or attrition (e.g. Brody *et al.* 1994; Marcus *et al.* 1990b; Wadden *et al.* 1994). Ho *et al.* (1995) even found that binge status had a significant protective effect against dropout in a six-month weight loss programme among 156 obese women. Binge eaters were half as likely to drop out of weight loss treatment as non-binge eaters.

However, studies focusing on weight reduction are confronted with the well-known problem of obesity being associated with poor long-term maintenance of weight reduction. The majority of individuals who attempt to lose weight are ultimately unsuccessful. From a medical standpoint, weight loss is of course still desirable since obesity is a relevant risk factor for e.g. cardiovascular disease. However, compared to patterns of large weight fluctuations with a gradual trend in the direction of increasing weight, relative weight stability or only small weight losses as little as 10 per cent of initial body weight can have many benefits in reducing the health-related morbidity of obesity and can be viewed as a desirable long-term outcome.

Very low calorie diets

Short-term weight loss with a VLCD is usually excellent with about 20 per cent of initial body weight lost (Yanovski et al. 1994); however, many patients rapidly regain any weight lost. With a VLCD, the limited exposure to food cues during the fasting period seems to suppress binge eating. LaPorte (1992) reported that none of the patients experienced an objective binge-eating episode while on the fast. However, Telch and Agras (1993) reported that during the refeeding phase of the VLCD, when food is gradually reintroduced, a significant proportion of binge eaters as well as non-binge eaters showed a temporary incline in binge episodes. At the three-month follow-up, 15 per cent of the patients without any overeating episodes pre-treatment reported regular binge eating, whereas 39 per cent of the patients with regular binge eating pre-treatment no longer reported binge eating problems. The authors note that the refeeding phase of a VLCD might induce binge eating in susceptible individuals; however, there is no indication that a VLCD worsens the condition in patients with BED. This is supported by Raymond et al. (2002), who found that one year after a VLCD 57 per cent of the individuals who met BED criteria at baseline no longer met the criteria. Yanovski et al. (1994) reported a greater likelihood for BED subjects to experience larger lapses in adherence during fasting and during refeeding and early major weight regain of lost weight. However, the overall amount of weight lost and regained did not differ between patients with and without BED. Since the refeeding period of a VLCD has been described as a vulnerable phase for the development of binge eating, de Zwaan et al. (in press) added ten sessions of CBT targeting binge eating during this phase. The addition of CBT did not improve the abstinence rates at the end of the CBT, which were high with 58 per cent in those who received the CBT and 74 per cent in those who did not receive the CBT.

Pharmacotherapy targeting weight

Several studies of serotonin reuptake inhibitors for obesity suggest that this medication results in short-term weight loss, but most patients regain most or all of their lost weight even while still taking the medication (e.g. Goldstein et al. 1994). Marcus et al. (1990b) found that fluoxetine 60 mg added to behaviour therapy enhanced weight loss in both obese binge eaters and non-binge eaters. Fluvoxamine in a dose of 100 mg did not have an additional weight loss benefit when added to dietary management or behaviour therapy for weight loss (de Zwaan et al. 1992). The combination of phentermine and d-fenfluramine was also tested in the binge eating subgroup of the obese and was proven effective with regard to weight loss (Alger et al. 1991). In addition, dexfenfluramine was found to be effective in reducing binge eating in an eight-week double-blind placebo-controlled trial (Stunkard et al. 1996a).

This reduction was not associated by weight loss and there was a rapid relapse once d-fenfluramine was stopped. However, the fenfluramides were withdrawn from the market worldwide due to the development of valvular heart disease and primary pulmonary hypertension.

Night Eating Syndrome

In their original article, Stunkard *et al.* (1955) reported that night eating was associated with a poor weight loss outcome and even with untoward reactions to a weight loss programme such as the development of psychotic depression and the onset of severe bronchial asthma. In addition, eight patients reported the emergence of depressive or anxiety symptoms during past attempts to lose weight. Consistent with the original report by Stunkard *et al.* (1955), Gluck *et al.* (2001) reported that night eaters lost less weight than the non-night eaters (4.4 vs 7.3 kg) over a one-month period. However, the dropout rate during weight loss did not differ between obese with and without NES.

Bariatric surgery

The weight reduction after bariatric surgery is achieved by restriction (small gastric pouch and small outlet which restricts the volume of ingestible food) and in the case of gastric bypass also by a "dumping physiology". Liquid of high energy density which passes unimpeded through the pouch dumps directly into the jejunum thereby causing discomfort, pain or other highly unpleasant symptoms which are believed to help patients control their intake. The patients avoid caloric-dense sweet foods and milk products to prevent the occurrence of these symptoms.

There are conflicting results concerning the importance of binge eating for weight loss and weight loss maintenance after bariatric surgery. Most studies demonstrate that in the short term bariatric surgery has a pronounced positive effect on binge eating and associated psychopathology (Dymek *et al.* 2001; Kalarchian *et al.* 1999). Only one study demonstrated that binge eaters lost significantly less weight during the first six months after gastric bypass compared to non-binge eaters (Dymek *et al.* 2001); however, the prevalence of binge eating dropped to zero shortly following surgery. On the other hand there is increasing evidence that binge eating may re-emerge later during follow-up (after two years or later) and may be correlated with more weight regain in the long run (Hsu *et al.* 1996, 1997; Mitchell *et al.* 2001; Pekkarinen *et al.* 1994). Patients are unable to maintain a reduced intake and regain weight once their pouch stretches (which is a normal development over time) and restriction loosens. Constant overeating might even promote pouch stretching. Others found that binge eating before surgery predicted a higher frequency of vomiting after gastric banding with a higher rate of complications (e.g. neostoma stenosis) (Busetto *et al.* 1996).

As with BED there is evidence that the reoccurence of NES and nocturnal eating might contribute to post-surgical weight regain (Hsu *et al.* 1996, 1997; Powers *et al.* 1999).

Direct comparisons between behaviour weight loss treatments and CBT for obese BED patients

Four studies have compared the effect of a behaviour weight loss treatment with moderate caloric restriction to CBT in treating both the eating disorder and the obesity (Agras *et al.* 1994; Goodrick *et al.* 1998; Marcus *et al.* 1995; Porzelius *et al.* 1995). After three months, behaviour weight loss treatment was significantly superior to CBT in reducing weight, whereas CBT was significantly superior in reducing binge eating frequency (Agras *et al.* 1994). The three months of CBT was followed by 24 weeks of behaviour weight loss treatment, whereas patients in the behaviour weight loss treatment group continued treatment for another 24 weeks. At the end of treatment, the two groups did not differ in per cent abstinent from binge eating or amount weight lost. Porzelius *et al.* (1995) reported that even though CBT had a somewhat better effect on weight loss in binge eaters, the reduction in binge eating frequency did not differ between the CBT for BED and a behaviour weight loss treatment. They also found a higher dropout rate for the CBT compared to the behaviour weight loss treatment. Marcus *et al.* (1995) found no differences in binge eating reduction between individual CBT and behaviour weight loss treatment. The latter resulted in significantly more weight loss but also more weight regain during follow-up. In line with these results, Goodrick *et al.* (1998) did not find a difference in reduction of weight or binge eating comparing a diet treatment (resembling behaviour weight loss treatment) with a non-diet approach (comprising CBT elements).

In summary, these four studies suggest that moderate caloric restriction does not exacerbate binge eating among obese BED patients. In fact, it appears that behaviour weight loss treatment is as effective as CBT for BED in reducing binge eating. The studies provide mixed weight loss results; however, overall the amount of weight lost and maintained was poor. Many of the behavioural components of behaviour weight loss treatment overlap with those for CBT for BED and it may be that the encouragement of regular meals and snacks, stimulus control etc. are per se effective in reducing binge eating in BED patients (Wilfley and Cohen 1997).

Treatment for binge eating

Studies focusing on binge eating and related psychopathology have usually applied treatment approaches that have been found useful for patients with

BN. In these studies, normal eating is prioritized over weight loss. However, BED treatment manuals were changed to address also weight control issues. The most common treatment strategies employed include CBT adapted for BED (Fichter *et al.* 1993, 1998; Smith *et al.* 1992; Telch *et al.* 1990; Wilfley *et al.* 1993, 2002), IPT (Wilfley *et al.* 1993, 2002), dialectical behaviour therapy (Telch *et al.* 2001) and pharmacotherapy, most commonly but not exclusively with antidepressant medication (see Carter *et al.* 2003). Treatment lengths were usually brief, ranging from 10 to 20 weeks, and a group format was used. Data indicate that short-term CBT adapted for BED as well as IPT are effective in significantly reducing the frequency of binge eating with abstinence rates of 50 per cent and more of BED patients. The CBT subjects had reductions in the number of episodes of binge eating ranging from 48 per cent to 98 per cent and abstinence rates from 28 to 79 per cent. In contrast, waiting list control (WLC) groups have reductions of binge eating and abstinence rates ranging from 9 to 22 per cent and 0 to 9 per cent (Wilfley and Cohen 1997). The WLC results suggest that very few individuals who suffer from BED significantly improve or recover without treatment.

Despite experiencing impressive reductions in binge eating, patients usually do not lose weight (e.g. Carter and Fairburn 1998; Loeb *et al.* 2000; Smith *et al.* 1992; Telch *et al.* 1990; Wilfley *et al.* 1993) and in several of the earlier studies there was even a small weight gain after a course of CBT (Agras *et al.* 1994; Telch *et al.* 1990; Wilfley *et al.* 1993). Although subjects are no longer ingesting excess calories from binge-eating episodes, they may have not reduced their overall food intake to a point that would permit weight reduction. Cessation of binge eating and improvement in self-acceptance can contribute to an increased sense of physical and emotional well being even without major weight loss. However, studies suggest that complete abstinence from binge eating results in significantly more weight loss (Agras *et al.* 1994; Smith *et al.* 1992). In addition, there is evidence that obese patients with BED might continue to gain weight when not successfully reducing the frequency of their binge-eating episodes.

Night Eating Syndrome

There are no controlled treatment studies to date targeting the night-time eating directly. In a retrospective documentation of naturalistic pharmacotherapy interventions in the community, O'Reardon *et al.* (2001) found that 85 per cent of 56 patients with NES reported that various drugs (melatonin, herbal medicines, SSRIs and hypnotics) were of no significant help. Open label studies in small sample sizes have been conducted using d-fenfluramine 15–50 mg (Manni *et al.* 1997; Spaggiari *et al.* 1994), gamma-hydroxybutyric acid (GHB) 25 mg/kg, and oxazepam 30 mg (Mazzetti di Pietralata *et al.* 2000) with some positive but mostly equivocal results.

There are ongoing studies employing melatonin and sertraline (O'Reardon *et al.* 2001, 2002).

Combined treatments

More recent studies focus on eating behaviour, associated psychopathology and weight in obese individuals with BED. These studies usually combine weight loss treatment or exercise with CBT (Agras *et al.* 1995, 1997; de Zwaan *et al.* in press; Eldredge *et al.* 1997), medication with CBT (Agras *et al.* 1994; Devlin 2002; Devlin *et al.* 2000; Grilo *et al.* 2002; Laederach-Hofmann *et al.* 1999; Ricca *et al.* 2001) or use medication which has shown to be effective in reducing weight and binge eating (Appolinario *et al.* 2003; McElroy *et al.* 2003b). Interestingly, medication does not seem to add to the efficacy of CBT in reducing binge eating frequency (Wonderlich *et al.* 2003).

A sequential treatment programme was evaluated by Agras *et al.* (1994) and is described above. Additional findings are that the addition of desipramine increased the amount of weight lost and that patients who entirely stopped binge eating during the CBT phase were able to maintain their weight loss. This suggests that treating the eating disorder first and then treating the overweight might be a useful approach to the management of the overweight binge eater. Because only one-half of patients stop binge eating after treatment with CBT a second-level treatment that would benefit poor responders to CBT might be useful. Agras *et al.* (1995) did not find an add-itional benefit of IPT, whereas an extended course of CBT had a beneficial effect in terms of abstinence rates (Eldredge *et al.* 1997) in non-responders to CBT.

Pharmacotherapy targeting binge eating and combined with CBT for BED

A sizeable literature supports the effect of antidepressants in the short-term treatment of BN. Most placebo-controlled trials have found medication to be superior to placebo in reducing binge eating and weight also in obese patients with BED. This includes desipramine (McCann and Agras 1990), d-fenfluramine (Stunkard *et al.* 1996a), fluvoxamine (Hudson *et al.* 1998), imipramine (Laederach-Hofmann *et al.* 1999), sertraline (McElroy *et al.* 2000), fluoxetine (Arnold *et al.* 2002), citalopram (McElroy *et al.* 2003a), and more recently topiramate (McElroy *et al.* 2003b) and sibutramine (Appolinario *et al.* 2003). Small or open studies are also available for paroxetine (Prats *et al.* 1994), inositol (Gelber *et al.* 2001), venlafaxine (Malhotra *et al.* 2002) and zonisamide (McElroy *et al.* 2004). In general, medication trials have either no or only a short follow-up period and there is not enough knowledge about the benefit of long-term treatment. Medication does not appear to add much to the effectiveness of CBT in reducing binge eating (Agras *et al.* 1994; Ricca *et al.* 2001). However, antidepressant medication may enhance weight loss beyond the effects of CBT (Agras *et al.* 1994; Devlin *et al.* 2000; Ricca *et al.* 2001). Attrition rates are generally higher for medication trials (23–54 per cent with a mean attrition rate of 31 per cent) than for the psychotherapy trials of BED (16–35 per cent with a mean attrition rate of 14 per cent) (Wilfley and Cohen 1997). In some studies, there was an extremely strong placebo effect with remission rates of more than 40 per cent (Alger *et al.* 1991; Hudson *et al.* 1998), which stresses the therapeutic value of weekly clinic visits.

Self-help

Although psychotherapy has been found to be beneficial in reducing binge eating symptoms, this type of intervention is costly in the treatment of eating disorders and may be unnecessarily intensive for some individuals with BED. In addition, it is unlikely that there will ever be sufficient specialist resources to deal with the large number of cases that exist. Self-help approaches are cost-effective and easily disseminated.

There are now early results also for patients with BED using various modes of service delivery, e.g. group format with videotapes (Peterson *et al.* 1998, 2001), in-person on a one-to-one basis (Carter and Fairburn 1998; Fairburn 1995; Loeb *et al.* 2000) and even by telephone (Wells *et al.* 1997). The results show a marked reduction in binge eating frequency as well as improvement in secondary outcome measures. Abstinence rates of 40–50 per cent can be achieved and maintained during short-term follow-up (Carter and Fairburn 1998; Loeb *et al.* 2000). Overall, guided self-help showed better results and there is no effect on weight.

The results suggest that it may be appropriate to initiate treatment by providing self-help material followed by more intensive treatment for those who do not respond to this approach. However, a stepped care strategy of this type might result in some people being delayed from receiving appropriate specialist help or being demoralized by treatment failure. However, self-help may promote entry into and engagement with treatment.

Conclusion

In summary, many treatments are effective in reducing binge eating frequency. Not unexpectedly, weight loss treatments are less successful. Various combined treatments of CBT/IPT, behaviour weight loss treatment and medication, sequential or parallel, might promise a somewhat better efficacy on both binge eating and weight.

References

Abbott, D.W., de Zwaan, M., Mussell, M., Raymond, N.C., Seim, H.C., Crow, S., Crosby, R.D. and Mitchell, J.E. (1998) "On the relationship between binge eating and dietary restraint", *Journal of Psychosomatic Research* 44, 367–74.

Adami, G.F., Gandolfo, P., Bauer, B. and Scopinaro, N. (1995) "Binge eating in massively obese patients undergoing bariatric surgery", *International Journal of Eating Disorders* 17, 45–50.

Adami, G.F., Meneghelli, A. and Scopinaro, N. (1999) "Night eating and binge eating disorder in obese patients", *International Journal of Eating Disorders* 25, 335–8.

Agras, W.S. and Telch, C.F. (1998) "The effect of caloric deprivation and negative affect on binge eating in obese binge eating disordered women", *Behavior Therapy* 29, 491–503.

Agras, W.S., Telch, C.F., Arnow, B., Eldredge, K., Wilfley, D.E., Reaburn, S.D., Henderson, J. and Marnell, M. (1994) "Weight loss, cognitive-behavioral, and desipramine treatments in binge eating disorder: an additive design", *Behavior Therapy* 25, 225–38.

Agras, W.S., Telch, C.F., Arnow, B., Eldredge, K., Detzer, M.J., Henderson, J. and Marnell, M. (1995) "Does interpersonal therapy help patients with binge eating disorder who fail to respond to cognitive behavioural therapy?", *Journal of Consulting and Clinical Psychology* 63, 356–60.

Agras, W.S., Telch, C.F., Arnow, B., Eldredge, K. and Marnell, M. (1997) "One-year follow-up of cognitive behavioural therapy for obese individuals with binge eating disorder", *Journal of Consulting and Clinical Psychology* 65, 343–7.

Alger, S.A., Schwalberg, M.D., Bigaouette, J.M., Michalek, A.V. and Howard, L.J. (1991) "Effect of a tricyclic antidepressant and opiate antagonist on binge eating behavior in normoweight bulimic and obese, binge eating subjects", *American Journal of Clinical Nutrition* 53, 865–71.

American Academy of Sleep Medicine (2000) *International Classification of Sleep Disorders, Revised: Diagnostic and Coding Manual*, Rochester, MN: American Sleep Disorders Association.

American Psychiatric Association (1994) *Diagnostic and Statistical Manual of Mental Disorders*, 4th edn (DSM-IV), Washington, DC: APA.

Antony, M.M., Johnson, W.G., Carr-Nangle, R.E. and Abel, J.L. (1994) "Psychopathology correlates of binge eating and binge eating disorder", *Comprehensive Psychiatry* 35, 386–92.

Appolinario, J.C., Bacaltchuk, J., Sichieri, R., Claudino, A.M., Godoy-Matos, A., Morgan, C., Zanella, M.T. and Coutinho, W.A. (2003) "Randomized, double-blind, pacebo-controlled study of sibutramine in the treatment of binge eating disorder", *Archives of General Psychiatry* 60, 1109–16.

Ardovini, C., Caputo, G., Todisco, P. and Dalle Grave, R. (1999) "Binge eating and restraint model: psychometric analysis in binge eating disorder and normal weight bulimia", *European Eating Disorders Review* 7, 293–9.

Arnold, L.M., McElroy, S.L., Hudson, J.I., Welge, J.A., Bennett, A.J. and Keck, P.E. (2002) "A placebo-controlled randomized trial of fluoxetine in the treatment of binge eating disorder", *Journal of Clinical Psychiatry* 63, 1028–33.

Aronoff, N.J., Geliebter, A. and Zammit, G. (2001) "Gender and body mass index as related to the night eating syndrome in obese outpatients", *Journal of the American Dietetic Association* 101, 102–4.

Barry, D.T., Grilo, C.M. and Masheb, R.M. (2002) "Gender differences in patients with binge eating disorder", *International Journal of Eating Disorders* 31, 63–70.

Birketvedt, G.S., Florholmen, J., Sundsfjord, J., Osterud, B., Dinges, D., Bilker, W. and Stunkard, A.J. (1999) "Behavioral and neuro-endocrine characteristics of the night-eating syndrome", *Journal of the American Medical Association* 282, 657–63.

Brody, M.L., Walsh, B.T. and Devlin, M.J. (1994) "Binge eating disorder: reliability and validity of a new diagnostic category", *Journal of Consulting and Clinical Psychology* 62, 381–6.

Bruce, B. and Agras, W.S. (1992) "Binge eating in females: a population-based investigation", *International Journal of Eating Disorders* 12, 365–73.

Bulik, C.M. and Reichborn-Kjennerud, T. (2003) "Medical morbidity in binge eating disorder", *International Journal of Eating Disorders* 34, 39–46.

Busetto, L., Valente, P., Pisent, C., Segato, G., de Marchi, F., Favretti, F., Lise, M. and Enzi, G. (1996) "Eating pattern in the first year following adjustable silicone gastric banding (ASGB)", *International Journal of Obesity* 20, 539–46.

Cachelin, F.M., Striegel-Moore, R.H., Elder, K.A., Pike, K.M., Wilfley, D.E. and Fairburn, C.G. (1999) "Natural course of a community sample of women with binge eating disorder", *International Journal of Eating Disorders* 25, 45–54.

Carter, J.C. and Fairburn, C.G. (1998) "Cognitive-behavioral self-help for binge eating disorder: a controlled effectiveness study", *Journal of Consulting and Clinical Psychology* 66, 616–23.

Carter, W.P., Hudson, J.I., Lalonde, J.K., Pindyck, L., McElroy, S.L. and Pope, H.G. (2003) "Pharmacological treatment of binge eating disorder", *International Journal of Eating Disorders* 34, 74–88.

Ceru-Björk, C., Andersson, I. and Rössner, S. (2001) "Night eating and nocturnal eating: two different or similar syndromes among obese patients?", *International Journal of Obesity* 25, 365–72.

Crow, S.J. (2002) "Does binge eating disorder exist?", paper presented at the Annual Meeting of the Eating Disorders Research Society, Charleston, SC, November.

Devlin, M. (2002) "Psychotherapy and medication for binge eating disorder", Plenary Session, International Conference on Eating Disorders in Boston, MA, 25–28 April.

Devlin, M.J., Goldfein, J.A., Carino, J.S. and Wolk, S.L. (2000) "Open treatment of overweight binge eaters with phentermine and fluoxetine as an adjunct to cognitive behavioural therapy", *International Journal of Eating Disorders* 28, 325–32.

de Zwaan, M., Nutzinger, D.O. and Schönbeck, G. (1992) "Binge eating in overweight females", *Comprehensive Psychiatry* 33, 256–61.

de Zwaan, M., Mitchell, J.E., Seim, H.C., Specker, S.M., Pyle, R.L., Crosby, R.B. and Raymond, N.C. (1994) "Eating related and general psychopathology in obese females with binge eating disorder (BED)", *International Journal of Eating Disorders* 15, 43–52.

de Zwaan, M., Burgard, M.A., Schenck, C.H., Blaine, T. and Mitchell, J.E. (2003a) "Nighttime eating: a review of the literature", *European Eating Disorders Review* 11, 7–24.

de Zwaan, M., Mitchell, J.E., Howell, L.M., Monson, N., Swan-Kremeier, L. and Crosby, R.D. (2003b) "Characteristics of morbidly obese patients before gastric bypass surgery", *Comprehensive Psychiatry* 44, 428–34.

de Zwaan, M., Mitchell, J.E., Mussell, M.P., Raymond, N.C., Seim, H.C., Specker, S.M. and Crosby, R.D. (in press) "Short-term cognitive behavioral treatment does not improve long-term outcome of a comprehensive very-low-calorie diet program in obese women with binge eating disorder", *Behavior Therapy*.

Drewnowski, A. (1995) "Metabolic determinants of binge eating", *Addictive Behaviors* 20, 733–45.

Dymek, M.P., le Grange, D., Neven, K. and Alverdy, J. (2001) "Quality of life and psychosocial adjustment in patients after Roux-en-Y gastric bypass: a brief report", *Obesity Surgery* 11, 32–9.

Eldredge, K.L. and Agras, W.S. (1996) "Weight and shape overconcern and emotional eating in binge eating disorder", *International Journal of Eating Disorders* 19, 73–82.

Eldredge, K.L., Agras, W.S., Arnow, B., Telch, C.F., Bell, S., Castonguay, L.G. and Marnell, M. (1997) "The effects of extending cognitive behavioural therapy for binge eating disorder among initial treatment nonresponders", *International Journal of Eating Disorders* 21, 347–52.

Fairburn, C.G. (1995) *Overcoming Binge Eating*, New York: Guilford Press.

Fairburn, C.G. and Cooper, Z. (1993) "The Eating Disorder Examination (12.0D)", in C.G. Fairburn and G.T. Wilson (eds) *Binge Eating: Nature, Assessment, and Treatment*, New York: Guilford Press.

Fairburn, C.G., Cooper, Z., Doll, H.A., Norman, P. and O'Connor, M. (2000) "The natural course of bulimia nervosa and binge eating disorder in young women", *Archives of General Psychiatry* 57, 659–65.

Fichter, M.M., Quadflieg, N. and Brandl, B. (1993) "Recurrent overeating: an empirical comparison of binge eating disorder, bulimia nervosa, and obesity", *International Journal of Eating Disorders* 14, 1–16.

Fichter, M., Quadflieg, N. and Gnutzmann, A. (1998) "Binge eating disorder: treatment outcome over a 6-year course", *Journal of Psychosomatic Research* 44, 385–405.

French, S.A., Jeffery, R.W., Sherwood, N.E. and Neumark-Sztainer, D. (1999) "Prevalence and correlates of binge eating in a nonclinical sample of women enrolled in a weight gain prevention program", *International Journal of Obesity* 23, 576–85.

Gelber, D., Levine, J. and Belmaker, R.H. (2001) "Effect of inositol on bulimia nervosa and binge eating", *International Journal of Eating Disorders* 29, 345–8.

Gladis, M.M., Wadden, T.A., Vogt, R., Foster, G., Kuehnel, R.H. and Bartlett, S.J. (1998) "Behavioral treatment of obese binge eaters: do they need different care?", *Journal of Psychosomatic Research* 44, 375–84.

Gluck, M.E., Geliebter, A. and Satov, T. (2001) "Night eating syndrome is associated with depression, low self-esteem, reduced daytime hunger, and less weight loss in obese outpatients", *Obesity Research* 9, 264–7.

Goldfein, J.A., Walsh, B.T., LaChaussee, J.L., Kissileff, H.R. and Devlin, M.J. (1993) "Eating behavior in binge eating disorder", *International Journal of Eating Disorders* 14, 427–31.

Goldstein, D.J., Rampey, A.H. Jr, Enas, G.G., Potvin, J.H., Fludzinski, L.A. and Levine, L.R. (1994) "Fluoxetine: a randomized clinical trial in the treatment of obesity", *International Journal of Obesity* 18, 129–35.

Goodrick, C.K., Poston, W.S.C., Kimball, K.T., Reeves, R.S. and Foreyt, J.P. (1998) "Nondieting versus dieting treatment for overweight binge eating women", *Journal of Consulting and Clinical Psychology* 66, 363–8.

Gormally, J., Black, S., Daston, S. and Rardin, D. (1982) "The assessment of binge eating severity among obese persons", *Addictive Behavior* 7, 47–55.

Greeno, C.G., Wing, R.R. and Marcus, M.D. (1995) "Nocturnal eating in binge eating disorder and matched-weight controls", *International Journal of Eating Disorders* 18, 343–9.

Grilo, C.M. and Masheb, R.M. (2000) "Onset of dieting vs binge eating in outpatients with binge eating disorder", *International Journal of Obesity and Related Metabolic Disorders* 24, 404–9.

Grilo, C.M., Masheb, R.M., Heninger, G. and Wilson, G.T. (2002) "Psychotherapy and medication for binge eating disorder", Abstract 095, International Conference on Eating Disorders in Boston, MA, 25–28 April.

Grissett, N.I. and Fitzgibbon, M.L. (1996) "The clinical significance of binge eating in an obese population: support for BED and questions regarding its criteria", *Addictive Behavior* 21, 57–66.

Hamburger, W.H. (1951) "Emotional aspects of obesity", *Medical Clinics of North America* 35, 483–99.

Hawkins, R.C. and Clement, P.F. (1980) "Development and construct validation of a self-report measure on binge eating tendencies", *Addictive Behavior* 5, 219–26.

Herpertz, S., Kielmann, R., Grigutsch, K., Dost, M., Siffert, W., Stang, A., Jockel, K.H., Wolf, A.M., Husemann, B., Hulisz, T., Machleit, U., Chen-Stute, A., Kemen, M., Stroh, C., Berg, T. and Senf, W. (2001) "Predictor variables of the course of weight – a multicenter, prospective, controlled trial", paper presented at the Eating Disorders Research Society Annual Meeting, Bernalillo, NM, 28 November – 1 December.

Ho, K.S.I., Nichaman, M.Z., Taylor, W.C., Lee, E.S. and Foreyt, J.P. (1995) "Binge eating disorder, retention, and drop out in an adult obesity program", *International Journal of Eating Disorders* 18, 291–4.

Hsu, L.K.G., Betancourt, S. and Sullivan, S.P. (1996) "Eating disturbances before and after vertical banded gastroplasty: a pilot study", *International Journal of Eating Disorders* 19, 23–4.

Hsu, L.K.G., Sullivan, S.P. and Benotti, P.N. (1997) "Eating disturbances and outcome of gastric bypass surgery: a pilot study", *International Journal of Eating Disorders* 21, 385–90.

Hudson, J.I., Pope, H.G., Wurtman, J., Yurgelun-Todd, D., Mark, S. and Rosenthal, N.E. (1988) "Bulimia in obese individuals: relationship to normal-weight bulimia", *Journal of Nervous and Mental Disorders* 176, 144–52.

Hudson, J.I., McElroy, S.L., Raymond, N.C., Crow, S., Keck, P.E., Carter, W.P., Mitchell, J.E., Strakowski, S.M., Pope, H.G., Coleman, B. and Jonas, J.M. (1998) "Fluvoxamine in the treatment of binge eating disorder", *American Journal of Psychiatry* 155, 1756–62.

Kalarchian, M.A., Wilson, G.T., Brolin, R.E. and Bradley, L. (1999) "Effects of bariatric surgery on binge eating and related psychopathology", *Eating and Weight Disorders* 4, 1–5.

Kinzl, J.F., Traweger, C., Trefalt, E., Mangweth, B. and Biebl, W. (1999) "Binge eating disorder in females: a population-based investigation", *International Journal of Eating Disorders* 25, 287–92.

Kornhaber, A. (1970) "The stuffing syndrome", *Psychosomatics* 11, 580–4.

Kuehnel, R.H. and Wadden, T.A. (1994) "Binge eating disorder, weight cycling, and psychopathology", *International Journal of Eating Disorders* 15, 321–9.

Laederach-Hofmann, K., Graf, C., Horber, F., Lippuner, K., Lederer, S., Michel, R. and Schneider, M. (1999) "Imipramine and diet counseling with psychological support in the treatment of obese binge eaters: a randomized, placebo-controlled double-blind study", *International Journal of Eating Disorders* 26, 231–44.

LaPorte, D.J. (1992) "Treatment response in obese binge eaters: preliminary results using a very low calorie diet (VLCD) and behavior therapy", *Addictive Behaviors* 17, 247–57.

Loeb, K.L., Wilson, G.T., Gilbert, J.S. and Labouvie, E. (2000) "Guided and unguided self-help for binge eating", *Behaviour Research and Therapy* 38, 259–72.

Lowe, M.R. and Caputo, G.C. (1991) "Binge eating in obesity: toward the specification of predictors", *International Journal of Eating Disorders* 10, 49–55.

McCann, U.D. and Agras, W.S. (1990) "Successful treatment of nonpurging bulimia nervosa with desipramine: a double-blind, placebo-controlled study", *American Journal of Psychiatry* 147, 1509–13.

McCann, U.D., Rossiter, E.M., King, R.J. and Agras, W.S. (1991) "Nonpurging bulimia: a distinct subtype of bulimia nervosa", *International Journal of Eating Disorders* 10, 679–87.

McElroy, S.L., Casuto, L.S., Nelson, E.B., Lake, K.A., Soutullo, C.A., Keck, P.E. Jr and Hudson, J.I. (2000) "Placebo-controlled trial of sertraline in the treatment of binge eating disorder", *American Journal of Psychiatry* 157, 1004–6.

McElroy, S.L., Hudson, J.I., Malhotra, S., Welge, J.A., Nelson, E.B. and Keck, P.E. (2003a) "Citalopram in the treatment of binge eating disorder: a placebo-controlled trial", *Journal of Clinical Psychiatry* 64, 807–13.

McElroy, S.L., Arnold, L.M., Shapira, N.A., Keck, P.E., Kamin, M., Karim, R., Rosenthal, N. and Hudson, J.I. (2003b) "Topiramate in the treatment of binge eating disorder associated with obesity: a randomized, placebo-controlled trial", *American Journal of Psychiatry* 160, 255–61.

McElroy, S.L., Kotwal, R., Hudson, J.I., Nelson, E.B. and Keck, P.E. (2004) "Zonisamide in the treatment of binge eating disorder: an open-label, prospective trial", *Journal of Clinical Psychiatry* 65, 50–6.

Malhotra, S., King, K.H., Welge, J.A., Brusman-Lovins, L. and McElroy, S.L. (2002) "Venlafaxine treatment of binge eating disorder associated with obesity: a series of 35 patients", *Journal of Clinical Psychiatry* 63, 802–6.

Manni, R., Ratti, M.T. and Tartara, A. (1997) "Nocturnal eating: prevalences in 120 insomniac referrals", *Sleep* 20, 734–8.

Marcus, M.D. (1993) "Binge eating in obesity", in C.G. Fairburn and G.T. Wilson (eds) *Binge Eating: Nature, Assessment and Treatment*, New York: Guilford Press.

Marcus, M.D., Wing, R.R. and Lamparski, D.M. (1985) "Binge eating and dietary restraint in obese patients", *Addictive Behaviors* 10, 163–8.

Marcus, M.D., Wing, R.R. and Hopkins, J. (1988) "Obese binge eaters: affect, cognitions, and response to behavioral weight control", *Journal of Consulting and Clinical Psychology* 56, 433–9.

Marcus, M.D., Wing, R.R., Ewing, L., Kern, E., Gooding, W. and McDermott, M. (1990a) "Psychiatric disorders among obese binge eaters", *International Journal of Eating Disorders* 9, 69–77.

Marcus, M.D., Wing, R.R., Ewing, L., Kern, E., McDermott, M. and Gooding, W. (1990b) "A double-blind, placebo-controlled trial of fluoxetine plus behavior modification in the treatment of obese binge-eaters and non-binge-eaters", *American Journal of Psychiatry* 147, 876–81.

Marcus, M.D., Smith, D., Santelli, R. and Kaye, W. (1992) "Characterization of eating disordered behavior in obese binge eaters", *International Journal of Eating Disorders* 12, 249–55.

Marcus, M.D., Wing, R.R. and Fairburn, C.G. (1995) "Cognitive treatment of binge eating versus behavioral weight control in the treatment of binge eating disorder", *Annals of Behavioral Medicine* 17, S090.

Masheb, R.M. and Grilo, C.M. (2000a) "Binge eating disorder: a need for additional diagnostic criteria", *Comprehensive Psychiatry* 41, 159–62.

Masheb, R.M. and Grilo, C.M. (2000b) "On the relation of attempting to lose weight, restraint, and binge eating in outpatients with binge eating disorder", *Obesity Research* 8, 638–45.

Masheb, R.M. and Grilo, C.M. (2002) "On the relationship of flexible and rigid control of eating to body mass index and overeating in patients with binge eating disorder", *International Journal of Eating Disorders* 31, 82–91.

Mazzetti di Pietralata, M., Florentino, M.T. and Leonardi, C. (2000) "Night eating syndrome: preliminary results", *Eating and Weight Disorders* 5, 92–101.

Miller, P.M., Watkins, J.A., Sargent, R.G. and Rickert, E.J. (1999) "Self-efficacy in overweight individuals with binge eating disorder", *Obesity Research* 7, 552–5.

Mitchell, J.E., Mussell, M.P., Peterson, C.B., Crow, S., Wonderlich, S.A., Crosby, R.D., Davis, T. and Weller, C. (1999) "Hedonics of binge eating in women with bulimia nervosa and binge eating disorder", *International Journal of Eating Disorders* 26, 165–70.

Mitchell, J.E., Lancaster, K.L., Burgard, M.A., Howell, L.M., Krahn, D.D., Crosby, R.D., Wonderlich, S.A. and Gosnell, B.A. (2001) "Long-term follow-up of patients status post-gastric bypass for obesity", *Obesity Surgery* 11, 464–8.

Molinari, E., Ragazzoni, P. and Morosin, A. (1997) "Psychopathology in obese subjects with and without binge eating disorder and in bulimic subjects", *Psychological Reports* 80, 1327–35.

Mussell, M., Mitchell, J., Weller, C., Raymond, N., Crow, S. and Crosby, R. (1995) "Onset of binge eating, dieting, obesity, and mood disorders among subjects seeking treatment for binge eating disorder", *International Journal of Eating Disorders* 4, 395–400.

Mussell, M.P., Mitchell, J.E., de Zwaan, M., Crosby, R.D., Seim, H.C. and Crow, S.J. (1996) "Clinical characteristics associated with binge eating in obese females: a descriptive study", *International Journal of Obesity and Related Metabolic Disorders* 20, 324–31.

Napolitano, M.A., Head, S., Babyak, M.A. and Blumenthal, J.A. (2001) "Binge eating disorder and night eating syndrome: psychological and behavioral characteristics", *International Journal of Eating Disorders* 30, 193–203.

O'Reardon, J., Allison, K.C., Stunkard, A.J. and Dinges, D. (2001) "Treatment of the night eating syndrome", *Obesity Research* 9, 69.

O'Reardon, J.P., Allison, K.C. and Stunkard, A.J. (2002) "Treatment options for the night eating syndrome", Abstract 1514, International Conference on Eating Disorders, Boston, MA, 25–28 April.

Pekkarinen, T., Koskela, K., Huikuri, K. and Mustajoki, P. (1994) "Long-term results of gastroplasty for morbid obesity: binge eating as a predictor for poor outcome", *Obesity Surgery* 4, 248–55.

Peterson, C.B., Mitchell, J.E., Engbloom, S., Nugent, S., Mussell, M.P. and Miller, J.P. (1998) "Group cognitive behavioral treatment of binge eating disorder: a comparison of therapist-led versus self-help formats", *International Journal of Eating Disorders* 24, 125–36.

Peterson, C.B., Mitchell, J.E., Engbloom, S., Nugent, S., Mussell, M.P., Crow, S.J. and Thuras, P. (2001) "Self-help versus therapist-led group cognitive behavioral treatment of binge eating disorder at follow-up", *International Journal of Eating Disorders* 30, 363–74.

Pike, K.M., Dohm, F.A., Striegel-Moore, R.H., Wilfley, D.E. and Fairburn, C.G. (2001) "A comparison of black and white women with binge eating disorder", *American Journal of Psychiatry* 158, 1455–60.

Polivy, J. and Herman, C.P. (1985) "Dieting and binging", *American Psychologist* 40, 193–201.

Porzelius, L.K., Houston, C., Smith, M., Arfken, C. and Fisher, E. (1995) "Comparison of a standard behavioral weight loss treatment and a binge eating weight loss treatment", *Behavior Therapy* 26, 119–34.

Powers, P.S., Perez, A., Boyd, F. and Rosemurgy, A. (1999) "Eating pathology before and after bariatric surgery: a prospective study", *International Journal of Eating Disorders* 25, 293–300.

Prats, M., Diez-Quevedo, C., Avila, C. and Planell, L.S. (1994) "Paroxetine treatment for bulimia nervosa and binge eating disorder", Abstract 308, Sixth International Conference on Eating Disorders, New York, April.

Rand, C.S.W. and Kuldau, J.M. (1986) "Eating patterns in normal weight individuals: bulimia, restraint eating and the night eating syndrome", *International Journal of Eating Disorders* 5, 75–84.

Rand, C.S.W. and Kuldau, J.M. (1993) "Morbid obesity: a comparison between a general population and obesity surgery patients", *International Journal of Obesity* 17, 657–61.

Rand, C.S.W., MacGregor, A.M.C. and Stunkard, A.J. (1997) "The night eating syndrome in the general population and among postoperative obesity surgery patients", *International Journal of Eating Disorders* 22, 65–9.

Raymond, N., Mussell, M., Mitchell, J.E., Crosby, R. and de Zwaan, M. (1995) "An age-matched comparison of subjects with binge eating disorder and bulimia nervosa", *International Journal of Eating Disorders* 18, 135–43.

Raymond, N., de Zwaan, M., Mitchell, J.E., Ackard, D. and Thuras, P. (2002) "Effect of a very low calorie diet on the diagnostic category of individuals with binge eating disorder", *International Journal of Eating Disorders* 31, 49–56.

Reeves, R.S., McPherson, R.S., Nichaman, M.Z., Harrist, R.B., Foreyt, J.P. and Goodrick, G.K. (2001) "Nutrient intake of obese female binge eaters", *Journal of the American Dietetic Association* 101, 209–15.

Ricca, V., Mannucci, E., Mezzani, B., Moretti, S., Di Bernardo, M., Bertelli, M., Rotella, C.M. and Faravelli, C. (2001) "Fluoxetine and fluvoxamine combined with individual cognitive-behaviour therapy in binge eating disorder: a one-year follow-up study", *Psychotherapy and Psychosomatics* 70, 298–306.

Schenck, C.H., Hurwitz, T., O'Connor, K.A. and Mahowald, M.W. (1993)

"Additional categories of sleep-related eating disorders and the current status of treatment", *Sleep* 16, 457–66.

Schlundt, D.G., Taylor, D., Hill, J.O., Sbrocco, T., Pope-Cordle, J., Kasser, T. and Arnold, D. (1991) "A behavioral taxonomy of obese female participants in a weight-loss program", *American Journal of Clinical Nutrition* 53, 1151–8.

Schwalberg, M.D., Barlow, D.H., Alger, S.A. and Howard, L.J. (1992) "Comparison of bulimics, obese binge eaters, social phobics, and individuals with panic disorder on comorbidity across DSM-III-R anxiety disorders", *Journal of Abnormal Psychology* 101, 675–81.

Smith, D.E., Marcus, M.D. and Kaye, W. (1992) "Cognitive-behavorial treatment of obese binge eaters", *International Journal of Eating Disorders* 12, 257–62.

Spaggiari, M.C., Granella, F., Parrino, L., Marchesi, C., Melli, I. and Terzano, M.G. (1994) "Nocturnal eating syndrome in adults", *Sleep* 17, 339–44.

Specker, S., de Zwaan, M., Raymond, N. and Mitchell, J. (1994) "Psychopathology in subgroups of obese women with and without binge eating disorder", *Comprehensive Psychiatry* 35, 185–90.

Spitzer, R.L., Devlin, M.J., Walsh, B.T., Hasin, D., Wing, R., Marcus, M.D., Stunkard, A.J., Wadden, T., Yanovski, S., Agras, S., Mitchell, J. and Nonas, C. (1992) "Binge eating disorder: a multisite field trial of the diagnostic criteria", *International Journal of Eating Disorders* 11, 191–203.

Spitzer, R.L., Yanovski, S., Wadden, T., Wing, R., Marcus, M.D., Stunkard, A., Devlin, M., Mitchell, J., Hasin, D. and Horne, R. (1993) "Binge eating disorder: its further validation in a multisite study", *International Journal of Eating Disorders* 13, 137–53.

Spurrell, E.B., Wilfley, D.E., Tanofsky, M.B. and Brownell, K.D. (1997) "Age of onset for binge eating: are there different pathways to binge eating?", *International Journal of Eating Disorders* 21, 55–65.

Striegel-Moore, R.H. and Franko, D.L. (2003) "Epidemiology of binge eating disorder", *International Journal of Eating Disorders* 34, 19–29.

Striegel-Moore, R.H., Wilson, G.T., Wilfley, D.E., Elder, K.A. and Brownell, K.D. (1998) "Binge eating in an obese community sample", *International Journal of Eating Disorders* 23, 27–37.

Striegel-Moore, R.H., Dohm, F.A., Solomon, E.E., Fairburn, C.G., Pike, K.M. and Wilfley, D.E. (2000) "Subthreshold binge eating disorder", *International Journal of Eating Disorder* 27, 270–8.

Striegel-Moore, R.H., Cachelin, F.M., Dohm, F.A., Pike, K.M., Wilfley, D.E. and Fairburn, C.G. (2001) "Comparison of binge eating disorder and bulimia nervosa in a community sample", *International Journal of Eating Disorders* 29, 157–65.

Stunkard, A.J. (1959) "Eating patterns and obesity", *Psychiatry Quarterly* 33, 284–95.

Stunkard, A. and Messik, S. (1985) "The Three-Factor Eating Questionnaire to measure dietary restraint, disinhibition, and hunger", *Journal of Psychosomatic Research* 29, 71–83.

Stunkard, A., Grace, W.J. and Wolff, H.G. (1955) "The night-eating syndrome: a pattern of food intake among certain obese patients", *American Journal of Medicine* 19, 78–86.

Stunkard, A., Berkowitz, R., Tanrikut, C., Reiss, E. and Young, L. (1996a) "d-Fenfluramine treatment of binge eating disorder", *American Journal of Psychiatry* 153, 1455–9.

Stunkard, A., Berkowitz, R., Wadden, T., Tanrikut, C., Reiss, E. and Young, L. (1996b) "Binge eating disorder and the night eating syndrome", *International Journal of Obesity and Related Metabolic Disorders* 20, 1–6.

Tanofsky, M.B., Wilfley, D.E., Spurrell, E.B., Welch, R. and Brownell, K.D. (1997) "Comparison of men and women with binge eating disorder", *International Journal of Eating Disorders* 21, 49–54.

Telch, C.F. and Agras, W.S. (1993) "The effects of a very low calorie diet on binge eating", *Behavior Therapy* 24, 177–93.

Telch, C.F. and Stice, E. (1998) "Psychiatric comorbidity in women with binge eating disorder: prevalence rates from a non-treatment-seeking sample", *Journal of Consulting and Clinical Psychology* 66, 768–76.

Telch, C.F., Agras, W.S., Rossiter, E.M., Wilfley, D. and Kenardy, J. (1990) "Group cognitive-behavioral treatment for the nonpurging bulimic: an initial evaluation", *Journal of Consulting and Clinical Psychology* 58, 629–35.

Telch, C.F., Agras, W.S. and Linehan, M.M. (2001) "Dialectical behavior therapy for binge eating disorder", *Journal of Consulting and Clinical Psychology* 69, 1061–5.

Wadden, T.A., Foster, G.D. and Letizia, K.A. (1992) "Response of obese binge eaters to treatment by behavior therapy combined with very low calorie diet", *Journal of Consulting and Clinical Psychology* 60, 808–11.

Wadden, T.A., Foster, G.D., Letizia, K.A. and Wilk, J.E. (1993) "Metabolic, anthropometric, and psychological characteristics of obese binge eaters", *International Journal of Eating Disorders* 14, 17–25.

Wadden, T.A., Foster, G.D. and Letizia, A. (1994) "One-year behavioral treatment of obesity: comparison of moderate and severe caloric restriction and the effects of weight maintenance therapy", *Journal of Consulting and Clinical Psychology* 62, 165–71.

Wadden, T.A., Sarwer, D.B., Womble, L.G., Foster, G.D., McGuckin, B.G. and Schimmel, A. (2001) "Psychosocial aspects of obesity and obesity surgery", *Surgical Clinics of North America* 81, 1001–24.

Wells, A.M., Garvin, V., Dohm, F.A. and Striegel-Moore, R.H. (1997) "Telephone-based guided self-help for binge eating disorder: a feasibility study", *International Journal of Eating Disorders* 21, 341–6.

Wilfley, D.E. and Cohen, L.R. (1997) "Psychological treatment of bulimia nervosa and binge eating disorder", *Psychopharmacological Bulletin* 33, 437–54.

Wilfley, D.E., Agras, W.S., Telch, C.F., Rossiter, E.M., Schneider, J.A., Golomb Cole, A., Sifford, L. and Reaburn, S.D. (1993) "Group cognitive behavioural therapy and group interpersonal psychotherapy for the nonpurging bulimic individual: a controlled comparison", *Journal of Consulting and Clinical Psychology* 61, 296–305.

Wilfley, D.E., Friedman, M.A., Dounchis, J.Z., Stein, R.I., Welch, R.R. and Ball, S.A. (2000a) "Comorbid psychopathology in binge eating disorder: relation to eating disorder severity at baseline and following treatment", *Journal of Consulting and Clinical Psychology* 68, 641–9.

Wilfley, D.E., Schwartz, M.B., Spurrell, E.B. and Fairburn, C.G. (2000b) "Using the Eating Disorder Examination to identify the specific psychopathology of binge eating disorder", *International Journal of Eating Disorders* 27, 259–69.

Wilfley, D.E., Pike, K.M., Dohm, F.A., Striegel-Moore, R.H. and Fairburn, C.G. (2000c) "Bias in binge eating disorder: how representative are recruited clinical samples?" *Journal of Consulting and Clinical Psychology* 69, 383–8.

Wilfley, D.E., Welch, R.R., Stein, R.I., Spurrell, E.B., Cohen, L.R., Saelens, B.E., Dounchis, J.Z., Frank, M.A., Wiseman, C.V. and Matt, G.E. (2002) "A randomized comparison of group cognitive behavioural therapy and group interpersonal psychotherapy for the treatment of overweight individuals with binge eating disorder", *Archives of General Psychiatry* 59, 713–21.

Wilfley, D.E., Wilson, G.T. and Agras, W.S. (2003) "The clinical significance of binge eating disorder", *International Journal of Eating Disorders* 34, 96–106.

Wilson, G.T., Nonas, C.A. and Rosenblum, G.D. (1993) "Assessment of binge eating in obese patients", *International Journal of Eating Disorders* 13, 25–33.

Wing, R.R., Marcus, M.D., Epstein, L.H., Blai, E.H. and Burton, L.R. (1989) "Binge eating in obese patients with type II diabetes", *International Journal of Eating Disorders* 8, 671–9.

Winkelman, J.W., Herzog, D.B. and Fava, M. (1999) "The prevalence of sleep-related eating disorder in psychiatric and non-psychiatric populations", *Psychological Medicine* 29, 1461–6.

Wonderlich, S.A., de Zwaan, M., Mitchell, J.E., Peterson, C. and Crow, S. (2003) "Psychological and dietary treatments of binge eating disorder", *International Journal of Eating Disorders* 34, 58–73.

World Health Organization (1992) *ICD-10 Classification of Mental and Behavioural Disorders: Clinical Descriptions and Diagnostic Guidelines*, Geneva: WHO.

Yanovski, S.Z. (1995) "The chicken or the egg: binge eating disorder and dietary restraint", *Appetite* 24, 258.

Yanovski, S.Z. and Sebring, N.G. (1994) "Recorded food intake of obese women with binge eating disorder before and after weight loss", *International Journal of Eating Disorders* 15, 135–50.

Yanovski, S.Z., Leet, M., Yanovski, J.A., Flood, M., Gold, P.W., Kissileff, H.R. and Walsh, B.T. (1992) "Food selection and intake of obese women with binge eating disorder", *American Journal of Clinical Nutrition* 56, 975–80.

Yanovski, S.Z., Nelson, J.E., Dubbert, B.K. and Spitzer, R.L. (1993) "Association of binge eating disorder and psychiatric comorbidity in obese subjects", *American Journal of Psychiatry* 150, 1472–9.

Yanovski, S.Z., Gormally, J.F., Leser, M.S., Gwirtsman, H.E. and Yanovski, J.A. (1994) "Binge eating disorder affects outcome of comprehensive very low calorie diet treatment", *Obesity Research* 2, 205–12.

Chapter 6

Patterns of change in eating disorders

A process view on eating disorders symptomatology

Stephanie Bauer, Matthias Richard, Hans Kordy and COST Action B6

Introduction

Standard assessment systems like the *Diagnostic and Statistical Manual of Mental Disorders* (APA 1994) or the International Statistical Classification of Diseases and Related Health Problems (WHO 1992) define Bulimia Nervosa and Anorexia Nervosa as complex syndromes composed of several symptoms (see Appendix for diagnostic criteria). The diagnostic criteria relate to characteristic symptom patterns as well as to aspects of time such as minimum frequency or minimum duration. For example, the diagnosis "Bulimia Nervosa" requires a duration of at least three months with at least two binge-eating episodes per week. Although time is explicitly mentioned, eating disorders are rather conceptualized as state diagnoses. The duration is taken into account rather to control for fluctuations of symptoms over time than to shift attention to the course of symptoms.

The processes of getting ill and getting well again are actually not considered of diagnostic relevance. This may be due to the main purpose of these assessment systems, which is to evaluate a patient's actual status at a single point of time, e.g. when she or he presents for treatment. Such snapshots of a developmental process may suggest diagnostic diversity where actually just different stages of the process are observed. Up to now it remains open whether the diagnostic categories such as Eating Disorder Not Otherwise Specified, Binge Eating Disorder, BN and AN describe different disorders or various stages or variants of one common pathology (e.g. Crow *et al.* 2002; Striegel-Moore *et al.* 2000).

In our opinion, neglecting the time perspective leads to a substantial loss for the clinical understanding of an individual's eating disorder and for an optimal treatment. For the individual patient – and the treatment – it may be important whether she (or he) moved quickly to a full syndrome eating disorder or whether this process took several years with periods of various length on various levels of symptoms, with perhaps ups and downs before eventually developing a full disorder. Surprisingly, little is known about the processes of falling ill, getting well, and staying well. The search for risk factors is still dominated by cross-sectional designs; prospective longitudinal approaches are still an exception (e.g. Tyrka *et al.* 2002). Data on the process of change in treatment are still meagre (e.g. Wilson *et al.* 2002). And follow-up research still aims rather on the stability of treatment gains than on a better understanding of the "course" of staying well (e.g. Halmi *et al.* 2002; Strober *et al.* 1997).

This chapter introduces a longitudinal approach to describe patterns of change in the eating disorder symptomatology over time. This allows new insights in the course of eating disorder in general and EDNOS in particular:

Course of illness

Patients whose symptomatology does not fit the criteria of AN or BN at the time of assessment are diagnosed as EDNOS, i.e. EDNOS is conceptualized as "residual category". However, it remains open whether patients diagnosed as suffering from EDNOS form a distinct population or rather just happen to not meet the full criteria at this moment.

Eating disorders are severe and complex diseases with heterogeneous courses. Many patients experience more than one episode in their life. Some will just go through brief phases of mild to moderate symptoms, others may develop problems of clinical significance although not meeting criteria for any of the eating disorder diagnoses, and some will suffer from recurrence of some or all of the symptoms for long enough to be diagnosed as EDNOS, BED, BN or AN. Therefore it would be helpful to have a definitional scheme that can be applied to patients with multiple episodes over a lifetime as well as to patients who experience only a single episode. The relevance of this temporal focus was first stated by Frank *et al.* (1991) for major depression. Their definitions of the concepts remission, recovery, relapse and recurrence have been adapted to the field of eating disorder by Kordy *et al.* (2002). In these definitions, two aspects are central: the severity of the symptomatology, i.e. number and intensity of symptoms and the duration of symptom improvement or deterioration. Assessing longitudinal data and observing change in symptoms as it was done in the present study are the preconditions to allow the application of such concepts, which in a second step have to undergo clinical validation strategies.

Symptoms, symptom severity and symptom combinations

Even within the diagnostic categories of BN and AN a repeated discussion concerns the question whether it can be justified to consider these diagnoses as distinct categories. For example, the symptomatology of a patient diagnosed with AN of the bingeing subtype is often very similar to that of a patient diagnosed as BN. Similarly, the boundaries between BED and the non-purging form of BN are often indistinct (Hay 1998).

Although these topics are still under debate, studies on eating disorder usually treat their samples of anorectic or bulimic patients as if they were homogeneous groups. However, it has been shown repeatedly that diagnostic categories often mean nothing more than putting a certain label to a group of patients that often vary largely in their symptomatology, and in the degree of impairment. In randomized clinical trials strict inclusion and exclusion criteria somehow create an artificial homogeneity. But naturalistic study designs often reveal that a substantial proportion of subjects do not fit to any of the predefined (ICD or DSM) diagnoses. In addition, those studies often include patients who do not undergo standardized screening procedures that in a way could lead to reliable diagnoses. The consequence is that samples often do not consist of "similar" patients even though they have identical diagnoses. In some investigations at least some attention is paid to these aspects by e.g. dividing samples of anorectic patients in different BMI groups or by considering different extents of anorectic attitudes. However, the syndromal character is not taken into consideration. Thus, not much is known on the patterns of symptoms that underlie the syndromes and how these patterns change over time. Our present approach will operationalize such patterns and investigate the frequencies of these patterns at different time points.

Changes during treatment

Although some studies have been published on the long-term outcome of treatment of patients with eating disorder (e.g. Halmi *et al.* 2002; Herzog *et al.* 1999; Strober *et al.* 1997), studies with prospective longitudinal designs are still rare, and thus, little is known about the underlying factors that determine the heterogeneous courses of illness. In addition, inconsistency in the conceptualization and definition of the above mentioned concepts such as relapse, remission and recovery makes findings difficult to interpret and comparisons between studies are hardly possible (Kordy *et al.* 2002).

While the lack of long-term observation of the process of staying well might be understandable, because of the great effort and costs of such research, the lack of process-outcome research in efficacy and effectiveness research is more surprising. Little is known about the process of change during treatment. Do symptoms change independently of each other? Do they change at the same time and at the same speed? Do they change in a certain sequence? Are changes in certain symptoms of higher importance for outcome than others? And so on.

This chapter addresses these questions by considering different combinations of the key symptoms of AN and BN and the changes in these combinations during treatment in a large European naturalistic study. As "key symptoms" in AN, the BMI, the fear of weight gain, and the body perception distortion are taken into account. For BN, the frequencies of binge-eating episodes, compensatory behaviours, and concern about weight and shape are chosen.

In detail, the questions investigated in the present analyses address (1) the distribution of patients to different symptom combinations (patterns) at the beginning and end of treatment and (2) change of this distribution over time, plus (3) the transition between specific patterns of symptoms over time.

Patterns of change

Sample

The sample derives from a large naturalistic longitudinal European study on eating disorders conducted between 1994 and 2001 (COST Action B6). Data from 14 countries (Czech Republic, Denmark, Finland, France, Germany, Great Britain, Iceland, Italy, Poland, Portugal, Romania, Spain, Switzerland and The Netherlands) were included. The number of patients as well as the duration of treatment varied across countries. Overall, information on 1181 patients suffering from AN and on 1768 suffering from BN was gathered. However, information was sufficiently complete for the present analyses on only 557 (47.2 per cent) anorectic and 875 (49.5 per cent) bulimic patients; data analyses were conducted using these samples.

Criteria

Patients filled out questionnaires on their physical and psychological impairment at the beginning and at end of treatment. Questions on the eating disorder symptomatology were formulated on basis of the DSM-III-R criteria for AN and BN (APA 1987). For both diagnoses three key symptoms were assessed. Each symptom is divided in three levels (1 to 3) indicating low, medium and high impairment respectively.

Anorexia Nervosa

First, patients with AN were classified according to their BMI: patients with a BMI of 14 or below were assigned to level 3. The medium level 2 was defined by a BMI higher than 14 but lower than or equal to 17.5. Patients with a BMI higher than 17.5 were assigned to level 1. Second, fear of weight gain was considered (1 = never or sometimes fear, 2 = almost always fear, 3 = always extreme fear). Finally, body perception distortion was taken into account by comparison of the actually measured BMI and patient's report on how she perceives her own body appearance (6 point rating scale, 1 = much too thin, 6 = much too fat). The discrepancy was then translated to another trichotomous scale.

Bulimia Nervosa

Patients with BN reported on their number of binge-eating episodes during the past week. Three categories were defined according to the extent of binge-eating episodes: more than five binge-eating episodes (level 3), between one and five (level 2) and not more than one binge-eating episode (level 1). Second, patients' compensatory behaviours during the past week were assessed (3 = daily or more, 2 = between twice and six times, 1 = once or not at all). Finally patients' concerns about weight and shape were rated according to their answers to three −6/+6 rating scale questions on attractiveness/ unattractiveness, femininity/lacking femininity and muscularity/flabbiness (3 = all answers in negative direction, 2 = two answers negative direction, 1 = one or no answer in negative direction).

Operationalization of patterns

Since each of the three key symptoms can be assessed on three levels, twenty-seven logically possible combinations of symptom status can be distinguished. Figures 6.1 and 6.2 display the distribution of these combinations for AN and BN respectively. The figures reveal that we structured the multitude

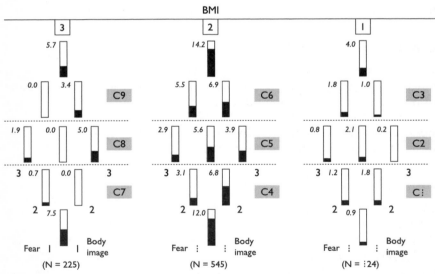

Figure 6.1 Distribution of symptom combinations (percent) at beginning of treatment for Anorexia Nervosa.

Note: BMI = body mass index (1 = BMI > 17.5, 2 = 14 < BMI ≤ 17.5, 3 = BMI ≤ 14), fear = fear of weight gain (1 = slight or no fear, 2 = medium fear, 3 = strong fear), body image = disturbance in body image (1 = slight or no disturbance, 2 = medium disturbance, 3 = strong disturbance), C = cluster.

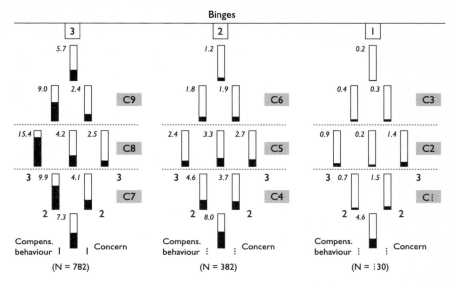

Figure 6.2 Distribution of symptom combinations (percent) at beginning of treatment for Bulimia Nervosa.

Note: binges = frequency of binge-eating episodes per week (1 = less than one episode, 2 = one to five episodes, 3 = more than five episodes), concern = concerns about weight and shape (1 = slight or no concerns, 2 = medium concerns, 3 = strong concerns), compens. behaviour = frequency of compensatory behaviours per week (1 = not more than once, 2 = twice to six times, 3 = daily or more), C = cluster.

of combinations in a certain way: by application of the concepts of contiguity and (semantic) principal components from facet theory (Borg 1977) we created a semi-order according to an implicit concept of severity. As principal components, BMI was used for AN and the frequency of binge-eating episodes for BN. The corresponding semi-orders are represented by three lattices each (Figures 6.1 and 6.2).

This choice apparently influences the resulting grouping of the combinations in Figures 6.1 and 6.2, i.e. it determines which combinations are in the nearer and further neighbourhood. Only those which are connected can be ordered according to severity. In both figures the most severe symptom combination is displayed in the upper left indicating that a patient has the highest rating in each of the three symptoms. Figures 6.1 and 6.2 describe the sample at the beginning of treatment. The boxes are filled according to the percentage with which a certain combination occurred.

Transition matrixes

The grouping of the twenty-seven symptom combinations gives a detailed and structured overview of the sample's status at a certain time point, e.g. as

Figures 6.1 and 6.2 show, at the beginning of treatment. But when one thinks of change over time, twenty-seven combinations are far too many to keep the overview. In addition one would need a very large sample size. By choosing the two principal components we already decided to take these aspects as our main criteria. Concerning the change over time this order leads to the assumption that a change in the category BMI or binge eating is less likely than a change in the other variables within a certain BMI or binge eating category. To reduce the number of categories, the remaining two variables were treated as one criterion for each diagnosis (again three levels) indicating the degree of psychological impairment. From these procedures nine clusters resulted for each diagnosis as each of the three levels of the principal component was combined with the three levels of psychological impairment.

For both diagnoses the resulting nine clusters were defined as follows (to better understand which three of the twenty-seven combinations were summarized to get nine clusters, see also Figures 6.1 and 6.2):

- Cluster 9: high impairment in BMI (AN) or binge-eating episodes (BN), and high psychological impairment
- Cluster 8: high impairment in BMI (AN) or binge-eating episodes (BN), and medium psychological impairment
- Cluster 7: high impairment in BMI (AN) or binge-eating episodes (BN), and low psychological impairment
- Cluster 6: medium impairment in BMI (AN) or binge-eating episodes (BN), and high psychological impairment
- Cluster 5: medium impairment in BMI (AN) or binge-eating episodes (BN), and medium psychological impairment
- Cluster 4: medium impairment in BMI (AN) or binge-eating episodes (BN), and low psychological impairment
- Cluster 3: low impairment in BMI (AN) or binge-eating episodes (BN), and high psychological impairment
- Cluster 2: low impairment in BMI (AN) or binge-eating episodes (BN), and medium psychological impairment
- Cluster 1: low impairment in BMI (AN) or binge-eating episodes (BN), and low psychological impairment

In both diagnoses patients in cluster 9 show the strongest impairment, and patients in cluster 1 the lowest. Clusters 9, 6 and 3, as well as 8, 5 and 2, and 7, 4 and 1 are equivalent with respect to the extent of psychological impairment (high, medium, low). However, they differ from each other with respect to BMI level or the level of binge-eating episodes that have been chosen as main criteria.

The transition matrixes (Figures 6.3 and 6.4) describe the (transition) probabilities for moving from one cluster to another. Figures 6.3 and 6.4 can

End of treatment

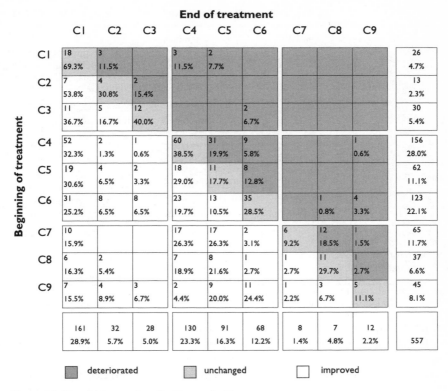

Beginning of treatment	C1	C2	C3	C4	C5	C6	C7	C8	C9	Total
C1	18 69.3%	3 11.5%		3 11.5%	2 7.7%					26 4.7%
C2	7 53.8%	4 30.8%	2 15.4%							13 2.3%
C3	11 36.7%	5 16.7%	12 40.0%			2 6.7%				30 5.4%
C4	52 32.3%	2 1.3%	1 0.6%	60 38.5%	31 19.9%	9 5.8%			1 0.6%	156 28.0%
C5	19 30.6%	4 6.5%	2 3.3%	18 29.0%	11 17.7%	8 12.8%				62 11.1%
C6	31 25.2%	8 6.5%	8 6.5%	23 19.7%	13 10.5%	35 28.5%		1 0.8%	4 3.3%	123 22.1%
C7	10 15.9%			17 26.3%	17 26.3%	2 3.1%	6 9.2%	12 18.5%	1 1.5%	65 11.7%
C8	6 16.3%	2 5.4%		7 18.9%	8 21.6%	1 2.7%	1 2.7%	11 29.7%	1 2.7%	37 6.6%
C9	7 15.5%	4 8.9%	3 6.7%	2 4.4%	9 20.0%	11 24.4%	1 2.2%	3 6.7%	5 11.1%	45 8.1%
	161 28.9%	32 5.7%	28 5.0%	130 23.3%	91 16.3%	68 12.2%	8 1.4%	27 4.8%	12 2.2%	557

■ deteriorated   ▨ unchanged   ☐ improved

Figure 6.3 Transition matrixes for Anorexia Nervosa.

be understood as graphic representations of cross tables. They show the nine clusters at two time points (beginning and end of treatment) and the resulting nine by nine combinations. In addition the percentages and numbers of patients that showed a certain combination are displayed. The percentages always refer to percentage of patients who started treatment in a certain cluster (i.e. percentage of patients in a certain row of the matrix). In the diagonals are the numbers of patients who were classified in the same cluster at beginning and at end of treatment. In the upper part above the diagonal are patients who showed a "higher" cluster at end of treatment than at beginning, i.e. those who showed deterioration. In the lower part of the matrix are those patients who finished treatment in a "lower" cluster, i.e. in an improved state.

End of treatment

Beginning of treatment		C1	C2	C3	C4	C5	C6	C7	C8	C9	Total
	C1	50 / 76.9%	3 / 4.6%		9 / 13.8%			3 / 4.6%			65 / 7.4%
	C2	8 / 42.1%	4 / 21.1%		3 / 15.3%	3 / 15.3%			1 / 5.3%		19 / 2.2%
	C3	3 / 37.5%	2 / 25.0%			1 / 12.5%		1 / 12.5%		1 / 12.5	8 / 0.9%
	C4	104 / 69.7%	1 / 0.7%		31 / 20.8%	4 / 2.7%		8 / 6.0%	1 / 0.7%		149 / 17.0%
	C5	38 / 54.3%	10 / 14.3%		7 / 10.0%	6 / 8.8%	2 / 2.8%	3 / 4.3%	4 / 5.7%		70 / 8.0%
	C6	10 / 34.5%	3 / 10.3%	2 / 6.9%	7 / 24.1%	3 / 10.3%	3 / 10.3%	1 / 3.4%			29 / 3.3
	C7	144 / 61.5%	8 / 3.4%		47 / 20.1%	3 / 1.6%		26 / 11.1%	2 / 0.9%	4 / 0.9%	234 / 26%
	C8	78 / 44.6%	10 / 5.7%		37 / 21.1%	7 / 4.0%	1 / 0.6%	21 / 12.0%	20 / 11.4%	1 / 0.6%	175 / 20.0
	C9	46 / 36.5%	10 / 7.9%	6 / 4.8%	17 / 13.5%	8 / 6.3%	7 / 5.6%	9 / 7.1%	9 / 7.1%	14 / 11.1%	126 / 14.4%
		480 / 54.9%	51 / 5.8%	8 / 0.9%	158 / 18.1%	35 / 4.0%	13 / 1.5%	73 / 8.3%	37 / 4.2%	20 / 2.3%	875

◼ deteriorated   ▢ unchanged   ☐ improved

Figure 6.4 Transition matrixes for Bulimia Nervosa.

Results

Patterns at beginning of treatment

Anorexia Nervosa

Figure 6.1 shows the frequencies of different symptom combinations at beginning of treatment. Obviously most patients start treatment in the BMI range 14 to 17.5. The most frequent combination in the total sample is this medium BMI either combined with strong fear of weight gain and severe body perception distortion (14 per cent) or combined with low ratings in both other symptoms (12 per cent). Between 3 per cent and 7 per cent of patients show a comparable BMI together with one of the remaining combinations of psychological impairment. In the group of patients with severe underweight (BMI < 14) again mostly the extreme ratings in fear of weight gain and body perception distortion are observed (6.7 per cent and 7.5 per cent respectively).

Bulimia Nervosa

Figure 6.2 illustrates the frequencies of initial symptom combinations in BN. The majority of patients (N = 782; 60.4 per cent) suffer from severe bingeing. Concerning psychological impairment within this group, most patients display slight concern about body and shape. The most frequent symptom combination in the total sample (15.4 per cent) is strong impairment concerning bingeing and compensatory behaviours in combination with slight concerns about weight and shape. A considerable proportion of patients (N = 130; 10 per cent) reports no or only slight bingeing at the beginning of treatment.

Changes over time

Anorexia Nervosa

Concerning the changes in symptomatology from beginning to end of treatment, Table 6.1 gives a first overview. It shows the distribution of patients to the three BMI groups and to the three groups of psychological impairment at beginning and at end of treatment.

Table 6.1 shows that 12.4 per cent of the patients started treatment with a BMI in the normal range (above 17.5), 61.2 per cent with a medium rating (14 < BMI ≤ 17.5) and 26.4 per cent with a high rating, i.e. with severe underweight (BMI ≤ 14); 44.3 per cent of patients begin treatment with slight or no impairment concerning the variables "fear of weight gain" and "disturbance in body image", 20 per cent display medium and 35.5 per cent severe psychological impairment. At the end of treatment still 8.4 per cent of the anorectic patients suffer from severe underweight. About half of the patients (52 per cent) show a BMI between 14 and 17.5, and 40 per cent above 17.5. Concerning psychological impairment, 19 per cent show severe psychological

Table 6.1 Percentages (numbers) of AN patients in different groups at beginning and at end of treatment

	BMI			Fear/body		
	3	2	1	3	2	1
Begin of treatment	26.4 (147)	61.2 (341)	12.4 (69)	35.5 (198)	20.1 (112)	44.3 (247)
End of treatment	8.4 (47)	51.9 (289)	39.7 (221)	19.4 (108)	26.9 (150)	53.7 (299)

Notes: BMI = body mass index, BMI 3 = BMI ≤ 14, BMI 2 = 14 < BMI ≤ 17.5, BMI 1 = BMI > 17.5, Fear = fear of weight gain, body = disturbance in body image, Fear/body 3 = high rating for both symptoms or one severe and one medium rating, i.e. severe impairment, Fear/body 2 = medium rating for both symptoms or one high and one low rating, i.e. medium impairment, Fear/body 1 = low rating for both symptoms or one low and one medium rating, i.e. slight or no impairment.

distress at the end of treatment, 27 per cent of the patients are classified as medium and 54 per cent as slightly or not impaired. In summary, the results confirm the expectation that the proportion of extremely impaired patients decreases from beginning to end of treatment.

The transition matrix for AN (Figure 6.3) gives a clearer picture of the changes from beginning to end of treatment than just the frequency table. The right column shows the distribution of patients to the nine clusters at beginning of treatment, the bottom row the distribution at the end of treatment.

The following example may illustrate the principle of the transition matrix and facilitate reading it: 8.1 per cent of the patients (N = 45) start treatment in cluster 9 i.e. with the severest combination of symptoms. Of this group, 5 patients are in the same cluster at the end of treatment, 4 are improved in their psychological impairment (clusters 8 and 7) but not in their BMI category; 22 patients improve from BMI level 3 to level 2 (clusters 4, 5, 6), 14 even to BMI group 1 (clusters 1, 2, 3). While 14 patients improve with respect to their BMI group (from cluster 9 to 6 or 3 respectively) without improving in their psychological impairment, 22 improve in their BMI as well as in their psychological impairment (from cluster 9 to 5, 4, 2, 1).

At the beginning of treatment the most frequent clusters are clusters 4 and 6, with 50 per cent of patients starting with one of these symptom combinations. That is most patients show a BMI between 14 and 17.5 at the beginning of treatment, combined with either severe or slight psychological impairment.

A considerable proportion of patients starting treatment with the most frequent combination (i.e. cluster 4) finish treatment in an unchanged or a worsened state (38.5 per cent and 26.3 per cent respectively). This leads to the lowest improvement rate among all clusters (35.2 per cent).

As one could expect the rates of patients who reach cluster 1 at end of treatment increase with decreasing cluster number at beginning of treatment: while only 15.5 per cent of patients starting treatment in cluster 9 finish treatment in cluster 1, 53.8 per cent of those starting in cluster 2 improve to this state.

At the end of treatment most patients are located in cluster 1 (28.9 per cent), 4 (23.3 per cent) and 5 (16.3 per cent), i.e. they show medium or slight psychological distress in combination with either a normal or medium BMI.

Overall 29 per cent of the patients were classified in the same cluster at end of treatment as at beginning, i.e. 29 per cent show an unchanged symptomatology, 14.4 per cent finish treatment in a deteriorated state, and 56.6 per cent in an improved state compared to beginning of treatment.

Bulimia Nervosa

The frequencies of the three binge-eating episode groups and the groups of psychological impairment at both time points are shown in Table 6.2.

Table 6.2 Percentages (numbers) of BN patients in different groups at beginning and at end of treatment

	Binges			Comp./Conc.		
	3	2	1	3	2	1
Begin of treatment	61.1 (535)	28.3 (248)	10.5 (92)	18.6 (163)	30.2 (264)	51.2 (448)
End of treatment	14.9 (130)	23.5 (206)	61.6 (539)	4.7 (41)	14.1 (123)	81.3 (711)

Notes: Binges = frequency of binge-eating episodes, binges 3 = more than five binge-eating episodes per week, binges 2 = one to five binge-eating episodes per week, binges 1 = less than one binge-eating episode per week, comp. = frequency of compensatory behaviours, conc. = concerns about weight and shape, comp./conc. 3 = high rating for both symptoms or one severe and one medium rating, i.e. severe impairment, comp./conc. 2 = medium rating for both symptoms or one high and one low rating, i.e. medium impairment, comp./conc. 1 = low rating for both symptoms or one low and one medium rating, i.e. slight or no impairment.

At the start of treatment almost 90 per cent of patients report between one and five binge-eating episodes (28.3 per cent) or more than five binge-eating episodes (61.1 per cent) in the past week. At the end of treatment these rates are reduced to 23.5 per cent and 14.9 per cent respectively. Concerning psychological impairment, about half of the patients start treatment in group 1, i.e. with slight or no impairment, 30 per cent show medium, 19 per cent severe symptoms concerning compensatory behaviours and concerns about weight and shape. At the end of treatment only 4.7 per cent of patients are classified as severely impaired. The vast majority of patients (81.3 per cent) show hardly any impairment in these dimensions. As in AN the proportion of slightly or not impaired patients clearly increases from beginning to end of treatment.

The transition matrix for BN (Figure 6.4) shows that in all clusters the greatest percentages improve to cluster 1 at end of treatment. This improvement rate is biggest for patients starting with medium extent of binge-eating episodes and slight/no impairment concerning compensatory behaviours and concerns about weight and shape (cluster 4).

To reach cluster 1 at end of treatment is most difficult for patients starting treatment with severe impairment in the variables "compensatory behaviours" and "concerns about weight and shape". The probability of improving to cluster 1 is comparable for clusters 3, 6 and 9 (34.5 per cent to 37.5 per cent), i.e. patients starting treatment with a high rating in the dimensions "compensatory behaviours" and "concerns about weight and shape" have a 35 per cent chance to improve to a state with minimum impairment independently of the extent of binge-eating episodes at beginning of treatment.

At the beginning of treatment most patients are located in clusters 7 and 8, i.e. they suffer from heavy bingeing and show slight or medium impairment concerning compensatory behaviours and concerns about weight and shape. Of each of these groups 11 per cent of patients remain unchanged at end of treatment, and about 20 per cent improve to cluster 4, i.e. they improve with respect to the number of binge-eating episodes to the medium group and show little impairment in the other dimensions. Most patients starting in the most frequent clusters 7 and 8 improve to cluster 1 at end of treatment (62 per cent and 45 per cent respectively).

At the end of treatment most patients are located in clusters 1 (54.9 per cent), 4 (18.1 per cent) and 7 (8.3 per cent), i.e. most patients are more or less symptom free concerning compensatory behaviours and concerns about weight and shape.

In the sample of bulimic patients deteriorations are rare. Overall only 6.3 per cent of patients are located in a higher cluster at the end of treatment compared to the beginning. The rates of deterioration are highest in clusters 2 and 3, i.e. in patients that report only few or no binge-eating episodes but medium or severe psychological impairment. But the number of patients starting in these clusters is small: 7.4 per cent of patients start treatment in cluster 1, i.e. with the lowest possible impairment. More than 75 per cent of these patients display an unchanged state at the end of treatment. In the total sample 17.6 per cent of patients were classified as unchanged at end of treatment, 6.3 per cent as deteriorated, and 76.1 per cent as improved.

Discussion

The central aim of this exploration was to illustrate the necessity and the advantage of considering both the patterns of symptoms (i.e. the syndromal character of the disorders) and time when conducting research on eating disorder symptoms, diagnoses, outcome and systematic treatment planning. In the present analyses only two points of time, beginning and end of treatment, were included, to illustrate the strategy. By adding assessments during treatment to the analyses, one could monitor patients' treatment progress in detail. The exploration of the data by transition matrixes reveals an interesting illustration of the patterns of change. The figures display in detail the distribution of patients to the different clusters at two points of time, as well as the (extent of) movements between clusters.

In congruence with earlier research findings the results of the study show that outcome is better in BN compared to AN: while 76 per cent of bulimic patients finish treatment in an improved cluster compared to their state at beginning of treatment, this rate is 20 per cent lower in anorectic patients. About 30 per cent of anorectic patients show the same combination of symptoms at the end of treatment as at beginning. In BN only 18 per cent are classified as unchanged. These rates of no change indicate that patients changed neither in their binge-eating episodes or their BMI group respectively, nor in the extent of psychological impairment. About twice as many anorectics (14 per cent) finish treatment in a deteriorated cluster compared to bulimics (6 per cent).

Besides these overall numbers the results show the typical symptom combinations and patterns of change of patients undergoing treatment for BN or AN in the institutions participating in the present study. In BN this is typically the combination of severe bingeing with slight (cluster 7, 27 per cent) or medium (cluster 8, 20 per cent) impairment with respect to compensatory behaviours and concerns about weight and shape. Another frequent combination (17 per cent) is that of medium bingeing and slight impairment in the other variables (cluster 4). It should be noted that a substantial proportion of the patients (51 per cent) started treatment without reporting psychological symptoms. But if patients engage in compensatory behaviours and suffer from concerns about weight and shape this is negatively related to outcome: improvement rates to cluster 1 decrease within each binge-eating episode group with increasing psychological impairment.

In AN the most frequent clusters are the combination of a BMI between 14 and 17.5 and either slight or severe psychological impairment (cluster 4 and 6); 50 per cent of the patients start treatment with one of these symptom combinations. Cluster 4 can be used to illustrate the potential advantage of conducting this kind of data analysis: cluster 4 is at the same time the most frequent combination at beginning of treatment and the combination with the lowest rates of improvement. Almost two-thirds of patients starting with this combination are classified in the same cluster at end of treatment (39 per cent) or even worse (26 per cent). Patients in this group are at high risk of deteriorating with respect to their psychological impairment. Only one patient showed deterioration in her BMI. This result can give important information to practitioners: patients who start treatment in a comparatively healthy state apparently do not benefit as much as they could. A hypothesis could be that they do not get as much or as intense treatment as more disturbed patients.

Studies on large samples of eating disorder patients, as the one presented here, can help in identifying symptom combinations that are at an increased risk for negative outcomes. This could suggest tailored treatment elements that could help these patients to better benefit from psychotherapeutic treatment. Implications of the method used in the present investigation for systematic treatment planning are obvious: symptom combinations at the beginning of treatment are related to outcome. This leads to the conclusion that patients in different clusters at the beginning of treatment may need different treatment modalities or intensities. The present study creates a basis for the development of stepped care models. Patients located in clusters with low impairment could be treated with less intense treatments first. Several studies have shown that there are subsets of eating disorder patients who benefit from e.g. self-help or psycho-educational programmes. So far, it is not clear which characteristics predispose patients to benefit from this kind of minimum interventions. Further investigations could explore if these subsets of patients consist of patients who are located in certain clusters.

In both diagnoses a remarkably high proportion of patients start treatment without fulfilling the diagnostic criteria required by the international classification systems: 7.4 per cent of the bulimic patients and 4.7 per cent of the anorectic patients are even located in cluster 1 at the beginning of treatment apparently representing symptom free patients. More than 10 per cent in both diagnoses start with a BMI in the normal range (AN) or with a maximum of one binge-eating episode in the past week (BN) respectively. These facts are probably due to the naturalistic study design and the fact that these patients may have reached an improved health status between the first interview that led to the diagnosis and assignment for treatment and the actual start of treatment (i.e. first assessment). Several studies have shown that across a variety of therapies, disorders and symptoms, changes in well-being can be observed before treatment officially starts (e.g. Howard *et al.* 1993; Ilardi and Craighead 1994). These findings put additional emphasis on the relevance of assessing longitudinal data: apparently, symptoms fluctuate rapidly and frequently. Cross-sectional designs give only a status display and fall short of the heterogeneous and complex courses of mental illnesses. Similarly diagnoses according to the standard assessment systems focus only on a patient's status at one single point in time.

Strictly speaking, in our data set, only patients located in cluster 9 could be diagnosed as suffering from AN (11.1 per cent) and BN (14.4 per cent) respectively. All other symptom combinations would have to be classified as EDNOS.

More than 50 per cent of the bulimic patients are evaluated as having no or only mild psychological impairment at the beginning of treatment. As all patients underwent psychotherapeutic treatment this rate is probably an underestimation, i.e. the conceptualization of the variables "compensatory behaviours" and/or "concerns about weight and shape" should probably be revised in subsequent studies.

Conclusion

The present study calls for an evaluation of patterns of changes rather than changes on single dimensions. But in addition to the face validity it is necessary to validate the conceptualization used in the present investigation. One could e.g. analyse the concordance between the outcome according to the transition matrixes and clinical ratings of treatment outcome. Patients who moved across more clusters in the matrix should be judged by a clinical expert as showing greater benefit. Continuous monitoring would allow the discovery of the pathways followed by patients moving through the clusters.

Furthermore it is of research interest to find out whether certain clusters are associated with an increased risk of relapse or an increased chance for long-term recovery after finishing.

References

American Psychiatric Association (1987) *Diagnostic and Statistical Manual of Mental Disorders*, 3rd edn revised (DSM-III-R), Washington, DC: APA.

American Psychiatric Association (1994) *Diagnostic and Statistical Manual of Mental Disorders*, 4th edn (DSM-IV), Washington, DC: APA.

Borg, I. (1977) "Some basic concepts of facet theory", in J.C. Lingoes (ed.) *Geometric Representation of Relational Data*, Ann Arbor, MI: Mathesis Press.

Crow, S.J., Agras, W.S., Halmi, K., Mitchell, J.E. and Kraemer, H. (2002) "Full syndromal versus subthreshold AN, BN, and Binge Eating Disorder: a multicenter study", *International Journal of Eating Disorders* 32, 309–18.

Frank, E., Prien, R.F., Jarrett, R.B., Keller, M.B., Kupfer, D.J., Lavori, P.W., Rush, A.J. and Weissman, M.M. (1991) "Conceptualization and rationale for consensus definitions of terms in major depressive disorder: remission, recovery, relapse, and recurrence", *Archives of General Psychiatry* 48, 851–5.

Halmi, K., Agras, W.S., Mitchell, J. E., Wilson, T.G., Crow, S., Bryson, S.W. and Kraemer, H. (2002) "Relapse predictors of patients with BN who achieved abstinence through cognitive behavioral therapy", *Archives of General Psychiatry* 59, 1105–9.

Hay, P. (1998) "The epidemiology of eating disorder behaviours: an Australian community-based survey", *International Journal of Eating Disorders* 23, 371–82.

Herzog, D.B., Dorer, D.J., Keel, P.K., Selwyn, S.E., Ekeblad, E.R., Flores, A.T., Greenwood, D.N., Burwell, R.A. and Keller, M.B. (1999) "Recovery and relapse in anorexia and bulimia nervosa: a 7.5-year follow-up study", *Journal of the American Academy of Child and Adolescent Psychiatry* 38, 829–37.

Howard, K.I., Lueger, R.J., Maling, M.S. and Martinovich, Z. (1993) "A phase model of psychotherapy outcome: causal mediation of change", *Journal of Consulting and Clinical Psychology* 61, 678–85.

Ilardi, S.S. and Craighead, W.E. (1994) "The role of nonspecific factors in cognitive-behavior therapy for depression", *Clinical Psychology: Science and Practice* 1, 138–56.

Kordy, H., Krämer, B., Palmer, R.L., Papezova, H., Pellet, J., Richard, M., Treasure, J. and COST Action B6 (2002) "Remission, recovery, relapse and recurrence in eating disorders: conceptualization and illustration of a validation strategy", *Journal of Clinical Psychology* 58, 833–46.

Striegel-Moore, R.H., Dohm, F.A., Solomon, E.E., Fairburn, C.G., Pike, K.M. and Wifley, D.E. (2000) "Subthreshold binge eating disorder", *International Journal of Eating Disorders* 27, 270–8.

Strober, M., Freeman, R. and Morrell, W. (1997) "The long-term course of severe anorexia nervosa in adolescents: survival analysis of recovery, relapse, and outcome predictors over 10–15 years in a prospective study", *International Journal of Eating Disorders* 22, 339–60.

Tyrka, A.R., Waldron, I., Graber, J. and Brooks-Gunn, J. (2002) "Prospective predictors of the onset of anorexic and bulimic syndromes", *International Journal of Eating Disorders* 32, 282–90.

Wilson, G.T., Fairburn, C.C., Agras, W.S., Walsh, B.T. and Kraemer, H. (2002) "Cognitive behavioural therapy for bulimia nervosa: time course and mechanisms of change", *Journal of Consulting and Clinical Psychology* 70, 267–74.

World Health Organization (1992) *ICD-10 Classification of Mental and Behavioural Disorders: Clinical Descriptions and Diagnostic Guidelines*, Geneva: WHO.

Chapter 7

Clarifying the nature of EDNOS
Cluster analysis, diagnosis and comorbidity

David Clinton, Eric Button, Claes Norring and Bob Palmer

The problem of the classification of eating disorders

Since the original key papers in the 1870s on what is now known as Anorexia Nervosa, a number of new terms have been introduced to describe a range of clinical conditions akin to AN. Some hundred years later, Russell's (1979) seminal article on Bulimia Nervosa heralded a new wave of terminology to describe a related clinical problem, which shared some of the features of AN, but in which the dominant phenomenon centred around so-called "binge eating".

Nylander (1971) was one of the first authors to draw attention to the concept of a continuum of eating disorders in his research on dieting and feeling fat in a Scandinavian teenage school population. Button and White-house (1981) extended such thinking in their study of British female college students. They identified a substantial number of young women who had many of the symptoms of AN without fulfilling strict criteria. They suggested that AN may be something of a tip of an iceberg and introduced the term "subclinical anorexia nervosa" to describe this group. Holmgren *et al.* (1983) examined the entire eating disorders spectrum, and introduced a continuum model of eating disorders (the ABC-model), which included the so-called "anorexic-like" patients. Szmukler (1983) also recognized this group, but preferred the term "partial syndrome". Such partialness of disorder also applies to bulimic disorders, as exemplified by the term "Binge Eating Disorder" in which binge eating is present, but without the accompanying compensatory behaviours associated with BN. It is now widely recognized that there is a spectrum or continuum of problems aligned to the two major disorders. The current DSM-IV (APA 1994) favours the term "Eating Disorder Not Otherwise Specified". This is something of a catch-all diagnosis that covers any eating disorder of clinical severity, the symptomatology of which does not meet criteria for AN or BN. The ICD-10 (WHO 1992) contains the terms atypical AN and atypical BN to cover broadly the same range of disorders (see Appendix for diagnostic criteria).

The diagnostic criteria for eating disorders used within the DSM and ICD systems tend to be based on clinical opinion and consensus.

The question, therefore, arises of whether prevailing diagnostic categories reflect the natural groupings of patients who seek help for eating problems. Such empirical study of the patterns occurring in the real world may provide a useful commentary upon our familiar and well-used diagnostic concepts, and may even help to clarify the picture of residual categories such as EDNOS. Both factor analysis and cluster analysis have been used for many years by psychiatric researchers investigating problems of diagnosis (Everitt and Landau 1998). Recent examples of factor analytic approaches to diagnostic questions within the field of eating disorders are the studies by van der Ham *et al.* (1997) and Williamson *et al.* (2002). While factor analysis reveals patterns among variables, cluster analysis focuses on groupings of individuals. In the field of eating disorders, four relevant studies have used cluster analysis with eating disordered patients. Hay *et al.* (1996) used cluster analysis to investigate the classification of bulimic disorders in a community sample of 250 young women. Stice and Agras (1999) subtyped 265 patients with BN into two subgroups using cluster analysis. Their findings were subsequently replicated by Grilo *et al.* (2001) in a sample of 48 patients with BN. Cluster analysis was also used by Mizes and Sloan (1998) to investigate subgroups within a sample of 53 EDNOS patients presenting to psychotherapy clinics for the treatment of an eating disorder. Using another method aimed at uncovering naturally occurring groups of patients, latent class analysis, Bulik *et al.* (2000) examined the empirical typology of eating disorder symptoms among female twins from a population-based twin register.

These studies provide some useful empirical indicators about the classification of eating disorders, however they also have important shortcomings. They have tended to focus on specific diagnoses (Hay *et al.* 1996), or subgroups of diagnoses (Grilo *et al.* 2001; Mizes and Sloan 1998; Stice and Agras 1999) rather than the entire spectrum of eating disorders. Samples have often been small (Grilo *et al.* 2001; Mizes and Sloan 1998; van der Ham *et al.* 1997) or based on non-clinical cases with doubtful relevance to clinical eating disorders (Bulik *et al.* 2000).

Another approach to studying questions related to classification is called taxometrics. However, where the previously mentioned methods are exploratory, trying to uncover naturally occurring groups of subjects or variables, taxometrics uses predefined groups (e.g. diagnoses) and tries to determine whether these groups are actually discrete classes or concepts with a more dimensional quality. There are three relatively recent studies applying taxometric methods to the eating disorder classification (Gleaves *et al.* 2000a, 2000b; Williamson *et al.* 2002). The study by Williamson and co-workers is unique in that it first applies both exploratory and confirmatory factor analysis and then taxometric methods in an attempt to shed more light on the problem of eating disorder classification. In a similar vein, Crow *et al.* (2002) used stepwise discriminant analysis to distinguish between groups of patients (total N = 385) with full and partial syndromes of AN, BN and BED. They could differentiate the full syndromes from each other, but failed to discriminate the partial from the full syndromes for AN and BED. While these studies give important indications about the underlying structure of the presently used eating disorder classification, they are of less value in illuminating questions about the natural groupings of eating disorder patients, and have failed to provide clues about EDNOS.

Our approach to the classification of eating disorders has been based on cluster analysis (Everitt *et al.* 2001). In this chapter we present data from two studies. In the first study, which is reported in detail elsewhere (Clinton *et al.* 2004), we attempted to explore natural groupings of patients who present to a wide range of eating disorder services, using data on key diagnostic variables routinely collected on series of patients presenting to a number of centres in Sweden and to one centre in England. There was sufficient overlap between the assessment methods and variables studied in both countries to enable us to make relevant comparisons. Primary aims of the first study were to generate and compare the cluster solutions based on ten key diagnostic variables from two similar but unrelated data sets of eating disordered patients, and to compare the most appropriate of these cluster solutions to the diagnostic eating disorder classification of DSM-IV in order to explore the relevance of alternative diagnostic classifications. In the second study, the clinical utility of our clusters was explored by extending comparisons of clusters and diagnostic categories to include other relevant eating disorder variables and aspects of comorbidity assessed initially and subsequently after 6 and 36 months. Owing to differences in assessment and follow-up routines between the two samples these analyses could be carried out only on the Swedish data.

A cluster analytic approach to the classification of eating disorders

Participants

Two samples of female patients from Sweden (N = 631) and England (N = 472) were used in the first study. The Swedish sample was collected within the framework of the Coordinated Evaluation and Research at Specialist Units for Eating Disorders in Sweden (CO-RED) Project. This is a longitudinal naturalistic study of the treatment of eating disorders at 15 specialist centres. The units offer a wide variety of treatment forms such as inpatient, day patient, outpatient, individual psychotherapy, family and group therapy, psychoactive drugs, expressive forms of treatment, etc. At the conclusion of the six-year data collection period in December 2002, 946 patients with eating disorders were included in the project. In order to conduct appropriate cluster analysis, patients with missing data on one or more of the ten variables used in the study were excluded; this left 631 patients. In the majority of excluded cases (71 per cent) data were lacking on just one of the variables. The distribution of DSM-IV diagnoses was: AN (N = 137, 22.8 per cent), BN (N = 240, 39.9 per cent), BED (N = 31, 5.2 per cent) and EDNOS (N = 193, 32.1 per cent). All subjects provided informed consent to take part in the CO-RED study. Age ranged from 14 to 49 years (M = 24.5 years, S.D. = 6.4), and all participants were female. Mean duration of eating disorder at presentation was 8.2 years (S.D. = 6.7).

The English sample came from Leicester, and was drawn from a series of patients referred to a specialized service for eating disorders within the British National Health Service. For some years the service has collected and electronically recorded standard clinical information on all patients assessed. This allowed for the identification of 890 potential participants. The data files and clinical records of these patients were used to extract data on the standard variables shared with the Swedish sample. Patients with missing data on one or more of the ten standard variables, as well as those with a diagnosis other than an eating disorder, were excluded in order to be consistent with the Swedish sample. This left 472 Leicester patients with complete data on all the relevant variables. Mean scores on clinical and demographic characteristics were very similar to another cohort of consecutive referrals to the same service previously published (Button et al. 1997). The sample was, therefore, reasonably representative of patients referred to the service. The distribution of DSM-IV diagnoses was: AN (N = 82, 17.4 per cent), BN (N = 163, 34.5 per cent), BED (N = 8, 1.7 per cent) and EDNOS (N = 219, 46.4 per cent). Age ranged from 15 to 61 (M = 25.1, S.D. = 7.8). There were no systematic differences in terms of eating disorder, psychiatric or background variables between cases with and without complete data.

In the second study only patients from the Swedish sample who had not been identified as outliers in the first step of cluster analysis were used (see below for details). These patients had completed a number of psychometric measures that had not been administered to the English sample (see below). Of these 601 Swedish patients, 349 had been assessed on the same measures after 6 months, and 322 subsequently at 36 months after initial assessment. The distribution of initial DSM-IV diagnoses at 6-month follow-up was: AN (N = 86, 24.6 per cent), BN (N = 132, 37.8 per cent), BED (N = 24, 6.9 per cent) and EDNOS (N = 107, 30.7 per cent). Among the patients assessed after 36 months the distribution of initial DSM-IV was: AN (N = 75, 23.3 per cent), BN (N = 126, 39.1 per cent), BED (N = 16, 5.0 per cent) and EDNOS (N = 105, 32.6 per cent).

Instruments

Two separate semi-structured interviews with similar variables were used to assess key diagnostic variables. In the Swedish sample the Rating of

Anorexia and Bulimia (RAB) interview was used (Clinton and Norring 1999; Nevonen *et al.* 2003). The RAB is a 56-item semi-structured interview with graded response formats covering a wide range of eating disorder symptoms, related psychopathology and background variables; it generates operational DSM-IV eating disorder diagnoses, and is widely used in Sweden. It has satisfactory internal consistency and inter-rater reliability; kappa ranged from 0.47 to 0.92 (M = 0.74) for the variables used in the present study (Nevonen *et al.* 2003). In the English sample the Clinical Eating Disorders Rating Instrument (CEDRI) was used (Palmer *et al.* 1987), a semi-structured interview similar to the RAB. It has demonstrated high inter-rater reliability, with kappa ranging from 0.73 to 1.0 (M = 0.90) for the variables used in the present study (Palmer *et al.* 1996). From these instruments, ten essential clinical variables for the diagnosis of eating disorders according to DSM-IV were selected from both the RAB and CEDRI for subsequent cluster analysis. These variables were: BMI, fear of weight gain, restriction of food intake, avoidance of fattening foods, binge eating, self-induced vomiting, abuse of laxatives, compulsive exercise, amenorrhoea and body image disturbance. The phrasing of questions on the two interviews was similar and response formats were identical with the exception of questions pertaining to binge eating (RAB: 5-point graded scale; CEDRI: 4-point graded scale) and body image disturbance (RAB: 3-point graded scale; CEDRI: 4-point graded scale). Issues of duration and intensity of symptoms are dealt with similarly in the two instruments, and in a way that is in keeping with DSM-IV criteria.

In the second study further assessment of eating disorder symptoms was made using the self-report questionnaire Eating Disorders Inventory-2 (EDI-2: Garner *et al.* 1983). Psychiatric symptoms were measured using a shortened (63-item) version of the self-report questionnaire Symptom Check List-90 (SCL-90: Derogatis *et al.* 1973). The SCL was shortened by removing the subscales for Phobic Anxiety, Paranoid Ideation, Psychoticism and Additional Scales. Self-image was assessed using the Structural Analysis of Social Behaviour (SASB: Benjamin 1974, 1996). The SASB is a widely used personality measure that utilizes two axes, affiliation and interdependence, as well as three dimensions (or surfaces), each with a specific interpersonal focus (i.e. other, self and self-image). In the present study the SASB Intrex questionnaire for assessing self-image was used. The questionnaire comprises 36 self-referential statements, some framed positively and others negatively. Responses are given on a scale from zero to 100 with 10-point increments, and combine to form eight clusters (or subscales) of self-image: (1) Self-emancipation, (2) Self-affirmation, (3) Active self-love, (4) Self-protection, (5) Self-control, (6) Self-blame, (7) Self-hate and (8) Self-neglect.

Procedure

Data for both the Swedish and English samples were collected by staff from participating units. Interviewers had long experience in the assessment of eating disorders in a clinical setting using the respective instruments. For the most part interviewers were either qualified psychiatrists or clinical psychologists, although other professionals, such as experienced nurses and social workers, also took part. Training of interviewers took place at participating units. In the case of the Swedish data, centrally arranged project meetings and workshops were also used for training of interviewers and for making checks on how instruments were being used once the project was under way. In the first study, administration of measures took place at initial diagnostic assessment prior to treatment, or in the case of the Swedish series within two to four weeks of commencing treatment at the latest. In the second study utilizing the extended Swedish data set, the EDI-2 and SCL-63 were administered at initial assessment and then subsequently after 6 and 36 months. The SASB was administered only at initial assessment and 36-month follow-up.

Data analysis

Prior to computation of cluster analysis all variables were standardized, and standard scores were used for subsequent cluster analyses. Cluster analysis was conducted in a series of three steps using SLEIPNER (Bergman and El-Khouri 1998), a statistical package for person-based analysis, focusing on cluster analysis. Although other more common packages for cluster analysis are available, such as SPSS, SLEIPNER has the ability to identify outliers that may otherwise distort the normative pattern of results, and allows for a more flexible way of conducting non-hierarchical cluster analysis based on the initial results of hierarchical methods. Separate cluster analyses were conducted on each sample. We did not combine data from the two series. This allowed for a comparison of the pattern of results in one sample against the pattern of results in the other.

Study 1: classification of patients using cluster analysis

Step 1: identification of outliers

In the first step, residual analysis was conducted to identify outliers. This is an important step in cluster analysis, since it allows for the exclusion of statistically eccentric cases that may obscure the more normative patterns in the data. The procedure resulted in the identification of 30 outliers in each of the two samples. Outliers were a diverse group without common identifying features. Examples were: normal or overweight patients with amenorrhoea, bulimics with relatively normal BMI who reported low levels of compensatory behaviour, bulimics who reported high levels of compensatory behaviour but who were grossly overweight, low weight anorexics of the bulimic subtype who reported little in the way of caloric restriction, EDNOS patients with a high degree of laxative abuse, and EDNOS patients with clear binge-eating symptoms and compensatory behaviour but little body image disturbance. These outliers were excluded from subsequent cluster analysis.

Step 2: hierarchical cluster analysis

In the second step, hierarchical cluster analysis was computed using Ward's method. The resultant pattern of agglomeration was most interesting from five clusters down to two clusters. Results are presented in Table 7.1.

Looking first at the Swedish sample, the largest group in the five-cluster solution was what could be termed "generalized eating disorder" (N = 211). These patients presented with relatively normal BMI and relatively high levels of restriction, food avoidance, binge eating, vomiting, compulsive exercise and body image disturbance, along with low levels of laxative abuse and amenorrhoea. The second largest cluster was labelled "anorexics" (N = 178) and was distinguished by amenorrhoea and low BMI, along with higher than average restriction and food avoidance, plus low levels of bingeing and vomiting. The third largest cluster was termed "overeaters" (N = 94) and was characterized by high BMI, average bingeing, along with low levels of restriction, compensatory behaviour and amenorrhoea. The fourth largest cluster was labelled "binge eaters" (N = 90). These patients presented with the highest levels of binge eating, coupled with relatively average BMI, low restriction and high levels of vomiting. The smallest cluster was termed "laxative abusers" (N = 28) and was typified by relatively low BMI, high fear of fatness, high restriction, high levels of body image disturbance and markedly high levels of laxative abuse.

A generally similar pattern was found in the English sample. The largest cluster comprised "high weight bingers" (N = 152) and was characterized by high BMI and binge eating, as well as low levels of restriction and compensation. Unlike the Swedish sample, the second largest cluster comprised what could be termed "compulsive exercisers" (N = 93) and was typified by high levels of compulsive exercise and avoidance of fattening food, along with low levels of binge eating and compensation. The third largest cluster was termed "anorexics" (N = 76) and was characterized by high levels of amenorrhoea and low BMI, as well as low levels of binge eating and compensatory behaviour. The fourth largest cluster was labelled "restricting bulimics" (N = 63) and was characterized by high levels of binge eating and vomiting, along with high restriction and food avoidance. Like the Swedish sample, the smallest cluster comprised "laxative abusers" (N = 58) and was typified by

Table 7.1 Standard scores on essential clinical variables in relation to specific cluster solutions using Ward's method of hierarchical cluster analysis

	N	BMI	Weight phobia	Binge eating	Restriction	Fat avoidance	Vomiting	Laxative abuse	Compulsive exercise	Amenorrhoea	Body image
Five-cluster solution											
Swedish sample:											
Generalized ED	211	0.02	0.19	0.33	0.44	0.54	0.38	-0.19	0.29	-0.51	0.25
Anorexics	178	-0.53	-0.13	-0.87	0.24	0.20	-0.76	-0.12	0.10	0.91	0.29
Overeaters	94	0.90	-0.10	-0.03	-0.95	-1.04	-0.51	-0.27	-0.55	-0.97	-0.69
Binge eaters	90	0.12	-0.27	0.88	-0.73	-0.83	1.01	-0.26	-0.37	0.40	-0.60
Laxative abusers	28	-0.16	0.61	0.36	0.68	0.82	0.47	3.93	0.21	0.05	0.55
English sample:											
High weight bingers	152	0.56	-0.43	0.33	-0.41	-0.62	0.16	-0.36	-0.63	-0.47	-0.31
Compulsive exercisers	93	-0.04	0.10	-0.58	0.14	0.41	-0.39	-0.36	0.56	-0.56	0.11
Anorexics	76	-0.94	-0.17	-0.92	0.10	0.09	-0.80	-0.40	-0.22	1.78	-0.43
Restricting bulimics	63	0.01	0.68	0.92	0.46	0.56	0.94	-0.20	0.53	0.07	0.49
Laxative abusers	58	-0.18	0.44	0.26	0.23	0.23	0.24	2.24	0.46	-0.28	0.67
Four-cluster solution											
Swedish sample:											
Generalized ED	211	0.02	0.19	0.33	0.44	0.54	0.38	-0.19	0.29	-0.51	0.25
Anorexics	178	-0.53	-0.13	-0.87	0.24	0.20	-0.76	-0.12	0.10	0.91	0.29
High weight bingers	184	0.52	-0.18	0.41	-0.84	-0.94	0.23	-0.26	-0.46	-0.30	-0.64
Laxative abusers	28	-0.16	0.61	0.36	0.68	0.82	0.47	3.93	0.21	0.05	0.55
English sample:											
Generalized ED	156	-0.02	0.33	0.03	0.27	0.47	0.15	-0.29	0.55	-0.31	0.26
High weight bingers	152	0.56	-0.43	0.33	-0.41	-0.62	0.16	-0.36	-0.63	-0.47	-0.31
Anorexics	76	-0.94	-0.17	-0.92	0.10	0.09	-0.80	-0.40	-0.22	1.78	-0.43
Laxative abusers	58	-0.18	0.44	0.26	0.23	0.23	0.24	2.24	0.46	-0.28	0.67

Three-cluster solution

Swedish sample:

Generalized ED	239	0.00	0.24	0.33	0.47	0.57	0.39	0.30	0.28	-0.44	0.28
High weight bingers	184	0.52	-0.18	0.41	-0.84	-0.94	0.23	-0.26	-0.46	-0.30	-0.64
Anorexics	178	-0.53	-0.13	-0.87	0.24	0.20	-0.76	-0.12	0.10	0.91	0.29

English sample:

Generalized ED	214	-0.06	0.36	0.09	0.26	0.41	0.17	0.39	0.52	-0.30	0.37
High weight bingers	152	0.56	-0.43	0.33	-0.41	-0.62	0.16	-0.36	-0.63	-0.47	-0.31
Anorexics	76	-0.94	-0.17	-0.92	0.10	0.09	-0.80	-0.40	-0.22	1.78	-0.43

Two-cluster solution

Swedish sample:

Restrainers	417	-0.23	0.08	-0.18	0.37	0.41	-0.10	0.12	0.20	0.13	0.28
High weight bingers	184	0.52	-0.18	0.41	-0.84	-0.94	0.23	-0.26	-0.46	-0.30	-0.64

English sample:

Overeaters	366	0.19	0.03	0.19	-0.02	-0.02	0.17	0.08	0.05	-0.37	0.09
Anorexics	76	-0.94	-0.17	-0.92	0.10	0.09	-0.80	-0.40	-0.22	1.78	-0.43

markedly high levels of laxative abuse, along with high to moderate levels of pathology on most other variables.

When the two closest clusters were agglomerated at the four-cluster level in the Swedish sample, "binge eaters" merged with "overeaters" to produce a cluster of "high weight bingers" (N = 184). These patients were characterized by high BMI, high levels of binge eating and low levels of restriction and compensatory behaviour with the exception of vomiting, which was moderate. In the English sample at the four-cluster level, "compulsive exercisers" combined with "restricting bulimics" to produce a new cluster that could also be described as "generalized eating disorder" (N = 156). This cluster was characterized by compulsive exercise, avoidance of fattening foods and restriction, along with above average levels of vomiting. Although levels of binge eating were around the mean for this group, examination of raw values indicated that 60 per cent of these patients were binge eating, and 39 per cent were bingeing sufficiently frequently to meet criteria for BN.

When the next two closest clusters were agglomerated at the three-cluster level in the Swedish sample, "laxative abusers" merged with cases characterized by "generalized eating disorder" (N = 239). Because the former was such a small cluster the general pattern of results changed little, with the exception that the "generalized eating disorder" cluster as a whole now exhibited considerably higher levels of laxative abuse. In the English sample, the "generalized eating disorder" cluster also merged with the small cluster of "laxative abusers" to produce a cluster of patients that further accentuated the "generalized eating disorder" cluster (N = 214), which now exhibited markedly higher levels of laxative abuse. Although the levels of binge eating in this cluster were near the mean, examination of raw scores indicated clear problems with this symptom (63 per cent of the group were bingeing, and 43 per cent met binge eating criteria for BN).

When only two clusters were left in the Swedish sample, cases with "generalized eating disorder" merged with the "anorexics" to produce a cluster of "restrainers" (N = 417), characterized by moderately low BMI, along with relatively high restriction and food avoidance, plus moderately high levels of compulsive exercise and laxative abuse. In the English sample at the two-cluster level, cases with "generalized eating disorder" merged with "high weight bingers" to produce a cluster of "overeaters" (N = 366).

Determination of the optimal number of clusters was based on both the interpretability of the specific cluster solution (i.e. how meaningful it appeared) and by using the "variance ratio criterion" (Calinski and Harabasz 1974). The Variance Ratio Criterion (VRC) is a statistical aid for determining an optimal number of clusters, and is computed by calculating a ratio of the total Between Group Sum of Squares (BGSS) to the total Within Group Sum of Squares (WGSS) in relation to number of clusters (k) and sample size (n). The formula used was:

$$VRC = (BGSS/k–1) / (WGSS/n–k).$$

According to this method a statistically optimal number of clusters is reached at the point where the graph peaks. In both samples the statistical optimum appeared to be around three or four clusters. In the English sample the VRC peaked at three clusters and then declined, whereas in the Swedish sample the VRC peak came at four clusters. Of these two solutions, the three-cluster solution was chosen for further analysis based on the VRC, and the interpretability of the solution. Although the four-cluster solution was also potentially interesting, it was not chosen for further analysis since the cluster of laxative abusers was relatively small and appeared to constitute more of a subgroup of cases within the "generalized eating disorder" category.

Step 3: non-hierarchical cluster analysis

In the third step non-hierarchical cluster analysis using the relocation method was utilized to arrive at an optimal classification. This final step initially proceeded from the previous three-cluster solution using Ward's method. Using an iterative algorithm each case was examined in relation to cluster centroids in order to arrive at the optimal allocation of cases for a three-cluster solution. Conceptually, this step is akin to rotation in factor analysis. When relocation analysis is used in cluster analysis it tends to yield more homogeneous and conceptually distinct clusters compared to hierarchical methods. Results of this procedure, which can be considered as the final cluster results, are presented in Table 7.2.

Results of the non-hierarchical cluster analysis did indeed yield more homogeneous and distinct clusters. The three clusters were of more equal size. The "bulimic" aspect of the "generalized eating disorder" cluster in both samples was more evident in higher levels of binge eating compared to the hierarchical results. In many respects this cluster was now more classically bulimic as well as showing high levels of restriction and avoidance of fattening foods at the same time. Overall, the pattern of results in both samples after non-hierarchical cluster analysis was markedly similar. Nevertheless, there were some small differences between the two samples. English "anorexics" tended to exhibit more of the physical symptoms (i.e. a tendency toward lower BMI and greater degree of menstrual dysfunction), whereas their Swedish counterparts tended to exhibit more behavioural symptoms (i.e. a tendency toward greater restriction, avoidance of fattening foods, compulsive exercise and disturbed body image). Swedish patients in the "generalized eating disorder" cluster tended to be characterized by high levels of binge eating and vomiting, while their English counterparts had a tendency to be somewhat more anorexic (i.e. engage in compulsive exercise and avoidance of fattening foods, as well as express a higher degree of weight phobia).

Table 7.2 Standard scores on essential clinical variables in relation to three-cluster solution following non-hierarchical relocation analysis

Cluster labels	N	BMI	Weight phobia	Binge eating	Restriction	Fat avoidance	Vomiting	Laxative abuse	Compulsive exercise	Amenorrhoea	Body image
Swedish sample:											
Generalized ED	216	0.03	0.39	0.60	0.47	0.48	0.68	0.32	0.26	−0.24	0.64
Overeaters	193	0.65	−0.36	0.28	−1.03	−0.88	0.01	−0.25	−0.49	−0.33	−0.63
Anorexics	192	−0.68	−0.07	−0.96	0.51	0.35	−0.78	−0.11	0.20	0.61	0.29
English sample:											
Overeaters	171	0.55	−0.49	0.14	−0.59	−0.64	0.06	−0.23	−0.41	−0.47	−0.42
Generalized ED	170	−0.01	0.60	0.38	0.49	0.60	0.40	0.38	0.54	−0.37	0.66
Anorexics	101	−0.91	−0.19	−0.89	0.18	0.09	−0.78	−0.25	−0.21	1.41	−0.41

Step 4: comparison of clusters and diagnoses

Following cluster analysis we compared the results of the non-hierarchical cluster analysis at step 3, with the original clinical diagnoses according to DSM-IV. Figures 7.1a and 7.1b provide relevant data for the Swedish and English samples.

There was a high degree of correspondence between the two samples as well as substantial concordance between the clusters and clinical diagnosis. For the most part, patients with AN were found in the "anorexic" cluster, patients with BN were found in the "generalized eating disorder" cluster, and BED patients were found among the "overeaters". The large number of EDNOS patients, however, underwent a major reallocation, which also tended to differ somewhat between the two series of data. In the Swedish sample EDNOS patients tended to fall into the "overeater" and "anorexic" clusters, whereas in the English sample EDNOS patients tended to be found in the "overeater" and "generalized eating disorder" clusters.

Further comparisons of clusters and diagnoses can be made graphically by examining the profiles of the two samples on the key diagnostic variables used for cluster analysis. For the Swedish sample comparisons of clusters are to be found in Figure 7.2a and comparisons of DSM-IV diagnoses in Figure 7.2b. Corresponding comparisons for the English sample are presented in Figures 7.3a and 7.3b. These graphs illustrate how the cluster approach produces a pattern of results that is more homogeneous and distinct than when traditional diagnostic categories are used.

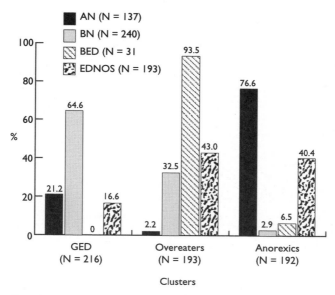

Figure 7.1a Distribution of DSM-IV diagnoses across clusters (Swedish data).

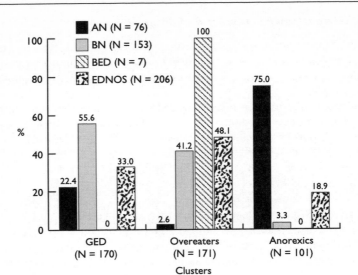

Figure 7.1b Distribution of DSM-IV diagnoses across clusters (UK data).

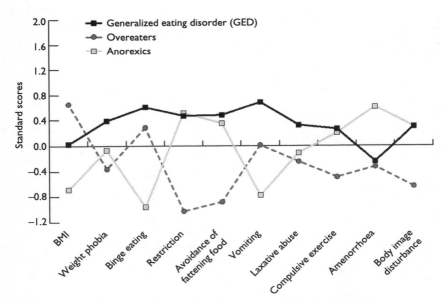

Figure 7.2a Comparisons of clusters on key diagnostic variables (Swedish data).

The utility of the cluster analytic approach is further underlined in Tables 7.3 and 7.4, which give the results of one-way ANOVA on the key diagnostic variables for both clusters and DSM-IV diagnoses.

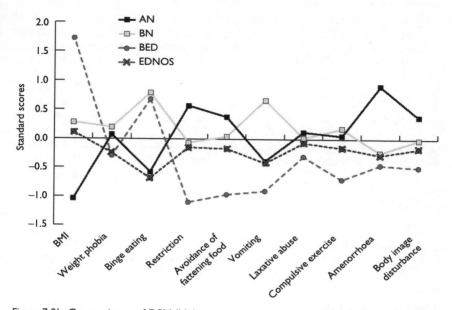

Figure 7.2b Comparisons of DSM-IV diagnoses on key diagnostic variables (Swedish data).

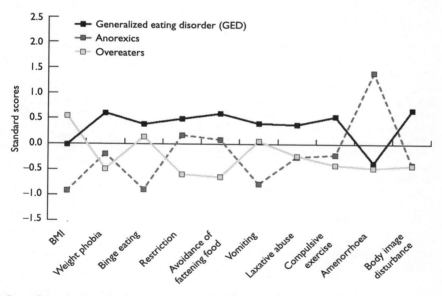

Figure 7.3a Comparisons of clusters on key diagnostic variables (UK data).

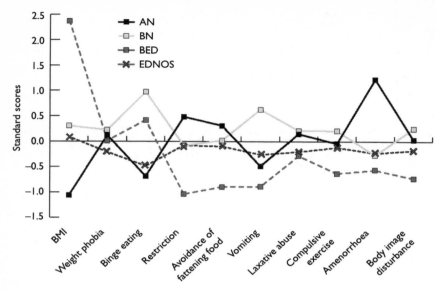

Figure 7.3b Comparisons of DSM-IV diagnoses on key diagnostic variables (UK data).

Table 7.3 Comparison of clusters and DSM-IV diagnoses on key diagnostic variables (Swedish sample)

Key diagnostic variable	Clusters[a]			DSM diagnoses[b]		
	F	p	h²	F	p	h²
BMI	119.5	<0.001	0.29	153.8	<0.001	0.44
Weight phobia	32.3	<0.001	0.10	8.5	<0.001	0.04
Binge eating	247.8	<0.001	0.45	198.1	<0.001	0.50
Restriction	301.2	<0.001	0.50	33.8	<0.001	0.14
Avoidance of fattening food	175.8	<0.001	0.37	19.7	<0.001	0.09
Vomiting	168.0	<0.001	0.36	89.0	<0.001	0.31
Laxative abuse	19.2	<0.001	0.06	2.0	NS	0.01
Compulsive exercise	38.5	<0.001	0.11	9.7	<0.001	0.05
Amenorrhoea	62.8	<0.001	0.17	65.0	<0.001	0.25
Disturbed body image	69.9	<0.001	0.19	11.4	<0.001	0.05

Notes:
a Clusters: Generalized ED, overeaters, anorexics.
b DSM diagnoses: AN, BN, BED, EDNOS.

As expected, F-values are significant across the board for virtually all variables, and for both clusters and diagnoses. What, however, is most interesting is a comparison of the effect sizes (h^2) of these variables in relation to clusters and diagnoses. A comparison of effect size gives an indication of how well the two approaches perform in their ability to account for variation in

Table 7.4 Comparison of clusters and DSM-IV diagnoses on key diagnostic variables (UK sample)

Key diagnostic variable	Clusters[a]			DSM diagnoses[b]		
	F	p	h²	F	p	h²
BMI	96.9	<0.001	0.31	67.7	<0.001	0.32
Weight phobia	70.0	<0.001	0.24	6.1	<0.001	0.04
Binge eating	71.7	<0.001	0.25	158.0	<0.001	0.52
Restriction	67.9	<0.001	0.24	9.7	<0.001	0.06
Avoidance of fattening food	93.7	<0.001	0.30	5.1	<0.01	0.03
Vomiting	56.0	<0.001	0.20	41.1	<0.001	0.22
Laxative abuse	21.9	<0.001	0.09	6.0	<0.01	0.04
Compulsive exercise	50.1	<0.001	0.19	4.2	<0.001	0.03
Amenorrhoea	316.1	<0.001	0.59	66.8	<0.001	0.31
Disturbed body image	84.1	<0.001	0.28	6.9	<0.001	0.04

Notes:
a Clusters: Generalized ED, overeaters, anorexics.
b DSM diagnoses: AN, BN, BED, EDNOS.

key eating disorder symptoms. When variables are examined in relation to DSM-IV diagnoses, high effect sizes were found in both samples for BMI, binge eating, vomiting and amenorrhoea, which would suggest that the DSM system is, not surprisingly, primarily relying on these variables to explain the variance in diagnostic categories. When variables are examined in relation to clusters, effect sizes were, on the whole, even higher and more evenly distributed across a wider range of variables. The only instances where variables achieved notably higher effect sizes in relation to diagnoses compared to clusters were BMI in the Swedish sample and binge eating in the English sample. Slightly higher effect sizes in relation to diagnoses were found for binge eating and amenorrhoea in the Swedish sample. In contrast, effect sizes were considerably higher for restriction and avoidance of fattening food in relation to clusters as opposed to diagnoses in both samples. Higher effect sizes of a somewhat lesser magnitude were found for weight phobia, compulsive exercise and disturbed body image.

Study 2: exploring the utility of clusters and diagnostic categories

Comparisons at initial assessment

The comparative utility of clusters and diagnostic categories was further explored in the second study using the Swedish data set by examining clusters and diagnoses in relation to other eating disorder variables and aspects of comorbidity. Using the EDI-2, SCL-63 and SASB, comparisons were first made at initial assessment using one-way ANOVA. These are presented in Table 7.5.

Overall, levels of significance and effect sizes were greater for clusters compared to diagnoses. On the EDI this was especially true of psychological subscales of the instrument. When pair-wise differences were examined for clusters using Scheffé tests (p < 0.05), "overeaters" scored for the most part significantly lower than patients in the "generalized eating disorder" cluster,

Table 7.5 Comparison of clusters and DSM-IV diagnoses on eating disorder symptoms (EDI-2), psychiatric comorbidity (SCL-63) and self-image (SASB) at initial assessment with one-way ANOVA on Swedish data

	Clusters[a]			DSM diagnoses[b]		
	F	p	h^2	F	p	h^2
EDI-2						
Drive for thinness	32.5	<0.001	0.10	15.2	<0.001	0.07
Bulimia	165.9	<0.001	0.36	76.6	<0.001	0.28
Body dissatisfaction	15.7	<0.001	0.05	13.3	<0.001	0.06
Ineffectiveness	17.0	<0.001	0.05	4.6	<0.01	0.02
Perfectionism	9.2	<0.001	0.03	0.7	NS	0.00
Interpersonal distrust	7.7	<0.001	0.02	0.9	NS	0.00
Introceptive awareness	18.2	<0.001	0.06	2.7	<0.05	0.01
Maturity fears	8.4	<0.001	0.03	6.5	<0.001	0.03
Asceticism	14.9	<0.001	0.05	3.3	<0.05	0.02
Disturbed impulse regulation	7.9	<0.001	0.03	2.8	<0.05	0.01
Social insecurity	7.3	<0.001	0.02	2.5	NS	0.01
Total ED	64.4	<0.001	0.18	39.1	<0.001	0.17
Total psychological	22.5	<0.001	0.07	3.9	<0.01	0.02
Total score	40.0	<0.001	0.12	10.4	<0.001	0.05
SCL-63						
Somaticism	20.0	<0.001	0.06	1.5	NS	0.01
Obsession-compulsion	8.3	<0.001	0.03	1.7	NS	0.01
Interpersonal sensitivity	19.0	<0.001	0.07	1.2	NS	0.01
Depression	12.4	<0.001	0.04	1.9	NS	0.01
Anxiety	14.3	<0.001	0.05	3.7	<0.05	0.02
Anger	5.7	<0.01	0.02	0.5	NS	0.00
Symptom index	20.5	<0.001	0.06	2.3	NS	0.01
SASB						
Self-emancipation	17.8	<0.001	0.06	3.7	<0.05	0.02
Self-affirmation	16.0	<0.001	0.05	4.1	<0.01	0.02
Active self-love	18.3	<0.001	0.06	3.7	<0.05	0.02
Self-protection	5.6	<0.01	0.02	0.6	NS	0.00
Self-control	18.1	<0.001	0.06	8.5	<0.001	0.04
Self-blame	16.8	<0.001	0.05	3.0	<0.05	0.01
Self-hate	21.5	<0.001	0.07	3.9	<0.01	0.02
Self-neglect	9.6	<0.001	0.03	0.7	NS	0.00

Notes:
a Clusters: Generalized ED, overeaters, anorexics.
b DSM diagnoses: AN, BN, BED, EDNOS.

while the latter scored significantly higher than "overeaters" and "anorexics". An important exception to this trend was found for the Bulimia subscale where "overeaters" scored significantly higher than "anorexics". Graphic comparisons between clusters and diagnoses on the EDI-2 are presented in Figures 7.4a and 7.4b.

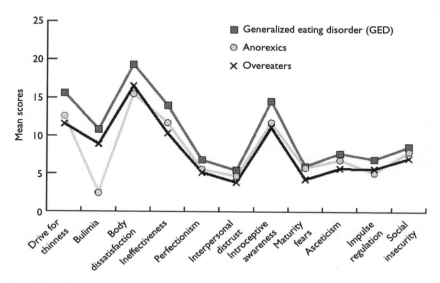

Figure 7.4a Mean scores for clusters on the EDI-2 at initial assessment (Swedish data).

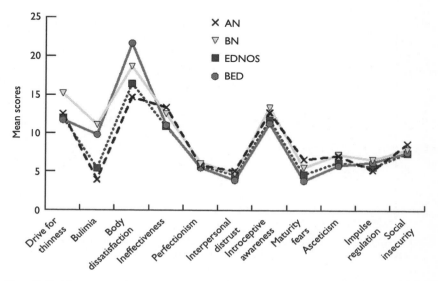

Figure 7.4b Mean scores for diagnoses on the EDI-2 at initial assessment (Swedish data).

Even when variables that have not been used for cluster analysis are compared, a more distinct and homogeneous pattern of between-group differences emerge in relation to clusters as opposed to diagnoses.

Similar, if not even more pronounced, results to those obtained on the EDI-2 were found for the SCL-63 (see Figures 7.5a and 7.5b) and SASB (see Figures 7.6a and 7.6b). On the SCL-63 significant differences between

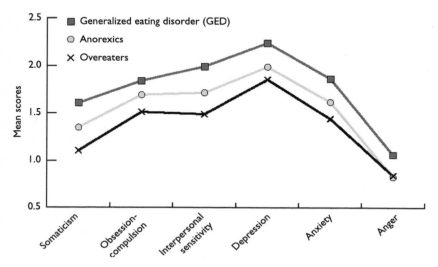

Figure 7.5a Mean scores for clusters on the SCL-63 at initial assessment (Swedish data).

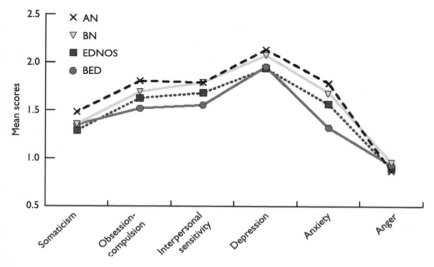

Figure 7.5b Mean scores for diagnoses on the SCL-63 at initial assessment (Swedish data).

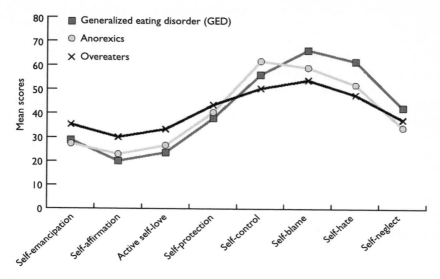

Figure 7.6a Mean scores for clusters on the SASB at initial assessment (Swedish data).

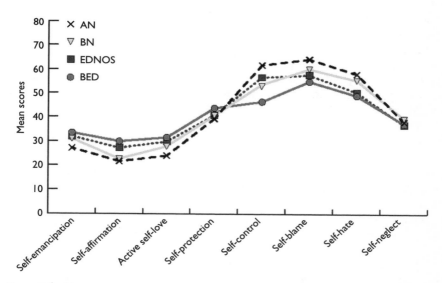

Figure 7.6b Mean scores for diagnoses on the SASB at initial assessment (Swedish data).

diagnostic categories were only found for the depression subscale, while all between-cluster differences were significant. When pair-wise comparisons were made for clusters, patients in the "generalized eating disorder" cluster scored significantly higher than "overeaters" on all subscales. "Anorexics" scored significantly higher than "overeaters" on Somaticism and Interpersonal sensitivity. "Anorexics" also scored significantly lower than "generalized eating disorder" patients on Somaticism, Interpersonal sensitivity, Depression, Anxiety and Anger. Once again, effect sizes were considerably greater for clusters compared to diagnoses. On the SASB, significant between-group differences were found for both clusters and diagnoses, yet once again the magnitude of these differences were clearly greater for the between-cluster comparisons. When clusters were compared, patients in the "generalized eating disorder" cluster exhibited the most pathological pattern of self-image and "overeaters" the least pathological. A notable exception was, however, Self-control, where "anorexics" scored significantly higher than patients in the "generalized eating disorder" cluster.

Comparisons after 6 and 36 months

Further comparisons of clusters and diagnoses were made by examining patients who had been followed-up after 6 and 36 months. Again one-way ANOVA was computed to make comparisons, and results are presented in Tables 7.6 and 7.7. Since only 58 per cent of patients could be followed up after 6 months and 54 per cent after 36 months, dropout analysis was conducted. Overall, when patients who could be assessed at follow-up were compared with dropouts on initial measures using one-way ANOVA, both groups were virtually indistinguishable with only a few exceptions. Patients who attended 6-month follow-up had reported significantly lesser (i.e. $p < 0.05$) fear of weight gain and laxative abuse at initial assessment. At 36-month follow-up, patients who could be assessed had previously reported significantly greater disturbed body image, and had scored significantly higher on EDI Asceticism and SASB Self-control.

After six months, levels of significance and effect sizes were diminished, but still suggested that clusters produced a more powerful categorization of patients than diagnoses. This was especially true of the SCL-63 where one-way ANOVA was significant on all subscales for clusters but none of the comparisons attained significance for diagnoses. What is more, effect sizes, although somewhat small, were at least twice as large for clusters as for diagnoses. After 36 months, however, the patterns that had been present at assessment and still after six months had been largely dissipated. On the EDI-2 significant between-cluster differences were still present on the Bulimia subscale, while significant between-diagnosis differences were found on Maturity fears. On the SCL-63 Anger was still significant for clusters, and on the SASB Self-control was significant for clusters, while Self-blame and Self-hate were significant for diagnoses.

Table 7.6 Six-month follow-up: comparison of clusters and DSM-IV diagnoses on eating disorder symptoms (EDI-2), and psychiatric comorbidity (SCL-63) with one-way ANOVA on Swedish data

	Clusters[a]			DSM diagnoses[b]		
	F	p	h²	F	p	h²
EDI-2						
Drive for thinness	11.5	<0.001	0.06	3.6	<0.05	0.03
Bulimia	20.5	<0.001	0.11	5.9	<0.001	0.05
Body dissatisfaction	4.1	<0.05	0.02	3.5	<0.05	0.03
Ineffectiveness	4.9	<0.01	0.03	3.7	<0.05	0.03
Perfectionism	2.0	NS	0.01	0.4	NS	0.00
Interpersonal distrust	5.2	<0.01	0.03	1.8	NS	0.01
Introceptive awareness	12.2	<0.001	0.06	2.9	<0.05	0.02
Maturity fears	5.0	<0.01	0.03	4.8	<0.01	0.04
Asceticism	4.7	<0.01	0.03	1.4	NS	0.01
Disturbed impulse regulation	2.6	NS	0.01	0.9	NS	0.01
Social insecurity	2.4	NS	0.01	2.0	NS	0.02
Total ED subscales	12.0	<0.001	0.07	4.8	<0.01	0.04
Total psychological subscales	7.6	<0.001	0.04	3.6	<0.05	0.03
Total score	9.8	<0.001	0.05	3.5	<0.05	0.03
SCL-63						
Somaticism	5.5	<0.01	0.03	1.6	NS	0.01
Obsession-compulsion	5.7	<0.01	0.03	1.1	NS	0.01
Interpersonal sensitivity	7.1	<0.001	0.04	2.3	NS	0.02
Depression	7.1	<0.001	0.04	2.5	NS	0.02
Anxiety	9.3	<0.001	0.05	1.8	NS	0.01
Anger	6.1	<0.01	0.02	1.6	NS	0.01
Symptom index	8.9	<0.001	0.06	1.5	NS	0.01

Notes:
a Clusters: Generalized ED, overeaters, anorexics.
b DSM diagnoses: AN, BN, BED, EDNOS.

Discussion

We have sought to contribute evidence relevant to the classification of eating disorders by examining natural groupings of patients on key diagnostic variables in two independent samples using cluster analysis, and by comparing clusters and diagnoses on a range of measures relating to eating disorders and comorbidity. In so doing we have also attempted to clarify the picture of EDNOS by exploring how these patients can be reallocated to more relevant alternative categories. Strengths of the first study were that samples were drawn from series of patients newly presenting to specialist eating disorders services in two countries – England and Sweden – and that they were analysed separately. Subjects were also assessed using interview schedules that were similar, yet not identical, which suggests that results are not due to some specific feature of the interview methodology, and hints at greater generalize-

Table 7.7 Thirty-six-month follow-up: comparison of clusters and DSM-IV diagnoses on eating disorder symptoms (EDI), psychiatric comorbidity (SCL-63) and self-image (SASB) with one-way ANOVA on Swedish data

	Clusters[a]			DSM diagnoses[b]		
	F	p	h^2	F	p	h^2
EDI-2						
Drive for thinness	2.6	NS	0.02	0.9	NS	0.01
Bulimia	4.2	<0.05	0.03	0.1	NS	0.00
Body dissatisfaction	0.8	NS	0.00	0.5	NS	0.00
Ineffectiveness	0.2	NS	0.00	2.0	NS	0.02
Perfectionism	2.1	NS	0.01	1.1	NS	0.01
Interpersonal distrust	0.8	NS	0.00	0.9	NS	0.01
Introceptive awareness	1.9	NS	0.01	0.3	NS	0.00
Maturity fears	0.9	NS	0.01	4.5	<0.01	0.04
Asceticism	0.4	NS	0.00	0.9	NS	0.01
Disturbed impulse regulation	0.3	NS	0.00	0.4	NS	0.00
Social insecurity	0.7	NS	0.00	0.8	NS	0.01
Total ED subscales	1.7	NS	0.01	0.2	NS	0.00
Total psychological subscales	0.3	NS	0.00	1.1	NS	0.01
Total score	0.1	NS	0.00	0.3	NS	0.00
SCL-63						
Somaticism	2.6	NS	0.02	0.6	NS	0.00
Obsession-compulsion	2.7	NS	0.02	1.4	NS	0.01
Interpersonal sensitivity	1.5	NS	0.01	1.5	NS	0.01
Depression	0.3	NS	0.00	0.7	NS	0.01
Anxiety	1.7	NS	0.01	0.7	NS	0.01
Anger	3.1	<0.05	0.02	0.1	NS	0.00
Symptom index	1.7	NS	0.01	0.7	NS	0.01
SASB						
Self-emancipation	1.6	NS	0.01	1.2	NS	0.01
Self-affirmation	0.8	NS	0.00	1.7	NS	0.01
Active self-love	0.9	NS	0.01	2.3	NS	0.02
Self-protection	0.8	NS	0.00	0.6	NS	0.01
Self-control	5.1	<0.01	0.03	1.5	NS	0.01
Self-blame	0.5	NS	0.00	3.1	<0.05	0.03
Self-hate	1.0	NS	0.01	3.1	<0.05	0.03
Self-neglect	0.2	NS	0.00	1.9	NS	0.02

Notes:
a Clusters: Generalized ED, overeaters, anorexics.
b DSM diagnoses: AN, BN, BED, EDNOS.

ability. However, since the samples were of patients presenting to secondary services, they may not be representative of all of those suffering from eating disorders in their respective communities. This is a weakness with regard to investigating the nature of eating disorders, but does, nonetheless, mean that the patterns found are likely to be of relevance to clinicians. Another weakness was the high number of patients excluded because of incomplete data, although examination of cases with and without complete data revealed no systematic bias in terms of eating disorder, psychiatric or background variables. Strengths of the second study were that clusters and diagnoses could be examined on relevant self-report measures of eating disorders, psychiatric symptoms and self-image, administered at initial assessment and again after 6 and 36 months. The fact that only a little more than half of these patients could be followed-up must be seen as a weakness.

Results of the first study suggested that a three-cluster solution with clusters of relatively equal size provided the most parsimonious classification of cases. The utility of the three-cluster solution was supported both statistically (i.e. using the variance ratio criterion) and heuristically (i.e. the most interpretable). It also produced clusters with markedly similar groupings of patients in both samples using hierarchical and non-hierarchical techniques. Both samples generated a cluster that broadly corresponded to a diagnosis of AN without bingeing or vomiting. Membership of this "anorexic" cluster was associated with a clinical diagnosis of AN in 55 per cent of cases. Conversely, of patients who received a clinical diagnosis of AN, three-quarters fell into the "anorexic" cluster and a quarter into the "generalized eating disorder" cluster in both series. However, 40 per cent of patients assigned to the "anorexic" clusters had received a clinical diagnosis of EDNOS.

The other two clusters were also similar between the two samples, and we felt justified in giving them the same labels, namely "generalized eating disorder" and "overeaters". The distinction between these two clusters seemed to be mainly one of severity and weight. Patients assigned to the "generalized eating disorder" cluster were rated as having more severe symptoms in almost every respect except weight. In broad terms, these clusters correspond to BN with restrictive tendencies and to a grouping of other states characterized by overeating and high weight. Of those subjects who had a diagnosis of BN, 61 per cent fell into the "generalized eating disorder" clusters and conversely 62 per cent of subjects in those clusters received a diagnosis of BN. Only relatively few of the subjects in either series had received a clinical diagnosis of BED, perhaps because of an inconsistency of practice as to whether or not to use this still provisional diagnostic category. Nevertheless, of the 38 subjects who did receive a clinical diagnosis of BED, 36 (94 per cent) were located in the "overeaters" clusters.

When interpreting these results it should be borne in mind that the labelling of clusters is as much an art as a science. The use of common labels in the final three-cluster solution does not imply identity between the data sets, and alternative labels could be applied. Nevertheless, our common labels do emphasize the continuity and surprising similarity between two independent samples of eating disorder patients.

Direct comparisons between the results of the first study and previous research are complicated by methodological factors. Previous studies using cluster analysis with eating disorders have used more restricted samples, focusing on the identification of subtypes, and are not strictly comparable (Grilo *et al.* 2001; Hay *et al.* 1996; Mizes and Sloan 1998; Stice and Agras 1999). There are, however, some important similarities between our results and those of others who have used other methodological approaches. Using latent class analysis in a community sample of non-clinical cases, Bulik *et al.* (2000) found three general classes resembling AN, BN and BED. A similar conclusion could be drawn from Crow *et al.* (2002), who showed that patients with partial AN and BED could not be readily differentiated from those with full syndromes. Williamson *et al.* (2002), who examined the underlying structure of symptoms rather than groupings of individuals, found three factors: binge eating, fear of fatness/compensatory behaviour, and drive for thinness. They also performed taxometric analyses and found support for conceptualizing the bulimic disorders (BN and BED) as discrete syndromes, whereas the evidence concerning AN was inconclusive. A similar conclusion was drawn by Gleaves *et al.* (2000b), who found that bulimic-type AN could be conceptualized on a continuum with BN but qualitatively distinguished from AN restricting type. Nevertheless, the present results are somewhat at odds with the findings of van der Ham *et al.* (1997) who found that the occurrence of bulimic symptoms was of greater relevance for distinguishing patients than anorexic symptoms. However, van der Ham and associates examined a relatively small number of eating disordered adolescents, the majority of which presented with anorexic forms of eating disorders, and focused on patterns of results over an extended period of time rather than initial clinical presentation, which might explain the apparent discrepancy.

Our analysis produced clusters that are recognizable from a clinical perspective. Although the results do not correspond precisely to the diagnoses generated by established diagnostic systems, they broadly support the distinction between AN, restricting type, and BN. In the present study, analyses of two large and distinct samples produced closely similar results. Patients presenting to differing eating disorder services in different countries had clinical features that fell into very similar patterns. This cross-sample similarity suggests that the patterns of symptoms reflected in the clusters are likely to be found in other samples. However, this might not be the case if the samples were drawn directly from the community rather than from the clinic. Nevertheless, the replication of clusters within the present study does allow some confidence that they may be meaningful, and not just chance findings. They may provide a parsimonious description of the symptomatology of clinical eating disorders. However, description is different to diagnosis.

Clinical diagnosis is a tool for use in aiding prognosis and treatment choice. The best description of a complex set of features may well involve dimensions or factors. Nevertheless, diagnosis favours categories over dimensions so that clinicians may assign an individual unambiguously. Clusters too involve individual membership. But clusters are different from categories. Categories are defined by their boundaries – by the fulfilment or non-fulfilment of particular criteria in the case of formal diagnoses. In regard to some eating disorder features, such as weight loss, a dimensional description is clearly optimal, but nevertheless a particular degree of weight or weight loss may need to be chosen as the boundary. Ideally, there should be a point of rarity at the boundary of diagnostic categories if it is not to be arbitrary. However, this ideal is often not the case, and may well not be so in this instance. Studies such as the present ones may suggest alternative categorizations. Yet it is probably expecting too much in such a complex and poorly defined field as eating disorders for true categories to be "discovered" or to reflect profound truths about underlying mechanisms. Rather they will need to be determined – provisionally – and then tested as to their utility (see Kendell and Jablensky 2003). On the whole, such decisions have tended to emerge from clinical experience, and have only sometimes been the result of systematic research. Nevertheless, empirical evidence should be able to help to inform the decision as to where appropriate boundaries should be drawn, and, perhaps as importantly, where they should not be drawn.

Empirical evidence from both our studies suggested that a cluster analysis approach generated categories that demonstrated a higher degree of utility than traditional diagnoses. The higher degree of association between key eating disorder symptoms and clusters as opposed to diagnoses suggests that clusters "out-performed" diagnoses in their ability to account for variability in important symptoms. This was the case at initial assessment, as well as at short-term follow-up after six months, and in relation to both a wider range of eating disorder psychopathology and important aspects of comorbidity. The ability of the cluster approach to generate a more homogeneous and powerful classification may be due to two important factors. First, cluster analysis attached greater importance to a wider range of psychological and behavioural characteristics of eating disorders in order to classify cases, as opposed to measures of weight, menstrual functioning, and binge eating. Classification of cases using cluster analysis put comparatively greater emphasis on restriction of eating, avoidance of fattening foods, weight phobia, disturbed body image, compulsive exercise and laxative abuse. Second, cluster analysis succeeded in clarifying the picture of EDNOS by generating and reallocating these patients to more relevant categories. By elucidating EDNOS we, therefore, illuminate the picture of eating disorders generally.

Conclusion

We must remain cautious about revising diagnostic categories in the light of our results. In particular, our findings suggest that there may be a special problem in categorizing eating disorders other than AN. Our "generalized eating disorder" and "overeating" clusters seem to be distinguished mainly by overall severity and weight. Such a distinction is unlikely to support clear boundaries. A system of classification should provide categories that are mutually exclusive and – ideally – they should also be collectively exhaustive. The present eating disorders categories largely fail these tests (Palmer 2003). The categories overlap in practice, or are prevented from doing so only by arbitrary rules. Certainly over time an individual may move from one diagnosis to another. Furthermore, the eating disorder diagnoses together cover the field only through the use of the wide catch-all category of EDNOS. Our findings as well as those of others (Bulik *et al.* 2000; Crow *et al.* 2002) could be seen as indicating that the present diagnostic classes are too narrowly defined, and that the relocation of a proportion of the patients today diagnosed as EDNOS would make sense from a clinical point of view. New categories would not need to be perfect to be an improvement. Clusters such as those that we have outlined may suggest new categories that could be clinically useful, such as "generalized eating disorder". To be useful, however, diagnostic categories need to be recognizable and workable. Our use of only key clinical characteristics necessary for establishing diagnosis and detectable at first interview is helpful in this respect. Yet the clusters found in the present study are not yet candidate syndromes or prototype disorders. Although they did demonstrate more consistent associations with other features and had better prognostic value compared to diagnoses, they still need to be defined in ways that could be used in clinical practice and related to treatment outcome. A proper conservatism prevails in the definition and adoption of new syndromes. However, there has been some slow extension of the diagnostic canon over the years, most notably with BN (Russell 1979), and the launching of BED as a candidate disorder. Moreover, there has been a good deal of tinkering involving changes of detail in successive revisions of diagnostic criteria. Hitherto, both the definition of new syndromes and their subsequent revision have been the work either of perceptive individual clinicians or of committees. This is likely to continue to be the case; although their decisions and proposals could benefit from a greater use of empirical research into classificatory systems. Diagnostic categories facilitate research, but research findings should also inform the definition of diagnostic categories. Our results suggest that patients presenting to eating disorder services in different countries have clinical features that fall into very similar patterns. Although clusters did resemble existing diagnostic categories, a more consistent and powerful pattern of results emerged for clusters compared to diagnoses. Clusters demonstrated greater utility than traditional diagnoses in relation to a wide range of variables pertaining to eating disorders, psychiatric comorbidity and self-image at both initial assessment and short-term follow-up. The greater utility of clusters was in important respects due to the reallocation of EDNOS patients to more relevant alternative categories. If we are serious about wanting to limit the number of eating disorder patients that are consigned to the residual category of EDNOS we may need to revise diagnostic systems to take better account of the psychological and behavioural aspects of eating disorders. Setting inclusion boundaries around such dimensions will not, however, be easy. In order to do so continued empirical research will be necessary.

References

American Psychiatric Association (1994) *Diagnostic and Statistical Manual of Mental Disorders*, 4th edn (DSM-IV), Washington, DC: APA.

Benjamin, L.S. (1974) "Structural analysis of social behavior", *Psychological Review* 81, 392–425.

Benjamin, L.S. (1996) *Interpersonal Diagnosis and Treatment of Personality Disorders*, New York: Guilford Press.

Bergman, L. and El-Khouri, B.M. (1998) *SLEIPNER: A Statistical Package for Pattern-Oriented Analysis*, Stockholm: Department of Psychology, Stockholm University.

Bulik, C.M., Sullivan, P.F. and Kendler, K.S. (2000) "An empirical study of the classification of eating disorders", *American Journal of Psychiatry* 157, 886–95.

Button, E.J. and Whitehouse, A. (1981) "Subclinical anorexia nervosa", *Psychological Medicine* 11, 509–16.

Button, E.J., Marshall, P.M., Shinkwin, R., Black, S. and Palmer, R.L. (1997) "One hundred referrals to an eating disorders service: progress and service consumption over a 2–4 year period", *European Eating Disorders Review* 5, 47–63.

Calinski, T. and Harabasz, J. (1974) "A dendrite method for cluster analysis", *Communications in Statistics* 3, 1–27.

Clinton, D.N. and Norring, C. (1999) "The Rating of Anorexia and Bulimia (RAB) interview: Development and preliminary validation", *European Eating Disorders Review* 7, 362–71.

Clinton, D.N., Button, E., Norring, C. and Palmer, R. (2004) "Cluster analysis of key diagnostic variables from two independent samples of eating disorder patients: evidence for a consistent pattern", *Psychological Medicine* 34, 1035–45.

Crow, S.J., Agras, W.S., Halmi, K., Mitchell, J.E. and Kraemer, H.C. (2002) "Full syndromal versus subthreshold anorexia nervosa, bulimia nervosa, and binge eating disorder: a multicenter study", *International Journal of Eating Disorders* 32, 309–18.

Derogatis, L.R., Lipman, R.S. and Covi, L. (1973) "SCL-90: an outpatient psychiatric rating scale-preliminary report", *Psychopharmacology* 9, 13–28.

Everitt, B.S. and Landau, S. (1998) "The use of multivariate statistical methods in psychiatry", *Statistical Methods in Medical Research* 7, 253–77.

Everitt, B.S., Landau, S. and Leese, M. (2001) *Cluster Analysis*, 4th edn, London: Arnold.

Garner, D.M., Olmsted, M.P. and Polivy, J. (1983) "Development and validation of a mulidimensional eating disorders inventory for anorexia nervosa and bulimia", *International Journal of Eating Disorders* 2, 15–34.

Gleaves, D.H., Lowe, M.R., Snow, A.C., Green, B.A. and Murphy-Eberenz, K.P. (2000a) "Continuity and discontinuity models of bulimia nervosa: a taxometric investigation", *Journal of Abnormal Psychology* 10, 56–68.

Gleaves, D.H., Lowe, M.R., Green, B.A., Cororve, M.B. and Williams, T.L. (2000b) "Do anorexia and bulimia nervosa occur on a continuum? A taxometric analysis", *Behavior Therapy* 31, 195–219.

Grilo, C.M., Masheb, R.M. and Berman, R.M. (2001) "Subtyping women with bulimia nervosa along dietary and negative affect dimensions: a replication in a treatment-seeking sample", *Eating and Weight Disorders* 6, 53–8.

Hay, P.J., Fairburn, C.G. and Doll, H.A. (1996) "The classification of bulimic eating disorders: a community-based cluster analysis", *Psychological Medicine* 26, 801–12.

Holmgren, S., Humble, K., Norring, C., Roos, B.-E., Rosmark, B. and Sohlberg, S. (1983) "The anorectic bulimic conflict: an alternative diagnostic approach to anorexia nervosa and bulimia", *International Journal of Eating Disorders* 2, 3–14.

Kendell, R. and Jablensky, A. (2003) "Distinguishing between the validity and utility of psychiatric diagnoses", *American Journal of Psychiatry* 160, 4–12.

Mizes, J.S. and Sloan, D.M. (1998) "An empirical analysis of eating disorder, not otherwise specified: preliminary support for a distinct subgroup", *International Journal of Eating Disorders* 23, 233–42.

Nevonen, L., Broberg, A., Clinton, D. and Norring, C. (2003) "A measure for the assessment of eating disorders: reliability and validity studies of the Rating of Anorexia and Bulimia interview – revised version (RAB-R)", *Scandinavian Journal of Psychology* 44, 303–10.

Nylander, I. (1971) "The feeling of being fat and dieting in a school population", *Acta Sociomedica Scandinavica* 3, 17–26.

Palmer, R.L. (2003) "Concepts of eating disorders", in U. Schmidt, J. Treasure and E. van Furth (eds) *Handbook of Eating Disorders*, 2nd edn, Chichester: Wiley.

Palmer, R.L., Christie, M., Cordle, C., Davies, D. and Kenrick, J. (1987) "The Clinical Eating Disorders Rating Instrument (CEDRI): a preliminary description", *International Journal of Eating Disorders* 6, 9–16.

Palmer, R., Robertson, D., Cain, M. and Black, S. (1996) "The Clinical Eating Disorders Rating Instrument (CEDRI): a validation study", *European Eating Disorders Review* 4, 149–56.

Russell, G.F.M. (1979) "Bulimia nervosa: an ominous variant of anorexia nervosa?", *Psychological Medicine* 9, 429–48.

Stice, E. and Agras, W.S. (1999) "Subtyping bulimic women along dietary restraint and negative affect dimensions", *Journal of Consulting and Clinical Psychology* 67, 460–9.

Szmukler, G.I. (1983) "Weight and food preoccupation in a population of English schoolgirls", in J.G. Bergman (ed.) *Understanding Anorexia Nervosa and Bulimia: Fourth Ross Conference on Medical Research*, Columbus, OH: Ross Laboratories.

van der Ham, T., Meulman, J.J., van Strien, D.C. and van Engeland, H. (1997) "Empirically based subgrouping of eating disorders in adolescents: a longitudinal perspective", *British Journal of Psychiatry* 170, 363–8.

Williamson, D.A., Womble, L.G., Smeets, M., Netemeyer, R.G., Thaw, J.M., Kutlesic, V. and Gleaves, D.H. (2002) "Latent structure of eating disorder symptoms: a factor analytic and taxometric investigation", *American Journal of Psychiatry* 159, 412–18.

World Health Organization (1992) *ICD-10 Classification of Mental and Behavioural Disorders: Clinical Descriptions and Diagnostic Guidelines*, Geneva: WHO.

Chapter 8

The biology of EDNOS

Janet Treasure and David Collier

Introduction

The aim of this chapter is to summarize the biology of Eating Disorders Not Otherwise Specified. This task seems to be either impossibly difficult or facile depending on one's mood. The task is impossible because there are very few studies that have been designed to examine this question. Most studies directly examining the biology in eating disorders choose study participants based on the clearly defined DSM-IV criteria (see APA 1994 and the Appendix). Moreover as the diagnostic criteria for Anorexia Nervosa or Bulimia Nervosa have become more or less specific, by default, the size of the group who do not exactly fulfil these diagnostic criteria, that is, eating disorder not otherwise specified, varies. Also the syndromes that lie within the current systems of clinical classification are probably biologically heterogeneous and include many phenocopies, i.e. phenotypically similar states with different underlying genotypes. The borderlines between the categories in the over-eating ranges are fuzzy. The presenting symptoms in the clinic are often unreliable and seem to defy the laws of thermodynamics.

The task seems more possible if one takes a more dimensional approach to the categorization of eating disorders. Then the group of patients whom we are describing represent those who have some symptoms, which do not lie at the extreme end of the pathological dimension. On the other hand some of their symptoms are similar in severity to full cases. This is illustrated by Figure 8.1 in which attitudes and behaviours relevant to eating disorders are conceptualized as dimensional such as dietary restraint, disinhibition of eating, use of methods to expend calories and dissatisfaction with weight or shape and so on. There may be several other dimensions which are relevant to consider such as the physiological adaptation to starvation, the value placed upon bodily perfection, the fear and disgust associated with eating, the level of persistence, anxiety and cautiousness.

Thus one of the main themes of this chapter is the concept of a clinical spectrum of eating disorders with a variety of underlying endophenotypes which can summate to produce a multiplexity of disorders with variable

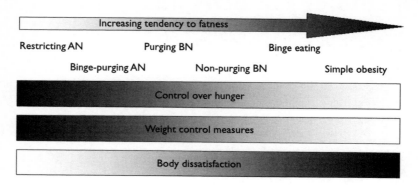

Figure 8.1 The diagnostic spectrum.

severity. An endophenotype, defined by Gottesman, is an internal phenotype discoverable by technology such as biochemical tests or microscopic examination (Gottesman and Gould 2003). Thus the concept of an endophenotype fills the gap between observable behaviours and descriptors and the underlying disease process. Not all endophenotypes are caused by genes although the concept has been used mainly in research with a genetic focus. Endophenotypes may be environmental, epigenetic or multifactorial in origin. The identification of endophenotypes can be useful in the construction of aetiological models and systems of classification.

Gottesman argues that optimally reduced measures of neuropsychiatric functioning (endophenotypes) should be more useful than diagnostic entities. The methods used for endophenotype analysis include neurophysiology, biochemistry, endocrinology, neuro-anatomy and cognitive neuropsychology. Gottesman has defined a set of five criteria that need to be met for a trait to be considered as a genetic endophenotype. These are:

1   The endophenotype is associated with illness in the population.
2   The endophenotype is heritable.
3   The endophenotype is primarily state-independent (manifests in an individual whether or not illness is active).
4   Within families, endophenotype and illness co-segregate.
5   The endophenotype found in affected family members is found in non-affected family members at a higher rate than in the general population.

Thus it is useful to test whether any putative risk factor for eating disorders fulfils these criteria. Within this framework, people with EDNOS probably share similar endophenotype markers but perhaps to a lesser degree, or other genes or environmental factors may have been protective and inhibited the full clinical presentation.

What are the observable physical aspects of eating disorders?

One of the key disturbances in AN is the severe persistent restriction of food intake such that weight falls to a level in which physiological adaptation to starvation occurs. (In women the most overt feature is amenorrhoea.) It is thought that this adaptation is orchestrated by a fall in plasma leptin levels. However, individuals in the atypical group may retain sufficient leptin at a low body mass index to maintain some neuro-endocrine function and menstruation while others may reduce their leptin levels to those which disrupt neuro-endocrine function even though their body mass index is greater than 17.5. Leptin levels are not merely a function of adipose tissue size and number.

Several types of eating behaviour are seen within the AN and the atypical AN groups. Restrictive AN individuals lose weight purely by dieting and exercise with no history of binge eating or purging. Other forms of anorexia include the presence of binge eating and/or purging behaviours. These latter groups also restrict their food intake to lose weight, but may experience a periodic disinhibition of restraint resulting in binge eating or may augment their restriction with purging behaviours.

By definition people with BN or atypical BN have a body weight above 85 per cent of average body weight (APA 1994). However, a subsection of this group do show some of the features of adaptation to starvation. Individuals with BN suffer recurring disinhibition of restraint resulting in cycles of binge eating and compensatory actions including self-induced vomiting, abuse of laxatives/diuretics, and excessive exercising. BN is not primarily associated with a primary, pathological increase in appetite; rather, like individuals with AN, individuals with BN have a seemingly relentless drive to restrict their food intake, an extreme fear of weight gain, and often have a distorted view of their actual body shape. Loss of control with overeating in individuals with BN usually occurs intermittently and typically only some time after the onset of dieting behaviour. AN and BN are not completely distinct.

As we move to the right of the spectrum, people with BED merge with some cases of obesity and do appear to have a tendency to overeat. The trend in obesity research over the recent decades has been to conceptualize it as a metabolic problem, i.e. a disorder of expenditure rather than a problem of intake, overeating. However, recent genetic research suggests that eating behaviours are a relevant part of obesity. Also the weight gain that is a side-effect of some of the new atypical neuroleptics illustrates how central mechanisms can interrupt weight and body composition homeostasis. This adds weight to the argument that places eating disorders on a spectrum with restrictive AN at one end and obesity at another.

The causes of eating disorders

One possible mechanism that underpins the various types of eating behaviours and disorders of body weight and composition is genetic variation and another is environmental exposure. These may have independent or interacting effects, which produce changes in brain and behaviour. Biological factors contribute to and interact with the various tiers of environmental input, interpersonal, societal and cultural to produce a broad array of unhealthy eating and nutritional balance. It can be difficult to unearth the underlying biological matrix of these complex behaviours.

In all of the disorders of eating and body composition there is a disruption in the pathophysiology of appetite, eating, satiation and metabolism. However, there is controversy as to whether these disturbances are primary or secondary. Hunger is a key drive in all living organisms. Eating is one of the basic primary reinforcers and has an impact on basal emotional tone producing pleasure. Thus the regulation of eating and emotions are intimately connected.

What are the eating behaviours, appetites and hunger?

Many experts dismiss the subjective and behavioural measures that are used as markers of appetite in people with eating disorders as unreliable and distorted. For example, Palmer (2000) suggests that appetite in AN is normal but kept under tight control. Others suggest that there must be some abnormality in the appetite control system in order to sustain such a negative homeostatic balance over time (Pinel *et al.* 2000). It is somewhat surprising that hunger and appetite in eating disordered people has received little systematic study so that each of these divergent views can be held with impunity.

Hunger and appetite across the spectrum

People who fulfil the criteria for AN and BN appear to lie at opposite ends of the biological response to appetite as illustrated in Figure 8.2. People with AN have higher levels of subjective fullness than a comparison group both before and after a meal (Robinson 1989). Other concomitants of decreased hunger and increased satiety are also present. Meals are prolonged, the rate of eating is slowed and there are more pauses within the meal (Sunday and Halmi 1996). People with AN salivate less than controls in response to olfactory food stimuli (LeGoff *et al.* 1988). Gastric emptying is delayed and as the subjective perception of fullness in AN correlates with gastric content this can explain the prolongation of satiety (Robinson *et al.* 1988).

Pinel and colleagues suggest that there is a decline in the positive incentive value of eating food to the left of the eating disorder spectrum. Taste has less

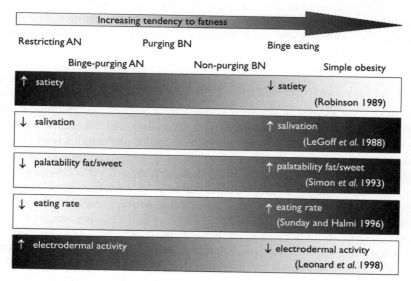

Figure 8.2 Response to food.

reward value (Sunday and Halmi 1990) and there is a reduced preference for high fat foods (Simon *et al.* 1993). Interestingly there is not a blanket, non-specific rejection of food. Food preferences vary appropriately with the metabolic context, thus sensory specific satiety occurs. This suggests that the response to food is subject to biological regulation albeit around an abnormal set point.

Not only do foods have less reward value but also the pleasurable emotional reaction to food is reversed to fear and disgust (Gomez *et al.* 2002). People with AN report anxiety when shown images of food (Ellison *et al.* 1998; Uher *et al.* 2002). Electrodermal activity increases during a meal (Leonard *et al.* 1998), which contrasts with the fall in electrodermal activity that occurs when a comparison group ate a meal in similar circumstances. Also an increase in autonomic arousal (as indicated by increased skin conductance) occurs during the Stroop "food" task (Perpina *et al.* 1998). The latter is completed more slowly by people with AN which indicates that food words interfere with cognitive tasks (Channon *et al.* 1988). In summary, the reaction to food in AN is unusual, as there are decreased preferences, a negative subjective emotional response, autonomic arousal and attentional bias.

The pattern of eating in people with BN is variable and dependent upon the environmental context. Under laboratory conditions people with BN restrict their intake (Rolls *et al.* 1997). However, if their eating is monitored over several days in an environment when they are free to binge and vomit then they eat significantly more than a comparison group (Hetherington *et al.*

1994). The positive incentive of food is increased in people who lie at this side of the spectrum. People with BN rate sweet tastes as more pleasant than a comparison group (Franko *et al.* 1994) and salivate more to olfactory stimuli than did a comparison group (LeGoff *et al.* 1988).

The neuro-endocrine response to eating

Various abnormalities in the neuro-endocrine response to a meal have been reported in AN. Insulin secretion to a meal or glucose is reduced in the acute state (Tamai *et al.* 1993; Uhe *et al.* 1992) and after recovery (Brown *et al.* in press). Pancreatic polypeptide levels (Uhe *et al.* 1992) and growth hormone (GH) are increased (Tamai *et al.* 1993). Research reports into cholecystokinin (CCK) release have been inconsistent. Some groups find a normal response (Geracioti *et al.* 1992; Pirke *et al.* 1994) whereas others report increased CCK (Harty *et al.* 1991; Phillipp *et al.* 1991; Tamai *et al.* 1993). It is uncertain how to account for these discrepancies. Possible reasons include the specificity of the assay, the type of meal or the patients. Many of these studies were completed before the distinction between the subtypes of AN was made in DSM-IV. Levels of ghrelin are high in acute AN as would be expected because of weight loss and are partially reduced by weight gain (Otto *et al.* 2001).

Leptin levels are decreased in AN (Baranowska *et al.* 1997; Lear *et al.* 1999; Monteleone *et al.* 2000b; Nakai *et al.* 1999) and the levels of soluble leptin receptor are increased (Jiskra *et al.* 2000). The binge purge subtype had higher levels of leptin than the restricting subtype (Mehler *et al.* 1999). Leptin levels correlate with fat cell mass and body mass index as would be expected. Leptin levels increase in AN with weight gain (Polito *et al.* 2000). There is a very weak effect for plasma leptin levels to be lower after full recovery in AN (Brown *et al.* in press) but this may be related to residual lower fat mass (Frey *et al.* 2000). People who have recovered from AN show an endocrine and metabolic response to a meal that is suggestive to increased sensitivity to insulin (Brown *et al.* 2003). No differences were found in cerebrospinal fluid (CSF) levels of leptin, neuropeptide Y and peptide YY after full recovery from all types of eating behaviour (Gendall *et al.* 1999).

Hunger and appetite in Bulimia Nervosa

Restraint theory has been one of the most influential models explaining the mechanisms of overeating in BN (Polivy and Herman 1985). This theory underpinned the cognitive behavioural model used in treatment (Fairburn *et al.* 1993). The essence of this model was that dietary restraint, during which weight fell below the biological set point or in the shorter term when the hunger drive was not inhibited by signals of satiety, predisposed to over-eating. This model is much less compelling in the case of BED when body weight is usually above the presumed biological set point. Furthermore, in

40 per cent of cases of BED there is no evidence that dieting or weight control precedes the onset of the disorder. Some people recall overeating when they were as young as 2 years old. Also treatments which focus on weight loss can be effective (Stice *et al.* 2003). The assumption of a homeostatic set point control of body weight would be that the hunger drive and predisposition to eat would be attenuated in states of overnutrition. Thus something other than forces regulating weight drives the overeating.

Food is one of the primary innate reinforcers. The detection of an internal imbalance such as low blood sugar in the case of hunger and the achievement or even the prospect of rectifying this imbalance usually initiates pleasure. Thus eating and related behaviours are tightly linked to positive emotions. It is therefore not surprising those emotional factors rather than hunger can trigger eating behaviours in some circumstances. People with BN respond to stressful imagery (personal rejection and loneliness) with an increase in hunger and the desire to binge (Tuschen-Caffier and Vogele 1999).

Meals (or glucose) produce less satiety in people with BN than in a comparison population (Kissileff *et al.* 1996). In many environmental settings a counter regulatory response occurs. The greater the size of the meal the stronger the desire to binge eat and a negative emotional reaction follows (Blouin *et al.* 1993; M.J. Devlin *et al.* 1997; Robinson 1989). Both the perception of gastric fullness and the rate of gastric emptying are abnormal in BN (Koch *et al.* 1998).

Neuro-endocrinology

People with BN have a blunting of cholecystokinin release following a meal (Geracioti and Liddle 1988). The levels of ghrelin appear to be higher than expected given the body mass index (Tanaka *et al.* 2002). If purging occurs insulin and glucose fall rapidly, this may serve to perpetuate the pattern of overeating (Johnson *et al.* 1994). Reduced leptin has been found in BN (Brewerton *et al.* 2000; Jimerson 2002; Monteleone *et al.* 2000a) even when weight and BMI were controlled for although some studies have found normal levels (Ferron *et al.* 1997). Low leptin levels persist after recovery from BN (Jimerson 2002). Brewerton *et al.* (2000) found that leptin levels were negatively correlated with baseline cortisol (not replicated by Monteleone *et al.* 2000b) and positively related to prolactin release following 5HT challenges. People with BN did not show such a profound reduction in leptin levels produced by acute fasting as a comparison group (Monteleone *et al.* 2000a).

Binge eating disorder

In a food laboratory people with BED eat more (in particular dessert and snack food) than people with simple obesity (Goldfein *et al.* 1993; Yanovski and Sebring 1994) but smaller quantities than those with BN (LaChaussee *et al.* 1992). People with BED have more difficulty in interpreting visceral sensations related to hunger and satiety (Eldredge and Agras 1994, 1996). Leptin levels are increased in BED (Monteleone *et al.* 2000b).

In conclusion the reaction to food in the BEDs contrasts to that in AN in that food retains its positive incentive. Eating behaviour is also dysregulated in that the satiety response is attenuated. As would be expected the leptin levels parallel body mass index and there is little evidence of any peripheral metabolic abnormalities.

The brain in people with eating disorders

The structural brain changes in people with eating disorders also appear to lie on a spectrum. People with AN have the most profound brain shrinkage (Dolan *et al.* 1988; Kohn *et al.* 1997) but the cerebral sulci are also widened in BN (Hoffman *et al.* 1989, 1990; Krieg *et al.* 1987). One MRI (magnetic resonance imaging) study found that the inferior frontal lobe cortex was reduced in size (Hoffman *et al.* 1989). To our knowledge there are no data on brain structure in BED. It is beyond the scope of this chapter to consider the neuro-anatomy relevant to eating disorders (for review see Uher *et al.* 2002). However, many atypical forms of eating disorders are associated with lesions in the prefrontal and temporal cortices and mesotemporal structures and hypothalamus predominantly on the right hand side.

The neural correlates of impaired appetite: brain scanning over the eating disorder spectrum

The basic biology of the neural correlates of appetite

The central information processing pathways for food stimuli in the visual, olfactory and gustatory modalities in the primate brain have been studied in depth. Rolls has summarized the findings from his meticulous series of experiments involving electrophysiological recording from individual neurones (Rolls and Baylis 1994). The initial processing of food stimuli occurs in the inferior temporal visual cortex (visual), olfactory bulb and piriform cortex (smell), and nucleus of the solitary tract, thalamus and insula (taste). These areas project to the amygdala, orbitofrontal cortex, lateral hypothalamus and striatum where the reward value of the stimuli is calibrated. The reward value assigned to food-related stimuli is modulated by integrated information from peripheral metabolism and the gastrointestinal tract.

The human biology of the neural correlates of appetite

A variety of scanning studies have investigated the human central appetite control system, which is composed of an orexigenic (i.e. appetite promoting) network and an inhibitory control (or anorexigenic) circuit; the balance between these two subsystems determines eating behaviour. Both external (visual, taste or olfactory) and internal appetite cues are associated with changes in blood flow in the orexogenic system. The orexigenic network (consisting of orbitofrontal and insular cortices, amygdala and hypothalamus) activates with fasting and it promotes feeding behaviour (Figure 8.3). The inhibitory, anorexigenic circuit consists of anterior ventromedial and dorso-lateral prefrontal cortices and acts to terminate eating, probably by direct inhibition of the orexigenic system (Del Parigi *et al.* 2002a, 2002b; Gautier *et al.* 2000; Gordon *et al.* 2000; LaBar *et al.* 2001; Liu *et al.* 2000; Morris and Dolan 2001; Small *et al.* 2001; Tataranni *et al.* 1999) (Figure 8.4).

The neural correlates of appetite in people with eating disorders

In response to food stimuli, patients with eating disorders (either AN or BN) recruit the orbitofrontal cortex and the anterior cingulate particularly on the left. Activation of the dorsolateral prefrontal area differs across eating disorder subtype and is reduced in BN. People who had recovered from AN also activated the orbitofrontal cortex and the anterior cingulate (Uher *et al.* 2003). This abnormal activation of the orbitofrontal cortex and anterior cingulate thus fulfils some of the criteria for an endophenotype. There are some interesting parallels between people with damage to the orbitofrontal cortex and people with AN. For example, people with ventral frontal lobe

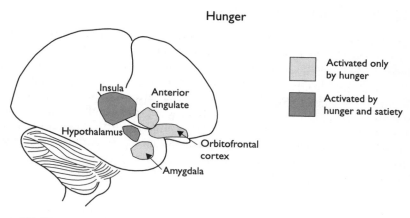

Figure 8.3 Orexigenic circuit.

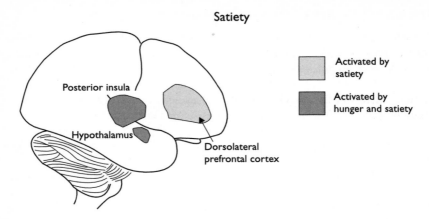

Figure 8.4 Anorexigenic circuit.

damage have impaired identification of facial and vocal expression. This disability correlates with the degree of alteration of their emotional experience (Hornak *et al.* 1996). Impaired identification of facial and vocal expression is present also in AN (Kucharska-Pietura *et al.* 2004). Animals with lesions of the prefrontal cortex experience an interceptive agnosia, an inability to determine how the body is reacting when faced with contrasting behavioural options. This resonates with the clinical descriptions of alexithymia (Cochrane *et al.* 1993; Troop *et al.* 1995) and poor interceptive awareness in AN (Bruch 1973). However, the orbitofrontal cortex is of key importance in many other aspects of brain function beside the control of appetite (Joseph 1999) and abnormal activation is found with other forms of psychopathology (Joseph 1999) and personality types (Cloninger 2002).

Brain function in eating disorders

Brain function has been examined in eating disorders using a wide array of tests of cognitive function (Lauer *et al.* 1999). The main conclusion from such studies is that many functional abnormalities disappear once weight is restored. However, there is a suggestion that there may be some abnormalities in executive function that remain present after weight restoration. For example, people with eating disorders have scores greater than one standard deviation from the norms on tests of perceptual rigidity, perseveration and set shifting and the neurological sign dysdiadokinesis (Tchanturia *et al.* 2001) which persist after recovery from AN (Tchanturia *et al.* 2002). Thus this is another possible endophenotype of relevance to eating disorders.

Neuro-endocrinology and neurotransmitters

The stress system: the hypothalamic pituitary adrenal axis in AN

Abnormalities in the regulation of the pituitary adrenal system have been implicated across the spectrum of eating disorder. Connan and colleagues have developed a neurodevelopmental model of AN (Connan and Treasure 1998; Connan *et al.* 2003). Early environmental experiences such as high levels of parental anxiety and insecure early attachments are thought to lead to a dysregulation and oversensitivity of the stress system. Stress later in life is though to result in high levels of cortisol, which is unresponsive to feedback. This effect is most pronounced in the subgroup with restrictive AN and it appears to remain after recovery which suggests that it is a vulnerability trait that is a candidate for endophenotype (Ward *et al.* 1998). However, a dysregulated stress response is not specific for AN but is also seen in depression. Connan argues that the specific problem in AN is a failure to switch ACTH secretagogue activity from CRH to AVP. Persistent high levels of CRH would disrupt appetite and weight homeostasis.

Neurotransmitters: Anorexia Nervosa

Several studies have examined the role of the central 5HT system in AN. Levels of plasma tryptophan are increased (Kaye *et al.* 2003) as are CSF levels of 5HIAA (Kaye *et al.* 1988). The release of prolactin is blunted to various 5HT challenges in acute AN (Brewerton and Jimerson 1996). Although the prolactin release to 5HT probes normalized after recovery (O'Dwyer *et al.* 1996; Ward *et al.* 1998) some aspects of 5HT-related appetite response remain abnormal either in the acute state (Brewerton and Jimerson 1996) or after long-term recovery (Ward *et al.* 1998). This suggests that some aspects of 5HT function may be dysregulated in AN. Tryptophan depletion produced a significant reduction in anxiety in both people acutely ill with AN and after recovery. Thus a dietary-induced reduction of TRP, the precursor of serotonin, is associated with decreased anxiety in people with AN (Kaye *et al.* 2003). Kaye speculates that restricting dietary intake may represent a mechanism through which individuals with AN modulate a dysphoric mood. The serotonin theory has also been tested by examining 5HT receptor levels in people who have recovered from an eating disorder. Reduced levels of 5HT2A binding were found in the mesial temporal cortex (including the amygdala and hippocampus) and to a lesser degree in the cingulate of women with a history of restricting AN (Frank *et al.* 2002). The mechanism underlying this phenomenon is unknown. The reduced receptor binding may be a process compensating for increased extra-cellular 5HT (Kaye *et al.* 1991). It is possible that increased 5HT activity is associated with compulsivity, which may predispose to dietary restriction.

Bulimia Nervosa

There has been very little work investigating the role of the HPA axis in BN. Some studies report pathophysiological changes similar to those found in AN (Kennedy *et al.* 1989) whereas others report normal values (Fichter *et al.* 1990).

There has been the suggestion that a low turnover of 5HT is linked to the severity of BN and that dieting-induced decreases in TRP availability may trigger the development of BN in susceptible individuals (Cowen and Smith 1999). Acute tryptophan depletion led to an increase in calorie intake and irritability in BN (Weltzin *et al.* 1995) and decreased mood, increased rating in body image concern and subjective loss of control of eating in people who had recovered from BN (Smith *et al.* 1999). The prolactin response to 5HT probes is reduced in BN (Jimerson *et al.* 1992). People with BN were found to have a 17 per cent reduction in the levels of serotonin transporter in the hypothalamus and thalamus and a 15 per cent reduction in levels of dopamine transporter in the striatum (Tauscher *et al.* 2001). A reduction in serotonin transporter was also found in obese binge eaters (Kuikka *et al.* 2001). People who had recovered from BN had reduced 5HT2A in the lateral and medial orbitofrontal cortex (Kaye *et al.* 2001). Furthermore this group of patients did not have the expected age-related decline in 5HT2A receptors. This reduction in 5HT tone may be related to the trait of impulsivity which in turn predisposes to binge eating. Steiger (2004) argues that state, trait and developmental influences impact on 5HT function in people with eating disorders, for example he cites evidence that suggests that traumatic experiences such as childhood abuse may affect serotonin functioning. In conclusion, the abnormalities in central 5HT function vary across the eating disorder spectrum. The persistent abnormalities after recovery suggest that 5HT function may be a marker of the endophenotype.

The underlying mechanisms: risk factors

We will now turn from some of these internal, biological markers, which may be aspects of the endophenotype or merely consequences of eating disorders and turn to some of the predisposing risk factors. Both extrinsic risk factors and intrinsic genetic vulnerability have been implicated in all conditions and may produce biological changes.

Genetic risk factors

It is only recently that the possibility of a genetic predisposition to eating disorders has been a serious subject of research interest. Many of the studies in this area are small or are limited because eating disorders have been added as a supplementary facet to a study of another condition.

The reliability of twin studies is limited because of low power. Most of these studies use a broad definition of cases in which the majority would fulfil the criteria of EDNOS rather than clinical cases of AN or BN. The best fit model for a broad anorexia-like phenotype (N = 77 out of 1030 twin pairs aged 29 from the Virginia twin registry) gave a heritability of 58 per cent (95 per cent CI 33–84 per cent) (Wade *et al.* 2000). In a second cohort of 672 female twins (age 17) the broad anorexia-like phenotype (N = 26) had a heritability of 74 per cent (95 per cent CI 33–94 per cent) and non-shared variance of 26 per cent (95 per cent CI 6–67 per cent) (Klump *et al.* 2000). In yet a third cohort of a population of 34,142 young Danish twins with self-reported AN or BN (total group N = 1270) the heritability of narrowly defined AN was 0.48, broad AN was 0.52 and BN was 0.61 (Kortegaard *et al.* 2001). When the broader phenotype of disordered eating attitudes and behaviours and BMI was modelled in two different age cohorts (age 11 and 17) of twins the pattern of variance differed. In the younger population shared environment dominated over genetic effects but this was reversed in the older cohort (Klump *et al.* 2000). The majority of the genetic variance on eating attitudes and behaviours in the older group was independent of genetic risk for BMI. Thus it is possible that a genetic risk factor, which increases the risk of abnormal attitudes to eating, is switched on by the hormonal changes at puberty.

Some of the genetic risk for eating disorders may be shared with other forms of psychopathology. For example there was a shared variance between AN and major depression of 34 per cent (95 per cent CI 13–71 per cent) (Wade *et al.* 2000). Unaffected MZ co-twins (N = 19) of people with AN-like phenotype had a increased risk of anxiety disorder compared to control MZ twins (N = 394) (OR 2.1; χ^2 = 4.5, p = 0.003) (Klump *et al.* 2001).

Unfortunately many of the family studies have not investigated the body size of family members. Hebebrand and Remschmidt (1995) marshal the evidence that there is a predisposition to leanness in the families of people with AN. It is not thought that this leanness is due to subclinical AN although the risk of AN (adjusted hazard ratio 11.4, 95 per cent CI 1.1–89; χ^2 = 5.3, p = 0.03) and BN (adjusted hazard ratio 3.5, 95 per cent CI 1.1–14; χ^2 = 3.9, p = 0.05) is increased in first-degree relatives of people with AN (Strober *et al.* 2000). The familial transmission between both types of eating disorder may be shared as the risk of AN (adjusted hazard ratio 12.1, 95 per cent CI 1.5–97; χ^2 = 8.8, p = 0.005) is increased in the first-degree relatives of people with BN (N = 171).

People with AN (N = 93, age 24 years) have first-degree relatives with a higher adjusted risk ratio of major depressive disorder (2.3, 95 per cent CI 1.1–4.8), generalized anxiety disorder (3.1, 95 per cent CI 1.5–6.8), obsessive-compulsive disorder (OCD: 4.1, 95 per cent CI 1.4–12.2) and obsessive-compulsive personality disorder (OCPD: 3.6, 95 per cent CI 1.6–8) (Lilenfeld and Kaye 1998). The rate of OCPD was similar in the relatives whether or not the person with AN was comorbid for OCPD. This suggests linked transmission for OCPD but not for the other forms of psychopathology.

Genetic vulnerability may involve factors relating to feeding and appetite, energy metabolism, development, personality and mood. Both genetic linkage analysis and association analyses have been performed. Genetic linkage analysis has identified a putative locus for restricting AN on human chromosome 1p (Grice *et al.* 2002) and for a composite quantitative phenotype, Drive for Thinness and Obsessionality, on human chromosome 1q (B. Devlin *et al.* 2002).

Candidate gene association analysis has identified a putative risk allele for AN in the serotonin receptor gene 5HT2A (Collier *et al.* 1997), but this has not been replicated in all subsequent studies (Gorwood *et al.* 2002) and in the Brain Derived Neurotrophic Factor gene (Ribases *et al.* 2004). Linkage, association and twin studies have been hampered by small sample size. Large-scale linkage studies in the United States and Europe are being performed with NIMH (National Institute of Mental Health) funding.

Early environmental risk factors

A case linkage study from Sweden found an increased risk of AN (ascertained from a psychiatric inpatient register) (N = 781) in girls born with a cephalohematoma (OR 2.4, 95 per cent CI 1.4–4.1) and those with prematurity (OR 3.2, 95 per cent CI 1.6–6.2) especially if the baby was small for gestational age (OR 5.7, 95 per cent CI 1.1–28.7) (Cnattingius *et al.* 1999).

Early environmental effects may set the level of activity of the appetite system. One such theory is that poor foetal and early postnatal growth may predispose to a thrifty genotype and metabolic problems in adult hood e.g. type 2 diabetes and the metabolic syndrome (Hales and Barker 2001) in the context of a later environment in which there is plenty. Small for gestational age infants appear to have reduced satiety as they drink a greater volume of milk (Ounsted and Sleigh 1975). This may be associated with the reduced levels of leptin seen in the cord blood of these infants (Ong *et al.* 1999). Thus poor nutrition in utero with access to better nutrition post-birth may predispose to overeating. In animals, poor postnatal nutrition can lead to a permanent reduction in appetite (Winick and Noble 1966). There is some evidence of a similar phenomenon in humans. Men who were exposed to the Dutch famine (1944–5) in the last trimester of pregnancy and early postnatal life had lower obesity rates at age 19 which contrasts with the higher obesity rates in those exposed to the famine in the first trimester (A.C. Ravelli *et al.* 1999; G.P. Ravelli *et al.* 1976). This effect remained in women aged 50 but not in the men from this cohort (Ravelli *et al.* 1999). Continuities in the patterns of eating do persist over childhood. For example, poor sucking in infancy is associated with picky eating at ages of 3.5 and 5.5 (Jacobi *et al.* 2003). In turn picky eating is associated with EDNOS AN type (Marchi and Cohen 1990).

Risk factors for Bulimia Nervosa

Genetics

A review of studies of BN suggests that between 31 and 81 per cent of the variance is accounted for by additive genetic effects (Bulik *et al.* 2000). There is thought to be a common genetic variance of approximately 20 per cent between depression and BN (Walters *et al.* 1992). There is a putative locus for BN on human chromosome 10p (Bulik *et al.* 2003). This locus is also implicated in obesity. Many of the genetic causes of obesity that are now being defined result from abnormalities in the central control of appetite with overeating as a consequence. For example, one of the commonest monogenic causes of obesity relates to mutations in the melanocortin receptor (Farooqi *et al.* 2000) and indeed a mutation on this receptor is associated with binge eating in obesity (Branson *et al.* 2003). Even outside these extremes of eating behaviours run in families. In a study on the Amish the heritability for disinhibition of eating was found to be 40 per cent and 30 per cent for restraint (Steinle *et al.* 2002).

The rate of parental obesity in women with BN or BEDs is increased (OR 4) (Fairburn *et al.* 1997). The risk of their parents suffering from depression, alcohol or substance abuse is also increased (OR 9–10) (Fairburn *et al.* 1997). Lilenfeld and Kaye (1998) review the evidence from family studies: the relative risk of mood disorders is increased twofold in the studies and the relative risk of substance abuse is weakly increased between one and twofold.

Developmental factors

High growth and a robust appetite may be part of the developmental endophenotype for BN and the binge-eating spectrum of disorders. For example, in a discordant sib-pair design, siblings with BN were more often overweight with less picky eating compared to their healthy siblings during childhood and this concurs with case control data in which the dieting domain (which included a personal and family history of obesity) was a specific risk factor for the bulimic disorders (Fairburn *et al.* 1997, 1998). The data on the offspring of mothers with BN are mixed: those who had a clinical eating disorder at the time of pregnancy tend to have infants that are lighter than average (Stein and Fairburn 1996) whereas in our pilot data in a epidemiological sample of mothers with a past history of BN we found them to be heavier. This may be linked to the predisposition to obesity which has been found to be linked to early patterns of eating behaviour. Adiposity in children at 2 and 6 years was found to be predicted by a vigorous feeding style at

2 weeks (Agras *et al.* 1990). Children from obese/overweight families had a higher preference for fatty foods (however the reported intake of fatty foods did not differ), a lower liking for vegetables and a more "overeating-type" eating style than children from lean parents (Wardle *et al.* 2001).

Conclusion

It is unclear where the borderlines of eating disorders in humans should now lie. For example it could be argued that the eating disorders and obesity can be conceptualized as lying on a continuum. It is probable that there is a complex interplay between genes and environment in all disorders of eating and body composition. There will be both quantitative and qualitative differences between individuals. For example, some people will have a higher loading on the genetic risk factors and yet others may encounter more severe environmental risks. Nevertheless it is interesting to note that some of the risk factors also lie on a continuum and there appear to be dose response relationships. Lean genes appear to run in families with AN whereas obesity or overeating genes run in families with overeating. Other risk factors do show these dose-related effects but produce specificity by virtue of their temporal impact. For example stress in the prenatal period may predispose to the undereating of AN whereas stress later in childhood may predispose to BN.

There are several possible biological traits that fulfil some of the criteria for being relevant endophenotypes. Thus a dysfunction in 5HT function and tests of executive function remain after recovery. Further work will need to establish whether such traits are heritable or whether they are scars from the illness.

It is hoped that a better understanding of the aetiological causes of risk factors will help people process and cope with the environmental adversities they encounter and alter their environment so that unhelpful interactions with their genetic propensities are minimized. It may be possible to match the individuals' needs with treatments offered.

Acknowledgements

We are grateful for the support of grant QLK1-1999-916 from the European Commission Framework V programme (http://www.cordis.lu/life/home.html); the Nina Jackson Eating Disorders Research Charity, and PPP foundation PPP grant – Ref. 1206/87 Gene and environmental factors in AN.

References

Agras, W.S., Kraemer, H.C., Berkowitz, R.I. and Hammer, L.D. (1990) "Influence of early feeding style on adiposity at 6 years of age", *Journal of Pediatrics* 116, 805–9.

American Psychiatric Association (1994) *Diagnostic and Statistical Manual of Mental Disorders*, 4th edn (DSM-IV), Washington, DC: APA.

Baranowska, B., Wasilewska-Dziubinska, E., Radzikowska, M., Plonowski, A. and Roguski, K. (1997) "Neuropeptide Y, galanin, and leptin release in obese women and in women with anorexia nervosa", *Metabolism* 46, 1384–9.

Blouin, A.G., Blouin, J., Bushnik, T., Braaten, J., Goldstein, C. and Sarwar, G. (1993) "A double-blind placebo-controlled glucose challenge in bulimia nervosa: psychological effects", *Biological Psychiatry* 33, 160–8.

Branson, R., Potoczna, N., Kral, J.G., Lentes, K.U., Hoehe, M.R. and Horber, F.F. (2003) "Binge eating as a major phenotype of melanocortin 4 receptor gene mutations", *New England Journal of Medicine* 348, 1096–103.

Brewerton, T.D. and Jimerson, D.C. (1996) "Studies of serotonin function in anorexia nervosa", *Psychiatry Research* 62, 31–42.

Brewerton, T.D., Lesem, M.D., Kennedy, A. and Garvey, W.T. (2000) "Reduced plasma leptin concentrations in bulimia nervosa", *Psychoneuroendocrinology* 25, 649–58.

Brown, N.W., Ward, A., Surwit, R., Tiller, J., Lightman, S., Treasure, J.L. and Campbell, I.C. (2003) "Evidence for metabolic and endocrine abnormalities in subjects recovered from anorexia nervosa", *Metabolism* 52, 296–302.

Brown, N., Ward, A., Surwit, R., Tiller, J., Lightman, S. and Treasure, J.L. (in press) "Evidence for the persistence of endocrine, metabolic and behavioural abnormalities in subjects recovered from anorexia nervosa", *International Journal of Eating Disorders*.

Bruch, H. (1973) *Eating Disorders: Obesity, Anorexia Nervosa and the Person Within*, New York: Basic Books.

Bulik, C.M., Sullivan, P.F., Wade, T.D. and Kendler, K.S. (2000) "Twin studies of eating disorders: a review", *International Journal of Eating Disorders* 27, 1–20.

Bulik, C.M., Devlin, B., Bacanu, S.A., Thornton, L., Klump, K.L., Fichter, M.M., Halmi, K.A., Kaplan, A.S., Strober, M., Woodside, D.B., Bergen, A.W., Ganjei, J.K., Crow, S., Mitchell, J., Rotondo, A., Mauri, M., Cassano, G., Keel, P., Berrettini, W.H. and Kaye, W.H. (2003) "Significant linkage on chromosome 10p in families with bulimia nervosa", *American Journal of Human Genetics* 72, 200–7.

Channon, S., Hemsley, D. and de Silva, P. (1988) "Selective processing of food words in anorexia nervosa", *British Journal of Clinical Psychology* 27, 259–60.

Cloninger, R.C. (2002) "Functional neuro-anatomy and brain imaging of personality and its disorders", in H. D'haenen, J.A. den Boer and P. Willner (eds) *Biological Psychiatry*, Chichester: Wiley.

Cnattingius, S., Hultman, C.M., Dahl, M. and Sparen, P. (1999) "Very preterm birth, birth trauma, and the risk of anorexia nervosa among girls", *Archives of General Psychiatry* 56, 634–8.

Cochrane, C.E., Brewerton, T.D., Wilson, D.B. and Hodges, E.L. (1993) "Alexithymia in the eating disorders", *International Journal of Eating Disorders* 14, 219–22.

Collier, D.A., Arranz, M.J., Li, T., Mupita, D., Brown, N. and Treasure, J. (1997) "Association between 5-HT2A gene promoter polymorphism and anorexia nervosa", *Lancet* 350, 412.

Connan, F. and Treasure, J.L. (1998) "Stress, eating and neurobiology", in H. Hoek, J. Treasure and M. Katzman (eds) *Neurobiology in the Treatment of Eating Disorders*, London: Wiley.

Connan, F., Campbell, I., Katzman, M., Lightman, S. and Treasure, J. (2003) "A neurodevelopmental model for the aetiology of anorexia nervosa", *Physiology and Behavior* 79, 13–24.

Cowen, P.J. and Smith, K.A. (1999) "Serotonin, dieting, and bulimia nervosa", *Advances in Experimental Medicine and Biology* 467, 101–4.

Del Parigi, A., Chen, K., Gautier, J.F., Salbe, A.D., Pratley, R.E., Ravussin, E., Reiman, E.M. and Tataranni, P.A. (2002a) "Sex differences in the human brain's response to hunger and satiation", *American Journal of Clinical Nutrition* 75, 1017–22.

Del Parigi, A., Gautier, J.F., Chen, K., Salbe, A.D., Ravussin, E., Reiman, E. and Tataranni, P.A. (2002b) "Neuroimaging and obesity: mapping the brain responses to hunger and satiation in humans using positron emission tomography", *Annals of the New York Academy of Sciences* 967, 389–97.

Devlin, B., Bacanu, S.A., Klump, K.L., Bulik, C.M., Fichter, M.M., Halmi, K.A., Kaplan, A.S., Strober, M., Treasure, J., Woodside, D.B., Berrettini, W.H. and Kaye, W.H. (2002) "Linkage analysis of anorexia nervosa incorporating behavioral covariates", *Human Molecular Genetics* 11, 689–96.

Devlin, M.J., Walsh, B.T., Guss, J.L., Kissileff, H.R., Liddle, R.A. and Petkova, E. (1997) "Postprandial cholecystokinin release and gastric emptying in patients with bulimia nervosa", *American Journal of Clinical Nutrition* 65, 114–20.

Dolan, R.J., Mitchell, J. and Wakeling, A. (1988) "Structural brain changes in patients with anorexia nervosa", *Psychological Medicine* 18, 349–53.

Eldredge, K.L. and Agras, W.S. (1994) "Instability of restraint among clinical binge eaters: a methodological note", *International Journal of Eating Disorders* 15, 285–7.

Eldredge, K.L. and Agras, W.S. (1996) "Weight and shape overconcern and emotional eating in binge eating disorder", *International Journal of Eating Disorders* 19, 73–82.

Ellison, Z., Foong, J., Howard, R., Bullmore, E., Williams, S. and Treasure, J. (1998) "Functional anatomy of calorie fear in anorexia nervosa", *Lancet* 352, 1192.

Fairburn, C.G., Marcus, M.D. and Wilson G.T. (1993) "Cognitive behavioural therapy for binge eating and bulimia nervosa: a comprehensive treatment manual", in C.G. Fairburn and G.T. Wilson (eds) *Binge Eating: Nature, Assessment and Treatment*, New York: Guilford Press.

Fairburn, C.G., Welch, S.L., Doll, H.A., Davies, B.A. and O'Connor, M.E. (1997) "Risk factors for bulimia nervosa: a community-based case-control study", *Archives of General Psychiatry* 54, 509–17.

Fairburn, C.G., Doll, H.A., Welch, S.L., Hay, P.J., Davies, B.A. and O'Connor, M.E. (1998) "Risk factors for binge eating disorder: a community-based, case-control study", *Archives of General Psychiatry* 55, 425–32.

Farooqi, I.S., Yeo, G.S., Keogh, J.M., Aminian, S., Jebb, S.A., Butler, G., Cheetham, T. and O'Rahilly, S. (2000) "Dominant and recessive inheritance of morbid obesity associated with melanocortin 4 receptor deficiency", *Journal of Clinical Investigation* 106, 271–9.

Ferron, F., Considine, R.V., Peino, R., Lado, I.G., Dieguez, C. and Casanueva, F.F. (1997) "Serum leptin concentrations in patients with anorexia nervosa, bulimia nervosa and non-specific eating disorders correlate with the body mass index but are independent of the respective disease", *Clinical Endocrinology* 46, 289–93.

Fichter, M.M., Pirke, K.M., Pollinger, J., Wolfram, G. and Brunner, E. (1990)

"Disturbances in the hypothalamo-pituitary-adrenal and other neuro-endocrine axes in bulimia", *Biological Psychiatry* 27, 1021–37.

Frank, G.K., Kaye, W.H., Meltzer, C.C., Price, J.C., Greer, P., McConaha, C. and Skovira, K. (2002) "Reduced 5-HT2A receptor binding after recovery from anorexia nervosa", *Biological Psychiatry* 52, 896–906.

Franko, D.L., Wolfe, B.E. and Jimerson, D.C. (1994) "Elevated sweet taste pleasantness ratings in bulimia nervosa", *Physiology and Behavior* 56, 969–73.

Frey, J., Hebebrand, J., Muller, B., Ziegler, A., Blum, W.F., Remschmidt, H. and Herpertz-Dahlmann, B.M. (2000) "Reduced body fat in long-term followed-up female patients with anorexia nervosa", *Journal of Psychiatric Research* 34, 83–8.

Gautier, J.F., Chen, K., Salbe, A.D., Bandy, D., Pratley, R.E., Heiman, M., Ravussin, E., Reiman, E.M. and Tataranni, P.A. (2000) "Differential brain responses to satiation in obese and lean men", *Diabetes* 49, 838–46.

Gendall, K.A., Kaye, W.H., Altemus, M., McConaha, C.W. and La Via, M.C. (1999) "Leptin, neuropeptide Y, and peptide YY in long-term recovered eating disorder patients", *Biological Psychiatry* 46, 292–9.

Geracioti, T.D. Jr, and Liddle, R.A. (1988) "Impaired cholecystokinin secretion in bulimia nervosa", *New England Journal of Medicine* 319, 683–8.

Geracioti, T.D. Jr, Liddle, R.A., Altemus, M., Demitrack, M.A. and Gold, P.W. (1992) "Regulation of appetite and cholecystokinin secretion in anorexia nervosa", *American Journal of Psychiatry* 149, 958–61.

Goldfein, J.A., Walsh, B.T., LaChaussee, J.L., Kissileff, H.R. and Devlin, M.J. (1993) "Eating behavior in binge eating disorder", *International Journal of Eating Disorders* 14, 427–31.

Gomez, P.P.S., Troop, N.A and Treasure, J.L. (2002) "Psychophysiology and eating disorders", in H. D'haenen, J.A. den Boer and P. Willner (eds) *Biological Psychiatry*, Chichester: Wiley.

Gordon, C.M., Dougherty, D.D., Rauch, S.L., Emans, S.J., Grace, E., Lamm, R., Alpert, N.M., Majzoub, J.A. and Fischman, A.J. (2000) "Neuroanatomy of human appetitive function: a positron emission tomography investigation", *International Journal of Eating Disorders* 27, 163–71.

Gorwood, P., Ades, J., Bellodi, L., Cellini, E., Collier, D.A., Di Bella, D., Di Bernardo, M., Estivill, X., Fernandez-Aranda, F., Gratacos, M., Hebebrand, J., Hinney, A., Hu, X., Karwautz, A., Kipman, A., Mouren-Simeoni, M.C., Nacmias, B., Ribases, M., Remschmidt, H., Ricca, V., Rotella, C.M., Sorbi, S. and Treasure, J. (2002) "The 5-HT(2A) –1438G/A polymorphism in anorexia nervosa: a combined analysis of 316 trios from six European centres", *Molecular Psychiatry* 7, 90–4.

Gottesman, I.I. and Gould, T.D. (2003) "The endophenotype concept in psychiatry: etymology and strategic intentions", *American Journal of Psychiatry* 160, 636–45.

Grice, D.E., Halmi, K.A., Fichter, M.M., Strober, M., Woodside, D.B., Treasure, J.T., Kaplan, A.S., Magistretti, P.J., Goldman, D., Bulik, C.M., Kaye, W.H. and Berrettini, W.H. (2002) "Evidence for a susceptibility gene for anorexia nervosa on chromosome 1", *American Journal of Human Genetics* 70, 787–92.

Hales, C.N. and Barker, D.J. (2001) "The thrifty phenotype hypothesis", *British Medical Bulletin* 60, 5–20.

Harty, R.F., Pearson, P.H., Solomon, T.E. and McGuigan, J.E. (1991) "Cholecystokinin, vasoactive intestinal peptide and peptide histidine methionine responses to feeding in anorexia nervosa", *Regulatory Peptides* 36, 141–50.

Hebebrand, J. and Remschmidt, H. (1995) "Anorexia nervosa viewed as an extreme weight condition: genetic implications", *Human Genetics* 95, 1–11.

Hetherington, M.M., Altemus, M., Nelson, M.L., Bernat, A.S. and Gold, P.W. (1994) "Eating behavior in bulimia nervosa: multiple meal analyses", *American Journal of Clinical Nutrition* 60, 864–73.

Hoffman, G.W., Ellinwood, E.H. Jr, Rockwell, W.J., Herfkens, R.J., Nishita, J.K. and Guthrie, L.F. (1989) "Cerebral atrophy in bulimia", *Biological Psychiatry* 25, 894–902.

Hoffman, G.W., Ellinwood, E.H. Jr, Rockwell, W.J., Herfkens, R.J., Nishita, J.K. and Guthrie, L.F. (1990) "Brain T1 measured by magnetic resonance imaging in bulimia", *Biological Psychiatry* 27, 116–19.

Hornak, J., Rolls, E.T. and Wade, D. (1996) "Face and voice expression identification in patients with emotional and behavioural changes following ventral frontal lobe damage", *Neuropsychologia* 34, 247–61.

Jacobi, C., Agras, W.S., Bryson, S. and Hammer, L.D. (2003) "Behavioral validation, precursors, and concomitants of picky eating in childhood", *Journal of the American Academy of Child and Adolescent Psychiatry* 42, 76–84.

Jimerson, D.C. (2002) "Leptin and the neurobiology of eating disorders", *Journal of Laboratory and Clinical Medicine* 139, 70–1.

Jimerson, D.C., Lesem, M.D., Kaye, W.H. and Brewerton, T.D. (1992) "Low serotonin and dopamine metabolite concentrations in cerebrospinal fluid from bulimic patients with frequent binge episodes", *Archives of General Psychiatry* 49, 132–8.

Jiskra, J., Haluzik, M., Svobodova, J., Haluzikova, D., Nedvidkova, J., Parizkova, J. and Kotrlikova, E. (2000) "Serum leptin levels and soluble leptin receptors in female patients with anorexia nervosa", *Casopis Lekaru Ceskych* 139, 660–3.

Johnson, W.G., Jarrell, M.P., Chupurdia, K.M. and Williamson, D.A. (1994) "Repeated binge/purge cycles in bulimia nervosa: role of glucose and insulin", *International Journal of Eating Disorders* 15, 331–41.

Joseph, R. (1999) "Frontal lobe psychopathology: mania, depression, confabulation, catatonia, perseveration, obsessive compulsions, and schizophrenia", *Psychiatry* 62, 138–72.

Kaye, W.H., Gwirtsman, H.E., George, D.T., Jimerson, D.C. and Ebert, M.H. (1988) "CSF 5-HIAA concentrations in anorexia nervosa: reduced values in underweight subjects normalize after weight gain", *Biological Psychiatry* 23, 102–5.

Kaye, W.H., Gwirtsman, H.E., George, D.T. and Ebert, M.H. (1991) "Altered serotonin activity in anorexia nervosa after long-term weight restoration. Does elevated cerebrospinal fluid 5-hydroxyindoleacetic acid level correlate with rigid and obsessive behavior?", *Archives of General Psychiatry* 48, 556–62.

Kaye, W.H., Frank, G.K., Meltzer, C.C., Price, J.C., McConaha, C.W., Crossan, P.J., Klump, K.L. and Rhodes, L. (2001) "Altered serotonin 2A receptor activity in women who have recovered from bulimia nervosa", *American Journal of Psychiatry* 158, 1152–5.

Kaye, W.H., Barbarich, N.C., Putnam, K., Gendall, K.A., Fernstrom, J., Fernstrom, M., McConaha, C.W. and Kishore, A. (2003) "Anxiolytic effects of acute tryptophan depletion in anorexia nervosa", *International Journal of Eating Disorders* 33, 257–67.

Kennedy, S.H., Garfinkel, P.E., Parienti, V., Costa, D. and Brown, G.M. (1989)

"Changes in melatonin levels but not cortisol levels are associated with depression in patients with eating disorders", *Archives of General Psychiatry* 46, 73–8.

Kissileff, H.R., Wentzlaff, T.H., Guss, J.L., Walsh, B.T., Devlin, M.J. and Thornton, J.C. (1996) "A direct measure of satiety disturbance in patients with bulimia nervosa", *Physiology and Behavior* 60, 1077–85.

Klump, K.L., McGue, M. and Iacono, W.G. (2000) "Age differences in genetic and environmental influences on eating attitudes and behaviors in preadolescent and adolescent female twins", *Journal of Abnormal Psychology* 109, 239–51.

Klump, K.L., Kaye, W.H. and Strober, M. (2001) "The evolving genetic foundations of eating disorders", *Psychiatric Clinics of North America* 24, 215–25.

Koch, K.L., Bingaman, S., Tan, L. and Stern, R.M. (1998) "Visceral perceptions and gastric myoelectrical activity in healthy women and in patients with bulimia nervosa", *Neurogastroenterology and Motility* 10, 3–10.

Kohn, M.R., Ashtari, M., Golden, N.H., Schebendach, J., Patel, M., Jacobson, M.S. and Shenker, I.R. (1997) "Structural brain changes and malnutrition in anorexia nervosa", *Annals of the New York Academy of Sciences* 817, 398–9.

Kortegaard, L.S., Hoerder, K., Joergensen, J., Gillberg, C. and Kyvik, K.O. (2001) "A preliminary population-based twin study of self-reported eating disorder", *Psychological Medicine* 31, 361–5.

Krieg, J.C., Backmund, H. and Pirke, K.M. (1987) "Cranial computed tomography findings in bulimia", *Acta Psychiatrica Scandinavica* 75, 144–9.

Kucharska-Pietura, K., Nikolaou, V., Masiak, M. and Treasure, J. (2004) "The recognition of emotion in faces and voice in anorexia nervosa", *International Journal of Eating Disorders* 35, 42–7.

Kuikka, J.T., Tammela, L., Karhunen, L., Rissanen, A., Bergstrom, K.A., Naukkarinen, H., Vanninen, E., Karhu, J., Lappalainen, R., Repo-Tiihonen, E., Tiihonen, J. and Uusitupa, M. (2001) "Reduced serotonin transporter binding in binge eating women", *Psychopharmacology* 155, 310–14.

LaBar, K.S., Gitelman, D.R., Parrish, T.B., Kim, Y.H., Nobre, A.C. and Mesulam, M.M. (2001) "Hunger selectively modulates corticolimbic activation to food stimuli in humans", *Behavioral Neuroscience* 115, 493–500.

LaChaussee, J.L., Kissileff, H.R., Walsh, B.T. and Hadigan, C.M. (1992) "The single-item meal as a measure of binge eating behavior in patients with bulimia nervosa", *Physiology and Behavior* 51, 593–600.

Lauer, C.J., Gorzewski, B., Gerlinghoff, M., Backmund, H. and Zihl, J. (1999) "Neuropsychological assessments before and after treatment in patients with anorexia nervosa and bulimia nervosa", *Journal of Psychiatric Research* 33, 129–38.

Lear, S.A., Pauly, R.P. and Birmingham, C.L. (1999) "Body fat, caloric intake, and plasma leptin levels in women with anorexia nervosa", *International Journal of Eating Disorders* 26, 283–8.

LeGoff, D.B., Leichner, P. and Spigelman, M.N. (1988) "Salivary response to olfactory food stimuli in anorexics and bulimics", *Appetite* 11, 15–25.

Leonard, T., Perpina, C., Bond, A. and Treasure, J. (1998) "Assessment of test-meal induced autonomic arousal in anorexic, bulimic and control females", *European Eating Disorders Review* 6, 188–200.

Lilenfeld, L.R. and Kaye, W.H. (1998) "Genetic studies of anorexia and bulimia nervosa", in H.W. Hoek, J. Treasure and M.A. Katzman (eds) *Neurobiology in the Treatment of Eating Disorders*, Chichester: Wiley.

Liu, Y., Gao, J.H., Liu, H.L. and Fox, P.T. (2000) "The temporal response of the brain after eating revealed by functional MRI", *Nature* 405, 1058–62.

Marchi, M. and Cohen, P. (1990) "Early childhood eating behaviors and adolescent eating disorders", *Journal of the American Academy of Child and Adolescent Psychiatry* 29, 112–17.

Mehler, P.S., Eckel, R.H. and Donahoo, W.T. (1999) "Leptin levels in restricting and purging anorectics", *International Journal of Eating Disorders* 26, 189–94.

Monteleone, P., Bortolotti, F., Fabrazzo, M., La Rocca, A., Fuschino, A. and Maj, M. (2000a) "Plamsa leptin response to acute fasting and refeeding in untreated women with bulimia nervosa", *Journal of Clinical Endocrinology and Metabolism* 85, 2499–503.

Monteleone, P., Di Lieto, A., Tortorella, A., Longobardi, N. and Maj, M. (2000b) "Circulating leptin in patients with anorexia nervosa, bulimia nervosa or binge eating disorder: relationship to body weight, eating patterns, psychopathology and endocrine changes", *Psychiatry Research* 94, 121–9.

Morris, J.S. and Dolan, R.J. (2001) "Involvement of human amygdala and orbito-frontal cortex in hunger-enhanced memory for food stimuli", *Journal of Neuroscience* 21, 5304–10.

Nakai, Y., Hamagaki, S., Kato, S., Seino, Y., Takagi, R. and Kurimoto, F. (1999) "Leptin in women with eating disorders", *Metabolism* 48, 217–20.

O'Dwyer, A.M., Lucey, J.V. and Russell, G.F. (1996) "Serotonin activity in anorexia nervosa after long-term weight restoration: response to D-fenfluramine challenge", *Psychological Medicine* 26, 353–9.

Ong, K.K., Ahmed, M.L., Sherriff, A., Woods, K.A., Watts, A., Golding, J. and Dunger, D.B. (1999) "Cord blood leptin is associated with size at birth and predicts infancy weight gain in humans. ALSPAC Study Team. Avon Longitudinal Study of Pregnancy and Childhood", *Journal of Clinical Endocrinology and Metabolism* 84, 1145–8.

Otto, B., Cuntz, U., Fruehauf, E., Wawarta, R., Folwaczny, C., Riepl, R.L., Heiman, M.L., Lehnert, P., Fichter, M. and Tschop, M. (2001) "Weight gain decreases elevated plasma ghrelin concentrations of patients with anorexia nervosa", *European Journal of Endocrinology* 145, 669–73.

Ounsted, M. and Sleigh, G. (1975) "The infant's self-regulation of food intake and weight gain: difference in metabolic balance after growth constraint or acceleration in utero", *Lancet* 1, 1393–7.

Palmer, R.L. (2000) *Helping People with Eating Disorders*, Chichester: Wiley.

Perpina, C., Leonard, T., Treasure, J., Bond, A. and Banos, R. (1998) "Selective processing of food and body related information and autonomic arousal in patients with eating disorders", *Spanish Journal of Psychology* 1, 3–10.

Phillipp, E., Pirke, K.M., Kellner, M.B. and Krieg, J.C. (1991) "Disturbed cholecystokinin secretion in patients with eating disorders", *Life Sciences* 48, 2443–50.

Pinel, J.P., Assanand, S. and Lehman, D.R. (2000) "Hunger, eating, and ill health", *American Psychologist* 55, 1105–16.

Pirke, K.M., Kellner, M.B., Friess, E., Krieg, J.C. and Fichter, M.M. (1994) "Satiety and cholecystokinin", *International Journal of Eating Disorders* 15, 63–9.

Polito, A., Fabbri, A., Ferro-Luzzi, A., Cuzzolaro, M., Censi, L., Ciarapica, D., Fabbrini, E. and Giannini, D. (2000) "Basal metabolic rate in anorexia nervosa:

relation to body composition and leptin concentrations", *American Journal of Clinical Nutrition* 71, 1495–502.

Polivy, J. and Herman, C.P. (1985) "Dieting and binging: a causal analysis", *American Psychologist* 40, 193–201.

Ravelli, A.C., Der Meulen, J.H., Osmond, C., Barker, D.J. and Bleker, O.P. (1999) "Obesity at the age of 50 y in men and women exposed to famine prenatally", *American Journal of Clinical Nutrition* 70, 811–16.

Ravelli, G.P., Stein, Z.A. and Susser, M.W. (1976) "Obesity in young men after famine exposure in utero and early infancy", *New England Journal of Medicine* 295, 349–53.

Ribases, M., Gratacos, M., Fernandez-Aranda, F., Bellodi, L., Boni, C., Anderluh, M., Cavallini, M.C., Cellini, E., Bella, D.D., Erzegovesi, S., Foulon, C., Gabrovsek, M., Gorwood, P., Hebebrand, J., Hinney, A., Holliday, J., Hu, X., Karwautz, A., Kipman, A., Komel, R., Nacmias, B., Remschmidt, H., Ricca, V., Sorbi, S., Wagner, G., Treasure, J., Collier, D.A. and Estivill, X. (2004) "Association of BDNF with anorexia, bulimia and age of onset of weight loss in six European populations", *Human Molecular Genetics* 13, 1205–12.

Robinson, P.H. (1989) "Perceptivity and paraceptivity during measurement of gastric emptying in anorexia and bulimia nervosa", *British Journal of Psychiatry* 154, 400–5.

Robinson, P.H., McHugh, P.R., Moran, T.H. and Stephenson, J.D. (1988) "Gastric control of food intake", *Journal of Psychosomatic Research* 32, 593–606.

Rolls, B.J., Hetherington, M.M., Stoner, S.A. and Andersen, A.E. (1997) "Effects of preloads of differing energy and macronutrient content on eating behavior in bulimia nervosa", *Appetite* 29, 353–67.

Rolls, E.T. and Baylis, L.L. (1994) "Gustatory, olfactory, and visual convergence within the primate orbitofrontal cortex", *Journal of Neuroscience* 14, 5437–52.

Simon, Y., Bellisle, F., Monneuse, M.O., Samuel-Lajeunesse, B. and Drewnowski, A. (1993) "Taste responsiveness in anorexia nervosa", *British Journal of Psychiatry* 162, 244–6.

Small, D.M., Zatorre, R.J., Dagher, A., Evans, A.C. and Jones-Gotman, M. (2001) "Changes in brain activity related to eating chocolate: from pleasure to aversion", *Brain* 124, 1720–33.

Smith, K.A., Fairburn, C.G. and Cowen, P.J. (1999) "Symptomatic relapse in bulimia nervosa following acute tryptophan depletion", *Archives of General Psychiatry* 56, 171–6.

Steiger, H. (2004) "Eating disorders and the serotonin connection: state, trait and developmental effects", *Journal of Psychiatry and Neuroscience* 29, 20–9.

Stein, A. and Fairburn, C.G. (1996) "Eating habits and attitudes in the postpartum period", *Psychosomatic Medicine* 58, 321–5.

Steinle, N.I., Hsueh, W.C., Snitker, S., Pollin, T.I., Sakul, H., St Jean, P.L., Bell, C. J., Mitchell, B.D. and Shuldiner, A.R. (2002) "Eating behavior in the Old Order Amish: heritability analysis and a genome-wide linkage analysis", *American Journal of Clinical Nutrition* 75, 1098–106.

Stice, E., Trost, A. and Chase, A. (2003) "Healthy weight control and dissonance-based eating disorder prevention programs: results from a controlled trial", *International Journal of Eating Disorders* 33, 10–21.

Strober, M., Freeman, R., Lampert, C., Diamond, J. and Kaye, W. (2000) "Controlled family study of anorexia nervosa and bulimia nervosa: evidence of shared liability and transmission of partial syndromes", *American Journal of Psychiatry* 157, 393–401.

Sunday, S.R. and Halmi, K.A. (1990) "Taste perceptions and hedonics in eating disorders", *Physiology and Behavior* 48, 587–94.

Sunday, S.R. and Halmi, K.A. (1996) "Micro- and macroanalyses of patterns within a meal in anorexia and bulimia nervosa", *Appetite* 26, 21–36.

Tamai, H., Takemura, J., Kobayashi, N., Matsubayashi, S., Matsukura, S. and Nakagawa, T. (1993) "Changes in plasma cholecystokinin concentrations after oral glucose tolerance test in anorexia nervosa before and after therapy", *Metabolism* 42, 581–4.

Tanaka, M., Naruo, T., Muranaga, T., Yasuhara, D., Shiiya, T., Nakazato, M., Matsukura, S. and Nozoe, S. (2002) "Increased fasting plasma ghrelin levels in patients with bulimia nervosa", *European Journal of Endocrinology* 146, R1–3.

Tataranni, P.A., Gautier, J.F., Chen, K., Uecker, A., Bandy, D., Salbe, A.D., Pratley, R.E., Lawson, M., Reiman, E.M. and Ravussin, E. (1999) "Neuroanatomical correlates of hunger and satiation in humans using positron emission tomography", *Proceedings of the National Academy of Sciences of the United States of America* 96, 4569–74.

Tauscher, J., Pirker, W., Willeit, M., de Zwaan, M., Bailer, U., Neumeister, A., Asenbaum, S., Lennkh, C., Praschak-Rieder, N., Brucke, T. and Kasper, S. (2001) "[123I] beta-CIT and single photon emission computed tomography reveal reduced brain serotonin transporter availability in bulimia nervosa", *Biological Psychiatry* 49, 326–32.

Tchanturia, K., Serpell, L., Troop, N. and Treasure, J. (2001) "Perceptual illusions in eating disorders: rigid and fluctuating styles", *Journal of Behavior Therapy and Experimental Psychiatry* 32, 107–15.

Tchanturia, K., Morris, R.G., Surguladze, S. and Treasure, J. (2002) "An examination of perceptual and cognitive set shifting tasks in acute anorexia nervosa and following recovery", *Eating and Weight Disorders* 7, 312–15.

Troop, N.A., Schmidt, U.H. and Treasure, J.L. (1995) "Feelings and fantasy in eating disorders: a factor analysis of the Toronto Alexithymia Scale", *International Journal of Eating Disorders* 18, 151–7.

Tuschen-Caffier, B. and Vogele, C. (1999) "Psychological and physiological reactivity to stress: an experimental study on bulimic patients, restrained eaters and controls", *Psychotherapy and Psychosomatics* 68, 333–40.

Uhe, A.M., Szmukler, G.I., Collier, G.R., Hansky, J., O'Dea, K. and Young, G.P. (1992) "Potential regulators of feeding behavior in anorexia nervosa", *American Journal of Clinical Nutrition* 55, 28–32.

Uher, R., Treasure, J. and Campbell, I.C. (2002) "Neuroanatomical basis of eating disorder", in H.A.D. D'haene, J.A. den Boer and P. Willner (eds) *Biological Psychiatry*, Chichester: Wiley.

Uher, R., Brammer, M.J., Murphy, T., Campbell, I.C., Ng, V.W., Williams, S.C. and Treasure, J. (2003) "Recovery and chronicity in anorexia nervosa: brain activity associated with differential outcomes", *Biological Psychiatry* 54, 934–42.

Wade, T.D., Bulik, C.M., Neale, M. and Kendler, K.S. (2000) "Anorexia nervosa and major depression: shared genetic and environmental risk factors", *American Journal of Psychiatry* 157, 469–71.

Walters, E.E., Neale, M.C., Eaves, L.J., Heath, A.C., Kessler, R.C. and Kendler, K.S. (1992) "Bulimia nervosa and major depression: a study of common genetic and environmental factors", *Psychological Medicine* 22, 617–22.

Ward, A., Brown, N., Lightman, S., Campbell, I.C. and Treasure, J. (1998) "Neuro-endocrine, appetitive and behavioural responses to d-fenfluramine in women recovered from anorexia nervosa", *British Journal of Psychiatry* 172, 351–8.

Wardle, J., Guthrie, C., Sanderson, S., Birch, L. and Plomin, R. (2001) "Food and activity preferences in children of lean and obese parents", *International Journal of Obesity and Related Metabolic Disorders* 25, 971–7.

Weltzin, T.E., Fernstrom, M.H., Fernstrom, J.D., Neuberger, S.K. and Kaye, W.H. (1995) "Acute tryptophan depletion and increased food intake and irritability in bulimia nervosa", *American Journal of Psychiatry* 152, 1668–71.

Winick, M. and Noble, A. (1966) "Cellular response in rats during malnutrition at various ages", *Journal of Nutrition* 89, 300–6.

Yanovski, S.Z. and Sebring, N.G. (1994) "Recorded food intake of obese women with binge eating disorder before and after weight loss", *International Journal of Eating Disorders* 15, 135–50.

Chapter 9

How family and twin studies inform the developing nosology of eating disorders

Cynthia M. Bulik and Charles B. Anderson

Introduction

The history of the nosology of eating disorders has been one of frequent change. These changes have occasionally been based on observation, such as the recognition of differences between "dieters" and "vomiters and purgers" (Beumont *et al.* 1976) or the identification of the bulimic subtype as an "ominous variant of anorexia nervosa" (Russell 1979). Other changes have been based more on opinion than on data. All modifications to the eating disorders nosological schema have not necessarily been improvements.

Much of the information that was used to inform changes to the DSM nosology for eating disorders (see Appendix for diagnostic criteria) came from clinical samples, which reflect only a small minority of affected individuals (Fairburn and Cooper 1982; Welch and Fairburn 1994). Further complicating the question of nosology in the eating disorders is a growing body of evidence suggesting that the range of presenting symptomatology may differ by gender.

This chapter will focus on how data from family and population-based twin studies can meaningfully inform questions regarding the nosology of eating disorders. As outlined in Bulik *et al.* (2000), there are three key questions regarding current nosology for eating disorders. First, how many eating disorders are there? Second, to what extent are the syndromes distinct or overlapping? Finally, given the fluidity of the boundaries across the eating disorders, how can we best account for changes in symptomatic presentation over time?

Family studies

Family studies, in their most basic form, are able to address the question, "Are eating disorders familial?" This is not, however, the limit to their informativeness as there are other questions related to nosology that can be addressed through the family study design. For example, in addition to identifying whether relatives of probands with an eating disorder are at increased risk for eating disorders themselves, family studies can also reveal whether relatives of probands with an eating disorder are also more likely to have had partial syndromes, sub-threshold conditions or atypical presentations. Such familial clustering can suggest aetiological overlap among various presentations of eating disorders. In addition, family studies can reveal whether individual eating disorders "breed true". That is, are relatives of individuals with AN only more likely also to have had symptoms of AN or might they also have had symptoms of BN? This can provide suggestive evidence of shared transmission of these two disorders and suggest aetiological overlap. The family design is limited however, in that it cannot provide information on the extent to which any of this observed familial aggregation is due to genetic or environmental factors.

So, what have the extant family studies told us about the current nosology of eating disorders? Most (Hudson *et al.* 1987; Kassett *et al.* 1989; Lilenfeld *et al.* 1998; Logue *et al.* 1989; Strober *et al.* 1990, 2000), but not all (Halmi *et al.* 1991; Stern *et al.* 1992) controlled family studies, have found a significantly greater lifetime prevalence of AN and BN among relatives of eating disordered individuals in comparison to relatives of controls. Studies which have not found elevated rates of eating disorders have been conducted using the family history method (whereby the proband acts as an informant for other family members), whereas those that have identified elevated relative risks have interviewed all family members directly.

Summarizing the above family literature as relevant to nosological issues, the following can be concluded. First, the prevalence of AN is significantly elevated in relatives of probands with AN. In the most comprehensive family study of AN to date, the rate of AN was 11.3 times as high in relatives of AN probands as in the relatives of comparison subjects. Moreover, the prevalence of partial AN syndromes was 5.7 times as high as in relatives of controls (Strober *et al.* 2000). The relative risk of AN in female relatives of males with AN was 20.3 (Strober *et al.* 2001). Second, the prevalence of BN is significantly elevated in relatives of probands with BN. In the Strober *et al.* (2000) study, the relative risk of BN in relatives of BN probands was 4.4. Third, the prevalence of BN appears to be elevated in relatives of probands with AN and the prevalence of AN appears to be elevated in relatives of probands with BN, suggesting some shared transmission of familial liability between these two disorders.

Substantially less is known about the familial aggregation of sub-threshold conditions, partial phenotypes and EDNOS in the families of probands with AN and BN. Early observations by Kalucy *et al.* (1977) suggested the presence of such sub-threshold and partial conditions in family members by noting either low adolescent weight, odd dieting habits, AN, or severe weight phobia in 27 per cent of mothers and 16 per cent of fathers of 56 cases of women with AN. Likewise, Strober *et al.* (1985) identified definite or probable (sub-threshold) AN in at least one first- or second-degree relative of

27 per cent of AN patients in comparison to 6 per cent of non-anorexic psychiatric controls. Large controlled family studies have found a significantly increased rate of sub-threshold eating disorders compared to relatives of controls (Lilenfeld *et al.* 1998; Strober *et al.* 2000). Lilenfeld *et al.* (1998) found significantly elevated rates of EDNOS and "any eating disorder diagnosis" (i.e. combined rates of AN, BN, BED and EDNOS) in first-degree relatives of anorexic and bulimic probands, suggesting that the eating disorders do not "breed true", but are expressed in families as a broad spectrum of eating-related pathology. Exploring this issue in greater depth, Stein *et al.* (1999) evaluated the complete spectrum of eating disorders among first-degree relatives of 47 probands with BN only (i.e. no history of AN). This study revealed the extent to which eating disorders syndromes overlap among family members. Among the bulimic probands, the most common diagnosis in female relatives was EDNOS. The nature of the EDNOS included bingeing or bingeing-purging symptomatology, restricting symptomatology, and a combination of bingeing-purging and restricting symptomatology.

On balance, evidence from family study data suggests there is an elevation in the lifetime prevalence of eating disorders among the relatives of people with eating disorders and that this aggregation is not necessarily disorder-specific. Moreover, suggestive evidence of the co-aggregation in families with AN, BN and sub-threshold eating disturbances raises the provocative possibility of shared aetiologic factors across these conditions. What family studies have not been able to address is factors that either contribute to an individual remaining "sub-threshold" versus developing a frank eating disorder (see twin studies in following section). For example, these findings might suggest the existence of a broad underlying genetic liability to disordered eating shaped, in part, by variability in unique environmental exposures across individuals within the same family. These questions, however, are beyond the scope of family study methodology.

Twin studies of eating disorders

The utility of twin studies in informing nosological decisions about eating disorders has only begun to be explored. In determining diagnostic "legitimacy" one criterion that has been applied is that of heritability (Robins and Guze 1970). That is, the heritability of a condition provides support for considering that syndrome to be a discrete diagnostic entity. Although this concept is limited and possibly flawed, heritability continues to be an important element in the equation weighing the validity of diagnostic schemas. In their most basic form, twin studies are capable of examining the extent to which liability to a disorder is due to genes and environment. There are, however, several additional nosology-related questions that have been addressed by various permutations of the twin design. The next section addresses the basic premise of twin studies, and is followed by a more elaborate discussion of how twin studies have helped us to further understand the phenomenology of eating disorders and their interrelationships.

Basics of twin studies

The goal of the classical twin study is to qualify and quantify similarities and differences between monozygotic (MZ) and dizygotic (DZ) twin pairs in order to identify and delineate genetic and environmental causes for a particular trait. Given that MZ twins have 100 per cent of their genes in common and DZ twins share, on average, half of their genes, any excess concordance in MZ twins over DZ twins suggests a genetic contribution to liability to the disorder. Conversely, any differences between MZ twins provides strong evidence for the role of environmental influences (Plomin *et al.* 1994), whereas differences between DZ twins can result from genetic and/or environmental effects. More complicated statistical modelling allows one to parse the variance in liability to illness into three sources: additive genetic effects (a^2), shared environmental effects (c^2) and unique environmental effects (e^2). Additive genetic effects reflect the cumulative impact on a trait of many individual genes each of which has a relatively small individual effect on the behavioural phenotype. The presence of a^2 is inferred when the correlation between MZ twins is greater than the correlation between DZ twins. By contrast, common environmental effects reflect aetiological influences to which both members of a twin pair are exposed, regardless of zygosity, and are implied when MZ and DZ correlations are equally high. Examples of such effects include the social class and religious preference of the family of origin. Unique environmental effects, on the other hand, result from aetiological influences to which one member of a twin pair is exposed but not the other, and contribute to differences between members of a twin pair. Examples include one member of a twin pair being exposed to a traumatic experience or a virus not shared with the co-twin.

Twin studies of Anorexia Nervosa

There are several case reports of clinically ascertained twins with AN (Askevold and Heiberg 1979; Nowlin 1983). The first systematic study of clinically ascertained twins with AN (Holland *et al.* 1984, 1988) found that MZ concordance was substantially greater than for DZ twins. We combined the data from all of these clinical reports and performed twin modelling in order to derive an approximate estimate of the heritability of AN. For the purpose of the analysis, we assumed a population prevalence of AN of 0.75 per cent and found evidence of familial aggregation with parameter estimates of 88 per cent (95 per cent CI 33–97) for a^2, 0 (95 per cent CI 0–59) for c^2 and 12 per cent (95 per cent CI 3–31) for e^2. Thus, these retrospective analyses suggested a rather strong contribution of genes to liability to AN.

In the first population-based twin analysis of AN, Walters and Kendler (1995) explored genetic and environmental contributions to the aetiology of AN. The concordance rates in MZ and DZ twins for a broad definition of AN were 10 per cent and 22 per cent suggesting no genetic contribution; however, the study was underpowered to draw firm conclusions regarding the contribution of genetic and environmental factors to the aetiology of AN. We later reanalysed these data following verification of zygosity status in the context of a bivariate twin analysis designed to explore the nature of the comorbid relation between AN and major depression (MD). In this analysis, the heritability of AN was estimated to be 58 per cent (95 per cent CI 33–84) and the genetic correlation between AN and MD was 0.58 indicating that the proportion of shared genetic variance between AN and MD was 34 per cent (95 per cent CI 13–71). Although the data are still preliminary, these twin studies suggest that liability to AN is indeed substantially influenced by the additive effects of genes and suggest that the familial aggregation observed in the family studies may be reflecting what is largely a genetic rather than an environmental effect.

Twin studies of Bulimia Nervosa

Similarly to our work on AN, we reanalysed three clinical case series of twins where one or both twins had BN (Fichter and Noegel 1990; Hsu *et al.* 1990; Treasure and Holland 1989). Each study showed greater MZ than DZ concordance for BN. Given the small numbers in each of the studies, we combined these data and performed classical twin modelling. In this model, assuming a population prevalence for BN of 2.5 per cent, BN showed evidence of familial aggregation with 47 per cent of the variance due to additive genetic effects, 30 per cent to shared environmental effects, and 23 per cent to unique environmental effects. The estimates were not precise as the confidence intervals around the parameter estimates were broad.

Table 9.1 includes our reanalyses of univariate twin analyses of BN. Two studies are from different waves of the Virginia Twin Registry (Bulik *et al.* 1998; Kendler *et al.* 1991) and one model from the Australian Twin Registry (Wade *et al.* 1999). There is reasonable consistency across these univariate models. The point estimates for a^2 are somewhat variable although the 95 per cent confidence intervals are overlapping (suggesting that the estimates are not widely variable). For c^2, the point estimates are near zero, but the confidence intervals (CIs) are broad and consistent across studies. There is a more substantial contribution of e^2 (which includes measurement error) as the confidence intervals did not contain zero.

The panel labelled "enhanced power" presents the three studies that used varying strategies to increase statistical power to detect a^2 and c^2 by including

Table 9.1 An analysis of twin studies of Bulimia Nervosa

Sample	Author	Sample size		Concordance		Full model		
		MZ	DZ	MZ	DZ	a^2	c^2	e^2
Univariate	Kendler et al. 1991	590	440	0.23	0.09	54 (0–77)	1 (0–65)	46 (23–77)
	Bulik et al. 1998	497	353	0.09	0.00	51 (0–86)	0 (0–68)	49 (14–100)*
		497	353	0.47	0.07	31 (0–54)	0 (0–35)	67 (46–94)**
	Wade et al. 1999	1232	747	0.08	0.00	32 (0–68)	0 (0–52)	68 (32–100)
Enhanced power	Kendler et al. 1995	590	440	n/a		28 (7–62)	37 (10–59)	35 (19–49)
	Bulik et al. 1998	(see text)		(see text)		83 (49–100)	0 (0–30)	17 (0–36)
	Wade et al. 1999	(see text)		(see text)		59 (36–68)	0 (0–11)	41 (33–48)

Source: Adapted from Bulik et al. (2000b).

Notes: MZ = monozygotic twin pairs, DZ = dizygotic twin pairs.
a^2 = additive genetic effects, c^2 = shared environmental effects, e^2 = unique environmental effects.
* = narrowly defined BN, ** = broadly defined BN.

BN diagnoses in a multivariate twin model (Kendler *et al.* 1995) or incorporating more than one occasion of measurement (Bulik *et al.* 1998; Wade *et al.* 1999). The effects of increasing statistical power are reflected in the narrower confidence intervals suggesting more precise estimates. It is critical to note that the two studies that corrected for measurement error had greater power to detect both c^2 and a^2. In these studies, the point estimates of a^2 were higher and the confidence intervals suggested a substantial contribution of additive genetic effects (a^2). The point estimates of c^2 were quite low, but the confidence intervals allowed for the possibility of some contribution of shared environment. In both studies the confidence intervals for the a^2 estimates and the c^2 estimates did not overlap. Controlling for measurement error and increasing statistical power, it appears that the contribution of a^2 to liability to BN is more substantive than the contribution of c^2. Therefore, similar to the twin studies of AN, in aggregate, these results suggest that the familiality of BN observed in family studies is largely due to the effects of genes rather than the effect of shared or common environment, lending legitimacy to the distinct diagnostic entity of BN as a heritable condition.

Boundaries and diagnostic overlap

Another key nosological issue in eating disorders is the extent to which AN and BN are aetiologically distinct. AN and BN are probably neither completely independent nor completely overlapping conditions. Despite the frequency with which the two disorders co-occur both concurrently and sequentially, we know little about the pattern and predictors of the observed comorbidity. A number of outcome studies of AN have been conducted which specifically address the percentage of patients who have developed BN at the time of follow-up assessment (Eckert *et al.* 1995; Gillberg *et al.* 1994; Herpertz-Dahlman *et al.* 1996; Hsu *et al.* 1992; Schork *et al.* 1994; Smith *et al.* 1993; van der Ham *et al.* 1994; Zipfel *et al.* 2000). The duration of the follow-up intervals ranged from 4 to 22 years and the percentage of individuals at follow-up who met diagnostic criteria for DSM-III BN or DSM-III-R BN ranged from 8 to 41 per cent. Across studies, the percentage of individuals with BN tended to be greater the longer the follow-up interval. In a pilot study with a very long observation period of 22 years, Hsu *et al.* (1992) reported that 19 per cent of women with AN met criteria for BN at follow-up. In addition to frank diagnoses of BN, 14–36 per cent of women in these studies met criteria for EDNOS (Gillberg *et al.* 1994; Herpertz-Dahlman *et al.* 1996; Schork *et al.* 1994; Smith *et al.* 1993) which includes women with bulimic symptoms of insufficient frequency or duration to qualify for a diagnosis of BN. Further evidence for the relation between AN and BN is reflected in the fact that a significant minority (22–37 per cent) of women with BN in clinical samples report a history of AN (e.g. Braun *et al.* 1994;

Fairburn and Cooper 1984; Pyle *et al.* 1981; Russell 1979; Schmidt *et al.* 1993; Sullivan *et al.* 1996). Finally, cross-sectional investigations have identified a range of symptom combinations ranging from the restricting subtype of AN, the mixed clinical picture of AN and BN, current BN with a history of AN, and BN with no history of AN (Braun *et al.* 1994; Herzog *et al.* 1992).

The above clinical studies are all subject to referral bias, which could conceivably inflate the observed frequency with which AN and BN co-occur either concurrently or sequentially. Arguing against this, however, are epidemiological studies of non-clinical populations indicating an elevated odds ratio between AN and BN (OR = 8.2) (Kendler *et al.* 1991; Walters and Kendler 1995).

Theoretically, twin studies are uniquely positioned to identify the nature of the relation between two related disorders such as AN and BN. However, an observed association between two disorders could result from numerous processes (Klein and Riso 1994; Neale and Kendler 1995). It is critical to note that not all of these processes represent causal associations (e.g. an observed association between two disorders might merely be due to chance or to biased sampling). More complex latent variable models (Neale and Kendler 1995) incorporating one or more underlying liability dimensions are also possible. For example, two seemingly separate disorders may be modelled as alternate forms originating from a common liability dimension. Alternatively, the existence of several liability dimensions can result in complex interrelations between two conditions. Assumptions about the nature of the association between two conditions are amenable to formal hypothesis testing and can be addressed using twin designs.

An illustrative example of how twin studies can elucidate the nature of comorbidity between two related disorders – and thus directly inform nosological issues – is the relation between MD and generalized anxiety disorder (GAD). Using bivariate twin modelling, Kendler *et al.* (1992) were able to determine that in women, liability to MD and GAD is influenced by the same genetic factors. In fact, they found that all of the genes that influence liability to MD also influence liability to GAD and vice versa. This means that there is a common genetically influenced neurobiological diathesis to both disorders. It appears that what determines whether those genetic vulnerabilities are expressed as either MD or GAD rests with environmental experiences. It is precisely this type of analysis that will have direct bearing on our understanding of the relation between AN and BN. Unfortunately, to date, no twin study has had sufficient statistical power to explore the extent to which genetic and environmental factors that contribute to liability to AN and BN are shared. Larger population-based twin samples are required in order to explore this question in these relatively low prevalence disorders.

Gender differences in symptom expression

Twin studies are also valuable tools in determining the extent to which a nosological system is equally applicable to males and females. As noted by Andersen and Holman (1997), "few disorders in general medicine are as skewed in gender distribution as eating disorders." Both clinical and case series (Braun *et al.* 1999) and epidemiological studies (Rastam *et al.* 1989) support a gender ratio for AN and BN of approximately 10:1. Of interest to the study of the epidemiology of eating disorders is the prevalence of sub-threshold eating disorder symptomatology as revealed in endorsement of symptoms of AN, BN and BED. For example, in a sample of college students, 1.3 per cent of females and 0.2 per cent of males met DSM-III-R criteria for BN, whereas the prevalence of bulimic symptomatology was 6.6 per cent for females and 3.6 per cent for males (Pemberton *et al.* 1996).

In addition, there may be differences in the ways eating disorders are expressed in males and females that have direct bearing on nosological issues. The history of eating disorders as a gender-bound construct has resulted in detailed explication of the varieties of clinical presentation among women with eating disorders (including binge eating, vomiting, laxatives, self-evaluation based on weight). However, the ways in which these well-documented presentations may differ from those found among males is just beginning to be explored. If differences in symptom frequency and expression do exist across genders, the current nosology could underestimate the prevalence of eating disorders in males.

A few studies have found similarities between males and females in the presentation of eating disorder symptoms and correlates such as body dissatisfaction, rates of familial psychiatric disorders, family dynamics, course of illness and treatment response (Olivardia *et al.* 1995; Pope *et al.* 1986; Woodside *et al.* 2001). However, these studies also identified gender differences with males being more likely to exercise excessively as a compensatory behaviour, more likely to be involved in professions or sports that emphasized weight, and less likely to use laxatives. One study of gender differences found similarities on demographic variables, and on the types of weight control programmes utilized, but found differences in dieting frequency and severity of post-binge emotional response (Rolls *et al.* 1991). A more commonly reported distinction is related to homosexuality or gender identity disturbance, which appears to be slightly more prevalent in males with eating disorders (Herzog *et al.* 1991; Mitchell and Goff 1984; Steiger *et al.* 1989; Yager *et al.* 1988). These reports are based on DSM diagnoses, which were developed primarily from observations of eating disorder presentations in females, and which may be upward-biased in females.

Twin studies which include all five zygosity groups (MZ female–female, DZ female–female, MZ male–male, DZ male–male, and DZ opposite sex) allow one to explore several nosologically relevant questions. First, what is the relation between the genetic and environmental determinants of eating disorders in women and men? Is the magnitude and the nature of the contribution of genes and environment similar or different across gender? Second, can we identify an underlying predisposition to illness that is transmitted within families that has gender-specific manifestations? Third, given high liability, do women tend to manifest eating disorders and men some other disorder?

We have recently completed the first in a series of investigations into the gender issue in twins. Reichborn-Kjennerud *et al.* (2003) studied binge eating, a core symptom in BN, to assess whether genetic and environmental effects are of equal importance for males and females and whether the same genetic risk factors predispose to binge eating in the two sexes. We used questionnaire data on 8045 same sex and opposite sex twins, aged 19 to 31 years, from a population-based registry of Norwegian twins. Results suggested that the magnitude of genetic and environmental effects on binge eating was the same for males and females. Heritability was 51 per cent (95 per cent CI 43–58) and the remaining 49 per cent (95 per cent CI 42–57) of the variance in liability was due to individual-specific environment. Of note, however, genetic risk factors for binge eating were not identical in men and women as the genetic correlation was estimated to be + 0.57. From this initial analysis, binge eating appears to be equally heritable in males and females, and although the majority of the genetic risk factors are shared between the sexes, there may exist gender-specific genetic effects on liability to binge eating.

Further studies along these methodological lines will assist us with understanding the gender imbalance in eating disorders and also allow us to address whether the current nosological systems accurately capture the nature of disordered eating in males.

Twin studies of component behaviours and related phenotypes

Another approach to dismantling the nosology of eating disorders is to perform twin modelling on component behaviours of eating disorders or to use continuous measures that may be aetiologically related to eating disorders (Neale and Cardon 1992). Sullivan *et al.* (1998b) used data from the Virginia Twin Registry to dismantle BN into its component behaviours of objective binge eating and self-induced vomiting. For binge eating, the parameter estimates were as follows: a^2: 46 per cent (95 per cent CI 22–58), c^2: 0 (95 per cent CI 0–18), and e^2: 54 per cent (95 per cent CI 42–68). For vomiting, the estimates were: a^2: 70 per cent (95 per cent CI 03–84), c^2: 0 (95 per cent CI 0–59), and e^2: 30 per cent (95 per cent CI 16–50). The genetic correlation between bingeing and vomiting was estimated to be 0.74. This means a rather high genetic contribution to both bingeing and vomiting and a substantial overlap in the genetic factors that influence liability to both behaviours. This approach is informative to nosology because the results are broadly consistent with current diagnostic schema for BN that include bingeing and vomiting under the same rubric. These two behaviours are strongly associated and the high genetic correlation between them suggests that they result from substantially overlapping genetic factors. The correlation of individual specific environmental factors that contributed to bingeing and vomiting was not as high, which suggests that there may be aetiological heterogeneity between the environmental factors that contribute to liability to binge eating and to vomiting.

Five studies have examined continuous measures of eating disorder-related behaviours and attitudes. The earliest study (Holland et al. 1988) examined the Eating Disorders Inventory (EDI: Garner et al. 1984) and only reported a heritability estimate for the "drive for thinness" scale which was "near 1.0", with large standard errors. Rutherford et al. (1993) reported heritability estimates ranging from 28 to 52 per cent for EDI subscales. In 11- and 17-year-old twins from the Minnesota Twin Study, there were marked differences between the age cohorts on the EDI (Klump et al. 2000). For the younger adolescents, there were contributions of both a^2 and c^2 to most subscales. For the older group, the contribution of a^2 outweighed the contribution of c^2. These results suggest the influence of developmental effects on the genetic and environmental sources of liability to eating disorders.

Studies from the Australian Twin Registry (Wade et al. 1998) examined measures of dietary restraint and concern about eating, weight and shape from the Eating Disorders Examination (Fairburn and Cooper 1993). The twin model including only additive genetic and unique environmental factors (AE model) provided the best fit for the total EDE score with a^2 estimated at 62 per cent (95 per cent CI 21–71). Individual variation of three of the EDE subscale measures was also best explained by the AE model, with heritability ranging from 32 to 62 per cent. The exception was the Weight Concern measure, best explained by a model incorporating only common and unique environment (no genetic effects – CE model) with the contribution of c^2 estimated to be 52 per cent (95 per cent CI 43–64).

These twin studies of related phenotypes are critical to nosology because it is highly unlikely that the human genome maps directly on to extant nosological systems. For example, it is unlikely that there are genes that code specifically for AN, BN and EDNOS. More plausible is a series of genes that contribute to the core features of these syndromes that then combine in various ways with each other and with environmental influences to manifest in the ultimate clinical presentation. These studies help us to discover which of these component symptoms are genetically influenced and which appear to be more the result of environmental influences.

From symptoms to syndromes

As noted in the earlier section on family studies, family members of probands with AN and BN often suffer from sub-threshold or partial syndromes. Twin studies allow one to dismantle a syndrome into stages and explore the extent to which the patterns and predictors of the initial stage of a disorder are similar to or different from patterns and predictors of the subsequent emergence of the full syndrome. We conducted these analyses with BN and explored the nature of risk factors for the emergence of binge eating in relation to the nature of risk factors that influence the transition from binge eating to frank BN (Wade *et al.* 2000). First, it appeared that the genetic risk factors that are important in the establishment of binge eating are also important in the transition from binge eating to BN. This is broadly consistent with the understanding of bulimic behaviours lying on a continuum of liability. Of particular interest, however, was that environmental factors experienced uniquely by each twin appear to be important in determining whether a person who has started to binge eat goes on to develop frank BN. This finding could assist in explaining the frequency with which partial syndromes appear in family members. Whereas an underlying shared genetic liability might influence the expression of these core symptoms (e.g. binge eating), it may be the presence or absence of evocative unique environmental events that determines whether a given genetically vulnerable individuals goes on to develop a full syndrome.

Diagnostic thresholds

Another nosological issue that twin studies can be used to address is the question of diagnostic thresholds. The eating disorders diagnostic schema has been plagued by somewhat arbitrarily determined duration and frequency criteria; however, the extent to which these thresholds are biologically meaningful has been unclear. These thresholds are important because they are used to delineate "caseness" from sub-threshold conditions. The most contentious threshold criterion for BN in the DSM-IV nomenclature is the "C" criterion which requires bingeing and purging, on average, twice per week for three months. The lack of empirical justification for this criterion has been widely noted (Garfinkel *et al.* 1996; Mitchell *et al.* 1996; Wilson and Eldredge 1991). Moreover, a number of studies support a "spectrum" concept of BN which suggests that individuals with bulimic behaviours below or above a certain threshold lie on a continuum and differ quantitatively but not qualitatively (Drewnowski *et al.* 1994; Fairburn and Beglin 1990; Garfinkel *et al.* 1995; Hay *et al.* 1996; Kendler *et al.* 1991; Sullivan *et al.* 1998a).

Sullivan *et al.* (1998a) optimized the twin design in order to empirically validate the usefulness of the frequency/duration criterion using Cox proportional hazard modelling. They varied the thresholds for binge eating and vomiting and calculated risk to co-twins across an array of thresholds. If an optimal threshold existed (i.e. one that reflects a true aetiological discontinuity and delineates a qualitative difference), they should have observed an obvious discontinuity in risk to co-twin at the empirically "best" threshold (Kendell and Brockington 1980). This was a direct test of whether the current DSM-IV thresholds actually reflect an underlying biological truth. Exploring a number of validators led to the following conclusion. First, there was no support for the current DSM thresholds. Second, there was one observed discontinuity in co-twin risk, which was associated with a binge frequency of once per week, which is half of that suggested by DSM-IV criteria. Restated, at the threshold of one binge per week, the risk of the same definition of binge eating in the co-twin was markedly greater. Third, there was no evidence for the twice per week threshold for vomiting. In fact, the data suggested that vomiting as infrequently as twice per month may be the optimal threshold as determined by risk to co-twin. This study perhaps represents the best example of how twin studies can have direct and relevant bearing on nosological questions.

Conclusion

Genetic epidemiological investigations of eating disorders, unfortunately, lag well behind those of other complex psychiatric phenotypes. In part this is due to delays caused by the prior ubiquitous conceptualization of AN and BN as disorders that were primarily of sociocultural origin. This delay means that although inroads have been made, that many of the potential applications of twin designs to questions of nosology remain theoretical at this point in time. As larger population-based twin studies emerge that incorporate more sophisticated measures of the phenotypes, our results will no doubt have more far-reaching impact on future decisions regarding the nosology of eating disorders.

References

Andersen, A.E. and Holman, J.E. (1997) "Males with eating disorders: challenges for treatment and research", *Psychopharmacology Bulletin* 33, 391–7.

Askevold, F. and Heiberg, A. (1979) "Anorexia nervosa: two cases in discordant MZ twins", *Psychotherapy and Psychosomatics* 32, 223–8.

Beumont, P.J.V., George, G.C.W. and Smart, D.E. (1976) " 'Dieters' and 'vomiters and purgers' in anorexia nervosa", *Psychological Medicine* 6, 617–22.

Braun, D.L., Sunday, S.R. and Halmi, K.A. (1994) "Psychiatric comorbidity in patients with eating disorders", *Psychological Medicine* 24, 859–67.

Braun, D.L., Sunday, S.R., Huang, A. and Halmi, K.A. (1999) "More males seek treatment for eating disorders", *International Journal of Eating Disorders* 25, 415–24.

Bulik, C.M., Sullivan, P.F. and Kendler, K.S. (1998) "Heritability of binge eating and broadly defined bulimia nervosa", *Biological Psychiatry* 44, 1210–18.

Bulik, C.M., Sullivan, P.F. and Kendler, K.S. (2000) "An empirical study of the classification of eating disorders", *American Journal of Psychiatry* 157, 886–95.

Drewnowski, A., Yee, D., Kurth, C. and Krahn, D. (1994) "Eating pathology and DSM-III-R bulimia nervosa: a continuum of behavior", *American Journal of Psychiatry* 151, 1217–19.

Eckert, E.D., Halmi, K.A., Marchi, P., Grove, W. and Crosby, R. (1995) "Ten-year follow-up of anorexia nervosa: clinical course and outcome", *Psychological Medicine* 25, 143–56.

Fairburn, C.G. and Beglin, S.J. (1990) "Studies of the epidemiology of bulimia nervosa", *American Journal of Psychiatry* 147, 401–8.

Fairburn, C.G. and Cooper, P.J. (1982) "Self-induced vomiting and bulimia nervosa: an undetected problem", *British Medical Journal* 284, 1153–5.

Fairburn, C.G. and Cooper, P.J. (1984) "The clinical features of bulimia nervosa", *British Journal of Psychiatry* 144, 238–46.

Fairburn, C.G. and Cooper, Z. (1993) "The Eating Disorder Examination, 12th edn", in C.G. Fairburn and G.T. Wilson (eds) *Binge Eating: Nature, Treatment and Assessment*, New York: Guilford Press.

Fichter, M.M. and Noegel, R. (1990) "Concordance for bulimia nervosa in twins", *International Journal of Eating Disorders* 9, 255–63.

Garfinkel, P., Lin, E., Goering, P., Spegg, C., Goldbloom, D., Kennedy, S., Kaplan, A. and Woodside, D. (1995) "Bulimia nervosa in a Canadian community sample: prevalence and comparison of subgroups", *American Journal of Psychiatry* 152, 1052–8.

Garfinkel, P., Kennedy, S. and Kaplan, A. (1996) "Views on classification and diagnosis of eating disorders", *Canadian Journal of Psychiatry* 40, 445–56.

Garner, D., Olmsted, M. and Polivy, J. (1984) *Eating Disorders Inventory Manual*, New York: Psychological Assessment Resources.

Gillberg, I.C., Rastam, M. and Gillberg, C. (1994) "Anorexia nervosa outcome: six-year controlled longitudinal study of 51 cases including a population cohort", *Journal of the American Academy of Child and Adolescent Psychiatry* 33, 729–39.

Halmi, K., Eckert, E., Marchi, P., Sampugnaro, V., Apple, R. and Cohen, J. (1991) "Comorbidity of psychiatric diagnoses in anorexia nervosa", *Archives of General Psychiatry* 48, 712–18.

Hay, P., Fairburn, C. and Doll, H. (1996) "The classification of bulimic eating disorders: a community-based cluster analysis study", *Psychological Medicine* 26, 801–12.

Herpertz-Dahlman, B., Wewetzer, C., Schulz, E. and Remschmidt, H. (1996) "Course and outcome in adolescent anorexia nervosa", *International Journal of Eating Disorders* 19, 335–45.

Herzog, D.B., Newman, K.L. and Warshaw, M. (1991) "Body image dissatisfaction in homosexual and heterosexual males", *Journal of Nervous and Mental Disease* 179, 356–9.

Herzog, D.B., Keller, M.B., Sacks, N.R., Yeh, C.J. and Lavori, P.W. (1992) "Psychiatric comorbidity in treatment-seeking anorexics and bulimics", *Journal of the American Academy of Child and Adolescent Psychiatry* 31, 810–18.

Holland, A.J., Hall, A., Murray, R., Russell, G.F.M. and Crisp, A.H. (1984) "Anorexia nervosa: a study of 34 twin pairs and one set of triplets", *British Journal of Psychiatry* 145, 414–19.

Holland, A., Sicotte, N. and Treasure, J. (1988) "Anorexia nervosa: evidence for a genetic basis", *Journal of Psychosomatic Research* 32, 561–71.

Hsu, G.L.K., Chesler, B.E. and Santhouse, R. (1990) "Bulimia nervosa in eleven sets of twins: a clinical report", *International Journal of Eating Disorders* 9, 275–82.

Hsu, L.K., Crisp, A.H. and Callender, J.S. (1992) "Psychiatric diagnoses in recovered and unrecovered anorectics 22 years after onset of illness: a pilot study", *Comprehensive Psychiatry* 33, 123–7.

Hudson, J.I., Pope, H.G., Jonas, J.M., Yurgelun-Todd, D. and Frankenburg, F.R. (1987) "A controlled family history study of bulimia", *Psychological Medicine* 17, 883–90.

Kalucy, R., Crisp, A. and Harding, B. (1977) "A study of 56 families with anorexia nervosa", *British Journal of Medical Psychology* 50, 381–95.

Kassett, J., Gershon, E., Maxwell, M., Guroff, J., Kazuba, D., Smith, A., Brandt, H. and Jimerson, D. (1989) "Psychiatric disorders in the first-degree relatives of probands with bulimia nervosa", *American Journal of Psychiatry* 146, 1468–71.

Kendell, R.E. and Brockington, I.F. (1980) "The identification of disease entities and the relationship between schizophrenic and affective psychoses", *British Journal of Psychiatry* 137, 324–31.

Kendler, K.S., MacLean, C., Neale, M.C., Kessler, R.C., Heath, A.C. and Eaves, L.J. (1991) "The genetic epidemiology of bulimia nervosa", *American Journal of Psychiatry* 148, 1627–37.

Kendler, K.S., Neale, M.C., Kessler, R.C., Heath, A.C. and Eaves, L.J. (1992) "Childhood parental loss and adult psychopathology in women: a twin study perspective", *Archives of General Psychiatry* 49, 716–22.

Kendler, K.S., Walters, E.E., Neale, M.C., Kessler, R.C., Heath, A.C. and Eaves, L.J. (1995) "The structure of the genetic and environmental risk factors for six major psychiatric disorders in women: phobia, generalized anxiety disorder, panic disorder, bulimia, major depression and alcoholism", *Archives of General Psychiatry* 52, 374–83.

Klein, D. and Riso, L. (1994) "Psychiatric disorders: problems of boundaries and comorbidity", in C. Costello (ed.) *Basic Issues in Psychopathology*, New York: Guilford Press.

Klump, K.L., McGue, M. and Iacono, W.G. (2000) "Age differences in genetic and environmental influences on eating attitudes and behaviors in preadolescent and adolescent female twins", *Journal of Abnormal Psychology* 109, 239–51.

Lilenfeld, L., Kaye, W., Greeno, C., Merikangas, K., Plotnikov, K., Pollice, C., Rao, R., Strober, M., Bulik, C. and Nagy, L. (1998) "A controlled family study of restricting anorexia and bulimia nervosa: comorbidity in probands and disorders in first-degree relatives", *Archives of General Psychiatry* 55, 603–10.

Logue, C.M., Crowe, R.R. and Bean, J.A. (1989) "A family study of anorexia nervosa and bulimia", *Comprehensive Psychiatry* 30, 179–88.

Mitchell, J.E. and Goff, G. (1984) "Bulimia in male patients", *Psychosomatics* 25, 909–13.

Mitchell, J., Hoberman, H., Peterson, C., Mussell, M. and Pyle, R. (1996) "Research on the psychotherapy of bulimia nervosa: half empty or half full", *International Journal of Eating Disorders* 20, 219–22.

Neale, M. and Cardon, L. (1992) *Methodology for the Study of Twins and Families*, Dordrecht: Kluwer.

Neale, M. and Kendler, K. (1995) "Models of comorbidity for multifactorial disorders", *American Journal of Human Genetics* 57, 935–53.

Nowlin, N. (1983) "Anorexia nervosa in twins: case report and review", *Journal of Clinical Psychiatry* 44, 101–5.

Olivardia, R., Pope, H., Mangweth, B. and Hudson, J. (1995) "Eating disorders in college men", *American Journal of Psychiatry* 152, 1279–85.

Pemberton, A.R., Vernon, S.W. and Lee, E.S. (1996) "Prevalence and correlates of bulimia nervosa and bulimic behaviors in a racially diverse sample of undergraduate students in two universities in southeast Texas", *American Journal of Epidemiology* 144, 450–5.

Plomin, R., DeFries, J.C., McClearn, G.E. and Rutter, M. (1994) *Behavioral Genetics*, 3rd edn, New York: W.H. Freeman.

Pope, H.G. Jr, Hudson, J.I. and Jonas, J.M. (1986) "Bulimia in men: a series of fifteen cases", *Journal of Nervous and Mental Disease* 174, 117–19.

Pyle, R.L., Mitchell, J.E. and Eckert, E.D. (1981) "Bulimia: a report of 34 cases", *Journal of Clinical Psychiatry* 42, 60–4.

Rastam, M., Gillberg, C. and Garton, M. (1989) "Anorexia nervosa in a Swedish urban region: a population-based study", *British Journal of Psychiatry* 155, 642–6.

Reichborn-Kjennerud, T., Bulik, C., Kendler, K., Maes, H., Roysamb, E., Tambs, K. and Harris, J. (2003) "Gender differences in binge eating: a population-based twin study", *Acta Psychiatrica Scandinavica* 108, 196–202.

Robins, E. and Guze, S.B. (1970) "Establishment of diagnostic validity in psychiatric illness: its application to schizophrenia", *American Journal of Psychiatry* 126, 107–11.

Rolls, B.J., Fedoroff, I.C. and Guthrie, J.F. (1991) "Gender differences in eating behavior and body weight regulation", *Health Psychology* 10, 133–42.

Russell, G.F.M. (1979) "Bulimia nervosa: an ominous variant of anorexia nervosa", *Psychological Medicine* 9, 429–48.

Rutherford, J., McGuffin, P., Katz, R. and Murray, R. (1993) "Genetic influences on eating attitudes in a normal female twin population", *Psychological Medicine* 23, 425–36.

Schmidt, U., Keilen, M., Tiller, J. and Treasure, J. (1993) "Clinical symptomatology and etiological factors in obese and normal weight bulimic patients: a retrospective case-control study", *Journal of Nervous and Mental Disease* 181, 200–2.

Schork, E.J., Eckert, E.D. and Halmi, K.A. (1994) "The relationship between psychopathology, eating disorder diagnosis, and clinical outcome at 10-year follow-up in anorexia nervosa", *Comprehensive Psychiatry* 35, 113–23.

Smith, C., Feldman, S., Nasserbakht, A. and Steiner, H. (1993) "Psychological characteristics and DSM-III-R diagnoses at 6-year follow-up of adolescent anorexia nervosa", *Journal of the American Academy of Child and Adolescent Psychiatry* 32, 1237–45.

Steiger, H., van der Feen, J., Goldstein, C. and Leichner, P. (1989) "Defense styles and parental bonding in eating disordered women", *International Journal of Eating Disorders* 8, 131–40.

Stein, D., Lilenfeld, L.R., Plotnicov, K., Pollice, C., Rao, R., Strober, M. and Kaye, W.H. (1999) "Familial aggregation of eating disorders: results from a controlled family study of bulimia nervosa", *International Journal of Eating Disorders* 26, 211–5.

Stern, S., Dixon, K., Sansone, R., Lake, M., Nemzer, E. and Jones, D. (1992) "Psycho-active substance use disorder in relatives of patients with anorexia nervosa", *Comprehensive Psychiatry* 33, 207–12.

Strober, M., Morrell, W., Burroughs, J., Salkin, B. and Jacobs, C. (1985) "A controlled family study of anorexia nervosa", *Journal of Psychiatric Research* 19, 239–46.

Strober, M., Lampert, C., Morrell, W., Burroughs, J. and Jacobs, C. (1990) "A con-trolled family study of anorexia nervosa: evidence of familial aggregation and lack of shared transmission with affective disorders", *International Journal of Eating Disorders* 9, 239–53.

Strober, M., Freeman, R., Lampert, C., Diamond, J. and Kaye, W. (2000) "Controlled family study of anorexia nervosa and bulimia nervosa: evidence of shared liability and transmission of partial syndromes", *American Journal of Psychiatry* 157, 393–401.

Strober, M., Freeman, R., Lampert, C., Diamond, J. and Kaye, W. (2001) "Males with anorexia nervosa: a controlled study of eating disorders in first-degree relatives", *International Journal of Eating Disorders* 29, 263–9.

Sullivan, P.F., Bulik, C.M., Carter, F.A., Gendall, K.A. and Joyce, P.R. (1996) "The significance of a prior history of anorexia in bulimia nervosa", *International Journal of Eating Disorders* 20, 253–61.

Sullivan, P.F., Bulik, C.M. and Kendler, K.S. (1998a) "The epidemiology of bulimia nervosa: symptoms, syndromes and diagnostic thresholds", *Psychological Medicine* 28, 599–610.

Sullivan, P.F., Bulik, C.M. and Kendler, K.S. (1998b) "The genetic epidemiology of binging and vomiting", *British Journal of Psychiatry* 173, 75–9.

Treasure, J. and Holland, A. (1989) "Genetic vulnerability to eating disorders: evi-dence from twin and family studies", in H. Remschmidt and M. Schmidt (eds) *Child and Youth Psychiatry: European Perspectives*, New York: Hogrefe & Huber.

van der Ham, T., van Strien, D. and van Engeland, H. (1994) "A four-year prospective follow-up study of 49 eating disordered adolescents: differences in course of illness", *Acta Psychiatrica Scandinavica* 90, 229–35.

Wade, T., Martin, N. and Tiggemann, M. (1998) "Genetic and environmental risk factors for the weight and shape concerns characteristic of bulimia nervosa", *Psychological Medicine* 28, 761–71.

Wade, T.D., Martin, N., Neale, M., Tiggemann, M., Trealor, S., Heath, A., Bucholz, K. and Madden, P. (1999) "The structure of genetic and environmental risk factors for three measures of disordered eating characteristic of bulimia nervosa", *Psychological Medicine* 29, 925–34.

Wade, T.D., Bulik, C.M., Sullivan, P.F., Neale, M.C. and Kendler, K.S. (2000) "The relation between risk factors for binge eating and bulimia nervosa: a population-based female twin study", *Health Psychology* 19, 115–23.

Walters, E.E. and Kendler, K.S. (1995) "Anorexia nervosa and anorexic-like syndromes in a population-based female twin sample", *American Journal of Psychiatry* 152, 64–71.

Welch, S.L. and Fairburn, C.G. (1994) "Sexual abuse and bulimia nervosa: three integrated case control comparisons", *American Journal of Psychiatry* 151, 402–7.

Wilson, G. and Eldredge, K. (1991) "Frequency of binge eating in bulimic patients: diagnostic validity", *International Journal of Eating Disorders* 10, 557–61.

Woodside, D.B., Garfinkel, P.E., Lin, E., Goering, P., Kaplan, A.S., Goldbloom, D.S. and Kennedy, S.H. (2001) "Comparisons of men with full or partial eating disorders, men without eating disorders, and women with eating disorders in the community", *American Journal of Psychiatry* 158, 570–4.

Yager, J., Landsverk, J., Edelstein, C.K. and Jarvik, M. (1988) "A 20-month follow-up study of 628 women with eating disorders: II. Course of associated symptoms and related clinical features", *International Journal of Eating Disorders* 7, 503–13.

Zipfel, S., Lowe, B., Reas, D.L., Deter, H.C. and Herzog, W. (2000) "Long-term prognosis in anorexia nervosa: lessons from a 21-year follow-up study", *Lancet* 355, 721–2.

Chapter 10

Cross-cultural perspectives on Anorexia Nervosa without fat phobia

Sing Lee and Kathleen Kwok

Introduction

Nowadays it is widely recognized that eating disorders are no longer confined to the developed West. Despite a low level of public awareness, Anorexia Nervosa and Bulimia Nervosa have become increasingly common clinical problems among young females in high-income Asian societies such as Japan, Hong Kong, Singapore and Taiwan. They have also appeared in the major cities of low-income Asian countries such as China, India, Malaysia, the Philippines and Indonesia. They have even been identified in such unexpected places as Africa (Nasser *et al.* 2001). Although accurate two-stage community estimates of eating disorders are usually lacking in these populations, preliminary estimates provide good reason for concern. Community studies in Hong Kong have indicated that 3–10 per cent of young females suffer from disordered eating. The trend is for this to increase with societal modernization (Lee and Lee 2000). This situation is characteristically attributed to the influx of Western cultural values that privilege slimness and weight control as being unquestionably desirable. AN is considered an imported illness that embodies such aesthetic ideals and impinges on those most vulnerable to fat concern, namely, young females.

Although the cultural fear of fatness doubtless shapes AN in multiple ways, increasing evidence suggests that the illness is phenomenologically variable in non-Western communities. Of particular interest is the finding that a varying proportion of non-Western patients with AN do not manifest the "fear of fatness" (termed "fat phobia" hereafter), which constitutes the raison d'être for self-starvation in the contemporary Western conceptualization of the illness (Lee 1995; Lee *et al.* 1993). Clinically, such non-fat phobic subjects were usually aware of their unsightly appearance. Instead of using fat phobia to legitimize food refusal, they often complained of stomach bloating and might even express an apparent wish to gain weight. This is in contrast to the DSM-IV stipulation that individuals with AN always manifest fat phobia that is not alleviated by weight loss (APA 1994; see also Appendix).

Mainstream researchers often cast doubt on the disease validity of non-fat phobic AN, or dismiss it as nothing more than a rare form of atypical eating disorder confined to the developing world (Habermas 1996; Vandereycken 1993). Others may not find it worthy of research. In this chapter, we present evidence that the condition demonstrates considerable historical, cross-cultural and longitudinal disease validity. Although our recent clinical experience suggests that non-fat phobic AN has become less common than before, we contend that it is not merely a historical remnant that will evolve into the typical "valid" form of AN following societal modernization. By problematizing the biomedical claim to universalism and constancy, non-fat phobic AN raises intriguing issues that can illuminate the diagnosis, research, treatment and prevention of eating disorders in general.

Historical evidence on non-fat phobic Anorexia Nervosa

Historical accounts provide a distinctive opportunity to study "non-DSMized" accounts of women with marked weight loss that followed self-starvation. They indicated that fat phobic AN as we conceptualize it today is a novel entity. Although subjective accounts were typically lacking, these studies have concluded that "miraculous maids" and "fasting girls" who exhibited obdurate food denial without fat phobia could be traced back to as early as the fifth century (Brumberg 1988; Hepworth 1999). During the trans-formation of AN from such sainthood to patienthood, the early patients were accorded various labels that had a visceral focus, such as "apepsia hysterica" (Gull 1874), "bradypepsia", "anorexia humoralis", "anorexia atonica", "gas-trodynia", "nervous dyspepsia", "dyspeptic neurasthenia", "dyspepsia ute-rina", "neuralgia and hyperaesthesias of the stomach" or simply "visceral neurosis" (Shorter 1987). C. Lasègue in particular made scrupulous descrip-tion of anorexic patients' "gastralgia" and the psychosocial origin of their food abstinence (Vandereycken and van Deth 1990). Likewise, Marcé wrote that

> these patients arrive at a delirious conviction that they cannot or ought not to eat . . . all the intellectual energy centres round the functions of the stomach . . . these unhappy patients only regain some amount of energy in order to resist attempts at alimentation.
>
> (quoted in Silverman 1989)

Charcot too thought that AN was a hysterical disorder of the stomach nerves (in Shorter 1987). Even in between the two world wars, most anorexic patients in London, Toronto, Rome and Berlin did not exhibit fat concern (Shorter 1994). In a learned review written as recently as the late 1950s, Nemiah (1958) made no allusion whatsoever to fat phobia, but attributed anorexic patients' psychogenic starvation to "the wish not to eat", "food phobia", "aversion to food" or "true loss of appetite" respectively. He added that "almost all of the patients are found to have a variety of other symptoms referable to the gastrointestinal tract."

The above historical evidence on women with morbid self-starvation is hard to refute. Moreover, apart from the lack of fat phobia, the overall resemblance between historical and modern accounts of AN is striking. Gastrointestinal disturbances, which were prominent in historical accounts, are common among modern anorexic patients. Robinson (1989) demonstrated that delayed gastric emptying produced "fullness" signals and satiety that in turn sustained anorexic behaviour. Unsurprisingly, a British anorexic patient who went on a diet had this to say about her poor food intake:

> as you eat less and less your stomach actually shrinks and so eventually, if you're persistent enough, what you do eat makes you feel full, so you think, "Oh, I ought to eat less", and you just go on like that ... when I went into hospital my stomach was about the size of a walnut.
>
> (MacSween 1993: 92)

In the absence of a permeating fear of fatness, biological constraints would thus oblige early anorexic patients to explain their non-eating in terms of appetitive dysfunctions. But the latter were not merely pathophysiology, but have to be interpreted within a social context. In the Victorian era, for example, these visceral complaints allowed young women to express feminine ideals and moral superiority much like fat phobia does nowadays (Brumberg 1988).

In more recent times, two major contributors to the conceptualization of AN both acknowledged and marginalized non-fat phobic AN. Based on a group of 70 patients, Bruch (1973) in the United States examined the distinction between primary and atypical AN. The former group (6 males, 45 females) all exhibited the "relentless pursuit of thinness" and "denial of even advanced cachexia as being too thin". The latter represented a mixed group of food-refusers (4 males, 15 females) who actually complained about the weight loss but were unable to eat because of "various symbolic misinterpretations of the eating function". Bruch subsequently concentrated on primary AN in her influential work that shaped the conceptual development of fat phobic AN. Yet, by the relentless pursuit of thinness, she did not refer to the increasingly common forms of fat phobic AN recognized in the contemporary diagnostic system. She admitted later that the form of the anorexic illness has "changed" and lost its former psychodynamic meanings since the 1980s (Bruch 1985).

In the United Kingdom, Arthur Crisp (1980) held that the essence of AN is the presence of an elicitable "weight phobia". This term was clinically derived from the theory of psychobiological regression. Unlike the phenomenologically based construct of fat phobia, it refers to anorexic patients' panicky avoidance of a normal body weight and the tasks of maturity it symbolizes. Specifically, Crisp hypothesized a sub-pubertal threshold weight of 38 to 41 kg, near which patients demonstrate defiance towards further weight gain in order not to reinstate the process of maturation. Accordingly, a patient who is non-fat phobic but nonetheless displays weight phobia during an intensive psychodynamic assessment qualifies for Crisp's diagnosis of AN. Arguably, a mild anorexic subject who admits to fat phobia but has no weight phobia may not have the illness. Thus, Crisp has never indicated that the DSM notion of fear of fatness is the core psychopathology of AN, though he appears to have been taken to mean so.

Cross-cultural evidence on non-fat phobic Anorexia Nervosa

Non-Western studies have strengthened the historical evidence on non-fat phobic AN. In a clinical study, 41 of 70 Chinese anorexic patients in Hong Kong, despite the overall resemblance to their Western counterparts, attributed food refusal to stomach bloating, loss of appetite, no hunger, and other non-fat phobic symptoms (Lee *et al.* 1993). A hospital-based survey revealed that about one-third of eating disordered patients in Japan still belonged to the "not otherwise specified" category (Nakamura *et al.* 2000). There were reports of non-fat phobic AN in Singapore, mainland China, Malaysia and India too (Katzman and Lee 1997; Lee 1995).

These observations were confirmed in a prospective study that examined the rationales for food refusal among Chinese patients with fat phobic and non-fat phobic AN in Hong Kong (Lee *et al.* 2001). This used a locally devised "rationale for food refusal questionnaire" (RFQ) to ask 48 anorexic patients to record the reasons for non-eating over three time points. The RFQ was a self-report instrument that allowed them to choose among eight rationales for food refusal twelve months previously, three months previously, and at clinical presentation. These rationales included "fear of food", "fat phobia", "stomach bloating", "stomach pain", "no hunger", "no appetite", "don't know" and "other reasons" respectively. Patients were classified as fat phobic (N = 32) or non-fat phobic (N = 16) according to whether they exhibited both of the following: (1) fear of fatness leading to weight control behaviour near the onset of their illness, and (2) an intense fear of fatness despite low body weight at the time of clinical presentation. This subtyping was done without knowledge of patients' response to the RFQ.

Results showed that the two groups of patients did not differ on ratings of general psychopathology. However, their explanations for non-eating were demonstrably different and, to some extent, changed over time. For the fat phobic group, by far the most commonly selected rationale for food refusal was "fat phobia". At one year, three months and "now", 71 per cent, 84 per cent and 52 per cent of patients endorsed this reason respectively. "Stomach bloating" (10 per cent, 29 per cent, 42 per cent), "stomach pain" (4 per cent, 13 per cent, 22 per cent) and "don't know" (8 per cent, 18 per cent, 23 per cent) were less popular reasons, but tended to become more common as the illness progressed. For the non-fat phobic group, the most commonly selected rationale was "stomach bloating". At the three time points, 32 per cent, 25 per cent and 44 per cent of patients endorsed this respectively, whereas only 19 per cent, 6 per cent and 6 per cent of patients chose fat phobia. When "no hunger", "no appetite" and "don't know" were averaged across the three time points, 35 per cent, 19 per cent and 32 per cent of patients chose these reasons respectively. Regarding group difference, at all three time points, significantly more fat phobic than non-fat phobic patients endorsed fat phobia. The study demonstrated that a subgroup of anorexic patients remained non-fat phobic throughout. It also suggested that fat phobic and non-fat phobic anorexic experiences were not mutually exclusive.

Western evidence on non-fat phobic Anorexia Nervosa

Kleinman (1987) admonished that psychiatric researchers are predisposed to exaggerate what is professionally defined to be universal in mental disorders and to de-emphasize what is culturally particular and often locally valid. Where it was reported in the English language literature at all, non-fat phobic AN was marginalized as "misleading variants" (Vandereycken 1993) or at best labelled as "atypical" AN (Bruch 1973; Mitchell *et al.* 1986).

But non-fat phobic AN has been described in Europe (Faltus 1986; Vandereycken 1993), the United Kingdom (Fosson *et al.* 1987; Palmer 1993; Russell 1995), Canada (Steiger 1993) and the United States (Banks 1992; Mitchell *et al.* 1986; Strober *et al.* 1999; Yager and Davis 1993). Experienced clinicians have honestly affirmed its existence. For example, Steiger (1993: 352) remarked:

> anyone who works with large numbers of anorexic sufferers knows that this disorder is not uniformly about a desire to be thin. Rather, the apparent pursuit of thinness or weight phobia seen in anorexia is often explicable in terms idiosyncratic to each case.

Among Western sufferers of childhood onset AN, fat phobia is not uncommonly absent but emerges as treatment progresses (Bryant-Waugh and Kaminski 1993). Others may simply not be able to articulate the reasons why they have lost weight (Lee *et al.* 1993; Treasure 1997). Palmer (1993) criticized the primacy given to weight concern in the modern Western understanding of AN. He cautioned that this could lead to a premature closure of the inquiry into the nature of the eating disorders in general.

Non-fat phobic AN was often reported from Eastern European countries where the medical profession was apparently under less immediate influence from the DSM. At an eating disorder unit in the former Czechoslovakia, aversion to food, refusal to eat, extreme emaciation, amenorrhoea and the absence of a primary disease, not fat phobia, were used for diagnosis (Faltus 1986). In a study of 42 female anorexic patients in Warsaw, Poland, the authors remarked that the illness was "a result of weight reducing diets" in only 22 (52 per cent) patients (Kasperlik-Zaluska *et al.* 1981).

Non-fat phobic AN also occurred in contemporary North America where the DSM system exercised considerable influence on clinical practice. Anthropologist Banks (1992) reported that asceticism grounded on particular religious symbols and idioms about food provided the context in which AN arose. She described two among several dozens of subjects who, coming from the religiously conservative traditions in the Twin Cities of Minnesota, exhibited typical clinical and psychodynamic features of AN, except that fat phobia was never a concern for them. By highlighting the disconnection between the DSM professional discourse and the subjective expressions of the illness, she challenged the assumption that secular ideals of slimness represent the exclusive hermeneutic context in which AN should occur in contemporary American society. She surmised that, when less narrowly conceived, the illness could occur in a wide range of contexts outside the West.

Evidence from outcome studies on non-fat phobic Anorexia Nervosa

Studying the outcome profile of a psychiatric disorder is a fundamental way of confirming or refuting its disease validity. In this regard, there are at least two outcome studies that supported the validity of non-fat phobic AN. In a 15-year longitudinal study, Strober *et al.* (1999) compared the long-term outcome of typical and atypical anorexic inpatients. Atypical AN was defined by the definite absence of fat phobia throughout inpatient stay. They found that atypical patients remained non-fat phobic, exhibited less bulimic tendencies, and had a more benign outcome than their fat phobic counterparts. This was the first systematic Western study to conclude that AN without fat phobia is a valid disease entity.

More recently, a study was conducted to determine the intermediate term outcome of Chinese patients with AN in Hong Kong (Lee *et al.* 2003). This involved a consecutive series of 88 patients who fulfilled the DSM-III-R criteria for typical (fat phobic, N = 63) and atypical (non-fat phobic, N = 25) AN. They were contacted at least four years after the onset of illness for semi-structured and self-rating assessments of outcome. Most (94 per cent) of the patients were successfully traced nine years after the onset of illness. Although their general psychopathology was similar, non-fat phobic AN was shown to be less likely to demonstrate BN, and had a better eating disorder outcome than fat phobic AN. In addition, non-fat phobic AN was symptomatically stable over time, while the presence of fat phobia independently predicted a poor outcome of illness. It was concluded that the cultural fear of fatness not only shaped the manifest content but also intensified the chronicity of the anorexic illness.

Qualitative studies

Most studies on atypical AN adopted a categorical approach that was insensitive to patients' subjective illness experience and the interpersonal milieu in which that experience was embedded. From an anthropological perspective, illness experience is an important way of validating clinical diagnosis. It can be studied using ethnographic or other experience-near methods of qualitative research. In a study of two patients with non-fat phobic AN in Hong Kong, Lee (1995) showed that nowhere from clinical examination, psychometric assessment and home visits was fat phobia relevant to their illness.

The first patient was sensitized to loss during a lonely childhood. In the patriarchal semi-rural milieu where she was brought up, having a timely marriage with a financially dependable man was every woman's duty in life. Yet, when she was 24, her boyfriend suddenly left for the United Kingdom without any explanation. The marked complaints of abdominal bloating and her staunch conviction that she could not eat were interpretable as somatopsychic symptoms that authenticated her chronic grief over a long-lost love. Her food denial conveyed sadness and relinquishment, not in the least fat phobia. The gruesome emaciation, self-neglect, social disconnection and unconquerable resistance toward treatment denoted a nearly extinguished interest in life itself. But the patient did not fulfil the diagnostic criteria for major depression. Lee argued that in her local world pleading abdominal discomfort was a more understandable idiom of distress than fat phobia.

The second patient's loss of interest in eating symbolized a loss of voice in a world perceived to be overwhelmingly oppressive. It echoed relational malaise, and allowed her to avoid and simultaneously resist a sexually abusive father at the dining table, where Chinese family members obligatorily met with one another every day. This was a profound act of communication by not communicating, and a non-confrontational style of expressing intra-familial hostility that did not breach Confucian values on demure female behaviour. Lee pointed out that at the age of 32, the patient's adoption of a permanently child-like look was expressive of a pseudo-power that both defeated and shielded her.

Qualitative studies further demonstrated that fat phobia was a labile experience. Bruch's account of how anorexic patients' explanations of non-eating could vacillate is riveting:

When the condition has existed for some time patients may be reluctant to give exact information or take delight in confusing "the experts," and patients with genuine anorexia will deny their "denial of thinness." I have observed this repeatedly when patients after many years of illness finally consent to one more consultation. They will describe in a submissive, pious-sounding voice how guilty they feel for having caused their family so much unhappiness. They say they know they are too thin and they want to regain their strength so that they can lead a normal life. They will promise that they will cooperate with whatever is necessary for them to get well. Within a few days, in particular if they gain a few pounds, the whole tone will change; they are concerned about weighing "too much," . . . and state outright "I am happy looking like a skeleton." A few patients with long-standing disease were shifted from one group to another when more detailed and exact information became available.

(Bruch 1973: 236)

Unsurprisingly, using qualitative techniques, Serpell *et al.* (1999) identified a number of illness themes, such as a sense of control and safety that transcended fat phobic concern among what appeared to be a homogeneous group of typical patients in the United Kingdom. Based on exploratory interviews, Szekely (1989) in Canada discovered that the pursuit of thinness among women was far from a unitary phenomenon. Instead, there were vast differences in their life situations and in some of the meanings thinness had for each of them. In Israel, Kaffman and Sadeh (1989) recognized that male anorexic patients did not have a clear distorted body image; they dieted not to acquire good looks, but to improve their athletic achievements, or to compete for recruitment into elite military units. Even in the United States, Yager and Davis (1993: 296) noted "how clinically difficult it can sometimes be to elicit a fat phobia in patients who have evolved a different type of attribution regarding why they are not eating." This observation is congruous with anorexic patients' own descriptions of their illness experience, which were diverse, changeable and at times contradictory (Hornbacher 1999; Way 1993).

Thus, anorexic patients do not live in a DSM-IV diagnostic laboratory. Our clinical experience indicated that as a fat phobic patient's emaciation became advanced, she could be blamed for risking her life and causing immense pain to family members. At that point, she might develop a different attribution about her food refusal. Cases like the following, in which a patient's positive subjectivity about thinness became neutralized by progressive weight loss and what was morally at stake in her local world, such as threatened filial duty, are commonly seen: Miss A was an 18-year-old student with a weight of 38.6 kg (BMI = 14.9 kg/m^2) at referral. With a premorbid weight of 49 kg, she equated slimness with beauty and a means to gain social acceptance. In contrast, fatness was considered an object of ridicule that would greatly hinder a woman's career and heterosexual relationships. Miss A came from a family in which she regarded herself as the less favoured of two children. Her chronic inferiority was exaggerated when her parents gave all of their attention to her elder sister, who developed AN six months previously. Against this backdrop, she emulated her sister's food restriction habit and lost weight steadily. She saw such weight reduction as a protest, and the sense of control gave her great satisfaction. Her peers' initial praise further boosted the sense of success. Contrary to her mother's apprehension, she saw amenorrhoea merely as convenience. However, when her weight decreased by over 5 kg, she felt no longer able to control her food intake, and was worried that without medical attention she could die. She was also saddened by her mother's self-blame and her sister's guilty feelings over having caused her illness. At this point, she was ashamed of her thin body and attributed her meagre food intake to stomach bloating rather than fat phobia. With family therapy, she gained weight to 44 kg, and learned how important family was to her. She lost her former fat phobia and decided to "eat and live in moderation" in the future.

Another patient, initially non-fat phobic, manifested fat phobia at a later stage of illness: Miss B was a 23-year-old university student with a nine-year history of AN. She came from a family of six who enjoyed stable income as well as relatively normal relationships. Prior to the onset of her anorexic illness, she was comfortable with being nicknamed a "fat little girl" and was satisfied with her body shape. At 13 and owing to examination pressures, she complained of epigastric pain that led to reduced food intake and progressive weight loss from 46.8 to 35.9 kg (BMI = 14.8 kg/m^2) within a few months. She became amenorrhoeic and constipated, as well as irritable towards her mother. She visited the emergency department because of a syncopal attack, but repeated medical investigations including upper endoscopy were negative. She did not engage in exercise, bingeing or vomiting to reduce weight. Major depression was absent. She responded to five months of outpatient counselling, during which she described her food refusal as an act of resistance against her mother. She maintained a weight of 41 kg and adequate social functioning. During Form Seven, she gained weight to 48 kg owing to eating snacks while studying for A levels in the evenings. She developed fat phobia, dieted, and engaged in self-induced vomiting and laxative abuse for four months. Her weight dropped to 36 kg. Worried that this could ruin her, she sought psychiatric help again and her weight returned to 48 kg. At 43 kg, she exhibited fat concern at the last follow-up.

Explanations for non-fat phobic Anorexia Nervosa

By assuming that fat phobia is the core psychopathology of AN, medical researchers "naturally" pose the question of why fat phobia should be absent among certain anorexic patients. Several ready-made explanations follow. The first and conceptually the simplest is that these patients are dishonest liars. They "deny" or merely conceal fat concern, thereby deceiving their doctors and/or family members. However, this speculation is not supported by our clinical and research experience, and certainly cannot be an adequate explanation for the majority of non-fat phobic patients. The second explanation is that non-fat phobic AN is a form of somatized depression. But this is contradicted by the lack of efficacy of antidepressant drugs and, more importantly, the fact that non-fat phobic and fat phobic patients demonstrated similar rates of depression in both cross-sectional and outcome studies (Lee *et al.* 2001, 2003). This is not to speak of the fact that depression rarely causes the substantial degree of weight loss and chronicity routinely seen in these patients. The third explanation is that non-fat phobic patients are premorbidly slim and less susceptible to the cultural delegitimation of fatness. This is supported by the fact that about 15 per cent of constitutionally slim young women in Hong Kong desired to gain rather than lose weight (Lee 1993). It is also strengthened by studies that compared the body shape of non-fat phobic and fat phobic anorexic patients. These consistently found that the former exhibited a lower BMI than the latter, being 18.5 kg/m^2 as opposed to 20.1 5 kg/m^2 (Lee *et al.* 1993). But this too cannot be the whole explanation because some non-fat phobic anorexic patients were not necessarily slim. It also cannot account for the variability of fat phobic experience within the same patient over time (Lee *et al.* 2001). The last explanation is that non-fat phobic patients come from subcultures in which fat phobia is not an effective idiom of distress (Kleinman 1987). Rather, rationales such as stomach bloating provide more irrefutable excuses for food refusal in their local interpersonal worlds (Lee 1995; Lee *et al.* 2001). Clearly, multiple contextual and individual factors have to be invoked to explain the variability of anorexic experience.

Validity of fat-focused research instruments and implications for epidemiological research

In a review of the epidemiology of eating disorders, Patton and Szmukler (1995) indicated that an over-reliance on fat phobia for diagnosis could result in a failure to recognize AN in broader cultural settings. The Study Group on Anorexia Nervosa (1995) further recommended that "it is important to take a wide view and not to focus specifically on identifying cases defined on narrowly based Western criteria" and that "there is a need to develop appropriate local instruments in the first instance."

There has been considerable doubt over the cross-cultural validity of the Eating Disorder Inventory (EDI) and Eating Attitudes Test (EAT), the two most commonly used instruments for assessing eating disorders (King and Bhugra 1989; Lee *et al.* 1998). In a German study, East Berlin anorexic patients were found to have significantly lower scores on most EDI subscales than West Berlin patients (Steinhausen *et al.* 1992). The authors believed that this discrepancy might reflect a lack of cross-cultural validity in the psychological constructs upon which the questionnaire was based. Other researchers who adhered to the fat phobia paradigm were obliged to ascribe anorexic patients' lack of psychometrically demonstrable fat rejection to a "deceptive tendency" or "denial of illness" (Castro *et al.* 1991; Greenfield *et al.* 1991; Habermas 1996; Vandereycken and Vanderlinden 1983). Neumarker *et al.* (1992) found that East Berlin anorexic patients scored atypically low compared to those of West Berlin, North America and Canada. Unexpectedly low EAT scores among anorexic patients were also found in Belgium (Vandereycken and Vanderlinden 1983), Spain (Castro *et al.* 1991) and the United States (Greenfield *et al.* 1991).

In Hong Kong, both the EDI and EAT have been shown to be problematic for Chinese anorexic patients. Lee *et al.* (1998) showed that although the EDI profile of fat phobic patients was similar to that of Canadian patients with restrictive AN, the EDI profile of non-fat phobic patients was anomalous. They displayed significantly more "general psychopathology" than control subjects, but exhibited even less "specific" psychopathology, as measured on the "drive for thinness" subscale. One study evaluated the EAT in screening Chinese patients with AN and BN in Hong Kong (Lee *et al.* 2002). A consecutive series of patients with BN (N = 67) and fat phobic (N = 65) and non-fat phobic (N = 44) AN underwent clinical assessment and completed the EAT-26. Results were compared with those of Chinese female undergraduates (N = 646). The findings showed that while bulimic and fat phobic anorexic patients' mean EAT scores were significantly higher than those of undergraduates, non-fat phobic anorexic patients scored unusually low. Classification and regression tree was then employed to identify significant predictors for differentiating the community subjects and the three groups of patients. The dieting and bulimia factor scores and body mass indices entered the classification tree. When compared to using the conventional EAT-26 cut-off, the misclassification rate for fat phobic AN, non-fat phobic AN and BN changed from 41.4 per cent to 52.3 per cent, 88.6 per cent to 43.2 per cent, and 23.9 per cent to 29.9 per cent respectively. The study showed that using the EAT-26 in the conventional manner would lead to an underestimate of non-fat phobic AN in community surveys. Complementary use of a classification tree based on EAT factor scores and body mass indices improved the prediction of this form of AN, but the EAT-26 remains a suboptimal screening instrument for the epidemiological study of AN in general.

Western community epidemiological surveys often yielded a lower than expected rate of AN (Hsu 1990). One reason can be that the existing screening instruments, such as the EAT and EDI, are based largely on the construct of fat phobia. Non-fat phobic and some formerly fat phobic patients might not endorse such familiar items as "I am terrified of gaining weight" and "I am preoccupied with the desire to be thinner" when they are manifestly emaciated. Consequently, they might be screened out as "non-cases".

One way to enhance the sensitivity of the fat-focused instruments is to create an additional subscale that is grounded in the different idioms used by starving subjects to explain food denial. Research in mainstream epidemiology has shown that small but culturally relevant changes in the stem questions of instruments originally based on the DSM system can result in significant changes in the detected rates of mental disorders (Regier *et al.* 1998). This approach to epidemiological work on eating disorders is yet to be explored.

A typology of anorexic phenomenology and implications for diagnosis

If non-fat phobic AN occurs globally, the current diagnostic systems cannot be considered adequate. Russell (1995: 10) admonished that "the time may be approaching when it will be advisable to retreat from our cherished diagnostic criteria of AN, as there may be a false precision in the current formulations of DSM-III-R and ICD-10." The DSM-IV Task Force also acknowledged that the DSM-IV "must not be culture specific but instead be applicable cross-culturally", and that "the highest purpose of the DSM-IV is that it encourages and facilitates the research that will render it obsolete" (Frances *et al.* 1991: 411).

Instead of a rigid fat phobic versus non-fat phobic dichotomy, a typology of anorexic phenomenology that may be of heuristic value for clinical practice and research is suggested as follows: (1) fat phobic type I (consistently fat phobic), (2) fat phobic type II (fat phobic changing to non-fat phobic presentation), (3) non-fat phobic type I (consistently non-fat phobic) and (4) non-fat phobic type II (non-fat phobic initially, but fat phobic later). The first type represents "typical" DSM-IV AN. It is arguably the most common form of the illness nowadays. The second type represents patients that clinicians often encounter, namely, fat phobia is present initially but diminishes or even vanishes as weight loss becomes advanced or chronic. The third type is "atypical" AN found in premorbidly slim patients, especially in non-Western societies where the cultural fear of fatness is not yet overwhelming. The fourth type adds to the diversity of anorexic phenomenology. As a formerly slim and non-fat phobic patient gains weight she may well develop fat concern that is collectively present among young females in modern societies, be they Western or non-Western.

This typology challenges the monothetic scheme of diagnosis adopted in the DSM-IV. Grounded in Aristotelian logic, monothetic classification imposes homogeneity and creates a sense of order over the polyphenomenal world. Polythetic classification, being based on reason by analogy, put emphasis on the uniqueness of each subject (Lock 1987). Medical diagnosis, usually monothetic and devoid of social constraints, is valuable for selecting precise therapies for specific organic problems (e.g. nitrates for angina pectoris). However, AN is not phenomenologically homogeneous, nor clearly organic in aetiology, or responsive to a specific form of therapy. Consequently, a monothetic diagnostic approach based on fat phobia not only will miss non-fat phobic patients but also is irrelevant to therapy.

Kirmayer and Young (1999) argued that the broad concept of psychiatric disorder is polythetic in nature. Accordingly, there need be no essential characteristic, criterion, or single prototype of disorder. Instead, multiple prototypes with varying features are used to group together a wide range of fuzzy phenomena by analogy. In the diagnosis of AN, a polythetic approach accommodates fat phobic as well as non-fat phobic rationales for food refusal. It promotes subjective expressions, explorations of social meanings, and the use of individualized therapeutics. From this perspective, the DSM-IV diagnosis of AN can be rendered polythetic by broadening its criteria "2" and "3". Instead of the mandatory requirement for fat phobia, a polythetic criterion would read something like: "the low body weight is caused by a voluntary reduction of food intake which may be variously attributed to fear of fatness, abdominal bloating/pain, loss of appetite, no hunger, fear of food, distaste for food, or 'don't know'." The list of rationales is expandable but not endless because the number of common initial rationales for food refusal is limited (Lee *et al.* 2001). This polythetic criterion is likely to have enhanced cross-cultural and clinical applicability. It does not devalue the vast amount of useful research work that accompanies fat phobic AN.

Beyond fat phobia: implications for treatment

Recent decades have witnessed little breakthrough in the treatment of AN (Hsu 1990). Except where medical complications warrant physical intervention, treatment usually consists of some form of psychotherapy. This depends less on a distinctive theoretical approach than a trusting and motivating therapist–client relationship. In the case of typical anorexic patients, the "core" psychopathology of fat phobia has ironically been suggested to be an unimportant clinical focus that needs no direct confrontation (Garner and Garfinkel 1981). Other experts have noted the difficulty of altering patients' fear of fatness, and would simply ask them to "live with it" (Hsu 1990: 146).

In the case of non-fat phobic patients, Lasègue emphasized that "the remedies appropriate to their gastralgia are absolutely inefficacious" Vandereycken and van Deth 1990: 904 and that "the moral medium amidst which the patient lives exercises an influence which it would be equally regrettable to overlook or misunderstand" (p. 905). Our experience in Hong Kong likewise indicated that although anorexic patients might present with stomach bloating, fear of food or amenorrhoea, their somatization is typically "facultative". That is, they presented with somatic symptoms initially but later admitted to their being embedded in a matrix of general psychopathology, developmental conflicts and interpersonal difficulties that could be dealt with during psychotherapy. These psychological difficulties often resemble those seen in fat phobic patients (Lee 1995). Therefore non-fat phobic AN should not be taken to constitute alexithymia or somatoform disorder in which patients with multiple physical complaints exhibit a notable inability to convey emotional difficulties. Based on content analysis of family therapy sessions with Chinese anorexic patients in Hong Kong, Ma *et al.* (2002) identified five main themes of self-starvation that are relevant to treatment, namely, self-sacrifice for family well-being, expression of control, filial piety over individuation, bridging of parental conflict and camouflage of family conflicts. Fat phobia was not a prominent theme of illness.

Tellingly, Bruch (1973) noted that, despite their different clinical presentation, "control" arose as an important issue during the psychological treatment of both primary and atypical AN. If this is so, will the psychological treatment of non-fat phobic AN shed light on the fundamental problems of control (e.g. subjective incompetence, disconnection, discrimination and helplessness) that beset anorexic sufferers and women generally? According to Katzman and Lee (1997), the portrait of AN as an appearance disorder incurred by young women lost in the world of calorie restricting is a belittling stereotype. It camouflages women's real worries and misses the universal power of food refusal, as in proclaiming needs for self-control in social positions of relative powerlessness. Unsurprisingly, anorexic patients' accounts of psychiatric treatment experience often indicated substantial treatment resistance because

> the solution is definitely not to take away the one and only one thing in her life she feels she has control over. It contradicts and defeats the entire purpose of what the anorexic needs to gain in recovery – positive coping skills to feel in charge of herself and her life.
>
> (Way 1993: 76)

What matters in treatment is a dialogue that transcends slim media ideals and food refusal to honour personal control, relational satisfaction and political position in the family and society at large. It is perhaps not coincidental that these factors were identified in empirical studies that asked patients to name the variables critical to successful treatment (Peters and Fallon 1994). Inasmuch as the anorexic body may be valued for its being proof of self-control, Katzman and Lee (1997) recommended substituting fat phobia with "no control phobia" in understanding patients with AN. Indeed, the latter often admitted that "letting go" of the illusory control that AN furnished them marked eventual recovery (Hornbacher 1999; Way 1993). Thus, the application of a multidimensional theory of control and control therapy (Shapiro 1998) to AN is worth exploring.

Conclusion

The emergence of AN in non-Western communities tells more than a story of Western cultural hegemony and assimilation. It elicits needed reflections among Western researchers who adhere to the paradigm of fat phobia that has guided research and treatment in the last several decades. Although fat concern has become a collective experience in the modern world, the anorexic illness is not phenomenologically constant. Non-fat phobic AN usefully challenges DSM's essentializing epistemology and can shed light on the diagnosis, treatment and research of eating disorders in general. It also draws necessary attention to the social forces that not only render young females vulnerable to pathological weight control but also have implications for the primary prevention of eating disorders.

Predictably, the rising rate of eating disorders will pose a new public health challenge to non-Western countries. At an outpatient psychiatric clinic where one of us (Lee) worked, the number of referrals of such patients clearly escalated since the early 1990s. Within the eighteen months (2000–2) that followed the opening of the Hong Kong Eating Disorders Center that is purposely located in a non-hospital area and decorated in a home-like style, over 300 individuals (including 9 males) sought help for eating disorders there. This indicates that eating disordered subjects are ready to seek help if specialized treatment facilities that do not carry significant psychiatric stigma are available. In most non-Western societies, however, such facilities are barely available. Patients often present with somatic symptoms and have to detour round practitioners before they receive limited psychological treatment from overworked psychiatrists who deal mostly with psychosis. Many more are not being treated. In this regard, more attention to the variable presentation of AN may enhance the early intervention and hence outcome of this disabling illness.

References

American Psychiatric Association (1994) *Diagnostic and Statistical Manual of Mental Disorders*, 4th edn (DSM-IV), Washington, DC: APA.

Banks, C.G. (1992) " 'Culture' in culture-bound syndromes: the case of anorexia nervosa", *Social Science and Medicine* 34, 867–84.

Bruch, H. (1973) *Eating Disorders: Obesity, Anorexia Nervosa, and the Person Within*, New York: Basic Books.

Bruch, H. (1985) "Four decades of eating disorders", in D.M. Garner and P.E. Garfinkel (eds) *Handbook of Psychotherapy for Anorexia Nervosa and Bulimia*, New York: Guilford Press.

Brumberg, J.J. (1988) *Fasting Girls: The Emergence of Anorexia Nervosa as a Modern Disease*, Cambridge, MA: Harvard University Press.

Bryant-Waugh, R. and Kaminski, Z. (1993) "Eating disorders in children: an overview", in B. Lask and R. Bryant-Waugh (eds) *Childhood Onset Anorexia Nervosa and Related Eating Disorders*, London: Plenum Press.

Castro, J., Toro, J., Salamero, M. and Guimera, E. (1991) "The eating attitudes test: validation of the Spanish version", *Psychological Assessment* 7, 175–90.

Crisp, A.H. (1980) *Anorexia Nervosa: Let Me Be*, London: Plenum Press.

Faltus, F. (1986) "Anorexia nervosa in Czechoslovakia", *International Journal of Eating Disorders* 5, 581–5.

Fosson, A., Knibbs, J., Bryant-Waugh, R. and Lask, B. (1987) "Early onset anorexia nervosa", *Archives of Disease in Childhood* 62, 114–18.

Frances, A., First, M., Widiger, T., Miele, G., Tilly, S., Davis, W. and Pincus, H. (1991) "An A to Z guide to DSM-IV conundrums", *Journal of Abnormal Psychology* 100, 407–12.

Garner, D.M. and Garfinkel, P.E. (1981) "Body image in anorexia nervosa: measurement, theory and clinical implications", *International Journal of Psychiatry and Medicine* 11, 263–84.

Greenfield, D.G., Anyan, W.R., Hobart, M., Quinlan, D.M. and Plantes, M. (1991) "Insight into illness and outcome in anorexia nervosa", *International Journal of Eating Disorders* 10, 101–9.

Gull, W.W. (1874) "Anorexia nervosa (apepsia hysterica, anorexia hysterica)", *Transactions of Clinical Society* 7, 22–8.

Habermas, T. (1996) "In defense of weight phobia as the central organizing motive in anorexia nervosa: historical and cultural arguments for a culture-sensitive psychological conception", *International Journal of Eating Disorders* 19, 317–34.

Hepworth, J. (1999) *The Social Construction of Anorexia Nervosa*, London: Sage.

Hornbacher, M. (1999) *Wasted – A Memoir of Anorexia and Bulimia*, London: Flamingo.

Hsu, L.K.G. (1990) *Eating Disorders*, New York: Guilford Press.

Kaffman, M. and Sadeh, T. (1989) "Anorexia nervosa in Kibbutz: factors influencing the development of a monoideistic fixation", *International Journal of Eating Disorders* 8, 33–53.

Kasperlik-Zaluska, A., Migdalska, B., Kazubska, M. and Wisniewska-Wozniak, T. (1981) "Clinical, psychiatric and endocrinological correlations in 42 cases of anorexia nervosa", *Psychiatria Polska* 15, 355–63.

Katzman, M. and Lee, S. (1997) "Beyond body image: the integration of feminist and transcultural theories in the understanding of self starvation", *International Journal of Eating Disorders* 22, 385–94.

King, M. and Bhugra, D. (1989) "Eating disorders: lessons from a cross-cultural study", *Psychological Medicine* 19, 955–8.

Kirmayer, L.J. and Young, A. (1999) "Culture and context in the evolutionary concept of mental disorder", *Journal of Abnormal Psychology* 108, 446–52.

Kleinman, A.M. (1987) "Anthropology and psychiatry: the role of culture in cross-cultural research on illness", *British Journal of Psychiatry* 151, 447–54.

Lee, S. (1993) "How abnormal is the desire for slimness? A survey of eating attitudes and behaviour among Chinese undergraduates in Hong Kong", *Psychological Medicine* 23, 437–51.

Lee, S. (1995) "Self-starvation in contexts: towards the culturally sensitive understanding of anorexia nervosa", *Social Science and Medicine* 41, 25–36.

Lee, S. and Lee, A.M. (2000) "Disordered eating in three communities of China: a comparative study of female high school students in Hong Kong, Shenzhen, and rural Hunan", *International Journal of Eating Disorders* 27, 317–27.

Lee, S., Ho, T.P. and Hsu, L.K.G. (1993) "Fat phobic and non-fat phobic anorexia nervosa: a comparative study of 70 Chinese patients in Hong Kong", *Psychological Medicine* 23, 999–1017.

Lee, S., Lee, A.M. and Leung, T. (1998) "Cross-cultural validity of the eating disorder inventory: a study of Chinese patients with eating disorder in Hong Kong", *International Journal of Eating Disorders* 23, 177–88.

Lee, S., Lee, A.M., Ngai, E., Lee, D.T. and Wing, Y.K. (2001) "Rationales for food refusal among Chinese patients with anorexia nervosa in Hong Kong", *International Journal of Eating Disorders* 29, 224–9.

Lee, S., Kwok, K., Liau, C. and Leung, T. (2002) "Screening Chinese patients with eating disorders using the eating attitudes test in Hong Kong", *International Journal of Eating Disorders* 32, 91–7.

Lee, S., Chan, Y.Y.L. and Hsu, L.K.G. (2003) "The intermediate term outcome of Chinese patients with anorexia nervosa in Hong Kong", *American Journal of Psychiatry* 160, 967–72.

Lock, M. (1987) "DSM-III as a culture-bound construct: commentary on culture-bound syndromes and international disease classifications", *Culture, Medicine and Psychiatry* 11, 35–42.

Ma, J.L., Chow, M.Y., Lee, S. and Lai, K. (2002) "Family meaning of self-starvation – themes discerned in family treatment in Hong Kong", *Journal of Family Therapy* 24, 57–71.

MacSween, M. (1993) *Anorexic Bodies: A Feminist and Sociological Perspective on Anorexia Nervosa*, London: Routledge.

Mitchell, J., Pyle, R.L., Hatsukami, D. and Eckert, E.D. (1986) "What are atypical eating disorders?", *Psychosomatics* 27, 21–8.

Nakamura, K., Yamamoto, M., Yamazaki, O., Kawashima, Y., Muto, K., Someya, T., Sakurai, K. and Nozoe, S. (2000) "Prevalence of anorexia nervosa and bulimia nervosa in a geographically defined area in Japan", *International Journal of Eating Disorders* 28, 173–80.

Nasser, M., Katzman, M. and Gordon, R. (eds) (2001) *Eating Disorders and Cultures in Transition*, London: Routledge.

Nemiah, J.C. (1958) "Anorexia nervosa: fact and theory", *American Journal of Digestive Diseases* 3, 249–74.

Neumarker, U., Dudeck, U., Vollrath, M., Neumarker, K.J. and Steinhausen, H.C. (1992) "Eating attitudes among adolescent anorexia nervosa patients and normal subjects in former West and East Berlin: a transcultural comparison", *International Journal of Eating Disorders* 12, 281–9.

Palmer, R.L. (1993) "Weight concern should not be a necessary criterion for the eating disorders: a polemic", *International Journal of Eating Disorders* 14, 459–65.

Patton, G.C. and Szmukler, G.I. (1995) "Epidemiology of eating disorders", in A. Jablensky (ed.) *Epidemiological Psychiatry, Baillière's Clinical Psychiatry – International Practice and Research*, London: Baillière Tindall.

Peters, L. and Fallon, P. (1994) "The journey of recovery: dimensions of change", in P. Fallon, M. Katzman and S. Wooley (eds) *Feminist Perspectives on Eating Disorders*, New York: Guilford Press.

Regier, D.A., Kaelber, C.T., Rae, D.S., Farmer, M.E., Knauper, B., Kessler, R.C. and Norquist, G.S. (1998) "Limitations of diagnostic criteria and assessment instruments for mental disorders: implications for research and policy", *Archives of General Psychiatry* 55, 109–15.

Robinson, P.H. (1989) "Perceptivity and paraceptivity during measurement of gastric emptying in anorexia and bulimia nervosa", *British Journal of Psychiatry* 154, 400–5.

Russell, G.F.M. (1995) "Anorexia nervosa through time", in G. Szmukler, C. Dare and J. Treasure (eds) *Handbook of Eating Disorders: Theory, Treatment and Research*, Chichester: Wiley.

Serpell, L., Treasure, J., Teasdale, J. and Sullivan, V. (1999) "Anorexia nervosa: friend or foe?", *International Journal of Eating Disorders* 25, 177–86.

Shapiro, D.H. (1998) *Control Therapy: An Integrated Approach to Psychotherapy, Health, and Healing*, New York: Wiley.

Shorter, E. (1987) "The first great increase in anorexia nervosa", *Journal of Social History* 21, 69–96.

Shorter, E. (1994) "Youth and psychosomatic illness", in E. Shorter (ed.) *From the Mind into the Body: The Cultural Origins of Psychosomatic Symptoms*, New York: Free Press.

Silverman, J.A. (1989) "Louis-Victor Marcé, 1828–1864: anorexia nervosa's forgotten man", *Psychological Medicine*, 19, 833–5.

Steiger, H. (1993) "Anorexia nervosa: is it the syndrome or the theorist that is culture- and gender-bound?", *Transcultural Psychiatric Research Review* 30, 347–58.

Steinhausen, H.C., Neumärker Vollrath, M., Dudeck, U. and Neumärker, U. (1992) "A transcultural comparison of the Eating Disorders Inventory in former East and West Berlin", *International Journal of Eating Disorders* 12, 725–30.

Strober, M., Freeman, R. and Morrell, W. (1999) "Atypical anorexia nervosa: separation from typical cases in course and outcome in a long-term prospective study", *International Journal of Eating Disorders* 25, 135–42.

Study Group on Anorexia Nervosa (1995) "Anorexia nervosa: directions for future research", *International Journal of Eating Disorders* 17, 235–41.

Szekely, E.A. (1989) "From eating disorders to women's situations: extending the boundaries of psychological inquiry", *Counselling Psychology Quarterly* 2, 167–84.

Treasure, J. (1997) *Anorexia Nervosa: A Survival Guide for Families, Friends and Sufferers*, Hove, East Sussex: Psychology Press.

Vandereycken, W. (1993) "Misleading variants in the clinical picture of anorexia nervosa", *European Eating Disorders Review* 1, 183–6.

Vandereycken, W. and Vanderlinden, J. (1983) "Denial of illness and the use of self-report measures in anorexia nervosa patients", *International Journal of Eating Disorders* 2, 101–7.

Vandereycken, W. and van Deth, R. (1990) "A tribute to Lasègue's description of anorexia nervosa (1873), with completion of its English translation", *British Journal of Psychiatry* 157, 902–8.

Yager, J. and Davis, C. (1993) "Letter to Sing Lee's review of 'Transcultural aspects of eating disorders' ", *Transcultural Psychiatric Research Review* 30: 295–6.

Way, K. (1993) *Anorexia Nervosa and Recovery: A Hunger for Meaning*, New York: Harrington Park Press.

Chapter 11

A psychoanalytic perspective on EDNOS

David Clinton

Introduction

Learning the lesson of EDNOS means learning that there exists unity within diversity. Our current diagnostic understanding, or perhaps more accurately lack of understanding, in relation to eating disorders demonstrates that these patients present with a wide range of both primary and secondary symptoms. EDNOS patients are characterized by psychopathology similar to, but not quite the same as, the familiar syndromes of Anorexia Nervosa and Bulimia Nervosa (see Appendix for diagnostic criteria). At the same time, there is something elusively "typical" about these "atypical" patients that allows us to apply the label of eating disorders in the first place. From a diagnostic perspective EDNOS raises the question of what indeed is typical about eating disorders. From a psychoanalytic perspective EDNOS raises the question of what a common core of symptoms may imply in terms of underlying personality structure. Put succinctly, we could ask whether a characteristic core of eating disorder symptoms also implies an underlying core unity of unconscious meaning among eating disorder patients. This chapter will explore these issues in relation to both the theoretical and empirical literature, and briefly discuss implications for the treatment of eating disorders.

Diversity of symptoms and diversity of meaning

A fundamental aspect of our knowledge about eating disorders is that we now know that patients who suffer from these problems are heterogeneous in terms of background, diagnostic features, comorbidity and personality functioning. The existence of EDNOS per se, and the fact that these patients comprise from perhaps 30 to 60 per cent of all eating disorder patients (Fairburn and Walsh 2002) is in itself testimony to the diversity of these problems. We know that age of eating disorder debut can vary considerably. The disorders are typical of adolescent and young adult females, but not uncommon in persons of considerably older and even younger age. Most, but by no means all, patients will initially develop a restricting form of eating disorder, and perhaps half of these restrictors will go on to develop binge eating. Depression can be a serious problem that may affect as many as half of all eating disorder patients at some point in their lives (Cooper 2002). Other often reported concomitant psychiatric problems include anxiety disorder and obsessional tendencies. Problems with drug and alcohol abuse are not unusual, especially among bulimics. Marked histories of impulsivity and self-destructiveness are to be found among some patients, while others show no traces of such problems. Personality functioning in general (Walsh and Garner 1997) and levels of ego functioning in particular (Norring *et al.* 1989) can vary considerably. Estimates of personality disturbance in eating disorders have been reported in between 23 and 93 per cent of cases (Rosenvinge *et al.* 2000).

This clinical diversity of eating disorders is mirrored in our emerging understanding of the complex aetiology of these problems. Most experts within the field would concur that the origin and development of eating disorders are not to be explained from the vantage point of one particular perspective. As the Maudsley group have expressed it, "we cannot focus exclusively on psyche or soma, but must pay close attention to a complex interaction between the two" (Ward *et al.* 2000). In the emerging picture biological, social and psychological factors act together to predispose, trigger and maintain eating disorders. The important aetiological questions no longer concern whether eating disorders are caused by biological, social or psychological factors, but rather how such factors interact over time to produce the diverse phenomena we meet in clinical practice.

Given both the clinical diversity, and multifactorial origins, of eating disorders, we might ask what a psychoanalytic perspective on eating disorders in general, and EDNOS in particular, has to offer. Psychoanalytic theories are traditionally based on individual analysts' close observation and interpretation of mental processes among a relatively small number of individuals over an extended period of time, and emphasize understanding the role of unconscious factors in a person's life. Psychoanalysts tend to work with their patients three to five times a week over a period of many years (five years or longer is not at all unusual). Similarly, those who work with psychoanalytic or psychodynamic forms of psychotherapy often meet their patients twice weekly over a period of several years or more. Clinically, the material that is generated from such observation is used to help patients understand, work through and change important factors that have contributed to the development and maintenance of their unique problems. Theoretically, such a method can provide a useful complement to the data that are collected by more objective means using the methodology of the natural sciences. As such psychoanalytic inquiry can help us to generate hypotheses on the development and maintenance of eating disorders. What's more, because of its emphasis on the unconscious, psychoanalysis can aid in better understanding common treatment problems that can arise within a wide range of therapeutic approaches.

The value of such an approach is discussed by Dare and Crowther (1995), who argue that a psychodynamic perspective can be seen in terms of how it helps us to understand what happens when a person meets with the possibility of becoming anorexic, and why "she clasps [this possibility] to her emaciated breast and makes it her own" (Dare and Crowther 1995: 126). They contend that the risk of embracing eating disorder symptoms (i.e. the availability of a symptom) is largely determined by social, cultural, familial, biological and cognitive factors. However, the need for the symptom can be understood in terms of "the developmentally understandable psychological qualities of the person". Psychoanalytic perspectives can, in this respect, help us to understand the individual's need for a symptom and the difficulties that person may have in relinquishing the symptom.

Nevertheless, there are a number of problems that must be addressed before exploring the wider possibilities of a psychoanalytic perspective on a specific psychiatric diagnosis such as EDNOS. Over the years psychoanalytic writers have developed ideas based on classical drive theory, self-psychology, object relations theory and interpersonal theory, among others. Within the field of eating disorders discussion has traditionally focused on AN, with BN receiving increased attention in recent years. Although there has been no specific discussion of EDNOS per se in psychoanalytic literature, a close inspection of relevant work suggests that many of the cases discussed would likely be classified as EDNOS if formal psychiatric criteria were to be applied. Within psychoanalysis, debate about eating disorders has largely focused on two general areas: the question of conflict versus deficit in the development of these problems, and the question of the underlying unconscious meaning of specific symptoms. Before going further it will be helpful to review these areas.

Conflict or deficit?

Freud himself never wrote explicitly about AN, the one diagnosable eating disorder of his time. However, in a paper with Breuer he did discuss what he called "chronic vomiting and anorexia carried to the point of refusal of food," which he saw as being of psychic origin (Breuer and Freud 1893: 4). In this early paper he maintained that "a painful affect, which was originally excited while eating but was suppressed, produces nausea and vomiting, and this continues for months as hysterical vomiting [which] accompanies a feeling of moral disgust." Later, in *The Interpretation of Dreams*, Freud (1900) described a patient who had chronic vomiting both in fulfilment of and self-punishment for a fantasy of being made continually pregnant by many men. He also discussed "hysterical vomiting" in his correspondence with Fliess (Freud 1899) and in the case of Dora (Freud 1905). Later still in his case study of the Wolf Man, Freud (1918: 106) mentioned a type of neurosis present in girls around the time of puberty and afterwards that "repudiates sexuality through anorexia".

In these early writings, Freud's implicit emphasis in relation to a psychologically derived disturbance of eating was on conflicts pertaining to sexual themes. During the 1940s several of his followers took up his ideas on the central role of repressed sexual conflicts in neurosis, and applied these explicitly to the ontogenesis of AN. Perhaps of greatest historical impact was the work of Waller *et al.* (1940: 6), who maintained that in AN "eating is symbolically equated with sexuality, particularly with [unconscious] fantasies of impregnation". The case material that they presented was described as "clear and unambiguous", and their work continued to exercise a pervasive influence into the 1960s and even beyond. During this time symptoms of disordered eating were seen as representing a neurotic compromise formation that attempted to bridge unconscious conflicts pertaining to oedipal development (i.e. the period of psychosexual development, around 3 to 5 years of age). Behind the symptom there was thought to be a forbidden unconscious sexual wish in relation to the parent of the opposite sex that had been repressed. Most psychoanalysts of the time probably took this to be "the whole truth". In a literature review from 1949 on feeding problems of psychogenic origin Lehman noted a "marked consensus" that AN reflects both a "repression of the sex drives" and an inhibition of eating because patients "unconsciously feel that eating is a sexual act" (1949: 469).

With time, however, the unassailable sexual conflict model of AN became more and more problematic. Gradually, less emphasis was placed on conflicts around sexual drives, while more emphasis was placed on early developmental deficits. Instrumental in this change of focus was Hilde Bruch. In her writings, Bruch (1973) emphasized the role of pervasive, but often subtly camouflaged, deficits in early development that formed a predisposition for AN. More specifically, she placed the emphasis on shortcomings in the early mother–child relationship, which she maintained forms a basis of vulnerability in relation to eating disorders. From the time of infancy the future anorexic's relationship with her mother was believed to be characterized by the mother's difficulties in adequately interpreting her child's signals. According to Bruch this pattern of early interaction results in difficulties for the child in identifying both emotional states and physiological signals, such as hunger. Further consequences involve a tendency for the child to become over-controlling in relation to his/her own needs, as well as predisposing to problems pertaining to separation and development of the self. Bruch saw symptoms of dieting and the need for weight loss during adolescence as providing the means for an individual with this particular vulnerability to assert control over her own body. Weight restriction is accordingly seen as representing a last attempt at asserting autonomy.

Contemporary applications of the deficit model of AN in particular, and eating disorders in general within psychoanalytic schools of thought have been many. Worth noting are the anthologies of Johnson (1991), which is largely within the tradition of self-psychology, and Petrucelli and Stuart (2001), in which contributors come from the tradition of interpersonal object relations theory. Another distinct extension of the deficit approach to eating disorders can be found in Lawrence (2001). Basing her work on the object relations theory of Melanie Klein, Lawrence develops the idea that eating disorders function to reinforce unconscious fantasies of control in relation to what she terms "the internalized parents" (i.e. the internalized mental images of early relationships with the mother and father). Establishing and maintaining control of these inner images is important because of the aggressive impulses that the eating disordered patient experiences towards these internal objects, and for which the patient feels guilt and fear.

The unconscious meaning of specific symptoms

Another major focus of interest in psychoanalytic writings on eating disorders has concerned the unconscious meaning of specific symptoms. Anna Freud's (1946) discussion of infantile feeding disturbances equated conflicts at particular stages of development with the subsequent emergence of specific eating-related symptoms. What symptoms an individual presented with depended on where he/she had run into developmental problems and at what age. More specifically, she argued that much of a child's problematic behaviour towards food originates in emotional conflicts towards the mother, which are transferred on to the food that is a symbol for her. During the earliest (pre-oedipal) period of development she seems to have seen feeding difficulties as somewhat less serious than those that arise later during the oedipal period. Ambivalence towards the mother during later development was thought to express itself as fluctuations between overeating and refusal of food, guilty feelings towards the mother and a consequent inability to enjoy her affection. This was thought to reflect an inability to enjoy food, as well as an obstinacy and hostility towards the mother and a struggle against being fed.

The psychological origin of fear of fatness has been taken up by Wilson *et al.* (1985). Working within the tradition of ego psychology Wilson saw this defining characteristic of AN as primarily caused by the ego's attempt to defend itself against an overwhelming terror of being fat. This fear of the patient's was seen as the result of identification with a parent who expressed a similar, but less intense, fear. According to this view a primitive, magical and omnipotent part of the ego is regressed, yet manifested in pre-oedipal conflicts and fantasies that are vehemently denied by the patient. Behind these symptoms Wilson saw unresolved oral sadomasochistic conflicts and the domineering and controlling personality of the mother (and/or the father) that profoundly warps and inhibits normal development. In Wilson's view, AN is a neurotic symptom complex that can be found in a variety of character disorders, largely caused by maternal and/or paternal over-control and overemphasis on food and eating as symbols of love.

As regards what we would now term binge eating in the early psycho-analytic literature, it tended to be seen as indicating a demand for love (Lehman 1949). In her early work on overeating, Bruch (1940: 761) wrote that obese children tend to regard "food as a comfort, as a means of combating unpleasant circumstances." She also found that "In some cases food seems to be the only source of satisfaction and the longing for it becomes an uncontrolled craving." She added that "Sometimes a feeling of helplessness and smallness makes a child crave more and more food in order to become as big and powerful as the person whom he fears." Compensatory vomiting has often been seen as the result of early oral sexual trauma, in which case the vomiting is understood in terms of a symbolized attempt to eliminate an unwanted penis. However, as was the case with AN, there has been a tendency among psychoanalytic writers to move away from explanations of bulimic behaviour that focus exclusively on oedipal sexual conflict. McDougall (2001), for example, emphasizes the role of maintaining control over the inner world. She sees symptoms of disordered eating as providing a means for dispelling, as rapidly as possible, feelings of anxiety, anger, guilt, depression, or any other affective state that is liable to give rise to psychic pain and tension.

A number of psychoanalytic authors have focused on distinguishing AN from BN. Johnson (1991) has maintained that developmental differences can be distinguished between the diagnoses. He sees this as largely having to do with the type of engagement that mothers have toward their children. According to this theory the anorexic's severe food restriction is a result of the mother's over-involvement with the child, whereas the bulimic's binge eating is a result of under-involvement during the early years. Even Lawrence (2001) attempts to make a developmental differentiation between AN and BN when she argues that in AN internalized objects are felt to be perman-ently in thrall, suspended or frozen, whereas in BN they are attacked in a frenzied and intermittent way.

Looking back on psychoanalytic writings on eating disorders over the years, authors have tended to espouse a wide range of ideas that have reflected the theoretical orientations of the time. Many of these approaches can indeed be seen as casting light on the unconscious internal world of individual sufferers. However, it is difficult to see these theories as providing generalizable ideas that are relevant to understanding the workings of all eating disorder patients. As we know, eating disorder patients are very hetero-geneous. The role of sexual conflicts or trauma may be important for creating predisposing factors in some patients, while key developmental deficits may be pertinent in others. Essentially, there is a problem when developmental theories are derived retrospectively from the observation of a limited number of adult individuals. Such an exercise may provide an essential heuristic for an individual who is endeavouring to understand his or her own past, and it may even help us to formulate some important hypotheses. But it is a hazardous procedure for developing generally applicable theories of psychopathology. An alternative approach, which will be elaborated below, concerns the rapprochement of psychoanalysis and empirical developmental psychology that is now taking place. This may offer the possibility of more generalizable and prospective theories concerning generally applicable predisposing and maintaining factors for eating disorders.

Another important problem for many theories of eating disorders, and by no means not just psychoanalytic ones, concerns the fate of symptoms over time. This is another one of the lessons of EDNOS. The presenting symptoms of eating disorder patients can change markedly over time, yet patients retain their eating disorders. Anorexics may become bulimic, bulimics may cease to compensate for their binges and develop a clinical picture typical of Binge Eating Disorder. Many EDNOS patients, in particular, may have previously fulfilled criteria for one of the major eating disorder syndromes. Such a state of affairs is problematic for theories that postulate differences in the underlying meaning of specific symptoms. The central questions here are first, whether there are central core symptoms to eating disorders, and second, whether there might be a common core of unconscious meaning to these central symptoms.

Uniformity of core symptoms and the question of common unconscious meaning

There has been considerable debate within the psychiatric literature about the diagnosis of eating disorders, a fact that this book in itself testifies to. Although questions about the optimal classification of these disorders are far from being resolved, there is a growing interest in attempting to distinguish a core of central symptoms that typify eating disorders. In many respects this development is largely due to EDNOS. The fact that this large group of patients can be considered eating disordered, without fulfilling full criteria for the two major syndromes, begs the question of what constitutes the common denominators of eating disorders. Surprisingly, this question has received relatively little attention in the empirical literature. However, Fairburn and Walsh (2002: 171) have proposed something so unusual as a definition of what defines an eating disorder. The central part of their definition emphasizes "a persistent disturbance of eating behaviour or behaviour intended to control weight, which significantly impairs physical health or psychosocial functioning."

Although being a clear step forward, their definition does have some problems. They put diagnostic emphasis on "behaviour intended to control weight". In a polemic on the hazards of undue focus on weight concern as a general defining criterion for eating disorders, Palmer (1993) made some important observations that may be relevant to Fairburn and Walsh's (2002) proposed definition. He observed that although "weight concern" has clear applicability to the diagnosis of AN and BN, it does have some important problems as a general criterion. Much the same can be said of "behaviour intended to control weight". As Palmer pointed out, the early-nineteenth-century accounts of AN did not emphasize, or often even mention, weight concern; cases of AN presenting in non-Western cultures are not known for the salience of weight concern; there are also clear examples of patients (usually classified as EDNOS) who otherwise appear to have classic eating disorders but who lack weight concern.

The over-investment of eating restraint

Despite Fairburn and Walsh (2002) putting emphasis on *behaviour to control* rather than *concern about* weight, the problem may be that they still miss the central diagnostic issue. And that issue may have to do more with eating than weight. In his polemic, Palmer (1993: 459) drew attention to what he called "eating restraint that is over-invested". Among other things he argued that eating restriction (or attempts at eating restriction) appears to be a universal finding in the histories of patients presenting for treatment of an eating disorder. It is obviously typical of patients presenting with AN. It is also a characteristic of the disorganized cycles of binge eating and compensatory behaviour typical of BN. Even in patients with BED where there is a lack of the behavioural manifestations of eating restraint, there will usually be found an emotionally laden issue around the desire to control and restrict eating, along with a history of failed attempts to do so. Moreover, as Palmer points out, the absence of appetite loss tends to be opposed by changes in the urge to eat. Palmer argues that persistence of restraint in the face of regulatory forces tends to increase these forces. As a result a vicious circle may develop if fear of the loss of control in the face of regulatory forces leads to an increase and persistence of restriction.

Clearly, resolution of the diagnostic issue of eating restraint versus weight concern will need to await further research. Nevertheless, we can, at least preliminarily, discern grounds for viewing eating restraint that is over-invested as forming a common core symptom characteristic of the two major eating disorder syndromes, and, by and large, the vast majority of those patients that we classify as EDNOS. But what might motivate this over-investment of eating restraint? This is an important question. At a conscious level, we can discern a plethora of motivators that we regularly meet in clinical practice. For example, anorexics will commonly maintain that they restrict their eating in order to avoid weight gain. Bulimics may express a need for greater control over disorganized eating habits. Other patients may focus on the need to purify themselves, talk about peer pressure or espouse commonly held cultural values about slimness.

From a psychoanalytic point of view, an interesting question arises when we ask what unconscious motivators may lay behind this over-investment of eating restraint. Might it be possible to discern an underlying core of unconscious meaning that creates a need for such an over-investment of eating restraint? What might this mean for the development and maintenance of eating disorders? Taking up this question, I would like to speculate on what could be an important unconscious dimension, which, together with other factors, provides a motivational basis for an over-investment of eating restraint. What's more, rather than developing this line of thought retrospectively on the basis of adult clinical material, I would like to draw on recent developments in theories of affect regulation, empirical infant research and object relations theory. Essentially, the idea I would like to explore is that the over-investment of eating restraint typical of eating disorders may reflect an underlying need to restrict affective experience in general and the experience of desire in particular. These ideas are admittedly speculative, but they may have some important implications, not only for the theoretical understanding of eating disorders, but also for clinical work and research. They can also offer a means of integrating our growing knowledge of eating disorders with advances in other areas.

Affect regulation and object relations

Not all psychoanalytic theories are based on retrospective reconstruction of the individual's early life through the interpretation of clinical material supplied during the adult years. Within psychoanalysis there has long been an interest in the direct observation of infants and children. Despite wide theoretical and clinical differences the work of Melanie Klein, Anna Freud, Margaret Mahler, John Bowlby and others has emphasized the importance of observing infants and children directly in order to better understand their inner experiences. More importantly for the present question, however, is the growing interest within psychoanalytic circles for empirical research on infant development (e.g. Emde and Fonagy 1997; Fonagy *et al.* 2002; Gergely and Watson 1996; Stern 1985).

Not so long ago, infants were conceived of as passive beings surrounded by a stimulus barrier that limited experience of the external world (e.g. Mahler *et al.* 1975). Now the emerging view is that infants enter life with a rich perceptual apparatus that is pre-wired to attend to and explore the external world, and which starts to build representations of the external world on the basis of that experience from the very beginning. For some relevant reviews of important research see, for example, Bower (1974), Emde (1988), Gergely (1992) or Stern (1985). A fundamental aspect of this growing empirical knowledge of early development has been the discovery of the infant's sensitivity to contingencies between the infant's own actions and the perceived effects these have in the world around. These contingencies can be seen as collections of expectations, or "if–then" conditional statements. A classic example was given by Watson (1972). He found that 2-month-old infants increase their rate of leg kicking when the kicking results in a contingent event (in Watson's study the movement of a mobile above the infant's bed). However, this will not happen when the infants experience a similar but non-contingent event. The implication is that detection of causal control over the mobile's movements is rewarding and stimulating in its own right. Another example pertaining directly to interpersonal aspects of behaviour concerns studies involving the still-face procedure (Tronick *et al.* 1978) or delayed feedback techniques (Murray and Trevarthen 1985). In these experimental situations of face-to-face interaction between infants and their mothers, the expected interpersonal contingencies are disrupted. The interpersonal exchange does not take place as the infant would expect, and considerable distress can be observed in the infants.

Of potential relevance to the understanding of eating disorders and the regulation of affect is the work of Fonagy and associates (2002). They present a social biofeedback theory of parental affect-mirroring, and discuss the way in which the infant's automatic emotion expression, along with the caregiver's consequent affect-reflective facial and vocal reactions, comes to be linked in the infant's mind through the detection of interpersonal contingencies that gradually become internalized. The forging of such contingency links is thought to have two important effects: first, infants come to associate the control they have over their parents' mirroring behaviour with a resulting improvement in their emotional state, leading, eventually, to an experience of the self as a regulating agent, and second, the basis for affect regulation and impulse control is established through second-order representations of feeling states. As a result, affects can be manipulated and discharged internally, as well as through action. Even more importantly, affects can be experienced as something recognizable and shareable. Expressions of affect by the parent that are not contingent on the infant's affect will tend to undermine the appropriate labelling of internal states, which may remain confusing, unsymbolized and difficult to regulate.

The Fonagy group further develop their ideas in relation to the pathological pathways that affect-mirroring can take. Essentially, they argue that the emergence of particular interpersonal contingencies create predisposing factors for the emergence of psychopathology later on in development. They identify two main types of pathological contingencies. The first is associated with borderline personality disorder, and receives considerable attention in their work. It is thought to arise when a caregiver is overwhelmed by the negative affect generated in response to the infant, and presents a reaction that lacks "markedness". This concept of markedness designates a response to the infant that indicates that the caregiver's reaction is "not real", i.e. the reaction is not an indication of what the caregiver feels, but rather an indication of what the infant is feeling. If the caregiver displays an overly realistic emotionally arousing reaction (i.e. one that that lacks markedness), then the infant will be led to believe that the reaction is an indication of how the caregiver actually feels. This, in turn, is thought to undermine, not only the infant's possibility of creating a secondary representation of his/her inner state, but also the sense of boundary between infant and caregiver. As Fonagy and co-workers put it, when a caregiver's reaction lacks markedness the infant's "internal experience suddenly becomes external through the experience equivalent to contagion." The second type of pathological mirroring, which receives less systematic attention, is thought to predispose to the development of narcissistic disorders. When affect-mirroring is appropriately "marked" but is non-contingent (i.e. the infant's emotion is misperceived by the caregiver), the infant is thought to experience the caregiver's mirroring as mapping onto his/her primary emotional state. However, since the mirrored state is incongruent with the infant's actual feelings, the secondary representation will tend to be distorted. The infant will, thus, mislabel the primary emotional state, and representations of the self will not have strong ties to the underlying emotional state. Consequently, the infant may convey an impression of reality, but since the primary affective state has not been recognized (or attuned to) by the caregiver, the self will feel empty and lack secondary representations of affect.

Of course, one may wonder what all of this has to do with eating disorders. Generally speaking, the ideas that the Fonagy group have put forward can help us to understand how the naturally occurring internal process of affect regulation can break down, leaving an individual without the means of appropriately identifying and acting on internal feeling states. Many clinicians will certainly recognize problems that patients have with identifying and expressing affects in eating disorders. It may be that early difficulties in the regulation and mentalization of inner states result in a need to restrict and control the experience of affect generally. The idea being that if an individual cannot differentiate the inner feeling states that are stimulated in a particular interpersonal exchange he/she will need to restrict experience of affects generally in order to avoid being overwhelmed by diffuse feelings that cannot be identified or understood. The idea of problems with affect regulation being involved in the origins of eating disorders is not new. Bruch's (1973) theories about the development of AN focused, among other things, on the role of how a mother perceives and responds to her infant's signals. More recently, Dare and Crowther (1995) as well as McDougall (2001) have also drawn attention to the relationship between eating disorders and the regulation of unpleasant and undifferentiated affect.

Nevertheless, although we might envisage how difficulties in the regulation and mentalization of affect during early development might put a person at risk for developing psychiatric symptoms generally, it remains unclear how such difficulties might contribute to the development of eating disorders specifically. Are there particular interpersonal contingencies that might predispose toward an over-investment of eating restraint? On the one hand, it is entirely possible that there are, in fact, none. It may be that problems of affect regulation in general, when combined with other factors (e.g. societal, biological vulnerability, family dynamics, etc.), are entirely sufficient to create a tendency for an individual to over-invest eating restraint during later development. On the other hand, it is difficult to see how these factors could combine to produce the resilient and overwhelming need to restrict eating, without the presence of some sort of factor that could predispose to the salience of this symptom. It may, therefore, be fruitful to consider identifying particular sorts of contingencies that might help to make eating restraint so appealing.

One possibility is that affect mirroring that takes deviant pathways in relation to the experience of *desire* may have a particular bearing on the propensity to over-invest eating restraint. The role of desire is not dealt with explicitly by the Fonagy group. They seem to see the concept as similar to, yet clearly distinct from, affect. However, the experience and regulation of desires may well be governed by similar interpersonal contingencies during early development. We can use the models of borderline and narcissistic psychopathology that the Fonagy group develops as a point of departure. Applying the borderline model we might speculate that when an infant desires something that the caregiver accurately perceives and reacts to, but without appropriate markedness, the infant will succeed in adequately labelling the desire. But at the same time, it will be difficult for the infant to distinguish whose desire is being experienced. Such a confusional state implies a lack of boundaries between self and other, and might predispose to a tendency to focus on the desires of others. Applying the narcissistic model we might speculate that when the infant desires something, and the caregiver responds with appropriate markedness, but non-contingently (i.e. in relation to a different desire that the caregiver perceives), the infant may perceive the desire as his/her own, but mislabel it.

A complicating factor for this model concerns the nature of desire itself. Desire is something that is experienced in relation to something else. It has an object. The object of desire can be said to have both psychological and physiological aspects. For example, in a threatening situation that causes the infant intense discomfort, the infant may desire both a physiological soothing function and a psychological interactive function. In other words, a particular manner of interacting with the caregiver may be desired in order to achieve a reduction in a particular state of physiological arousal. Putting it another way, the infant desires both soothing and someone who soothes. Problems may develop if the caregiver is unable to distinguish between the two. For example, if the caregiver accurately perceives the physiological aspect of desire (e.g. need for soothing), but misperceives the psychological aspect of desire (e.g. relates in a non-congruent fashion). An example might be when a mother accurately perceives her infant's distress, but attempts to soothe the infant by offering food or distracting the infant, rather than by comforting and showing appropriate holding behaviour. The use of food or distraction may reduce the displeasurable physiological state, but without the appropriate comforting and holding. The absence of this relational response may undermine the development of a self-soothing mechanism, and make the infant more dependent on the sort of response that is available (e.g. use of food or distraction).

At this point, object relations theory can help us to understand the fate of the person that is responding to the infant. Roots of this school of psycho-analysis can be found in the writings of Klein (1975) and Fairbairn (1952), while contemporary applications in relation to eating disorders have been described by Lawrence (2001). According to object relations theory, a person's psychology is not merely a function of the interpersonal relationships that arise between individuals in the external world, but also a function of the intrapersonal relations that exist within the internal world of subjective experience. Both these internal and external worlds are engaged in reciprocal interaction, where experiences of relationships in the external world are thought to influence the structuring of experience, and where inner structures provide the means of interpreting external reality. One of the key ideas within this school of thought is that objects in the outside world become internalized as "inner objects". In the context of the present discussion, the infant is thought to gradually internalize images of the actions of the caregiver, which come to guide patterns of experiencing and relating. What this implies, among other things, is that the sorts of interpersonal contingencies that Fonagy *et al.* (2002) discuss will also have implications for the fate of the caregiver within the infant's inner world. As regards the question of the regulation of desire, as discussed above, we might conjecture that a caregiver who tends to respond to the infant's expressions of desire without appropri-ate markedness or non-contingently, will tend to become internalized accord-ingly. As a result the infant may come to expect others to behave in a similar fashion.

If it is important what happens with the psychological aspects of desire, it is equally important what happens with the physiological aspects. If a person finds it difficult to differentiate internal states, and is not sure what he/she is experiencing, then the detection of hunger and regulation of eating may become challenging. What's more, a person who has early in life experienced a non-contingent form of affect mirroring, may find it difficult to distinguish between the psychological and physiological aspects of desire. Discriminating sensations of hunger and experiencing the desire to eat may therefore become particularly demanding, since such experiences may also symbolically awaken a deep ambivalent desire in relation to the caregiver, who in a sense promised to, but failed to, help the patient develop sufficient regulatory mechanisms to deal with the patient's inner world. Physiological processes such as hunger may, therefore, symbolically remind the patient of a painful psychological reality that must be controlled in order to avoid being overwhelmed. The result may be a tendency to over-invest eating restraint in order to help keep such feelings at bay. On the one hand, the patient is reminded of the desire for a good object, i.e. a caregiver who is attuned to what is going on inside the infant, and who can provide for the psychological and relational aspects of desire. On the other hand, the patient is reminded of the reality of a bad object, i.e. a caregiver who failed to satisfy desire in a congruent manner.

Treatment issues

The over-investment of eating restraint has a number of implications for treatment. Being a cardinal symptom of eating disorders in and of itself, tackling the over-investment of eating restraint constitutes an important treatment goal. Not many practitioners would disagree with this. However, the ideas developed above about the unconscious factors that may motivate this over-investment raise other key treatment issues. These issues pertain to both patients and those who endeavour to help patients in the recovery process. Understanding these issues may not only be of value to practitioners of psychoanalytic and psychodynamic forms of treatment, but even to clinicians working with other therapeutic approaches.

Helping patients

If the ideas developed in this chapter about the psychological origins of eating restraint are correct, then it will also be important for clinicians to focus attention on questions concerning the regulation of affect in general and desire in particular. It may be useful to help patients explore and express undifferentiated affects and desires, with an aim to making these inner states more recognizable and communicable. Such therapeutic work is by no means the exclusive preserve of psychoanalytically based forms of treatment. Therapists from a wide range of backgrounds could integrate such work into their own treatment approaches.

Otherwise, there are a number of treatment issues that do have a more direct relevance for psychoanalytic forms of treatment, although even here a general understanding of the forces involved may help other therapists. One such issue concerns transference. Essentially, transference refers to a person's tendency to repeat past forms of relating in the present. In psychotherapy this can be seen in forms of relating that the individual wishes to get away from, but which despite valiant efforts are repeated time and time again. This can be witnessed both outside the psychotherapeutic setting, but most especially within it in relation to the therapist. In a somewhat paradoxical sense trans-ference can be viewed as an adaptive striving, the idea being that the indi-vidual repeats apparently maladaptive patterns of relating in an attempt to overcome difficulties that were faced long ago and thereby move on in life.

However, since the individual lacks the tools to resolve these difficulties the maladaptive patterns repeat themselves. The psychoanalytically trained therapist will, therefore, help the individual to become aware of these patterns and aid in the development of tools (such as the development affect regulative functions) that will help to resolve the difficulties, thereby rendering further repetition unnecessary.

In eating disorders important transference issues may pertain to the expression of affect and how the patient relates to the object of desire. In many senses eating disorder patients are caught in a bind. They need to develop tools for integrating and expressing undifferentiated affect, but to do this they must approach what they are frightened of, not just behaviourally in terms of facing a fear of eating or weight gain. They also need to approach what they are frightened of emotionally in an intersubjective sense. Put another way, they must approach and experience the disorganized feeling states they would otherwise so like to control and repress, in order to find new ways of regulating and integrating these feeling states. Transference comes into play when the therapist attempts to deal with these problems. Exploration of affects and desires tends not to be welcomed with open arms in eating disorder patients. Since the patient will likely have internalized an image of a caregiver who failed to facilitate the regulation of affects and desires, she may tend to expect this pattern to be repeated in treatment. In other words, the therapist will be tested, and expected to fail. How the therapist deals with this challenge can have decisive bearing on his/her possibilities to be trusted by the patient and allowed access to the particular areas of inner affective life that are so problematic and elusive.

Other transference issues that may arise pertain to specific sorts of interpersonal contingencies. Patients whose early development was characterized by affect regulative contingencies that lacked markedness may find it possible to distinguish particular affects and desires, but find it difficult to be able to sense whether these are truly their own. In an attempt to establish some sense of boundaries these patients may tend to focus attention on the therapist in an attempt to ascertain what the therapist is feeling or desiring. What they see, however, may not reflect the therapist's own subjective reality, and the resultant pattern of interaction may largely come to be characterized by projective identification. That is, the patient may come to see in the therapist many of the feeling states that originate in her own inner world, but which she cannot recognize as her own. Consequent episodes of acting out may be unavoidable, and may be used by the patient to provoke the therapist into disclosing projected feelings. Such a pattern of interaction, which the therapist may experience as invasive and provocative to say the least, may also be an essential prerequisite for some patients to subsequently initiate examination and delineation of their own feelings and desires. How the therapist deals with such challenges may prove to be a litmus test of the treatment. In such situations it is imperative that the therapist understands not only what is going on in the patient, but also what is going on in him/herself. This can limit the risk of the therapist getting caught up in a destructive pattern of acting out. On the one hand, it may be necessary for the therapist to appropriately express emotion so the patient can form a clearer picture of the boundaries between herself and the therapist. On the other hand, it will be imperative for the therapist to shift focus back on to the patient so she can initiate exploration and delineation of her own feelings.

Helping those who help

Working with eating disorders can be extremely rewarding. It can also be extremely demanding. In work with eating disorder patients it can be as important to help those who help, as it is to help patients. One of the most important aspects of helping health care professionals to work with eating disorders is providing them with tools that can make the patient's behaviour, and the therapist's own reactions to the patient, more understandable and predictable. Clinical supervision is, of course, an important means to this end. Another important tool involves understanding the role of countertransference. Roughly speaking, countertransference is the therapist's counterpart to transference. It involves the notion that the therapist will react to the patient in ways that the therapist is not entirely conscious of. These patterns of reaction may involve the therapist experiencing feelings and behaving in a manner in which he/she consciously does not desire. Critically reflecting over such patterns, and endeavouring to understand the manner in which the patient's difficulties may be reflected in the therapist's own emotional reactions can be an important part of dealing with difficult treatment issues. By understanding not only how the patient is reacting to the therapist, but also how and why the therapist is reacting in a certain way, it may be possible to limit the risk of the therapist acting out and endangering the goal of helping the patient take steps away from established patterns of self-destructiveness. This may also help to make the demanding task of helping eating disorder patients more bearable.

Summary and conclusion

EDNOS teaches us that there is a unity of common symptoms within the clinical diversity of eating disorders. The very fact that this sizeable ragbag diagnostic category exists raises the question of what it is about these atypical eating disorders that makes them typical enough to be classified as eating disorders in the first place. In is chapter it has been argued that an "over-investment of eating restraint" constitutes an important common denominator, characteristic of eating disorders as a whole. Given this common core of symptomatology, we can begin to explore it from a psychoanalytic perspective, and ask what the underlying unconscious motivators of such an over-investment might be. Of course, given the complex and multidetermined nature of eating disorders in general, any conjectures that we formulate along these lines must be viewed as providing only a partial answer. Nevertheless, recent advances in the integration of psychoanalytic theory and empirical research on infancy, and in particular the work of the Fonagy group on the development of affect regulation may be of help. It is proposed that the over-investment of eating restraint typical of eating disorders may reflect an under-lying need to restrict affective experience in general, and the experience of desire in particular. These ideas are, of course, speculative. Nonetheless, they may help us to increase our understanding of eating disorders, as well as aid an integration of our knowledge of these disorders with other scientific developments. They may have important implications for clinical work, especially in regard to how the therapist helps the patient to discriminate, integrate and express inner feeling states. Finally, as with all ideas that are speculative, continued research within, and even outside, the eating disorders field will be essential for further development.

References

Bower, T.G.R. (1974) *Development in Infancy*, San Francisco, CA: W.H. Freeman.

Breuer, J. and Freud, S. (1893) *On the Psychical Mechanism of Hysterical Phenomena: Preliminary Communication, Standard Edition of the Complete Works of Sigmund Freud* (volume 2), London: Hogarth Press.

Bruch, H. (1940) "Obesity in children: physiologic and psychologic aspects of the food intake of obese children", *American Journal of Diseases in Children* 59, 739–81.

Bruch, H. (1973) *Eating Disorders: Obesity, Anorexia Nervosa and the Person Within*, New York: Basic Books.

Cooper, P.J. (2002) "Eating disorders and their relationship to mood and anxiety disorders", in C.G. Fairburn and K.D. Brownell (eds) *Eating Disorders and Obesity: A Comprehensive Handbook*, 2nd edn, New York: Guilford Press.

Dare, C. and Crowther, C. (1995) "Psychodynamic models of eating disorders", in G. Szmukler, C. Dare and J. Treasure (eds) *Handbook of Eating Disorders: Theory, Treatment and Research*, Chichester: Wiley.

Emde, R. (1988) "Development terminable and interminable: 1. Innate and moti-vational factors from infancy", *International Journal of Psycho-Analysis* 69, 23–42.

Emde, R. and Fonagy, P. (1997) "An emerging culture for psychoanalytic research?" (editorial), *International Journal of Psycho-Analysis* 78, 643–51.

Fairburn, C.G. and Walsh, B.T. (2002) "Atypical eating disorders (eating disorder not otherwise specified)", in C.G. Fairburn and K.D. Brownell (eds) *Eating Disorders and Obesity: A Comprehensive Handbook*, 2nd edn, New York: Guilford Press.

Fairbairn, W.R.D. (1952) *An Object-Relations Theory of the Personality*, New York: Basic Books.

Fonagy, P., Gergely, G., Jurist, E.L. and Target, M. (2002) *Affect Regulation, Mentalization and the Development of the Self*, New York: Other Press.

Freud, A. (1946) "The psychoanalytic study of infantile feeding disturbances", *Psychoanalytic Study of the Child* 2, 119–32.

Freud, S. (1899) Extracts from the Fliess Papers, *Standard Edition of the Complete Works of Sigmund Freud* (volume 1), London: Hogarth Press.

Freud, S. (1900) *The Interpretation of Dreams, Standard Edition of the Complete Works of Sigmund Freud* (volumes 4 and 5), London: Hogarth Press.

Freud, S. (1905) *Fragment of an Analysis of a Case of Hysteria, Standard Edition of the Complete Works of Sigmund Freud* (volume 7), London: Hogarth Press.

Freud, S. (1918) *From the History of an Infantile Neurosis, Standard Edition of the Complete Works of Sigmund Freud* (volume 7), London: Hogarth Press.

Gergely, G. (1992) "Developmental reconstructions: infancy from the point of view of psychoanalysis and developmental psychology", *Psychoanalysis and Contemporary Thought* 15, 3–55.

Gergely, G. and Watson, J. (1996) "The social biofeedback model of parental affect-mirroring", *International Journal of Psycho-Analysis* 77, 1181–212.

Johnson, C. (1991) *Psychoanalytic Treatment of Anorexia Nervosa and Bulimia*, New York: Guilford Press.

Klein, M. (1975) *Developments in Psychoanalysis*, London: Hogarth Press.

Lawrence, M. (2001) "Loving them to death: the anorexic and her objects", *International Journal of Psychoanalysis* 82, 43–55.

Lehman, E. (1949) "Feeding problems of psychogenic origin: a review of the literature", *Psychoanalytic Study of the Child* 4, 461–88.

McDougall, J. (2001) "The psychic economy of addiction", in J. Petrucelli and C. Stuart (eds) *Hungers and Compulsions: The Psychodynamic Treatment of Eating Disorders and Addictions*, Northvale, NJ: Jason Aronson.

Mahler, M., Pine, F. and Bergman, A. (1975) *The Psychological Birth of the Human Infant: Symbiosis and Individuation*, New York: Basic Books.

Murray, L. and Trevarthen, C. (1985) "Emotional regulation of interactions between two-month-olds and their mothers", in T.M. Field and N.A. Fox (eds) *Social Perception in Infants*, Norwood, NJ: Ablex.

Norring, C., Sohlberg, S., Rosmark, B., Humble, K., Holmgren, S. and Nordqvist, C. (1989) "Ego functioning in eating disorders: description and relation to diagnostic classification", *International Journal of Eating Disorders* 6, 607–21.

Palmer, R.L. (1993) "Weight concern should not be a necessary criterion for the eating disorders: a polemic", *International Journal of Eating Disorders* 14, 459–65.

Petrucelli, J. and Stuart C. (2001) *Hungers and Compulsions: The Psychodynamic Treatment of Eating Disorders and Addictions*, Northvale, NJ: Jason Aronson.

Rosenvinge, J.H., Martinussen, M. and Ostensen, E. (2000) "The comorbidity of eating disorders and personality disorders: a meta-analytic review of studies published between 1983 and 1998", *Eating and Weight Disorders* 5, 52–61.

Stern, D. (1985) *The Interpersonal World of the Infant: A View from Psychoanalysis and Developmental Psychology*, New York: Basic Books.

Tronick, E., Als, H., Adamson, L., Wise, S. and Brazelton, T. (1978) "The infant's response to entrapment between contradictory messages in face-to-face interaction", *Journal of Child Psychiatry* 17, 1–13.

Waller, J.V., Kaufman, R. and Deutsch, D. (1940) "Anorexia nervosa: a psycho-somatic entity", *Journal of Psychosomatic Medicine* 2, 3–16.

Walsh, B.T. and Garner, D.M. (1997) "Diagnostic issues", in D.M. Garner and P.E.

Garfinkel (eds) *Handbook for Treatment of Eating Disorders*, New York: Guilford Press.

Ward, A., Tiller, J., Treasure, J. and Russell, G. (2000) "Eating disorders: psyche or soma?", *International Journal of Eating Disorders* 27, 279–87.

Watson, J. (1972) "Smiling, cooing, and 'the game' ", *Merrill-Palmer Quarterly* 18, 323–39.

Wilson, C.P., Hogan, C.C. and Mintz, I.L. (1985) *Fear of Being Fat*, Northvale, NJ: Jason Aronson.

Chapter 12

Eating disorders in children

Dasha Nicholls

Do adult diagnostic criteria fit children?

Diagnostic criteria, like rules, are no sooner defined than their boundaries are tested. This chapter considers the way that children with eating disorders do and do not fit within the criteria originally described for adults, and then explores, by way of clinical examples, the range of eating problems seen in childhood and early adolescence and their relationship to eating disorders, specified or unspecified.

Despite the evident inadequacy of diagnostic criteria, eating disorders are relatively successful in terms of what diagnoses aim to do. For example, Anorexia Nervosa in adolescence is very reliably diagnosed in clinical practice. McCabe *et al.* (1996) found that in a sample of 276 adolescent inpatients, out of all psychiatric diagnoses only for AN (11 per cent of the cohort) was diagnostic confidence acceptably high at 90 per cent, the next highest being for conduct disorder at 50 per cent. McCabe *et al.* (1996) also found that the number of comorbid or other possible diagnoses in the AN group was lowest, in contrast with psychotic and affective disorders. No doubt the cases in this inpatient sample study were at an extreme end of the spectrum of clinical severity, but the study does suggest that established AN is not hard to recognize and diagnose in adolescence.

Problems really start to arise in younger adolescents and children, where, even in the most extreme clinical cases, diagnostic criteria are not always applicable. As DiNicola *et al.* (1989) have said "it is inadequate to simply portray children's cases that do not fit into a narrow adult standard as atypical." Each successive version of DSM and ICD has been adapted in the face of increasing knowledge about eating disorders in childhood, yet problems remain (Nicholls *et al.* 2000).

First, there is the issue of recognition. Failure to recognize AN in younger patients is likely to be the result of failure to expect the disorder in pre-adolescence, rather than to complexity in the diagnosis or differences in presentation (Bryant-Waugh *et al.* 1992). This may be less a problem of diagnostic applicability and more one of awareness. What it may further reflect, however, is that on the whole, emotional and behavioural disorders of childhood are identified on the basis of observable characteristics rather than the subjective report of the child. This point is illustrated by the rare childhood disorder of "hyperphagic short stature" (Skuse *et al.* 1996). One important feature of the disorder is the relationship between hyperphagic episodes and psychosocial stress. In the study the children (aged 3.8 to 13.7 years) were not interviewed about their own experience of eating. However, it emerged that a number of mothers of the hyperphagic children reported having Bulimia Nervosa (David Skuse, personal communication), although this was not systematically studied. Hyperphagic episodes in children are therefore described on the basis of observed behaviour, binge episodes on the basis of subjective report, and the relationship between the two remains unknown.

This emphasis on objective and observable phenomena as a basis for problem definition in children also highlights the potential problem of validity of self-report in younger children. Gallelli *et al.* (1997) found that premenarcheal subjects with AN and their parents disagreed substantially on the presence of subjective diagnostic features such as fear of becoming fat and body image distortion and if either report alone were considered, diagnosis rates were as low as 53 per cent (Gallelli *et al.* 1997). Therefore, despite a wealth of instruments designed to detect disordered eating behaviour in children and adolescents, in both interview and self-report questionnaire form (e.g. the Children's Eating Attitude Test (ChEAT: Smolak and Levine 1994); the Eating Disorder Inventory for Children (EDI-C: Thurfjell *et al.* 2003); the Stirling Eating Disorders Scales (SEDS: Campbell *et al.* 2002); and the Eating Disorders Examination interview (Bryant-Waugh *et al.* 1996; Cooper *et al.* 1989) and questionnaire (Carter *et al.* 2001) they would rarely be the sole source of information. Thus a GP or other health care professional listening to a parent's report of reduced food intake may not always consider talking to a young child about their understanding of the problem.

Second, problems remain with diagnostic criteria themselves when applied to children. Reservations about the applicability of current DSM-IV criteria to children have been documented over time (Bryant-Waugh and Lask 1995; Irwin 1981; Treasure and Thompson 1988), with continuing improvement and development of the criteria. The DSM-IV definition of AN (see Appendix) allows for the inclusion of children and premenarcheal adolescents in criterion A – "failure to make expected weight gain during period of growth." This does not take into account failure to make expected height during growth. If growth arrest has occurred, weight would be interpreted in relation to the child's actual (reduced) height, or in relation to the population norms for age, which may be inappropriate from parental or racial characteristics. The ideal would be to relate weight to predicted height for age from previous growth centile but this is often unknown. In premenarcheal, in contrast to postmenarcheal, onset AN there has often been insidious weight loss and growth retardation for some time prior to presentation (Swenne and Thurfjell 2003).

Criterion D of the DSM-IV diagnostic criteria describes the impact of hypothalamic-pituitary-gonadal dysregulation for postmenarcheal women, but does not offer alternative signs for premenarcheal women or for males, be they adult or child, such as failure to progress in sexual development, or regression of ovarian and uterine maturity.

In ICD-10 diagnostic criteria for AN, features relevant to children and adolescents include:

> Body weight is maintained at least 15 per cent below that expected (either lost or never achieved) or Quetelet's body mass index is 17.5 or less. Pre-pubertal patients may show failure to make expected weight gain during the period of growth [and] if onset is pre-pubertal, the sequence of pubertal events is delayed or even arrested (growth ceases; in girls the breasts do not develop and there is primary amenorrhoea; in boys the genitalia remain juvenile). With recovery, puberty is often completed normally but the menarche is late.

> (World Health Organization 1992: 177)

Both DSM-IV and ICD-10 use 15 per cent below expected body weight for diagnostic weight loss criteria. This in itself is deceptively complex. First, there is the issue of how expected body weight is defined in childhood. In adult patients, Quetelet's BMI is used fairly universally, but in adolescents and children BMI, BMI centiles, per cent ideal body weight (IBW) or per cent weight for height (using various methods of calculation) are all used, making comparisons difficult across the literature. Until now the convention in the European literature on children and adolescents with eating disorders has been to use per cent weight for height (Cole's method: Cole *et al.* 1981), which uses a power index weight/height^n to adjust weight for height at each age, meaning the centiles of the index can be calculated at each age. This is the basis of the British BMI charts and per cent BMI = per cent weight for height by this method. In the United States the tradition has been to use percentage of IBW obtained from the somewhat out-of-date US Vital and Health Statistics Series 11 data, although increasingly BMI centiles are being used. However, many studies continue to report nutritional status for children and adolescents in terms of BMI alone, which can lead to misleading findings. For example, a BMI of 16 at 11 years is only 0.7 standard deviations (SDs) below the median, whereas the same BMI at 14 years is 1.7 SDs below the median, and at 19 years is 2.7 SDs below the median.

It is to be hoped that per cent BMI or BMI centiles will soon replace the various forms of weight for height and per cent IBW that have been used to date, and begin to establish an international definition of underweight in children and adolescents for screening purposes, as is the case for definitions of obesity (Cole *et al.* 2000). The WHO Expert Committee, in their guidelines on the use and interpretation of anthropometry in infants and children, recommended the use of weight-for-height indices as screening instruments, with +2SDs as cut-off for overweight (WHO 1995). Screening at the lower end of the weight spectrum was not mentioned. In adults, chronic energy deficiency is defined as BMI below 18.5 (James *et al.* 1988), but no such equivalent definition for children exists. The poor correlation between BMI and other measures of body fat begs further questions about the usefulness of BMI centiles in clinical practice in those with established malnutrition. At this level of clinical complexity, separate evaluation of fat mass and fat free mass is appropriate and account should be taken of the size and developmental stage of the patient.

Even with a satisfactory definition of malnutrition in childhood established, evidence for 85 per cent body weight as the boundary for healthy weight in children is limited, if it exists at all. DSM-III-R described this weight criterion as "arbitrary but useful" (APA 1987: 65), while DSM-IV states that "it is unreasonable to specify a single standard for minimally normal weight that applies to all individuals of a given age and height" (APA 1994: 540). Until 1987 (before DSM-III-R), the weight loss criterion was to 75 per cent of IBW or below. Irwin (1984), one of the main proponents for change, argued that children differ from adults and from each other in their relative amount of body fat and that malnutrition may therefore be present at higher body weights. Taking this argument one step further Lask and Bryant-Waugh (2000) have suggested that in children both rate of weight loss and weight loss relative to previous weight are perhaps more relevant than absolute body weight. Thus a child at 100 per cent weight-for-height may show signs of starvation if she/he was previously 125 per cent weight-for-height.

Difficulties with the cognitive and behavioural aspects of classification are no less complex. ICD-10 requires one or more compensatory behaviours in addition to food restriction for the diagnosis of AN to be met. In the early 1980s, Pugliese *et al.* (1983) described a syndrome they called "fear of obesity syndrome". The authors argued that the children in their sample, 14 children presenting with short stature and delayed puberty, did not suffer from AN because of the absence of compensatory behaviours. All had weights below the fifth centile, and 11 had heights below the fifth centile; the mean weight for height 89.9 per cent (±6.6 per cent). A lack of compensatory behaviours is not unusual in the childhood presentation of AN, but on the other hand excluding these very clear markers of abnormal behaviour from the diagnostic criteria would lead to an over- rather than an under-inclusive diagnostic grouping.

ICD-10 also requires body image distortion and fear of becoming fat, features not always present despite otherwise typical characteristics of AN (Gallelli *et al.* 1997; Nielsen *et al.* 1997). To describe body image distortion requires the ability to think in self-evaluative terms, a capacity not always present in early onset subjects. The same applies to the capacity to describe the importance of weight and shape in self-evaluation. A further difference in the presentation of children is the tendency to generalize food avoidance to include fluid, which Irwin (1984) argues is a result of problems with abstraction and difficulty in understanding the relationship between calories and food intake. The skill of young people with AN at "logical" reasoning (and to engage in legalistic style arguments about facts and figures) is not matched either by their level of abstract reasoning or the capacity to evaluate complex arguments, with all their pros and cons. "Explanations" for behaviour such as avoidance of fluid can often seem confused or illogical.

Awareness of these and other developmental differences were considerations in adapting the eating disorders examination for use in childhood (Bryant-Waugh *et al.* 1996). The other important modification in the EDE-child was to reformulate some of the questions to assess intent rather than actual behaviour. This is because a child may not be permitted to perform certain actions despite having a clear wish to do so. For example, it is very hard for a child to abstain from food for eight hours without an adult intervening, but the intention to do so will be important to determine.

What a child intends compared to what actually occurs is even more important when considering diagnostic criteria for BN as they apply to children. For a diagnosis of BN to be made according to DSM-IV requires both binge episodes, at a frequency of twice a week for three months, and compensatory behaviours. Compensatory behaviours have been discussed above; in addition the difficulties a child may have in accessing laxatives or diuretics are worth noting. In terms of binge episodes there are a number of considerations. First, the child would need to be able to access, freely, large quantities of food. While this may be possible as a one-off, it would be unusual for such behaviour to occur over an extended period of time without it being noticed and prevented. However, we have seen a small number of children present with scavenging behaviour, including eating out of dustbins and stealing food from shops. Second, there is capacity to describe a sense of lack of control. In order to lose control a child would need to have had control in the first place, or at least the possibility of control. This raises the whole issue of how much real control a child has in any given situation. Finally, the frequency criteria are problematic, both because opportunities for behaviours to occur are less frequent, and also because child self-report for an extended period of time such as three months is unlikely to be accurate. Again, this is taken into account in the childhood modification of the EDE but not in the diagnostic criteria.

In ICD-10 BN is conceptualized in terms of its original description as a variant of AN, with emphasis on preoccupation with eating, cravings, compensatory behaviour and fear of weight gain. Normal weight BN, with binge and purge behaviours as the main clinical characteristics, might be classified in ICD-10 as "atypical". It remains unclear how much there is continuity between AN and BN in terms of direct developmental pathways, i.e. whether the emergence of binge eating is evidence of a newly developed capacity for self-reflection and attempts at conscious urge control in subjects with AN or whether it represents a failure of developmental progression. The lack of BN in clinical samples of younger patients does suggest that a degree of developmental maturity is required for BN to occur.

In summary therefore, childhood who fit a typical picture of an eating disorder, either AN or BN, and who show functional impairment in physical, psychological and social domains may not meet full criteria for an eating disorder for developmental reasons. Most would therefore be classified in the final eating disorder diagnostic category in DSM-IV, Eating Disorder Not Otherwise Specified. The examples given in the DSM manual all include abnormal cognitive preoccupation with weight, shape and food, with differences in the behavioural and somatic syndromes. Some might suggest that the majority of early onset cases should be correctly diagnosed as EDNOS. We are inclined to think that EDNOS should reflect severity, stage of illness or variation in clinical profile rather than the age of the sufferer.

Research has tended to focus on those who fit diagnostic criteria, with atypical cases excluded. A fairly consistent finding is that over 50 per cent of children presenting with severe eating problems do not fit DSM-IV diagnostic criteria (Nicholls *et al.* 2000), figures not much different from those reported for adult specialist clinic samples (Clinton and Glant 1992; Ricca *et al.* 2001). This means that little information is available about the substantial number of nutritionally compromised children who do not meet diagnostic criteria for even childhood appropriate definitions of AN, despite their poor prognosis (Higgs *et al.* 1989). Recent study of the nosology of eating difficulties in middle childhood (Cooper *et al.* 2002), together with increasing sophistication of measures of childhood eating psychopathology (Bryant-Waugh *et al.* 1996), have enabled specific psychological subgroups to be better identified and defined, although much more work is needed in this field. Preoccupation with food intake for reasons other than its influence on weight and shape in this age group is discussed further below. Bryant-Waugh and Lask (1995: 191) have proposed a broader definition for eating disorders in childhood that would include many more children with marked eating pathology: "excessive concern with the control of body weight and shape, and/or food intake, accompanied by a grossly inadequate, irregular or chaotic food intake." The remainder of this chapter will consider the range of clinical presentations seen in children and adolescents, and their relationship to current nosological concepts.

How do childhood onset eating disorders differ from adult onset?

Anorexia Nervosa: special features in children

True eating disorders present in children as young as 7 years old. By true eating disorders we mean disorders characterized by grossly disordered or chaotic eating behaviour associated with morbid preoccupation with body weight and shape. Overall, the clinical presentation is similar to presentation in adults. Nevertheless, important differences in presentation merit attention, reflecting differences that, in our view, are accounted for by age and gender rather than to differences in the disorder. The features described here might typically be expected in a 10- or 11-year-old premenarcheal girl or a boy up to 13 or 14 years old. This age difference by gender reflects the approximate two-year difference between boys and girls in terms of timing of pubertal development.

In AN common weight control behaviours in children include restricted food intake, restraint around eating behaviour, excessive exercising and self-induced vomiting. It is particularly common for children to restrict fluid as well as food, resulting in a different level of medical urgency to that engendered through controlled weight loss. Compensatory behaviours such as laxative or diuretic misuse are less common in younger children, and the restrictive subtype of AN is seen more commonly than the binge-purge subtype. Other common features of AN in children include preoccupation with food, eating and calories, a distorted view of "normal" amount of food, guilt associated with eating, increased interest in food preparation and recipes, concern about eating in front of others and low self-esteem. Some of these features are less marked than in older adolescents, reflecting developmental differences in terms of self-awareness and autonomy, as discussed above.

Despite these slight differences in emphasis and expression of AN with age, the disorder remains clearly identifiable. However, the conceptualization of AN as a "dieting disorder" (Beumont *et al.* 1994) would restrict applicability to young children, since children may be intensely anxious about their weight and shape in the absence of dieting intent.

Case example: Emma

Emma was an 11-year-old girl with a six-month history of a restricted eating pattern associated with obsessional behaviour, largely checking around her body shape. In addition to measuring the width of her waist she also rested her ribs on the table to gauge the angle between her ribs and her stomach — at its worst she was doing this every second. She was reported to be on her feet most of the time apart from when she was eating. Emma was found in distress by her mother, saying "I can't stop looking at myself. I want to be normal." The children's version of the Eating Disorders Examination (EDE) was used to explore Emma's beliefs further. The report reads as follows:

Emma denied any body image distortion or concern stating that, if anything, she becomes more distressed if she loses weight as everyone becomes upset. She added that she has never felt fat and she doesn't really understand why she began cutting back on her diet. Indeed, when I asked Emma if she had ever wanted a flat tummy she looked rather puzzled by what I meant and asked for further clarification.

This fairly typical description of AN in preadolescence is in keeping with the findings of Arnow et al. (1999), who compared 26 premenarcheal with 69 postmenarcheal subjects with AN. On the EDI, premenarcheal subjects scored lower on drive for thinness, but not on body dissatisfaction or perfectionism. The level of disordered eating (by parental report) was higher in the younger group. In addition, premenarcheal subjects in this study described a greater internal locus of control, greater wish for social desirability and a more mature defence style. This somewhat surprising finding, the authors concluded, may reflect the "pseudomaturity" observed in this patient population, which is even more marked than that of older subjects. The data could be understood as supporting the notion that premenarcheal onset AN represents a similar but more "pure" form of the neurobiological phenotype, where the biological trigger of puberty has not been necessary for the disorder to manifest. These premenarcheal differences would appear to reflect maturational stage rather than age per se; Gowers et al. (1991) compared 30 patients with primary amenorrhoea (Group 1) with age-matched patients (<14 years) with secondary amenorrhoea (Group 2) versus all other AN patients (Group 3). Gowers et al. (1991) found that the premenarcheal Group 1 differed from Groups 2 and 3 in terms of manifesting less abstinence, less vegetarianism, less bingeing and less difficulty eating with others, but no difference in terms of frequency of vomiting or on measures of severity using Morgan Russell Global scales. Younger patients were almost all living at home, and had fewer parents who were separated, divorced or expressing dissatisfaction. Overall, weight loss, vomiting and severity of illness were equal across all age groups, with fear of puberty a prevailing concern in terms of subjective precipitants.

Cases such as Emma enable a closer consideration of the developmental vulnerabilities that predispose to AN, which may differ from those predisposing to BN. For example, Jacobs and Isaacs (1986) identified greater pre-morbid feeding problems and more behavioural problems before becoming ill in pre-pubertal children with AN, while the illness is very similar in the pre- and post-pubertal children in terms of sexual anxiety, and self-injury rates (Jacobs and Isaacs 1986). An increased association with low mood has been variously described in early onset populations (Fosson *et al.* 1987; Irwin 1984), as have difficulties with expression and emotional language.

The hypothesis here is that the factors that make adolescent girls preferentially vulnerable to eating disorders may not be present to the same extent in younger patients or in boys. These factors may be cultural – pressure around body weight and shape in teenage girls is acknowledged to be greater in girls than in boys; biological – the relationship between onset of puberty and psychopathology in general, and shape concern in particular is well documented; or psychological – although the capacity to self-evaluate and compare oneself to peers is not unique to girls, the parameters by which a young person evaluates themselves may be.

Case example: Julie

Julie was a 10-year-old girl with AN characterized by a particularly morbid preoccupation with her shape. There was a rapid deterioration in Julie's eating during her birthday sleepover. Julie's best friend had ignored her and Julie felt isolated and humiliated in front of her peers. Julie's mother described lying awake, being aware that something was wrong, and retained a sense of guilt for some time afterwards about having been unable to prevent Julie's distress.

The experience of social rejection is a common trigger event in this age group, while puberty and fear of maturation or teasing about weight and shape may not be a feature, as in Julie's case. Background conditions, individual vulnerability and trigger events may be of greater importance in this group of patients, and less gender specific.

Biology

The role of biological triggers for eating disorders, while no longer considered absolutely necessary, remains important. Crisp's conceptualization of AN as a phobic avoidance of pubertal development has support in terms of the close association of eating disorders and puberty from epidemiological and endocrine studies (Graber *et al.* 1999) but the mechanisms by which this occur are not yet clear. What is known from other fields of human study is that oestrogen plays an important regulatory role in stress response systems and brain development (Stratakis *et al.* 1995).

In addition to being exposed to oestrogen and testosterone in varying quantities, the young person is learning to cope with changes in body shape and body composition. Percentages of lean body mass, skeletal mass and body fat are roughly equal between pre-pubertal boys and girls. Moving into adolescence, changes in lean body mass precede changes in fat mass. By completion of puberty, boys have on average 1.5 times the skeletal mass of girls, while women have roughly twice as much body fat as men (Grumbach and Styne 1992). Thus for girls, increase in weight continues after growth in stature had slowed down, increases in BMI equating to actual changes in body size and shape. Predisposition to overweight is an identified risk factor for BN (Fairburn *et al.* 1997) and it is easy to understand how rapid changes in body shape could induce anxiety in those predisposed to larger body size in adulthood, particularly in the context of low self-esteem. The relationship between restrictive AN and premorbid body weight is less clear, but is probably very different from that of BN, with a tendency to underweight more likely than to overweight.

More recently there has been a resurgence of interest in possible infectious and immune triggers for a range of neurodevelopmental disorders of childhood and adolescence, including eating disorders (Sokol 2000). The acronym PANDAS (for paediatric autoimmune neuropsychiatric disorders associated with streptococcal infections) was originally coined to describe a group of patients with OCD and/or tic disorder, pre-pubertal symptom onset, sudden onset or episodic course of symptoms, temporal association between streptococcal infections and neuropsychiatric symptom exacerbations, and associated neurological abnormalities. The proposed model of pathophysiology has implications for treatment strategies, including the use of antibiotic prophylaxis to prevent streptococcal-triggered exacerbations, and the use of immunomodulatory interventions such as plasma exchange.

Although the term PANDAS is relatively new, febrile illness as a trigger for AN has been previously described (Irwin 1984), and there is no suggestion that the illness is in any way "atypical" in its presentation following a biological rather than psychological trigger event. A related but as yet little reported phenomenon is the association between chronic fatigue symptoms (and syndrome) and eating disorders (Griffiths *et al.* 1996).

Case example: Fiona

Fiona was a 14-year-old girl with a history of chronic fatigue syndrome (CFS) with onset during her first term at secondary school. After two years of worsening symptoms she began slowly to recover, and began rehabilitation to school, initially two days per week. Her mother noticed that Fiona started to hide food after meals and would often comment on her own body shape. She lost 4 kg in weight, but had regained this by the time of presentation.

The similarly complex aetiology as well as overlap in presenting features of the two disorders suggests that the link may not be coincidental, but further work is needed in this area to understand more fully what, if any, association exists. CFS should be differentiated from pervasive refusal syndrome (Lask *et al.* 1991), which is defined as "a profound and pervasive refusal to eat, walk, talk or engage in self care." This rare condition has been conceptualized as both an extreme post-traumatic stress reaction in cases of evident or suspected abuse (Lask *et al.* 1991), and as a form of learned helplessness (Nunn and Thompson 1996). Unlike for CFS, viral illness as a trigger has not been reported.

Gender

As outlined above, the relationship between eating disorders and gender differs when looked at developmentally. A number of studies suggest that boys are over-represented in the younger age group presenting with severe eating disorders (Fosson *et al.* 1987; Higgs *et al.* 1989; Jacobs and Isaacs 1986). AN in boys may be characterized by concern around fitness and health, dietary restriction related to "healthy" diet (e.g. related to worries about heart disease), and shape is often more important than weight. Excessive exercising is very common and there is a strong association with obsessive-compulsive disorder (Shafran *et al.* 1995). Bryant-Waugh (1993) has argued that boys with AN may be particularly vulnerable in terms of predisposing factors, given the relative lack of pubertal and sociocultural triggers that have been suggested in aetiological models of AN in young girls. Thus characteristics such as increased sensitivity to food smells and textures, intense attachments and separation anxiety, and rigidity of style are not uncommon findings in boys with restrictive eating patterns.

Case example: Jon

Last year Jon changed schools and found it difficult to settle down. He was an extremely bright child in an area where there were quite a few underachievers. Jon would often help them as the teachers refused to believe that he was bored. In October Jon was diagnosed with vertigo. The doctor said that in an older person he would have said it was stress. As things were starting to get a bit better, Jon needed to have a tonsillectomy, then after the operation he got shingles.

Shortly after this Jon started eating strangely, reading the packets of food, and refusing to eat things that were high in fat. Then he started getting faddy about food, changing from vegetarian foods to couscous then to diet foods and gradually the weight began to drop off. His mother kept going to the GP but it was not until Jon had lost a lot of weight that they were sent to see a psychologist. Jon ate minute amounts at a time. When getting a drink he would not just walk to the fridge, but would tiptoe. He has rituals for doing certain things and given the chance he would be exercising the whole time.

Case example: Tom

Tom was a 14-year-old boy whose problems began at the age of 10 following a healthy eating talk at school which analysed the fat content in different foods. Tom began to alter his eating habits and his weight started to drop. At about the same time Tom began to suffer severe verbal bullying at school. Tom's parents thought that in temperament Tom was very like his father, quiet and introverted, bottling up his feelings, feeling the odd one out, but he was closer to his mother, a relationship that intensified during his illness. His mother described herself as his only friend. Both felt that Tom related better to women.

The relative paucity of cases means that many studies of eating disorders simply exclude male subjects. Boys present a particular challenge when it comes to understanding and treatment however, and may be particularly important for understanding the biological vulnerabilities that underlie these disorders (see Rosen, 2003 for a review of eating disorders in adolescent males).

Family patterns

Family patterns and their relationship to eating problems are a complex issue that can be considered at many levels, from genetic transmission through modelling to narratives and expectations.

Case example: Kate

Kate presented at the age of 9 with weight loss to 85 per cent BMI, associated with food restriction but no compensatory behaviours. She restricted the range of meals she would eat, only accepting three or four types of evening meal, and eating the same thing every day for breakfast and for lunch, and was quite "clingy", worried about leaving her mother's side. Kate's mother had had AN as an adolescent, and so quickly recognized the symptoms. In addition Kate's paternal cousin had had AN. Although Kate regained the weight she had lost quite quickly, the concern that her eating difficulties would return in adolescence was high.

Although this sort of family pattern is not unique to early onset cases, those vulnerable from a genetic or other familial mechanism might be expected to be over-represented in the early onset group. The early recognition that previous experience of an eating disorder affords may mean that cases present before they have become "full blown", and one can only speculate as to how, when and even whether such cases would have presented in a less attuned family. Stein's work on parenting styles of mothers with eating disorders, and the associated general and specific risks to their children, in particular whether the risks for girls differ from those for boys, is of interest and relevance here (Patel *et al.* 2002). Offspring of parents with past or present eating disorders are obvious candidates for prevention or early intervention. In terms of family factors that exacerbate or maintain eating difficulties once they arise, the role of parental anxiety (Shoebridge and Gowers 2000) and the effectiveness of supporting parents are clear (Eisler *et al.* 2000). Clinical experience tells us that intervening with the maintaining factors may be sufficient for recovery, without the need to address predisposing or precipitating factors.

Bulimia Nervosa: childhood considerations

BN is very unusual in children below the age of 12, although premenarcheal BN has been reported in the literature (Kent *et al.* 1992). As for AN, clinical presentation is similar to that in adults and weight control behaviours similar to those in AN, although with more laxative abuse (probably related to slightly older age). Most bulimic children engage in bingeing with compensatory vomiting. BN is often associated with "teenage" problems, such as underage drinking, smoking, sexual activity, etc. Depression and self-harm are often a feature. Occasionally chaotic and disordered eating in conjunction with vomiting may be suggestive of BN, although rarely is the full syndrome seen.

Case example: Karen
Karen was a 12-year-old girl who was reported by her mother to be skipping meals, vomiting secretly and eating junk foods. She was also increasingly argumentative with her parents, particularly her stepfather,

wanting to be out at night with her friends. Her mother thought she might be smoking and was worried about Karen being thought of as older than her age.

Perhaps more striking than differences in presenting features is the relationship to help seeking in this age group. Although BN may begin in the late teens, it is often many years before the sufferer presents for help. Attempts to target young people with BN have been met with a number of problems, including lack of ownership of the problem, and a reluctance for the problem to be shared (and hence of confidentiality). It is perhaps not surprising therefore that the models of treatment effective in adults seeking help have been difficult to generalize to younger patients. As yet, as good model for treatment of BN in this age group is lacking, in particular in relation to the issue of family involvement in treatment.

Of the eating disorders described in DSM-IV, Binge Eating Disorder is not usually seen in this age group, although binge eating has been described as a feature of childhood obesity (Decaluwe *et al.* 2003).

Variations on eating disorders presenting in childhood and early adolescence

Eating disorder presentations with unusual features

Occasionally a child may meet criteria for an eating disorder, and yet features of the illness suggest that the usual treatment and prognosis are not applicable. Examples might include very short-lived episodes of weight loss and exercising in relation to specific life stresses, or where the symptoms appear to be mimicking those of a friend or acquaintance. This latter is a particular feature of inpatient units or institutions such as boarding schools, when a sufferer from AN can be seen to be having an impact on their more vulnerable peers. The clinician is usually alerted by the presentation of more than one member of a school, and intervention may be more appropriately directed to the institution than to the young person and their family. Cases such as this are by no means trivial, and assessment will identify those at further risk.

Also within this group are young people in whom the problem starts as an eating disorder but where other factors begin to play an increasingly important role.

Case example: Rebecca

Rebecca was a 12-year-old girl who presented with chaotic eating behaviour, and deliberate restriction of food and fluid intake motivated by the wish to avoid calorie intake and necessitating hospitalization. Concerns about Rebecca's affect and communication style, together with the complexities of her family story, led the treating team to question her diagnosis. By the time of assessment neither she nor her mother reported eating difficulties. Looking back, the development of Rebecca's eating problem coincided with the deterioration in her father's mental health, with his being detained for treatment at the peak of Rebecca's dieting behaviour. He was coming home on leave as Rebecca was building up towards her school exams. Rebecca's weight reached its lowest level when her father was being moved towards a rehabilitation home.

Food restriction for reasons other than weight and shape concern

This section describes types of eating problem that cannot be considered an eating disorder but for whom no other classification is adequate and in which the primary presenting symptom is a difficulty in eating. There are a number of ways of conceptualizing this group of patients, depending on whether it is mechanisms, interventions or developmental stage that are the primary concern.

Primary versus secondary

It can be useful to differentiate unusual but habitual eating patterns from those in which there has been a clear change from previous eating, i.e. primary or secondary. While the clinical features at presentation may be the same, subtle differences may be discernible particularly in terms of emotional contributions to the problem. Examples of eating problems that may be primary or secondary include selective eating, restrictive eating and failure to thrive. Selective eating describes extreme selectivity in preferred foods and resistance to trying new foods (food neophobia), resulting in a highly limited range of foods eaten (Bryant-Waugh 2000; Nicholls *et al.* 2001). The terms "picky", "faddy" and "perseverative feeding disorder" are also used in the literature to describe this type of eating pattern.

Case example: Simon

Simon had difficulties feeding since the introduction of solid foods. At the age of 10 his range of foods consisted of chicken nuggets, toast and peanut butter and milk. He showed no interest in changing his eating habits and had not considered the ways in which his selective eating may influence his life adversely as he grew older.

Case example: Chris

Chris had eaten normally until the age of 3, when he was admitted to hospital with diarrhoea and vomiting. His mother reported a definite change in his eating from that day, even though the illness itself was short lived. His range of foods was crisps, cheese and crackers, chips, cereal and fruit juice. He has tried to eat new foods but gags or retches when they are presented. On questioning he described a fear of vomiting with unfamiliar foods.

Restrictive eating is a term that Bryant-Waugh and Lask (1995) have used to describe children with a constitutionally small appetite, who show limited interest in food, have small appetites, and who grow and develop normally in the lower centiles for weight and height and can therefore be considered a normal variant. They present clinically due to anxiety about growth, and indeed feeding practices such as coercion to eat, excessive pressure to gain weight and conflict over food can precipitate food refusal and failure to thrive.

The more serious condition of failure to thrive describes a pattern of faltering development as a result of poor weight gain. Although malnutrition is the end point, disentangling the complex contributions of child, parent and their interactions is not always straightforward. Failure to thrive can be, but is not always, associated with other evidence of neglect and deprivation.

Each of these primary eating problems is more common in, but not exclusive to, children with learning disability and developmental delay. Secondary eating problems can superimpose themselves on primary eating problems.

Case example: Nina

Nina was a 15-year-old girl whose pattern of restrictive eating and underweight went back many years, possibly to the age of 6. Her body had adapted to chronic underweight, as demonstrated by the fact that she had progressed through puberty and menstruated despite her low weight. In order to maintain the level of intake required, Nina needed extensive support from her family in being fed. In the 12 months prior to presentation Nina's weight had dropped slowly to around 67 per cent BMI. The most likely trigger for the weight loss was the arrival in the family of two younger siblings, which meant that Nina's parents were no longer able to provide as much support for her with eating.

Underweight versus normal weight

In terms of management, one of the key organizing factors in clinical decision making with children is the presence or absence of malnutrition, and distinguishing acute malnutrition, chronic malnutrition and no malnutrition is one of the first steps in determining management. Measures such as per cent BMI can be valuable pointers and screening instruments, but may be a poor reflection of a child's fat reserves, which in turn will vary with stage of development. Clinical judgement, together with vital signs (pulse, blood pressure, temperature and peripheral circulation), may be the best indicators. Even in postmenarcheal patients, amenorrhoea is less helpful than in adults, as adolescents often miss three or more cycles in the first one or two years. Skinfold thickness and other measures of body composition add a further level of refinement when per cent BMI and clinical findings do not tally. For example, a child may be exercising sufficiently to maintain body mass, while having so little fat reserve that endocrine function (and hence growth and puberty) are disturbed. Apart from AN, conditions that can present with underweight include food avoidance emotional disorder (see below), food phobias, functional dysphagia and psychogenic vomiting.

Specific cognitions versus "somatization"

There are a number of children who develop specific circumscribed fears in relation to food, which are associated with specific cognitions. The nature of the specific fear or belief will vary with, among other things, the child's developmental stage, but it is probably the case that other severe food phobias are more common than phobic fear of fatness in the 8 to 11 years old age group. Phobias involving food occur in isolation (i.e. as simple phobias), or as part of a more generalized anxiety disorder. The fears that are common are a fear of vomiting and a fear of contamination or poisoning, such that only certain family members can be entrusted to prepare foods. Lifshitz (1987), writing on the subject of nutritional dwarfing, identifies two additional syndromes: failure to thrive because of specific parental health beliefs, and failure to grow because of malnutrition resulting from dietary restrictions that are based on a fear of the consequences of hypercholesterolaemia.

Case example: John

John, 15, presented with an eight-year history of abdominal pain and intermittent diarrhoea. Over an 18-month period he developed yellow pigmentation, maculopapular rash, profound weight loss (7 kg) and growth arrest (height falling from the fiftieth to the second centile). He was referred with frequent episodes of "collapse" with profound brady-cardia, hypotension and hypothermia. After extensive investigation as an inpatient, a feeding challenge was undertaken. Nasogastric feeding for three weeks resulted in weight gain and precipitated over-exercising and interfering with the feeding. The patient revealed a phobic avoid-ance of fatty foods and obsessive exercising after eating any fat in order to prevent "cholesterol furring up my arteries". He attributed these beliefs to having witnessed his father's heart attack and resuscitation.

Obsessive-compulsive disorder can present as food-related obsessions, with-out or without comorbid AN. In children, factors determining the degree of elaboration of OCD rituals include how others respond to the rituals and other contextual factors.

By contrast, there are children who avoid food but are unable to identify specific beliefs or fears to explain their behaviour. In 1989 Higgs *et al.* coined the term "food avoidance emotional disorder" (FAED) to encompass a wide range of other eating difficulties in which the unifying feature was the avoid-ance of food for primarily psychological reasons. Over the years Lask and Bryant-Waugh (2000) have used and adapted the term FAED, restricting it to children who avoid food that results in weight loss, in the absence of specific fears about food or weight gain, and thus excluding children with chronic low weight. Unlike AN patients, children with FAED know that they are under-weight, would like to be heavier, and may not know why they find this difficult to achieve. In our clinical experience, families from non-white British back-grounds are over-represented in this patient group. They are more likely to have other medically unexplained symptoms, and their parents may attribute weight loss to an undiagnosed physical disorder.

Case example: Carole

Carole was a 13-year-old girl with a two-year history of medically unexplained symptoms of headache, dizziness, nausea and abdominal pain. Her poor food intake and weight loss dated back six months and were associated with abdominal pains. She was reported to be eating the same food but in smaller portions, and to feel nauseated after eating. No problems with swallowing were described. Carole had a self-imposed diet restricting wheat and dairy foods, in response to the abdominal pain. She reported that when she ate dairy products she felt bloated afterwards, and described herself as having lactose intolerance. There have been no investigations confirming this.

FAED sufferers are also more likely than AN sufferers to show generalized anxiety, unrelated to food. It is likely that children with FAED are a heterogeneous group of children, a minority of whom may later develop true eating disorders. However, direct continuity has not been demonstrated. This form of active food avoidance differs from the loss of appetite that can occur in depression. We have come to use the term FAED when food avoidance is marked and merits treatment in its own right.

Functional dysphagia is a term used to describe difficulty swallowing associated with a fear of choking. This symptom is found clinically in patients with FAED, selective eating and sometimes AN. It is also found as a new symptom of acute onset, often following trauma. The validity of functional dysphagia as a separate entity needs clarification.

Feeding problem versus eating problem

While DSM-IV and ICD-10 make a distinction between feeding disorders and eating disorders, the point at which the responsibility for food intake changes from parent to child is by no means easy to define. In DSM-IV, "feeding and eating disorders of infancy or early childhood" (including pica and rumination) are included in "disorders usually first diagnosed in infancy, childhood or adolescence." The diagnostic criteria require that the child be under 6 years of age when the problem starts, and that there is concern about the child's nutritional status. Eating disorders, in their current form, probably apply to children as young as 7 years, but in reality there are a large number of children presenting in middle childhood who fit neither into feeding disorders nor into eating disorder categories.

Jaffe and Singer (1989) described a group of such children, emphasizing the level of dysfunction: "intractable, adamant refusal to eat, with resultant conflict with families or teachers, and disruption of home or family life" (Jaffe and Singer 1989: 576). Of eight children, six girls and two boys (mean age 8.5 years), were all short in stature or failing to thrive. None had a fear of fatness. One 5-year-old was suspected to be binge eating and also had one episode of self-induced vomiting. Eating behaviours included cutting up food very small, hiding food, arranging food in patterns, slow eating (up to 3–4 hours) and overt, obstinate, combative refusal to eat. One had frank dysphagia. Relevant features included overt family conflict, a history of eating disorder in mother, and normal IQ. High scores were found for internalizing symptoms; somatic complaints, hyperactivity and externalizing behaviours were also common. The authors report a wide and inconsistent variety of comorbid diagnoses, stating

> we can only surmise the future courses of our patients, but the association of their eating disorders with other potentially serious, chronic psychological disorders, occurring in a milieu of significant familial and psycho-social distress, suggests a poor prognosis.
>
> (Jaffe and Singer 1989: 581)

Eating difficulties in combination with organic disorder

The association of eating disorders and organic disorders, particularly diabetes, are discussed in detail elsewhere in this book. Clearly organic disorders co-occurring can make eating difficulties more problematic to manage.

Case example: Ryan

Ryan, age 12, presented with severe restricting AN characterized by restraint and excessive exercising, in the context of restricted food intake associated with ulcerative colitis since the age of 6. Ryan had not been a particularly fussy eater in the early years. When he did start having eating difficulties, it took some time trying various exclusion diets until he was eventually diagnosed with ulcerative colitis. Ryan was described as having been miserable and having missed a lot of school around this time. Ryan's recalled first bleeding was after a spicy meal, and it was also reported that he had vomited after large meals from an early age, almost daily. As Ryan's ulcerative colitis became more medically under control the variety of foods he ate increased steadily. Ryan reported that he had always found it difficult to try new foods, and that there had been large periods in his life when he had had restricted diets imposed on him. The present illness manifested through a self-imposed restricted diet, with an increased emphasis on "healthy" eating.

With some of the eating patterns described thus far, medical symptoms are common, although rarely is clear additional organic pathology found. One case series described four patients presenting with eating problems who were subsequently identified with brain tumours (De Vile *et al.* 1995). In retrospect these cases did have additional signs and symptoms and highly atypical eating presentations, but emphasize the edict that absence of organic pathology is not evidence of psychological pathology.

Towards a developmental framework for eating disorders

A developmental framework within which to integrate sociocultural, bio-genetic, personality, family and behavioural studies remains lacking in the field of eating disorders, and as a result cases whose presentation differs from older adolescents and adults for developmental reasons are by necessity classified as atypical. Below are just three aspects relevant to eating disorders that would need to be considered to improve our developmental and systemic understanding, and to enable the "atypical" cases described above to be understood within a theoretical framework.

Identity and personality development, including gender identity

Theory suggests that parental attachment influences peer attachment and later identity in relationships, through the experience of trust, commitment, communication and exploration. Attachment to parents remains strong into late adolescence for both males and females, although increasingly peers play an important role. Identity in terms of relationships becomes consistently stronger as adolescents grow older, while for other aspects of identity such as school role and vocational identity there is less developmental consistency. For girls in particular, identity through peer relationships is more important than school or occupational identity (Meeus and Dekoviic 1995). Peer attachment has a strong effect on self-image particularly in areas that gain prominence during this developmental period, such as body image, vocational goals and sexuality. Most of the literature on identity formation addresses the evolution of self in relation to peers, gender, culture, vocational role, and family during adolescence. A developmental approach would need also to consider the background factors that influence the successful negotiation of identity formation, including development of self-theory.

Developmental and systemic aspects of control

Some children will try, and succeed, in controlling their food intake from an early age, while others do so only at times of stress and change. Learning to manage control over self and others is also an important developmental task and in a developmental framework food represents a vehicle for exploration and regulation of basic needs, including attachment relationships. Abnormal eating behaviours are often observed in young children and are usually benign, self-limiting, minor behavioural aberrations associated with attempts at mastery of a particular developmental stage, such as making choices or meeting new peers. Understanding how eating disorders arise requires consideration of how these more basic mechanisms of emotional regulation are evoked and how contextual and personality issues such as the valuing of self-control can reinforce these responses.

Emotional language and alexithymia

Alexithymia describes impairment of the ability to identify and communicate one's emotional state, and is believed to influence how emotions are regulated. Individual differences in emotionality and regulation are central to concepts of temperament and personality. Understanding the roles of emotional regulation (i.e. extrinsic and intrinsic monitoring and adjusting of emotion) and emotional understanding (i.e. comprehension of the signs of, causes of, and ways to regulate emotion) are central to an understanding of eating disorders. How negative emotionality is mediated and modulated is of importance in terms of the way in which dispositional characteristics interact to predict outcomes such as social functioning, and also in terms of how such interactions can be influenced by means of family or individual psychotherapy. From a development standpoint, this means considering not only how emotions are experienced and received, but also the sophistication of language, communication and relationships required to identify and share feelings.

Conclusion

This chapter has reviewed current criteria for eating disorders as applied to children, and by way of case examples considered those children for whom current diagnostic categories are insufficient. The range of eating difficulties found in the ages between toddler faddiness and eating disorders of adolescence are described. What remains unclear is how they should be described. The interactional nature of feeding is of relevance well into the teens and beyond, while "eating" suggests a level of autonomy many of our patients are some way from being able to attain. A developmental and systemic framework is necessary for the understanding and management of all types of eating problem in this age range.

References

American Psychiatric Association (1987) *Diagnostic and Statistical Manual of Mental Disorders*, 3rd edn revised (DSM-III-R), Washington, DC: APA.
American Psychiatric Association (1994) *Diagnostic and Statistical Manual of Mental Disorders*, 4th edn (DSM-IV), Washington, DC: APA.
Arnow, B., Sanders, M.J. and Steiner, H. (1999) "Premenarcheal versus postmenarcheal

anorexia nervosa: a comparative study", *Clinical Child Psychology and Psychiatry* 4, 403–14.

Beumont, P.J.V., Garner, D.M. and Touyz, S.W. (1994) "Diagnoses of eating or dieting disorders: what may we learn from past mistakes?", *International Journal of Eating Disorders* 16, 349–62.

Bryant-Waugh, R. (1993) "Anorexia nervosa in boys", *Neuropsychiatrie de l'Enfance* 41, 287–90.

Bryant-Waugh, R. (2000) "Overview of the eating disorders", in B. Lask and R. Bryant-Waugh (eds) *Anorexia Nervosa and Related Eating Disorders in Childhood and Adolescence*, 2nd edn, Hove, East Sussex: Psychology Press.

Bryant-Waugh, R. and Lask, B. (1995) "Eating disorders in children", *Journal of Child Psychology and Psychiatry* 36, 191–202.

Bryant-Waugh, R., Lask, B., Shafran, R. and Fosson, A. (1992) "Do doctors recognize eating disorders in children?", *Archives of Disease in Childhood* 67, 103–5.

Bryant-Waugh, R., Cooper, P., Taylor, C. and Lask, B. (1996) "The use of the eating disorder examination with children: a pilot study", *International Journal of Eating Disorders* 19, 391–7.

Campbell, M., Lawrence, B., Serpell, L., Lask, B. and Neiderman, M. (2002) "Validating the Stirling Eating Disorders Scales (SEDS) in an adolescent population", *Eating Behaviors* 3, 285–93.

Carter, J.C., Stewart, D.A. and Fairburn, C.G. (2001) "Eating disorder examination questionnaire: norms for young adolescent girls", *Behaviour Research and Therapy* 39, 625–32.

Clinton, D.N. and Glant, R. (1992) "The eating disorders spectrum of DMSR-III-R: clinical features and psychosocial concomitants of 86 consecutive cases from a Swedish urban catchment area", *Journal of Nervous and Mental Disease* 180, 244–50.

Cole, T.J., Donnet, M.L. and Stanfield, J.P. (1981) "Weight-for-height indices to assess nutritional status: a new index on a slide-rule", *American Journal of Clinical Nutrition* 34, 1935–43.

Cole, T.J., Bellizzi, M.C., Flegal, K.M. and Dietz, W.H. (2000) "Establishing a standard definition for child overweight and obesity worldwide: international survey", *British Medical Journal* 320, 1240–3.

Cooper, P.J., Watkins, B., Bryant-Waugh, R. and Lask, B. (2002) "The nosological status of early onset anorexia nervosa", *Psychological Medicine* 32, 873–80.

Cooper, Z., Cooper, P.J. and Fairburn, C.G. (1989) "The validity of the eating disorder examination and its subscales", *British Journal of Psychiatry* 154, 807–12.

Decaluwe, V., Braet, C. and Fairburn, C.G. (2003) "Binge eating in obese children and adolescents", *International Journal of Eating Disorders* 33, 78–84.

De Vile, C.J., Sufraz, R., Lask, B. and Stanhope, R. (1995) "Occult intracranial tumours masquerading as early onset anorexia nervosa", *British Medical Journal* 311, 1359–60.

DiNicola, V.F., Roberts, N. and Oke, L. (1989) "Eating and mood disorders in young children", *Psychiatric Clinics of North America* 12, 873–93.

Eisler, I., Dare, C., Hodes, M., Russell, G., Dodge, E. and le Grange, D. (2000) "Family therapy for adolescent anorexia nervosa: the results of a controlled comparison of two family interventions", *Journal of Child Psychology and Psychiatry* 41, 727–36.

Fairburn, C.G., Welch, S.L., Doll, H.A., Davies, B.A. and O'Connor, M.E. (1997) "Risk factors for bulimia nervosa: a community-based case-control study", *Archives of General Psychiatry* 54, 509–17.

Fosson, A., Knibbs, J., Bryant-Waugh, R. and Lask, B. (1987) "Early onset anorexia nervosa", *Archives of Disease in Childhood* 62, 114–18.

Gallelli, K.A., Solanto, M.V., Hertz, S.H. and Golden, N.H. (1997) "Eating-related and comorbid symptoms in premenarchal anorexia nervosa", *Eating Disorders: The Journal of Treatment and Prevention* 5, 309–24.

Gowers, S.G., Crisp, A.H., Joughin, N. and Bhat, A. (1991) "Premenarcheal anorexia nervosa", *Journal of Child Psychology and Psychiatry* 32, 515–24.

Graber, J.A., Brooks-Gunn, J. and Warren, M.P. (1999) "The vulnerable transition: puberty and the development of eating pathology and negative mood", *Women's Health Issues* 9, 107–14.

Griffiths, R.A., Beumont, P.J.V., Moore, G.M. and Touyz, S.W. (1996) "Chronic fatigue syndrome and dieting disorders: diagnosis and management problems", *Australian and New Zealand Journal of Psychiatry* 30, 834–8.

Grumbach, M.M. and Styne, D.M. (1992) "Puberty: ontogeny, neuroendocrinology, physiology and disorders", in J.D. Wilson and D.W. Foster (eds) *Williams Textbook of Endocrinology*, 8th edn, Philadelphia, PA: W.B. Saunders.

Higgs, J.F., Goodyer, I.M. and Birch, J. (1989) "Anorexia nervosa and food avoidance emotional disorder", *Archives of Disease in Childhood* 64, 346–51.

Irwin, M. (1981) "Diagnosis of anorexia nervosa in children and the validity of DSM-III", *American Journal of Psychiatry* 138, 1382–3.

Irwin, M. (1984) "Early onset anorexia nervosa", *Southern Medical Journal* 77, 611–14.

Jacobs, B.W and Isaacs, S. (1986) "Pre-pubertal anorexia nervosa: a retrospective controlled study", *Journal of Child Psychology and Psychiatry* 27, 237–50.

Jaffe, A. and Singer, L. (1989) "Atypical eating disorders in young children", *International Journal of Eating Disorders* 8, 575–82.

James, W.P., Ferro, L.A. and Waterlow, J.C. (1988) "Definition of chronic energy deficiency in adults: report of a working party of the International Dietary Energy Consultative Group", *European Journal of Clinical Nutrition* 42, 969–81.

Kent, A., Lacey, J.H. and McCluskey, S.E. (1992) "Pre-menarchal bulimia nervosa", *Journal of Psychosomatic Research* 36, 205–10.

Lask, B. and Bryant-Waugh, R. (eds) (2000) *Anorexia Nervosa and Related Eating Disorders in Childhood and Adolescence*, 2nd edn, Hove, East Sussex: Psychology Press.

Lask, B., Britten, C., Kroll, L., Magagna, J. and Tranter, M. (1991) "Pervasive refusal in children", *Archives of Disease in Childhood* 66, 866–9.

Lifshitz, F. (1987) "Nutritional dwarfing in adolescents", *Growth, Genetics and Hormones* 3, 1–5.

McCabe, R.J.R., Rothery, D.J., Wrate, R.M., Aspin, J. and Bryce, J.G. (1996) "Diagnosis in adolescent inpatients: diagnostic confidence and comparison of diagnoses using ICD-9 and DSM-III", *European Child and Adolescent Psychiatry* 5, 147–54.

Meeus, W. and Dekoviic, M. (1995) "Identity development, parental and peer support in adolescence: results of a national Dutch survey", *Adolescence* 30, 931–44.

Nicholls, D., Chater, R. and Lask, B. (2000) "Children into DSM-IV don't go: a comparison of classification systems for eating disorders in childhood and early adolescence", *International Journal of Eating Disorders* 28, 317–24.

Nicholls, D., Christie, D., Randall, L. and Lask, B. (2001) "Selective eating: symptom, disorder or normal variant?", *Clinical Child Psychology and Psychiatry* 6, 257–70.

Nielsen, G.B., Lausch, B. and Thomsen, P.H. (1997) "Three cases of severe early-onset eating disorder: are they cases of anorexia nervosa?", *Psychopathology* 30, 49–52.

Nunn, K.P. and Thompson, S. (1996) "The Pervasive Refusal Syndrome: learned helplessness and hopelessness", *Clinical Child Psychology and Psychiatry* 1, 121–32.

Patel, P., Wheatcroft, R., Park, R.J. and Stein, A. (2002) "The children of mothers with eating disorders", *Clinical Child and Family Psychology Review* 5, 1–19.

Pugliese, M.T., Lifshitz, F., Grad, G., Fort, P. and Marks-Katz, M. (1983) "Fear of obesity: a cause of short stature and delayed puberty", *New England Journal of Medicine* 309, 513–18.

Ricca, V., Mannucci, E., Mezzani, B., Di Bernardo, M., Zucchi, T., Paionni, A., Placidi, G.P., Rotella, C.M. and Faravelli, C. (2001) "Psychopathological and clinical features of outpatients with an eating disorder not otherwise specified", *Eating and Weight Disorders* 6, 157–65.

Rosen, D.S. (2003) "Eating disorders in adolescent males", *Adolescent Medicine* 14, 677–89.

Shafran, R., Bryant-Waugh, R., Lask, B. and Arscott, K. (1995) "Obsessive-compulsive symptoms in children with eating disorders: a preliminary investigation", *Eating Disorders: The Journal of Treatment and Prevention* 3, 304–10.

Shoebridge, P. and Gowers, S.G. (2000) "Parental high concern and adolescent-onset anorexia nervosa: a case-control study to investigate direction of causality", *British Journal of Psychiatry* 176, 132–7.

Skuse, D., Albanese, A., Stanhope, R., Gilmour, J. and Voss, L. (1996) "A new stress-related syndrome of growth failure and hyperphagia in children, associated with reversibility of growth-hormone deficiency", *Lancet* 348, 353–8.

Smolak, L. and Levine, M.P. (1994) "Psychometric properties of the children's eating attitudes test", *International Journal of Eating Disorders* 16, 275–82.

Sokol, M.S. (2000) "Infection-triggered anorexia nervosa in children: clinical description of four cases", *Journal of Child and Adolescent Psychopharmacology* 10, 133–45.

Stratakis, C.A., Gold, P.W. and Chrousos, G.P. (1995) "Neuroendocrinology of stress: implications for growth and development", *Hormone Research* 43, 162–7.

Swenne, I. and Thurfjell, B. (2003) "Clinical onset and diagnosis of eating disorders in premenarcheal girls is preceded by inadequate weight gain and growth retardation", *Acta Paediatrica* 92, 1133–7.

Thurfjell, B., Edlund, B., Arinell, H., Hagglof, B. and Engstrom, I. (2003) "Psychometric properties of Eating Disorder Inventory for Children (EDI-C) in Swedish girls with and without a known eating disorder", *Eating and Weight Disorders* 8, 296–303.

Treasure, J. and Thompson, P. (1988) "Anorexia nervosa in childhood", *British Journal of Hospital Medicine* 40, 362–9.

World Health Organization (1992) *ICD-10 Classification of Mental and Behavioural Disorders: Clinical Descriptions and Diagnostic Guidelines*, Geneva: WHO.

World Health Organization (1995) "Physical status: the use and interpretation of anthropometry. Report of a WHO Expert Committee", *World Health Organization Technical Report Series* 854, 1–452.

Chapter 13

Atypical eating disorders in female athletes

Jorunn Sundgot-Borgen

Introduction

There is a considerable body of research on the relationship between sports participation and eating problems in girls and women (for reviews see Beals and Manore 1994; Brownell 1995; Brownell and Rodin 1992; Slavin 1987; Smolack *et al.* 2000; Sundgot-Borgen 1994b). The data appear inconsistent, varying by sport, athletic performance level and methodology of the study. It often seems difficult to draw any conclusions. However, there are some negative relationship between athletics and eating problems such that special terms, including anorexia athletica (AA) and the female athlete triad, have been developed to capture the special risk of disordered eating and associated problems among athletes (Otis *et al.* 1997; Sundgot-Borgen 1994b).

Female athletes represent the group of girls and young women that most closely embodies the female "ideal" of physical perfection. However, not all athletes have a body that fits into the sport specific "ideal" and those athletes are likely to be under enormous pressure to achieve this ideal (Rodin and Larson 1992; Sundgot-Borgen 1994b). In addition to the sociocultural demands placed on all girls and women to achieve and maintain an ideal body shape, female elite athletes in particular are also under pressure to improve performance, conform to the specific requirements of their sport, and they are evaluated by "important" others such as coaches, every day (Sundgot-Borgen 1994b; Wilmore 1991).

For athletes competing in distance running, sprinting, cross-country skiing, jumping and cycling, a low body weight is thought to confer a competitive advantage. Dancers, gymnasts, figure skaters, divers and ballerinas, on the other hand, might feel that weight is important to performance, but they must also be concerned with appearance (Brownell and Steen 1992; Smolack *et al.* 2000; Sundgot-Borgen 1994a). In those sports, performance and appearance are rated by judges, and thus, the degree to which the athlete meets the sport-specific "ideal" for body shape may influence her score.

Therefore, some of the athletes might start dieting not because they are dissatisfied with their weight or body shape as long as they consider themselves ordinary girls/women. However, through their sport participation they experience specific demands that make them feel that their body weight/ composition is not like the ideal in their sport. Thus, for many female athletes who start dieting to improve performance, weight concerns, dieting and use of extreme weight control methods become the focal point of their athletic existence (Matejek *et al.* 1999). Some of these athletes may eventually be diagnosed with a clinical eating disorder according to the strict DSM-IV criteria (APA 1994; Brownell and Rodin 1992; Matejek *et al.* 1999; Sundgot-Borgen 1993).

Athletes who cannot be clinically classified as anorexic or bulimic will be the focus of this chapter. Therefore, research that has tried to elucidate the existence of subclinical eating disorder in athletes will be discussed in this chapter. This chapter seeks to answer the following questions:

1 How does the concept of anorexia athletica relate to Eating Disorder Not Otherwise Specified?
2 Should eating disorders in athletes be defined differently from those in the general population?
3 Are there empirical findings from the research on athletes that have bearing on the general nosological issue?

How does the concept of AA relate to EDNOS?

In general, individuals suffering from subclinical eating disorder do not meet the strict diagnostic criteria for AN or BN (see Appendix) but, nevertheless, present serious eating problems and body weight concerns. I shall propose a "continuum hypothesis" of eating/dieting behaviour in athletes which suggests that dieting may lead to disordered eating behaviours and use of one or more weight control methods such as vomiting after eating, the use of laxatives, diuretics, and diet pills, fluid restriction, dehydration, sweating and fasting, which, in turn, may lead to clinical eating disorders. One point along this continuum has been identified as a subclinical form of AN, AA (Sundgot-Borgen 1993). The concept of subclinical AN was first examined by researchers in the early 1970s in a population of female college students (Button and Whitehouse 1981). It was later identified in adolescents who fit a pattern of growth failure and/or delayed puberty due to malnutrition that resulted from self-imposed caloric restriction arising from a fear of becoming obese (Pugliese *et al.* 1983). Using case study data, Smith (1980) adapted the concept of subclinical AN to athletes. Subclinical anorexia was originally described by Smith (1980) as a young male athlete who was strongly committed to his sport and, as such, underwent extreme weight loss as a means of improving his chances of success.

AA allows identification of athletes with symptoms of eating disorders, who do not meet all diagnostic criteria for AN or BN (Sundgot-Borgen

1993). The main features of AA are an intense fear of gaining weight or becoming fat, even though the athlete is underweight (at least 5 per cent less than expected normal weight for age and height for the general population). This low body weight is accomplished by a reduction in energy intake, excessive exercising (more than is required to improve performance in the sport) or both. Although the weight of these AA athletes is not critically low, the percentage of body fat is usually too low to obtain regular menstrual cycles. In addition to the amount of training needed to enhance performance in sport, athletes with AA exercise excessively or compulsively to purge their bodies of the effect of eating. However, what is considered excessive training for the general population (>one hour five times a week) is not considered excessive training for athletes. The average amount of training for elite athletes is 15 hours per week (Sundgot-Borgen and Torstveit 2004). Most AA athletes use one or more weight control methods. These athletes frequently report binge eating and the use of vomiting, laxatives or diuretics (Sundgot-Borgen 1993). The binge eating is usually planned, and included in a strict training and study schedule. Furthermore, what these athletes often refer to as a binge is not more calories than they actually need to meet the energy requirement of their activity level. Therefore, follow-up questions or a 24-hour recall is often needed for more information regarding the athlete who reports binge eating.

AA athletes may also report that they are extremely dissatisfied with their body. This is usually related to the demand of the sport that this athlete represents. Furthermore, they report preoccupation with food, eating and dieting. This preoccupation is related to the fact that they try to eat nutritionally "correct" food but as few calories as possible. Also they are extremely preoccupied by when they have the different meals so that their training or competition is not influenced by stomach pain, nausea and so on. Furthermore, the preoccupation with weight could be due to the fact that athletes are supposed to compete in a certain weight class and have to reduce weight for an important competition. This might happen a number of times during the season. The athletes with a subclinical eating disorder may evidence some of the common psychological traits associated with the clinical eating disorder, such as high achievement orientation, obsessive-compulsive tendencies and perfectionism. However, these traits are generally expected and usually essential for competing successfully (Leon 1991).

Table 13.1 presents the criteria for identifying the athlete with AA. The absolute and relative criteria have been ascertained; however, the number of these criteria that an athlete must meet in order to be classified as having a subclinical eating disorder remains to be determined. In the list, absolute and relative criteria are noted with + and (+) signs, respectively.

Even the features of AA are somewhat ill defined and indiscriminate. Thus, at the present time, more research is needed to further delineate and define the unique characteristics of those with subclinical eating disorder.

Table 13.1 Criteria for the subclinical eating disorders EDNOS and anorexia athletica

Common features	EDNOS	Anorexia athletica
Weight loss (>5% of expected body weight)	−	+
Delayed puberty[a]	−	(+)
Menstrual dysfunction[b]	(+)	(+)
Gastrointestinal complaints	−	+
Absence of medical illness or affective disorder explaining the weight reduction		+
Distorted body image	(+)	(+)
Body dissatisfaction due to a sport-specific "ideal"	−	+
Excessive fear of becoming obese	(+)	+
Restriction of food (<1200 kcal/day)	−	+
Use of purging methods[c]	(+)	(+)
Bingeing[d]	(+)	(+)
Compulsive exercise[e]	(+)	(+)

Notes: + = absolute criteria; (+) = relative criteria; − = not used in diagnosis. [a]No menstrual bleeding at age 16 (primary amenorrhoea). [b]Primary amenorrhoea, secondary amenorrhoea, oligomenorrhoea. [c]Self-induced vomiting, laxatives and diuretics. [d]A caloric intake far above the need. [e]The amount of training is far above what is needed to improve performance.

As seen in Table 13.1, the differences between AA and EDNOS are the following: in the AA criteria weight loss, absence of medical illness or affective disorder explaining weight reduction, body dissatisfaction due to sport-specific ideal and restriction of food (<1200 kcal/day) are absolute criteria in AA and not required for diagnosing EDNOS (Table 13.1).

Individuals diagnosed with the clinical eating disorders of AN and BN exhibit severe emotional distress and/or specific psychopathologies that go beyond concerns about weight.

Therefore, the main distinction between behaviours (no matter how extreme) aimed principally at maintaining a low weight for reasons such as competing in a certain weight class and other performance issues (AA) and the central psychopathology of eating disorders.

Prevalence of pathological weight control methods, clinical and subclinical eating disorder in athletes

There has been controversy regarding the meaning of eating disorders among athletes. Some have raised alarm about high prevalence rates and others have suggested that eating disorders in athletes are a benign form of the clinical syndrome (Dale and Landers 1999; Hausenblas and Carron 1999).

Methodological weaknesses such as small size studies, lack of definition of the competitive level, type of sport(s) and lack of definition of the data collection method used characterize most of the studies attempting to study the prevalence of disordered eating and eating disorders. In addition to this, eating disorders are known to be secretive activities and many will not admit such a problem. Despite the methodological weaknesses, existing studies are consistent in showing that symptoms of disordered eating and pathogenic weight control methods are more prevalent in female athletes than non-athletes, and more prevalent in sports in which leanness or a specific weight are considered important, than among athletes competing in sports where these factors are considered less important (Dummer *et al.* 1987; Hamilton *et al.* 1988; Rosen and Hough 1988; Rosen *et al.* 1986; Smolack *et al.* 2000; Sundgot-Borgen 1993; Sundgot-Borgen and Corbin 1987; Wilmore 1991).

Most eating disorder questionnaires used in athletes assess only physical behaviours and ignore the psychological problems. Since AN, BN and EDNOS are included in the DSM-IV (APA 1994) it is obvious that eating disorders are mental disorders and must be examined and followed up accordingly.

In my research I examined risk factors for subclinical and clinical eating disorders among elite athletes representing all types of sports. The Eating Disorder Inventory was administered to all participants and careful steps were taken to address the issue of respondent truthfulness. Of the 522 elite female athletes participating in one phase of the study, 117 (22.4 per cent) were classified as "at risk" for an eating disorder based on scores on the drive for thinness and body dissatisfaction subscales of the EDI (Sundgot-Borgen 1994a). Of the 103 at-risk athletes who participated in a clinical interview, 48 per cent met criteria for AN or BN and 41 per cent met criteria for AA (8 per cent of the total sample). The prevalence of AN (1.3 per cent) seems to be within the same range as that reported in non-athletes (Andersen 1990), whereas BN (8.2 per cent) seems to be more prevalent among athletes than non-athletes. That study was performed in 1989–90 and the EDNOS criteria did not exist. Therefore AA was introduced and used for categorizing the athletes who had significant symptoms of disordered eating but no severe psychopathology.

In a more recent study, Sundgot-Borgen and Torstveit (2004) studied eating disorders in the entire population of male and female Norwegian elite athletes (N = 1620) and controls (N = 1696).

The diagnostic criteria for subclinical and clinical eating disorders were met by more athletes (10.5 per cent) than controls (3.2 per cent), and by more female (20 per cent) than male athletes (8 per cent) ($p < 0.05$). Corresponding values for controls were lower in both genders: females (9 per cent) and males (0.5 per cent). A higher percentage of both athletes (6.5 per cent) and controls (2 per cent) met the criteria for subclinical eating disorders (AA and EDNOS) as compared with the percentage meeting the DSM-IV criteria for AN or BN, 3.2 per cent for athletes and 1.1 per cent for controls (see Table 13.2).

Table 13.2 Prevalence of female athletes of different sports and controls meeting the criteria for AN, AA, BN and EDNOS (results are given in absolute numbers and percentage)

Female groups (N)	AN N (%)	BN N (%)	AA N (%)	EDNOS N (%)	Total N (%)	CI (95%)
Technical (72)		3 (4)	2 (–)	7 (10)	12 (17)	0.08–0.26
Endurance (102)	4 (4)	10 (10)	5 (5)	5 (5)	24 (24)	0.16–0.32
Aesthetic (52)	6 (12)	8 (12)	3 (6)	5 (10)	22 (42)	0.29–0.55
Weight class (53)		6 (11)	3 (6)	7 (13)	16 (30)	0.18–0.42
Ball (252)	1 (–)	9 (4)	10 (4)	19 (8)	39 (16)	0.11–0.19
Power (31)				1 (3)	1 (–)	–0.03–0.09
Anti-gravity (10)				1 (–)	1 (–)	–0.09–0.29
Total (572)	11 (2)	36 (6)	23 (4)	45 (8)	115 (20)	0.17–0.23
Controls (571)	1 (–)	17 (3)		34 (6)	52 (8)	0.07–0.11

Should eating disorders in athletes be defined differently from those in the general population?

Some argue that the symptoms of AA should be considered transient eating problems and not pathological eating disorders. No longitudinal data on the long-term consequences of AA exist.

My philosophical position is that while elite athletes physically and motivationally represent the extreme, they are not fundamentally different in physical or psychological make-up from non-athletes (i.e. the normal person shares more genetic similarities than differences). Accordingly, I am of the position that mental and physical health disorders among athletes should be defined essentially the same as among non-athletes. However, athletes are affected by all of the same risk factors encountered by their non-athlete counterparts, as well as risk factors unique to the athletic environment. In my opinion, athletes constitute a unique population and impact of factors such as performance pressure, effect of training, sport-specific demands, energy needs, definition of "bingeing", restriction of food intake/special diets and psychopathological profile must be evaluated differently from non-athletes (Matejek et al. 1999; Sundgot-Borgen 1993; Szmukler et al. 1985). It is important to determine whether the athlete's abnormal eating and dieting behaviour (AA) is a transient behaviour associated with the specific demands of the sport or if the symptoms are more stable and part of an eating disorder such as AA. Therefore, it is not enough to merely document behaviours; the emotional and psychological state of the athlete must also be examined.

For this reason, athletes are in need of special approaches to identification, diagnostic criteria, management, treatment and prevention. Thus, when the AA criteria were introduced EDNOS did not exist. Although the fact that the

EDNOS criteria include some of the criteria listed for AA, it is my opinion that we are still in need of the AA criteria for athletes.

No longitudinal data on the long-term consequences of AA exist. However, the symptom severity in these cases may be every bit as clinically significant as those that meet all the criteria (Garner *et al.* 1998).

Are there empirical findings from the research on athletes that have bearing on the general nosological issue?

Along with other researchers who have worked with elite athletes and dancers for years, I have found that most of the athletes with clinical eating disorder have been through a period of subclinical eating disorder such as AA or EDNOS (Sundgot-Borgen and Torstveit 2004).

When comparing athletes and non-athletes who are dissatisfied with their body, a significantly higher percentage of athletes than controls are using extreme weight control methods such as laxatives, vomiting and diet pills to reduce weight (Sundgot-Borgen and Larsen 1993). This indicates the high drive towards perfection. For many athletes the wish to improve performance by dieting usually is the first step into an eating disorder (Sundgot-Borgen 1994b).

Surveys of female students and athletes have indicated that extreme weight preoccupation and even self-induced vomiting may not be associated with the same level of psychopathology as that found in patients diagnosed as having clinical eating disorder (Garner *et al.* 1983; Holderness *et al.* 1994; Olmsted and Garner 1986). This raises the question of the clinical significance of pathogenic weight control behaviours in athletes and subclinical eating disorder such as AA. Szmukler *et al.* (1985) argued that ballet students with symptoms of AN only superficially resembled actual clinical cases because the students experienced considerable improvement in their eating disorder after one year without medical intervention. In a study of 49 female ballet students, Le Grange *et al.* (1994) identified 12.3 per cent of the sample as having AN or a "partial syndrome anorexia nervosa" and agreed with the Szmukler *et al.* (1985) interpretation that the disorders may not have the same clinical significance in the ballet students as they do in clinical samples. Rather than being conceptualized as an "illness", Le Grange *et al.* (1994) suggested that eating disorders in the ballet sample should be considered as "adaptive" because of the special "nutritional needs and body shape requirements" of ballet dancers.

In the Le Grange *et al.* (1994) study, just over half of the ballet students studied were underweight, perceived themselves to be fat, and controlled their food intake by dieting, vomiting and laxative or diuretic abuse. About one-third reported menstrual disturbance or delayed menarche, and (as mentioned earlier) these symptoms can lead to irreversible bone loss and other health risks. Finally, Le Grange *et al.* (1994) reported that those ballet students who had eating disorders continued to experience serious symptoms over the follow-up period.

Clinical interviews with athletes meeting the DSM-IV criteria for AN and BN also show that most of these athletes have had a history of subclinical eating disorder (Sundgot-Borgen and Torstveit 2004).

This is similar to an earlier prospective study by Garner *et al.* (1987), who found that young ballet students with elevated Drive for Thinness and Body Dissatisfaction scales on the EDI were at risk for developing or maintaining AN during a two- to four-year follow-up. In sum, the real physical risks of maintaining a low body weight mentioned earlier as well as the persistence of serious eating disorder symptoms should be sufficient to counter any argument that disordered eating and AA in any sport are benign. Thus, to identify athletes with disordered eating the AA diagnosis is needed.

Most athletes suffering from disordered eating are at or near normal weight but have low percentage of body fat. Athletes usually try to hide their disorder until they feel that they are out of control, or when they realize that the disordered behaviour negatively affects sport performance. Therefore, the team staff must be able to recognize the physical symptoms and psychological characteristics listed for athletes with subclinical or clinical eating disorder (Sundgot-Borgen and Torstveit 2004).

Most of the clinicians and researchers who have worked with dancers and athletes with subclinical eating disorder state that the suggestion that eating disorders might be thought of as benign or adaptive variants in certain environments is misguided (Garner *et al.* 1998).

Rather, serious questions need to be raised with the major sports regulatory bodies about the social and ethical implications of pressuring young women, many of whom are under the legal age to give consent, to lose body weight to meet the prevailing requirements for shape, weight and nutritional intake required in some sports. Indeed, the benign hypothesis seems unjustified in light of what is known about the irreversible skeletal damage caused by eating disorders (including osteoporosis, stress fractures and scoliosis) (Garner *et al.* 1998).

Added to this is the well-established risk of dancers and athletes developing serious eating disorders that can have devastating physical and psychological consequences.

Conclusion

Athletic participation – at least in certain sports – has been linked to a higher incidence of eating problems, including AA, EDNOS, AN and BN. It has been argued that success in these sports requires a particular appearance, especially a lean sometimes virtually pre-pubescent look, which may lead to direct pressure from judges, coaches and parents to be thin.

Athletes constitute a unique population, and special diagnostic considerations should be made when working with this group. An attempt has been made to identify athletes who show significant symptoms of disordered eating but who do not meet the criteria for AN or BN. These athletes have been classified as having a subclinical eating disorder termed AA.

Identifying disordered eating among athletes must go beyond focusing on those who meet formal diagnoses to include those who engage in a myriad of pathogenic weight control behaviours that have clinical significance and that can severely compromise health and performance.

References

American Psychiatric Association (1994) *Diagnostic and Statistical Manual of Mental Disorders*, 4th edn (DSM-IV), Washington, DC: APA.

Andersen, A.E. (1990) "Diagnosis and treatment of males with eating disorders", in A.E. Andersen (ed.) *Males with Eating Disorders*, New York: Brunner/Mazel.

Beals, K.A. and Manore, M.M. (1994) "The prevalence and consequences of subclinical eating disorders in female athletes", *International Journal of Sport Nutrition* 4, 175–95.

Brownell, K. (1995) "Eating disorders in athletes", in K. Brownell and C. Fairburn (eds) *Eating Disorders and Obesity: A Comprehensive Handbook*, New York: Guilford Press.

Brownell, K.D. and Rodin, J. (1992) "Prevalence of eating disorders in athletes", in K.D. Brownell, J. Rodin and J.H. Wilmore (eds) *Eating, Body Weight, and Performance in Athletes: Disorders of Modern Society*, Philadelphia, PA: Lea & Febiger.

Brownell, K.D. and Steen, S.N. (1992) "Weight cycling in athletes: effects on behavior, physiology and health", in K.D. Brownell, J. Rodin and J.H. Wilmore (eds) *Eating, Body Weight, and Performance in Athletes: Disorders of Modern Society*, Philadelphia, PA: Lea & Febiger.

Button, E.J. and Whitehouse, A. (1981) "Subclinical anorexia nervosa", *Psychological Medicine* 11, 509–16.

Dale, K.S. and Landers, D.M. (1999) "Weight control in wrestling: eating disorders or disordered eating?", *Medicine and Science in Sports and Exercise* 31, 1382–9.

Dummer, G.M., Rosen, L.W. and Heusner, W.W. (1987) "Pathogenic weight-control behaviors of young competitive swimmers", *Physician and Sportsmedicine* 5, 75–86.

Garner, D.M., Olmsted, M.P. and Garfinkel, P.E. (1983) "Does anorexia nervosa occur on a continuum?", *International Journal of Eating Disorders* 2, 11–20.

Garner, D.M., Garfinkel, P.E., Rockert, W. and Olmsted, M.P. (1987) "A prospective study of eating disturbances in the ballet", *Psychotherapy and Psychosomatics* 48, 170–5.

Garner, D.M., Rosen, L.W. and Barry, D. (1998) "Eating disorders among athletes: research and recommendations", *Child and Adolescent Psychiatric Clinics of North America* 4, 839–56.

Hamilton, L.H., Brocks-Gunn, J., Warren, M.P. and Hamilton, W.G. (1988) "The role of selectivity in the pathogenesis of eating problems in ballet dancers", *Medicine and Science in Sports and Exercise* 20, 560–5.

Hausenblas, H.A. and Carron, A.V. (1999) "Eating disorder indices and athletes: an integration", *Journal of Sport and Exercise Psychology* 21, 230–58.

Holderness, C.C., Brooks-Gunn, J. and Warren, M.P. (1994) "Eating disorders and substance use: a dancing vs a nondancing population", *Medicine and Science in Sports and Exercise* 26, 297–302.

Le Grange, D., Tibbs, J. and Noakes, T. (1994) "Implications of a diagnosis of anorexia nervosa in a ballet school", *International Journal of Eating Disorders* 15, 369–76.

Leon, G.R. (1991) "Eating disorders in female athletes", *Sports Medicine* 4, 219–27.

Matejek, N., Weimann, E., Witzel, C., Molenkamp, G., Schwidergall, S. and Bohles, H. (1999) "Hypoleptinaemia in patients with anorexia nervosa and in elite gymnasts with anorexia athletica", *International Journal of Sports Medicine* 20, 451–6.

Olmsted, M.P. and Garner, D.M. (1986) "The significance of self-induced womiting as a weight control method among nonclinical samples", *International Journal of Eating Disorders* 5, 683–700.

Otis, C., Drinkwater, B., Johnson, M., Loucks, A. and Wilmore, J. (1997) "Position stand on the female athlete triad", *Medicine and Science in Sports and Exercise* 29, i–ix.

Pugliese, M.T., Liftshitz, F., Grad, G., Fort, P. and Marks-Katz, M. (1983) "Fear of obesity: a cause for short stature and delayed puberty", *New England Journal of Medicine* 309, 513–18.

Rodin, J. and Larson, L. (1992) "Social factors and the ideal body shape", in K.D. Brownell, J. Rodin and J.W. Wilmore (eds) *Eating, Body Weight and Performance in Athletes: Disorders of Modern Society*, Philadelphia, PA: Lea & Febiger.

Rosen, L.W. and Hough, D.O. (1988) "Pathogenic weight-control behaviors of female college gymnasts", *Physician and Sportsmedicine* 16, 140–6.

Rosen, L.W., McKeag, D.B., Hough, D.O. and Curley, V. (1986) "Pathogenic weight control behavior in female athletes", *Physician and Sportsmedicine* 14, 79–95.

Slavin, J. (1987) "Eating disorders in athletes", *Journal of Physical Education, Recreation and Dance*, 58, 33–6.

Smith, N.J. (1980) "Excessive weight loss and food aversion in athletes simulating anorexia nervosa", *Paediatrics* 1, 139–42.

Smolack, L., Murnen, S. and Ruble, A.E. (2000) "Female athletes and eating problems: a meta-analysis", *International Journal of Eating Disorders* 27, 371–80.

Sundgot-Borgen, J. (1993) "Prevalence of eating disorders in elite female athletes", *International Journal of Sport Nutrition* 3, 29–40.

Sundgot-Borgen, J. (1994a) "Eating disorders in female athletes", *Sports Medicine* 17, 176–88.

Sundgot-Borgen, J. (1994b) "Risk and trigger factors for the development of eating disorders in female elite athletes", *Medicine and Science in Sports and Exercise* 26, 414–19.

Sundgot-Borgen, J. and Corbin, C.B. (1987) "Eating disorders among female athletes", *Physician and Sportsmedicine* 2, 89–95.

Sundgot-Borgen, J. and Larsen, S. (1993) "Nutrient intake of female elite athletes suffering from eating disorders", *International Journal of Sport Nutrition* 3, 431–42.

Sundgot-Borgen, J. and Torstveit, M.K. (2004) "Prevalence of eating disorders in elite athletes is higher than in the general polulation", *Clinical Journal of Sport Medicine* 14, 25–32.

Szmukler, G.I., Eisler, I., Gillies, C. and Hayward, M.E. (1985) "The implications of anorexia nervosa in a ballet school", *Journal of Psychiatric Research* 19, 177–81.

Wilmore, J.H. (1991) "Eating and weight disorders in the female athlete", *International Journal of Sport Nutrition* 1, 104–17.

Chapter 14

Eating disorders and type 1 diabetes

Robert Peveler and Hannah Turner

Introduction

The distinctive clinical features of patients who have both an eating disorder and type 1 diabetes mellitus (T1DM) were initially highlighted in a number of case reports published in the 1970s and early 1980s. Bruch published the first case description in 1973. The patient, who suffered from AN and T1DM, was described as having "serious medical complications" following poor treatment compliance (Bruch 1973). Subsequent case studies (Fairburn and Steel 1980; Garner 1980; Gomez *et al.* 1980) were added to by reports of the co-occurrence of BN with T1DM (Hudson *et al.* 1985). These reports were followed by a number of prevalence studies investigating whether or not clinical eating disorders are more common in young women with T1DM than in non-diabetic women (Fairburn *et al.* 1991; Jones *et al.* 2000). More recently, a small but growing number of longitudinal studies aimed towards exploring the clinical and psychological course of these patients have been conducted (Bryden *et al.* 1999; Peveler *et al.* in press; Rydall *et al.* 1997).

The considerable interest shown in this clinical group stems from the recognition that patients with an eating disorder and T1DM differ from their non-diabetic counterparts in two important respects: first, they have available to them an additional weight loss strategy, the underuse or omission of insulin; second, they appear to be at a high risk of mortality and morbidity from microvascular and macrovascular complications of diabetes.

This chapter will discuss the ways in which eating disorders in such patients differ from those in non-diabetic populations in respect of their clinical features, prevalence, clinical course, and diagnosis and management. The implications of research in diabetes mellitus for the diagnostic construct of EDNOS will also be commented upon.

Clinical features

AN, BN and EDNOS (see Appendix for diagnostic criteria) have all been described in patients with both type 1 and type 2 diabetes (Herpertz *et al.*

2001, Marcus and Wing 1990; Peveler 1996). In many respects the clinical features of eating disorders seen in T1DM patients resemble those of non-diabetic patients. The principal difference is that patients with T1DM have available to them an additional weight loss strategy, the underuse or omission of insulin leading to "self-induced glycosuria". This feature is common but not universal in diabetic patients with an eating disorder; it is also seen in up to about 30 per cent of female patients with T1DM but no eating disorder (Kaminer and Robbins 1989; Rodin *et al.* 1991). The initial effect of this behaviour on body weight is rapid, chiefly as a result of water loss.

Strict dieting, binge eating, vomiting, misuse of laxatives and diuretics, and self-induced glycosuria are all likely to impair glycaemic control, although a minority of patients do at times manage to maintain satisfactory control. Alternating periods of raised and lowered blood glucose level may go undetected by biochemical indices such as the glycated haemoglobin test. In the short term, poor control may be manifest as recurrent symptoms of hyperglycaemia (e.g. thirst or tiredness), frequent episodes of ketoacidosis (often requiring hospital admission) or hypoglycaemia (leading to uncon-sciousness if severe). Growth retardation and pubertal delay may occur in pre-pubertal children. Patients with eating disorders appear to be at increased risk of physical complications of diabetes, including retinopathy, nephropathy or neuropathy (Peveler *et al.* in press; Rodin *et al.* 1986).

Prevalence

The question of whether the clinical eating disorders AN, BN and EDNOS are more prevalent in patients with T1DM than in non-diabetic women has been widely debated. Given that the two conditions are both relatively com-mon, they might be expected to co-occur by chance reasonably frequently. However, there has been a strong clinical impression that eating disorders are over-represented in patients with T1DM. There are also some theoretical reasons to expect eating disorders to be more common in the diabetic popula-tion. First, the non-specific stress of physical illness may increase the risk. In addition, the availability of insulin underuse or omission as a means of weight control, the experience of rapid weight fluctuations around the time of diagnosis and the prescription of rigid dietary regimes may also serve as contributory risk factors. Insulin treatment itself may cause weight gain, probably as a result of the non-physiological route of administration. On the other hand, some factors may reduce the likelihood of developing an eating disorder: patients with diabetes are usually under closer professional and family surveillance, such that problems may be detected early and nipped in the bud. The known risks associated with diabetes may also discourage patients from bingeing, vomiting or dieting.

The argument that eating disorders are more prevalent in patients with T1DM appeared to be supported by early research studies (Hudson *et al.*

1985; Rodin *et al.* 1986; Rosmark *et al.* 1986). However, many of these studies have since been subject to considerable methodological criticism (Rodin and Daneman 1992). For example, the assessment of eating disorder features is often problematic, as self-report questionnaires assessing features such as dieting are prone to confounding by the presence of diabetes. Even in the non-diabetic population, the efficiency of screening instruments such as the Eating Attitudes Test is not high, and a clinical interview is required to ascertain diagnostic status. A further difficulty pertains to recruitment. Many studies have been conducted in specialist diabetes centres, in which patients with complicated diabetes, including those with eating disorders, are likely to be over-represented. Finally, few studies have included a well-matched non-diabetic control group, an essential component of a rigorous study design.

The findings from more recent studies, which have addressed most of the methodological limitations, remain varied. Results from two case-controlled studies suggest that rates of clinical eating disorders are not increased in the diabetic population (Fairburn *et al.* 1991; Peveler *et al.* 1992). However, this has not been supported by findings from a large multi-site controlled study, which found that DSM-IV and sub-threshold eating disorders were about twice as common in adolescent females with T1DM as in their age-matched peers (Jones *et al.* 2000). Findings from a meta-analysis in 2002 suggest that while AN does not appear to be over-represented in T1DM populations (although the statistical power of the studies may be insufficient to rule this out), there is a threefold increase in the odds ratio for BN (OR = 2.9; 95 per cent CI, 1.0 to 8.4) and a significant twofold increase in the odds ratio for both EDNOS and sub-threshold eating disorders (Nielsen 2002).

One explanation for the perceived high prevalence is concerned with sub-clinical disturbances in eating attitudes and behaviours. Given that sub-threshold eating problems, which might be regarded as relatively "mild" in the non-diabetic population, can lead to clinically significant disturbances in self-care and glycaemic control in diabetic patients, it is likely that T1DM may serve to shift the boundary of perceived "clinical significance". Such mild but clinically important disturbances of eating habits and attitudes may be present in up to 10 per cent of adolescent females and young women with T1DM. In line with this suggestion, findings from a recent study investigating the prevalence of eating disturbances in pre-teen and early teenage girls with T1DM, found that 8 per cent of girls with T1DM had a diagnosis of EDNOS or sub-threshold eating disorder, compared to 1 per cent of the non-diabetic control group (Colton *et al.* 2004).

There continues to be a lack of clarity concerning prevalence. While it is not possible to be confident that AN and BN occur more frequently in patients with T1DM, there is a strong suggestion that the prevalence of EDNOS and sub-threshold cases may be increased. Further longitudinal and cross-sectional studies with adequate sample size and statistical power, conducted in appropriate populations using the best available measures are required to demonstrate conclusively that there is an increased risk for diabetic subjects.

Clinical course

Since the mid-1990s a number of longitudinal studies have been published exploring the clinical course of symptoms in patients with diabetes and an eating disorder. Pollock and colleagues (1995) repeated clinical interviews over nine years and found a low rate of clinically significant eating disorders (4 per cent). They also found a relationship between "eating problems" and other psychiatric disorders, suggesting that a subgroup of young people may have difficulties coping with T1DM. In another follow-up study, conducted over four years, eating disordered behaviour was found to be common and persistent in young women with T1DM, and was associated with impaired metabolic control and increased risk of retinopathy (Rydall *et al.* 1997). Herpertz *et al.* (2001) reported a similar pattern of persistent eating disturbance in their two-year follow-up study of patients with type 1 and type 2 diabetes. They also reported an association between insulin-purging and higher levels of psychopathology (as measured by the EDI), higher BMI and poorer metabolic control in patients with T1DM. Although these studies report a number of interesting findings, all are limited in their conclusions by the selected clinic populations recruited, limited range of outcome measures and small sample sizes.

More recently, follow-up studies have been conducted on two community cohorts of patients initially recruited in the 1980s (Bryden *et al.* 1999, 2001, 2003). Results from the eight-year follow-up of adolescents with T1DM (Bryden *et al.* 1999) indicated a significant increase in BMI from adolescence to young adulthood; this was associated with a significant increase in body weight concern, shape concern and dietary restraint, as assessed using the Eating Disorder Examination (Cooper and Fairburn 1987; Rosen *et al.* 1990). Adolescents with T1DM have also been shown to have a poor prognosis in relation to clinical and psychological outcomes: behavioural problems such as aggression and antisocial conduct in adolescence have been found to be adversely associated with poorer glycaemic control during adolescence and young adulthood (Bryden *et al.* 2001).

The findings from a follow-up study of young adults (aged 17–25 years at baseline) also demonstrated poor clinical and psychiatric outcomes for many. One-quarter of the sample developed psychiatric morbidity and over one-third microvascular complications of diabetes, indicating a poor prognosis for many young adults with T1DM in their twenties and thirties (Bryden *et al.* 2003). Such adverse outcomes were often observed to occur even though attempts at treatment had been made. More recently, Peveler *et al.* (in press) have reported on the clinical course of disordered eating habits and attitudes in these populations, evaluating their impact on glycaemic control and microvascular complications over time. Findings suggest that the cumulative incidence of eating problems continues to increase after young adulthood, and is markedly higher than that suggested by earlier cross-sectional studies. A strong relationship between disturbed eating habits and attitudes, insulin misuse, poor glycaemic control and development of microvascular complications, was also found. This longitudinal study has revealed that, as there is some lability in clinical features and syndromal diagnosis over time, a greater proportion of patients will experience a period of poor self-care and impaired glycaemic control than is apparent from a cross-sectional study. Even a relatively brief period of poor control can produce a significant increase in the risk of subsequent microvascular complications, increasing the overall clinical impact above that expected from cross-sectional prevalence studies. Although this study has a number of methodological advantages over previous studies, its findings should be set within the context of a number of potential limitations. Additional longitudinal studies on larger patient groups with more frequent assessment are required in order to clarify the precise nature of the clinical course and outcome of this population.

Diagnosis and management

Identification

Although some patients with diabetes will volunteer information about eating psychopathology, illness-related factors such as ambivalence, denial, guilt and shame will lead many to be secretive about any problems they might have with their eating. Thus, the first step in management is concerned with successful detection. Poor metabolic control, repeated episodes of hypoglycaemia or ketoacidosis and weight fluctuations are important indicators of risk and their presentation should prompt sensitive but direct questioning relating to eating habits and attitudes, concerns about body weight and methods of weight control. The potential for eating disturbance should be borne in mind particularly when working with patients most at risk: adolescent and young adult females. Screening questionnaires such as the EAT (Garner and Garfinkel 1979) and the SCOFF (Morgan *et al.* 1999) may assist in the process of detection, but a psychiatric interview, such as the Structured Clinical Interview for DSM-IV (Spitzer *et al.* 1996) or EDE (Cooper and Fairburn 1987) is necessary to confirm a clinical diagnosis. Self-report instruments and interviews should be modified to take into account the presence of diabetes. In most instances it is good practice for specialist eating disorder teams to liaise closely with diabetes services. Only if good communication between teams can be established and maintained is treatment likely to be optimal for both conditions.

Principles of treatment

There is a lack of primary research concerning treatment of diabetic patients with an eating disorder. Advice is therefore based on the guidelines provided for the treatment of non-diabetic patients (National Collaborating Centre for Mental Health 2004), but this must take account of T1DM. Dietary counselling by a dietician or diabetes specialist nurse may be a helpful first approach, especially for patients presenting with milder forms of eating disturbance, but most cases will require specialist management. It is possible that diabetic patients with BN may benefit from a programme of evidence-based guided self-help (National Collaborating Centre for Mental Health 2004). In all cases close liaison between the therapist managing the eating disorder and the team managing the patient's diabetes is essential. It is also likely that treatment effectiveness will be enhanced when interventions are modified to include attention to insulin omission, diabetic control, body mass index, diabetes-related dietary restriction, relationships with family and medical staff, and feelings about having diabetes (Daneman *et al.* 2002). Although most patients can be managed on an outpatient basis, the risk of impaired physical health necessitating admission is increased among patients with T1DM. Clinical guidelines on the management of patients with an eating disorder and T1DM recommend intensive regular physical monitoring, given the high risk of complications and mortality (National Collaborating Centre for Mental Health 2004).

Bulimia Nervosa

Treatments for BN, particularly cognitive behavioural approaches, have been the subject of extensive research (National Collaborating Centre for Mental Health 2004). However, the suitability of cognitive behavioural therapy for patients with BN and T1DM has been assessed only in a small case series (Peveler *et al.* 1992).

The coexistence of diabetes with BN invariably complicates psychological interventions. For example, engaging patients in cognitive behavioural therapy can be more difficult than for non-diabetic patients. This may be linked to the compensatory weight gain that may accompany the initiation of insulin treatment, or the dietary restraint necessitated by diabetes management. Self-monitoring may also pose a challenge for patients with T1DM: for some it may draw unwanted attention to the increased risk of complications associated with high blood glucose, while others may not wish to indicate a commitment to respond with behavioural change. It is also possible that for some, the rapid nature of the initial weight loss induced by insulin omission serves as a particularly potent form of short-term self-esteem enhancement, leaving this behaviour particularly difficult to relinquish.

When using cognitive behavioural therapy with T1DM patients, a number of modifications must be made to the standard treatment approach. First, in addition to monitoring thoughts and eating habits, patients must also monitor insulin injections and blood glucose testing to facilitate the maintenance of adequate glycaemic control while eating habits and weight control behaviours are changing. In view of this, it is desirable that the therapist has some experience of the management of diabetes to make appropriate use of the information. Second, conflict may arise between the modifications to eating habits usually advocated for the treatment of BN, and the dietary advice often given for the management of diabetes. The cognitive model of BN is based on evidence that strict dieting predisposes individuals to engage in bingeing, and treatment is therefore aimed at lessening the patient's wish to diet and promoting a more flexible approach to eating. By contrast, conventional dietary management of diabetes is based on total avoidance of foods with a high sugar content and rigid observance of carbohydrate allowances. It can therefore be difficult to steer a course between these two extremes.

Other approaches to the treatment of BN include interpersonal psychotherapy and the use of pharmacological treatment, most commonly antidepressant drugs, especially those of the selective serotonin reuptake inhibitor class. Such treatment approaches have not been evaluated in diabetic patients, although clinical experience suggests that medication may be a useful adjunct to psychological treatment in some patients. This is also supported by clinical guidelines (National Collaborating Centre for Mental Health 2004). One empirical study has been conducted comparing psycho-education with "standard care" for people with BN and T1DM (Olmsted et al. 2002). Findings suggest that psycho-education was associated with a reduction in scores on the Restraint and Eating Concern subscales of the EDE, but not with improved metabolic control. Furthermore, although not routinely advocated for the treatment of BN, the potential effectiveness of an inpatient programme for patients with T1DM and BN has been evaluated. In their three-year follow-up study of "integrated inpatient therapy", Takki et al. (2003) reported sustained improvements in glycaemic control, depressive/anxiety and psychological/behavioural disturbances related to food in a group of T1DM patients. Although limited by a small sample size, such studies highlight a potentially interesting role for inpatient programmes in the treatment of T1DM females with BN.

Anorexia Nervosa

The treatment of AN has been subject to less systematic research than that of BN (National Collaborating Centre for Mental Health 2004), thus recommendations about management are based largely on clinical experience (Peveler and Fairburn 1989).

During the period of weight restoration, it is usually necessary to accept that glycaemic control will not be perfect but severe hypoglycaemia or hyperglycaemia must be avoided. It is helpful for the patient to monitor insulin dose and blood glucose level as eating habits and weight change. As with BN, it is desirable for the therapist to have some knowledge of the management of diabetes to assist the patient in maintaining adequate glycaemic control. Difficulties again arise in respect of dietary advice and it is important to steer a middle course between extreme dieting for weight control on the one hand and overly relaxed dietary management of diabetes on the other.

Eating Disorder Not Otherwise Specified

In the absence of research evidence to guide the treatment of those presenting with a diagnosis of EDNOS, it is currently recommended that clinicians follow the guidelines given for the treatment for the eating disorder the patient's presentation most closely resembles (National Collaborating Centre for Mental Health 2004). In line with this recommendation, the treatment of patients presenting with an atypical eating disorder and T1DM should follow that which most closely resembles the patient's clinical presentation. Again, close joint work with a representative of the diabetes team such as a diabetes specialist nurse is likely to be beneficial.

Sub-threshold cases

Little is known about the optimum management of patients with these more prevalent but less severe forms of eating disturbance. Although these conditions are seen as relatively unimportant when they occur in non-diabetic patients, they constitute an important clinical problem when they occur in conjunction with T1DM, as a relatively brief episode of eating disturbance and poor self-care can lead to serious physical morbidity. In view of this, it is regarded as essential that sub-threshold cases of an eating disorder in people with T1DM are treated alongside those with full diagnoses (National Collaborating Centre for Mental Health 2004). However, to date little systematic research has been conducted on the management of such patients. One published study evaluating a treatment intervention for this clinical group concluded that a six-session psycho-education programme was no more effective than a waiting list control group (Alloway et al. 2001). In view of the lack of published research, few recommendations can be made beyond the general principles described above.

Treatment of children and adolescents

Three cross-sectional studies investigating the association between family environment, eating disturbances and diabetes outcomes among adolescent girls have recently been conducted. Results suggest that family environment may increase the risk of eating disturbance through two interrelated pathways: first, through failing to adequately balance the adolescents' concurrent needs for independence and supportive parental guidance, and second, through modelling weight loss behaviours and reinforcing the values of thinness (Maharaj *et al.* 1998, 2001). It has also been suggested that the impact of family interaction on metabolic control may be moderated by the presence and severity of eating disturbances in girls with diabetes (Maharaj *et al.* 2000). These findings have led to recommendations that specifically tailored family-based interventions, aimed towards addressing issues such as limit-setting, communication skills and the development of self-esteem in domains beyond weight and shape, may be helpful for some female adolescents with T1DM (Daneman *et al.* 2002). However, such interventions have yet to be rigorously evaluated.

Implications for the construct of EDNOS

Though the debate over prevalence continues, few question the seriousness of a dual diagnosis of an eating disorder and T1DM. There also appears to be an emerging consensus regarding the higher occurrence of sub-threshold cases of eating disturbance among this clinical population. The potential for "mild" eating disorder psychopathology to give rise to clinically important disturbances of self-care and glycaemic control not only necessitates a shift in the boundaries of "clinical significance" but also prompts a need to redefine terms such as "subclinical". Similar issues may arise in other chronic physical conditions in which eating disorder psychopathology may affect outcome. For example, Pearson *et al.* (1991) reported high levels of AN in cystic fibrosis (CF) patients aged 8–15 years, and Pumariega *et al.* (1987) reported that 13 of 108 adolescents with cystic fibrosis described symptoms that were consistent with an atypical eating disorder. Other data suggest there is no evidence for elevated rates of "full syndrome" eating disorders in CF patients (Raymond *et al.* 2000).

Patients with an eating disorder and T1DM may present with an important additional feature, the underuse or omission of insulin as a means of weight control. Although some have suggested this clinical feature could be regarded as an additional diagnostic indicator (APA 1994) current research data suggest that this method of weight control might be more akin to dieting, its widespread occurrence across the eating disorder severity spectrum limiting its usefulness as a diagnostic indicator.

There is a paucity of research concerning the treatment of patients with an eating disorder and T1DM, and relatively little is known about the optimum treatment approach. Patients with T1DM who present with clinically severe or milder forms of eating psychopathology pose a significant clinical challenge, and more effort is required to address eating difficulties in this group if mortality and significant physical morbidity are to be prevented.

Conclusion

Disturbances in eating attitudes and behaviours in adolescents and young adults with T1DM are of major clinical importance. There is a clear need for further research, particularly longitudinal studies, including patients with the full spectrum of severity and evaluating outcome across all dimensions, and treatment trials. The clinical management of this group of patients remains a challenge, especially in the absence of good quality trial data. In relation to clinical management, the separation of diabetes teams and eating disorder teams into different provider organizations restricts collaboration and liaison, and limits effectiveness. Better methods of identification and treatment that are acceptable to patients are required if the potential for adverse outcomes within this clinical population is to be reduced.

References

Alloway, S.C., Roth, E.L. and Mccargar, L.J. (2001) "Effectiveness of a group psycho-education program for the treatment of subclinical disordered eating in women with type 1 diabetes", *Canadian Journal of Dietetic Practice and Research* 62, 188–92.

American Psychiatric Association (1994) *Diagnostic and Statistical Manual of Mental Disorders*, 4th edn (DSM-IV), Washington, DC: APA.

Bruch, H. (1973) *Eating Disorders: Obesity, Anorexia and the Person Within*, New York: Basic Books.

Bryden, K.S., Neil, H.A., Mayou, R.A., Peveler, R.C., Fairburn, C.F. and Dunger, D. (1999) "Eating habits, body weight, and insulin misuse: a longitudinal study of teenagers and young adults with type 1 diabetes", *Diabetes Care* 22, 1956–60.

Bryden, K.S., Peveler, R.C., Stein, A., Neil, H.A., Mayou, R.A. and Dunger, D. (2001) "Clinical and psychological course of diabetes from adolescence to young adulthood: a longitudinal study", *Diabetes Care* 24, 1535–40.

Bryden, K.S., Dunger, D., Mayou, R.A., Peveler, R.C. and Neil, H.A. (2003) "Poor prognosis of young adults with type 1 diabetes: a longitudinal study", *Diabetes Care* 26, 1052–7.

Colton, P., Olmsted, M., Daneman, D., Rydall, A. and Rodin, G. (2004) "Disturbed eating behaviour and eating disorders in pre-teen and early teenage girls with type 1 diabetes: a case-controlled study", *Diabetes Care* 27(7), 1654–9.

Cooper, Z. and Fairburn, C.F. (1987) "The eating disorder examination: a semi-structured interview for the assessment of the specific psychopathology of eating disorders", *International Journal of Eating Disorders* 6, 1–8.

Daneman, D., Rodin, G., Jones, D.J., Colton, P., Rydall, A., Maharaj, S. and Olmsted, M. (2002) "Eating disorders in adolescent girls and young adult women with type 1 diabetes", *Diabetes Spectrum* 15, 83–105.

Fairburn, C.F. and Steel, J.M. (1980) "Anorexia nervosa in diabetes mellitus", *British Medical Journal* 280, 1167–8.

Fairburn, C.G., Peveler, R.C., Davies, B.A., Mann, J.I. and Mayou, R.A. (1991) "Eating disorders in young adults with insulin dependent diabetes: a controlled study", *British Medical Journal* 303, 17–20.

Garner, S. (1980) "Anorexia nervosa in diabetes mellitus", *British Medical Journal* 281, 1144.

Garner, D.M. and Garfinkel, P.E. (1979) "The eating attitudes test: an index of the symptoms of anorexia nervosa", *Psychological Medicine* 9, 273–9.

Gomez, J., Dally, P. and Issacs, A.J. (1980) "Anorexia nervosa in diabetes mellitus", *British Medical Journal* 281, 61–2.

Herpertz, S., Albus, C., Kielmann, R., Hagemann-Patt, H., Lichtblau, K., Kohle, K., Mann, K. and Senf, W. (2001) "Comorbidity of diabetes mellitus and eating disorders: a follow-up study", *Journal of Psychosomatic Research* 51, 673–8.

Hudson, J.I., Wentworth, S.M., Hudson, M.S. and Pope, H.G. (1985) "Prevalence of anorexia nervosa and bulimia among young diabetic women", *Journal of Clinical Psychiatry* 46, 88–9.

Jones, J.M., Lawson, M.L., Daneman, D., Olmsted, M.P. and Rodin, G. (2000) "Eating disorders in adolescent females with and without type 1 diabetes: cross sectional study", *British Medical Journal* 320, 1563–6.

Kaminer, Y. and Robbins, D. R. (1989) "Insulin misuse: a review of an overlooked psychiatric problem", *Psychosomatics* 30, 19–24.

Maharaj, S., Rodin, G.M. and Olmsted, M. (1998) "Eating disturbances, diabetes and the family: an empirical study", *Journal of Psychosomatic Research* 44, 479–90.

Maharaj, S., Rodin, G.M., Connolly, J.A., Olmsted, M. and Daneman, D. (2000) "Eating disturbances among girls with type 1 diabetes mellitus (DM): examining the role of family dysfunction and mother's eating and weight control behaviors as contributing risk factors", *Diabetes Research and Clinical Practice* 50 (suppl. 1) S227.

Maharaj, S., Rodin, G.M., Connolly, J.A., Olmsted, M. and Daneman, D. (2001) "Eating problems and the observed quality of mother–daughter interactions among girls with type 1 diabetes", *Journal of Consulting and Clinical Psychology* 69, 950–8.

Marcus, M.D. and Wing, R.R. (1990) "Eating disorders and diabetes", in C.S. Holmes (ed.) *Neuropsychological and Behavioural Aspects of Diabetes*, New York: Springer-Verlag.

Morgan, J., Reid, F. and Lacey, J.H. (1999) "The SCOFF questionnaire: assessment of a new screening tool for eating disorders", *British Medical Journal* 319, 1467–8.

National Collaborating Centre for Mental Health (2004) *Eating Disorders: Core Interventions in the Treatment and Management of Anorexia Nervosa, Bulimia Nervosa and Related Eating Disorders*, London: British Psychological Society.

Nielsen, S. (2002) "Eating disorders in females with type 1 diabetes: an update of a meta-analysis", *European Eating Disorders Review* 10, 241–54.

Olmsted, M., Daneman, D., Rydall, A.C., Lawson, M.L. and Rodin, G. (2002) "The effects of psychoeducation on disturbed eating attitudes and behaviour in young women with type 1 diabetes mellitus", *International Journal of Eating Disorders* 32, 230–9.

Pearson, D.A., Pumariega, A.J. and Seilheimer, D.K. (1991) "The development of psychiatric symptomatology in patients with cystic fibrosis", *Journal of the Academy of Child and Adolescent Psychiatry* 30, 290–7.

Peveler, R.C. (1996) "Eating disorders in patients with insulin-dependent diabetes mellitus", *Practical Diabetes* 13, 128–30.

Peveler, R.C. and Fairburn, C.F. (1989) "Anorexia nervosa and diabetes mellitus", *Bulletin of the Royal College of Psychiatrists* 13, 17.

Peveler, R.C., Fairburn, C.F., Boller, I. and Dunger, D. (1992) "Eating disorders in adolescents with insulin-dependent diabetes mellitus", *Diabetes Care* 15(10), 1356–60.

Peveler, R.C., Bryden, K., Neil, H.A., Fairburn, C.F., Mayou, R.A., Dunger, D. and Turner, H.M. (in press) "The relationship of disordered eating habits and attitudes to clinical outcome in young adult females with type 1 diabetes", *Diabetes Care*.

Pollock, M., Kovacs, M. and Charron-Prochownik, D. (1995) "Eating disorders and maladaptive dietary/insulin management among youths with childhood-onset insulin-dependent diabetes mellitus", *Journal of the Academy of Child and Adolescent Psychiatry* 34, 291–6.

Pumariega, A.J., Pursell, J., Spoke, A. and Jones, D.J. (1987) "Eating disorders in adolescents with cystic fibrosis", *Journals of the American Academy of Child Psychiatry* 25, 269–75.

Raymond, N.C., Chang, P., Crow, S.J., Mitchell, J.E., Dieperink, B.S., Beck, M.M., Crosby, R.D., Clawson, C.C. and Warwick, W.J. (2000) "Eating disorder patients with cystic fibrosis", *Journal of Adolescence* 3, 359–63.

Rodin, G.M. and Daneman, D. (1992) "Eating disorders and IDDM: a problematic association", *Diabetes Care* 15, 1402–12.

Rodin, G.M., Johnson, L.E., Garfinkel, P.E., Daneman, D. and Kenshole, A.B. (1986) "Eating disorders in female adolescents with insulin dependent diabetes mellitus", *International Journal of Psychiatry in Medicine* 16, 49–57.

Rodin, G., Craven, J., Littlefield, C., Murray, M. and Daneman, D. (1991) "Eating disorders and intentional insulin undertreatment in adolescent females with diabetes", *Psychosomatics* 32, 171–6.

Rosen, J.C., Vara, L., Wendt, S. and Leitenberg, H. (1990) "Validity studies of the eating disorder examination", *International Journal of Eating Disorders* 9, 519–28.

Rosmark, B., Berne, C., Holgren, S., Lago, C., Renholm, G. and Sohlberg, S. (1986) "Eating disorders in patients with insulin-dependent diabetes mellitus", *Journal of Clinical Psychiatry* 47, 547–50.

Rydall, A.C., Rodin, G.M., Olmsted, M.P., Devenyi, R.G. and Daneman, D. (1997) "Disordered eating behavior and microvascular complications in young women with insulin-dependent diabetes mellitus", *New England Journal of Medicine* 336, 1849–54.

Spitzer, R., Williams, J. and Gibbons, M. (1996) *Instruction Manual for the Structured Clinical Interview for DSM-IV*, New York: New York State Psychiatric Institute.

Takki, M., Uchigata, Y., Komaki, G., Nozaki, T., Kawai, H., Iwamoto, Y. and Kubo, C. (2003) "An integrated inpatient therapy for type 1 diabetic females with bulimia nervosa: a 3-year follow-up study", *Journal of Psychosomatic Research* 55, 349–56.

Chapter 15

EDNOS

A neurodevelopmental perspective

Kenneth Nunn and Melissa Hart

Introduction

The understanding of eating disorders has grown substantially since the early 1970s. Nevertheless, the eating disorders remain syndromes associated with high morbidity and mortality. Progress has been made in our understanding of the psychological characteristics associated with eating disorders and of the physiological effects associated with these illnesses. Little progress, however, has been made in the understanding of aetiological factors and the evidence for effective treatments.

Previous chapters in this book have identified a significant variety of altered eating patterns and behaviours, proposed causal factors and potential biological mechanisms involved in eating disorders. However, most of these chapters address a more narrowly defined notion of eating disorders. If we broaden eating disorders to encapsulate a greater diversity of phenomena and conditions, we may clarify some of the unanswered questions around eating disorders. We can do this by identifying mechanisms in common and differential points of disruption in the pathways and processes of eating.

We start this chapter looking at brain abnormality associated with various disorders. However, as the chapter proceeds we attempt a tentative synthesis in relation to the normal, developing brain. Hypotheses relating to the normal development of brain function are the starting point for future inquiry. Considering the behaviours, psychological features, physiology and pathology in the context of our understanding of the normal functioning brain may provide a better, more useful framework for classifying the disorders of eating, allow targeted research into specific areas of disordered eating and the development of more effective treatments. This chapter aims to integrate literature to date on disordered eating behaviour from both medical and psychiatric perspectives with special reference to aetiology, prognosis and effective interventions.

The more typical eating disorders

Anorexia Nervosa, Bulimia Nervosa and similar disorders

Often, when we think about eating disorders, we think of the more typical eating disorders, Anorexia Nervosa (AN), Bulimia Nervosa (BN) and the slightly atypical forms of these disorders (see Appendix for diagnostic criteria). Even within the typical eating disorders, a variety of altered eating behaviours and physical aspects may be seen. Behaviours may include restrictive eating, food selectivity, altered preference for higher fat foods, preference for sweet tasting foods, negative emotional responses associated with eating, bingeing, purging, reduced rate of eating and increased exercise. Physical aspects may include amenorrhoea, weight changes and altered appetite and satiety. There may also be abnormalities in the neuro-endocrine response to eating, other neuro-endocrine abnormalities (such as in the hypothalamic-pituitary-adrenal system), neurotransmitter abnormalities (such as in the central serotonin and noradrenergic systems) and brain changes. The brain changes may include brain shrinkage in AN, cerebral sulci widening and involvement in the orbitofrontal cortex, anterior cingulate and dorsolateral prefrontal areas of the brain (see Chapter 8).

These more typical categories have been useful in targeting our research efforts and furthering our knowledge and understanding of AN and BN. The largest group however, the EDNOS category, remains a "mixed bag". This is a residual category and it is not clear what does *not* constitute an eating disorder, leaving open a wide range of possible disorders, which often overlap with other illnesses.

Disordered eating from a neurodevelopmental perspective

A range of disordered eating behaviours can be found in neurodevelopmental disorders. Abnormal brain function has been found in many of these cases, which may shed light on the altered eating behaviours encountered.

Kleine-Levin Syndrome: episodic bingeing without expressing hunger or guilt

Uncontrollable eating and binge episodes may be seen in Kleine-Levin Syndrome, a disorder characterized by daytime sleepiness, hyperphagia and behavioural disturbance (Lask *et al.* 2003; Strub *et al.* 1988). People with Kleine-Levin Syndrome will typically eat any food in sight during the waking hours and appear to have a voracious appetite without any clear mention of hunger and guilt about eating (Gillberg 1995).

Specific brain involvement has been reported in the literature. The main implicated brain structures are the frontal lobes and the hypothalamus (Arias *et al.* 2002; Landtblom *et al.* 2002; Mayer *et al.* 1998). SPECT (single photon emission computed tomography) scan has shown hypoperfusion of the frontal lobes, which may or may not be secondary to diencephalic (thalamus and hypothalamus) dysfunction (Arias *et al.* 2002; Landtblom *et al.* 2002). Hypoperfusion has also been seen in the temporal lobes (especially on the left side) and the right parietal lobe (Landtblom *et al.* 2002). Results of MRI scans have been variable with some studies showing no abnormalities, while another study reported a large and asymmetric mamillary body (Landtblom *et al.* 2002; Mayer *et al.* 1998). One autopsy has shown lesions in the medial thalamus (Strub *et al.* 1988).

It has been proposed that hypothalamic dysfunction, and abnormalities in central serotonin and dopamine metabolism, contribute to the pathogenesis (and voracious appetite) of Kleine-Levin Syndrome (Dauvilliers *et al.* 2002; Muller *et al.* 1998). This is supported by the appetite and sleep symptoms, the occurrence mostly in the teenage period, the sex differences (seen mostly in boys) and some EEG findings (Gillberg 1995). Disturbances in food intake, appetite, activity, sleep, hormonal levels and thermoregulation in AN have been shown to be similar to the physiological effects of oestrogen. Opposite disturbances in Kleine-Levin Syndrome are producible with andro-gens, implicating hypothalamic hypersensitivity to sex steroids in both AN and Kleine-Levin Syndrome (Young 1975). Abnormalities in prolactin, growth hormone and luteotropic hormone as well as other hormonal changes in the symptomatic period suggest a reduced hypothalamic dopaminergic tone during the acute phase (Muller *et al.* 1998). They have proposed that a general dopaminergic dysfunction, affecting both hypothalamic and nigros-triatal dopaminergic neurons, induced Kleine-Levin Syndrome in one sub-ject. The marked response to mood stabilizers such as lithium and sodium valproate reported by clinicians treating these disorders raises the possibility that hyperphagia and delirium in the young are a manifestation of mood disorder on the one hand or that hyperphagia generally may be responsive to mood stabilizers even if not part of a broader picture of mood disorder.

Kluver-Bucy Syndrome: hyperorality, hyperphagia and pica

Kluver-Bucy Syndrome is characterized by an excessive and insatiable appe-tite, the placing of non-food items in the mouth and chewing (hyperorality) and ingestion of inedible objects such as metal and faeces (Fogel *et al.* 1996; Mendez and Foti 1997; Varon *et al.* 2003). Cases of death associated with hyperoral behaviour in Kluver-Bucy Syndrome have been reported (Mendez and Foti 1997).

The amygdala and temporal lobes have been implicated in the aetiology and pathophysiology associated with Kluver-Bucy Syndrome (Fogel *et al.* 1996; Lopez *et al.* 1995; Mendez and Foti 1997; Varon *et al.* 2003). Monkeys with amygdala lesions develop Kluver-Bucy Syndrome symptoms of continuous olfactory and oral exploration and inability to distinguish food from non-food items (Fogel *et al.* 1996). Kluver-Bucy Syndrome behaviours were also seen in a 19-year-old man after a temporal lobectomy (for a seizure disorder) who developed an insatiable appetite (Fogel *et al.* 1996). Structural lesions in the medial, inferior and anterior temporal cortex are often found in autopsy of Kluver-Bucy Syndrome (Varon *et al.* 2003). Mendez and Foti (1997) propose that the hyperoral behaviour seen in Kluver-Bucy Syndrome results from damage to the amygdala in the anterior temporal lobes. The hyperorality of Kluver-Bucy Syndrome needs to be contrasted with the hyperphagia of Kleine-Levin Syndrome.

Prader-Willi Syndrome: increased hunger, decreased satiety and hoarding

Infantile hypotonia and failure to thrive, with subsequent hyperphagia due to an insatiable appetite, obesity and hoarding, are characteristic in Prader-Willi Syndrome (Kohn *et al.* 2001; Lask *et al.* 2003). The normal satiety response appears both delayed and impaired (Daenen *et al.* 2002). Behavioural problems occur from a young age and are mainly related to food. Such behaviours may include stealing food and eating inedible objects such as animal food and eating out of garbage cans. Obsessive-compulsive features seen in Prader-Willi Syndrome are believed to interact with the incessant hunger and lack of satiety to engender the intense preoccupation with food and incessant food-seeking (Dimitropoulos *et al.* 2000).

Biological findings have been implicated in the obsessionality and altered satiety response in Prader-Willi Syndrome, which is a congenital disorder caused by an abnormality of chromosome 15 (Counts 2001; Kohn *et al.* 2001). Hypothalamic dysfunction has been implicated in Prader-Willi Syndrome because of the overeating, hypogonadism and short stature (Gillberg 1995). Depressed plasma growth hormone levels (but not thyroid-stimulating hormone) have been found in Prader-Willi Syndrome children with short stature supporting this hypothesis (Gillberg 1995). Dimitropoulos *et al.* (2000) have proposed that the genetic material on chromosome 15 may alter synthesis, release, metabolism or other activities of specific neurotransmitters involved in modulating feeding. In this formulation, serotonin has been implicated in eating behaviours as an increased concentration of the serotonin metabolite 5-HIAA has been found in CSF in Prader-Willi Syndrome. They point out that elevated blood GABA has been found, along with high densities of GABA-A receptors in the anterior or medial hypothalamus. If sub-units of the GABA-A receptor are absent, there may be a compensatory feedback-induced increase in GABA release. Dimitropoulos *et al.* (2000) have suggested that failure of GABAnergic inhibition of dopaminergic, serotonergic and glutaminergic pathways between frontal cortex and basal ganglia are involved in obsessive symptoms in Prader-Willi Syndrome. Cells in the paraventricular nucleus of the hypothalamus are associated with satiety and meal size in animals and paraventricular peptides may be associated with abnormal eating patterns in Prader-Willi Syndrome. Again, Dimitropoulos *et al.* (2000) found reduced oxytocin neurons in the hypothalamic paraventricular nuclei in Prader-Willi Syndrome with elevated CSF oxytocin.

Autism: restricted, rigid repertoire with neophobia

The eating behaviours of autism are characterized by an extremely limited food repertoire, repetitive eating patterns, a lack of willingness to try new foods, mouthing of objects and rituals around eating (Cornish 2002; Field *et al.* 2003; Williams *et al.* 2000). People with autism may also stop eating from time to time, eat what are generally considered as non-edible substances, and choose food specifically for colour, brand or preparation features (Cornish 2002). The eating behaviours observed in autism are consistent with general rigid patterns of interest and activities and an obsessive drive for routine and order, and may be associated with sensory regulatory difficulties and desire for sameness (Williams *et al.* 2000). Body weight and growth can be variable in these patients, though one study showed normal body mass index distribution for females and lower than average for males (Cornish 2002; Mouridsen *et al.* 2002).

A variety of areas in the brain has been implicated in autism. The brain-stem and temporal lobes have been associated; prefrontal areas, cerebellum and basal ganglia are thought also to play a role (Gillberg 1995). Each of these areas may contribute in quite different ways.

The amygdala in the temporal lobes has been implicated in autism. One study has shown rats lesioned in the amygdala resulted in reduced social play behaviour as seen in autism (Daenen *et al.* 2002). The amygdala is involved in the discrimination of objects necessary for survival, such as food (Santrock 1996). Neurons fire selectively at the sight of edible food and lesions of the amygdala can cause animals to eat inappropriate objects (Santrock 1996).

The cerebellum may play a role in autistic behaviours. A direct pathway exists between the fastigial nucleus of the cerebellum, the septal nuclei and the amygdala, suggesting a role of the cerebellum in emotion and behaviour (Koves *et al.* 2002). The cerebellum has also been shown to modulate sensory input at the level of the brainstem, thalamus and cerebral cortex (Gillberg and Svennerholm 1987). Functional and sensory dysregulation are both central to autism.

Cerebral atrophy has also been reported with loss or abnormal development of Purkinje cell count which may be responsible for some behaviours in autism and will affect neurotransmitters and neuropeptides (Koves *et al.* 2002). The brain's dopamine and serotonin systems have been reported to be abnormal in autism (Gillberg 1995; Koves *et al.* 2002). Increased serotoninaemia and hyper-beta-endorphinaemia has been observed (Koves *et al.* 2002). Elevated levels of 5-HT (5-hydroxytryptamine; serotonin) are also reported in 30–50 per cent of children with autism (Abu-Akel 2003).

Other hypotheses include a pathogenic model involving hyperfunction of dopaminergic nerve fibres in the brainstem (Gillberg and Svennerholm 1987). The brainstem and pontine nuclei are sites of convergence of taste and visceral information (Capaldi 1996). Another hypothesis is that an incomplete breakdown of gluten- and casein-containing foods passes the blood brain barrier decreasing the breakdown of neurotransmitters, increasing opioid activity leading to abnormal behaviours seen in autism (Cornish 2002). Decreased ability to effectively metabolize phenolic amines (such as dopamine, tyramine and serotonin) has also been postulated (Alberti *et al.* 1999). Such substances function as neurotransmitters, are toxic for the central nervous system and may exacerbate behaviour.

Dementia: selective disruptions progressing to comprehensive disruption of eating

The early stages of dementia are associated with excessive eating, a change in food preferences and eating bizarre and inappropriate substances. This is followed by difficulty with eating, refusal to eat and finally an inability to self-feed at all. One study has shown hyperorality in 6 per cent of dementia patients and binge eating in 10 per cent (Fogel *et al.* 1996). The final stages may also involve Kluver-Bucy Syndrome features with constant mouthing (Hope *et al.* 1989).

Changes in eating are less common in Alzheimer's dementia (AD) (except anorexia), though in fronto-temporal dementia, changes in eating behaviours are common. Frontal variant fronto-temporal dementia (fvFTD) has been associated with gluttony and overeating, whereas the temporal variant, semantic dementia (SD), shows increased selectivity, food fads and the eating of inedible objects (Ikeda *et al.* 2002; Mummery 2002). In fvFTD the first symptom may be changes in food preference or increased appetite while in SD developmental patterns include initial changes in food preferences, followed by increased appetite, altered eating habits and other oral behaviour, and finally swallowing problems (Ikeda *et al.* 2002). The same authors found weight increases in 30 per cent of fronto-temporal dementia, while significant weight loss has been found in 10 per cent of AD. One study has shown that eating non-edible substances in dementia is associated with frontal and occipital atrophy (Cullen *et al.* 1997).

Common eating behaviour changes are seen in fvFTD and SD (altered food preference, especially for sweet foods, appetite and eating behaviour) and the ventral frontal lobe, temporal pole and amygdala are damaged in both syndromes (Mummery 2002). As previously seen, degeneration of the amygdala in monkeys and the surgical removal of the temporal lobes in humans have both resulted in Kluver-Bucy Syndrome (Fogel *et al.* 1996). Some human studies have implicated orbitofrontal cortex, frontal operculum/insula and amygdala in processing taste, which may account for some of the preference for sweet foods developed in the fronto-temporal dementias (Ikeda *et al.* 2002).

Hypothalamic syndromes and appetite

Idiopathic hypothalamic syndromes do not appear to be a homogeneous group (Nunn *et al.* 1997). Some children present with multiple endocrine abnormalities while others may entail circumscribed salt and water regulatory difficulties. The majority of cases have reported obesity and some have reported loss of food discrimination and a voracious appetite. Small children may gain tens of kilograms in weight and death may result from difficulties in breathing due to both mechanical obstruction and central brain causes of hypoventilation. At least one mechanism for this occurring is an auto-immune reaction of the body to the brain triggered by tumour development in the sympathetic chain of the autonomic nervous system. The body sets up an immune inflammatory response to the tumour, which has elements similar to the brain and the brain is attacked inadvertently, especially in the region of the hypothalamus and brainstem but also in areas of the limbic system including the amygdala.

Head injury and frontal lobe disorders: inhibition and dyscontrol of eating

Bulimic behaviour, hyperorality and depressed taste intensities (due to central damage) may be seen in severe head injury (Capaldi 1996; Gillberg 1995; Strub *et al.* 1988). Acceleration/deceleration of the brain can cause contusions of the nervous system, haemorrhage, shearing stress, cerebral oedema, infection and degeneration of cerebral white matter (Gillberg 1995). Some patients with extensive frontal lobe degeneration develop a frontal syndrome with inappropriate behaviour (Strub *et al.* 1988). The frontal lobes form part of the brain system that inhibits unacceptable behaviour. Therefore, loss of normal inhibitions together with increased orality may lead to overeating in much the same way as Kluver-Bucy Syndrome.

Epilepsy

Eating difficulties can relate to the treatment for epilepsy or to epilepsy itself. Weight gain is observed with valproate and weight loss with topiramate. One mouse study looked at injection of tetanus toxin into the amygdala which led to an epileptiform syndrome (Mellanby *et al.* 1999). During the active epilepsy, occasional "paroxysmal eating" was observed and less neophobia around new foods. This was not observed with injections to the hippocampus (Mellanby *et al.* 1999). In humans, smells may be sensed during epilepsy when the nose has not been stimulated (Tortora 1990).

Deprivation

Disordered eating behaviour may also be found in deprivation or neglect. Voracious appetite, overeating, lack of control over eating and eating unusual combinations of food are often seen. Disturbances of body image have also been found, which may be seen as a difficulty in proper definition of the self (van der Kolk *et al.* 1994).

It is known that neglect affects the biologically based capacity to regulate the intensity of affective responses (van der Kolk *et al.* 1994). It has been suggested that those lacking early parental responsiveness (and left to regulate their own physiological states) may develop persistent deficits in the ability to modulate physiological arousal (van der Kolk *et al.* 1994). This may in part explain the inability to regulate food seen in deprivation disorders.

Disruptions of attachment in early life are known to have long-term effects on neurochemical responses to subsequent stress, including the catecholamine response and the cortisol response (van der Kolk *et al.* 1994). Low cortisol levels have been found in post-trauma victims and that long-term effects on other systems have been found, including the serotonin and the endogenous opioid systems. Low serotonin may play a role in the dysregulation of affects and impulses.

Slow growth has been associated with family conflict and may result from a hypothalamic regulatory process (Montgomery *et al.* 1997). Mechanisms by which stress can influence growth are not fully understood. Montgomery *et al.* (1997) observed basal levels of growth hormone in monkeys with chronic psychological stress and also saw hippocampal degeneration in monkeys due to increased glucocorticoid levels associated with chronic stress.

Case example: John

John was a 12-year-old boy who was admitted to a Child Psychiatric Inpatient Unit for assessment. Initially, it was difficult to hold a conversation. John found it difficult to maintain concentration for more than a few seconds at a time. It was also hard to understand John as his speech appeared incoherent at times. Careful observation revealed altered eating behaviours. John had a voracious appetite, ate food rapidly and had difficulty controlling his intake of food. Unusual combinations of foods and indiscriminate urges to try all available foods were evident. Inability to use a knife and fork and lack of facial cleanliness were also observed.

John gained a significant amount of weight during the admission (up to 2 kg per week), appeared to take pride in weight gain and continued to enquire if he was "fat yet". After several weeks, John's behaviours became less abnormal, with a slowing of eating, less use of unusual food combinations and improved speech and concentration. John had disclosed that food had been withheld for long periods at home and the ingestion of paper and a cockroach had suppressed appetite. He was systematically neglected and starved.

Disordered eating in psychiatry

Drug induced disordered eating

Many drugs interact with the endogenous opioid systems, and it is thought there may be common neural substrates between food and drug reward within these systems (Kelley *et al.* 2002). Opiates, such as morphine and heroin, convert to morphine in the brain and depress central nervous system (CNS) activity and in the longer term, appetite. Appetite is, however, increased in the short term. (Santrock 1996). Stimulants (such as caffeine, amphetamines and cocaine) on the other hand increase CNS activity and reduce appetite.

Morphine has stimulatory effects on feeding (short term) that are in part mediated by the mesolimbic dopamine system (Sills and Vaccarino 1998). Neurotransmitters most dramatically affected are the endorphins. For several hours after taking an opiate, a person feels euphoric and has an increased appetite for food and sex (Santrock 1996). Endogenous opioids have a similar physiological profile to exogenous opioid drugs such as heroin (Kelley *et al.* 2002). Opiate agonists augment feeding while opiate antagonists have been shown to decrease feeding. Opioid peptides appear to influence palatability of food, and ingestion of sweet food (or perhaps any palatable food) has been shown to produce analgesic effects (Pelchat 2002). Kelley *et al.* (2002) have proposed that opiates regulate palatability or hedonic evaluation of food, especially of foods rich in fat, sugar or salt. Animal literature demonstrates a relationship between drug self-administration and preference for sweets (Pelchat 2002). Rats with low sugar intake at baseline show an increase in sugar intake when administered morphine, but rats with high sugar intake at baseline were unaffected (or less sensitive) by the morphine (Sills and Vaccarino 1998). Human drug addiction programmes recommend use of sweets to reduce drug cravings (Pelchat 2002).

Opioids and GABA-A agents appear to promote feeding behaviour by acting on receptors in the nucleus accumbens (Kurup and Kurup 2003;

Soderpalm and Berridge 2000). The nucleus accumbens (implicated in drug addiction) and associated circuitry are associated with motivational behaviours such as drinking, eating and sexual behaviour. Kelley *et al.* (2002) have shown morphine infusion into the nucleus accumbens accentuates feeding, and that opioids within the accumbens are involved in preferences for foods rich in fat. The nucleus accumbens has direct input from the cortical taste area, which is found in the anterior insular/perirhinal areas of the cortex. The accumbens also receives direct input from the nucleus of the solitary tract, the first structure relaying taste signals to other brain regions.

The stimulants, on the other hand, are involved in reducing appetite. Low doses of amphetamine in rats with low sugar intake at baseline results in a sugar selective effect (Sills and Vaccarino 1998). Cocaine increases extracellular dopamine, norepinephrine and serotonin by inactivating neuronal membrane transporter proteins, and is associated with inducing hypophagia (Wellman *et al.* 2002). Cocaine increases synaptic dopamine levels, which can inhibit eating when localized within the lateral hypothalamus. Hypophagic activities of cocaine, however, are not completely mimicked by dopamine receptor agonists in rats, suggesting action, in part, on non-dopaminergic substrates. Wellman *et al.* (2002) have proposed norepinephrine systems and adrenoceptors as mechanisms in the mediation of cocaine-induced hypophagia. Activity in the orbitofrontal cortex, which receives projections from rewards circuits such as the nucleus accumbens, is also associated with cocaine craving (Pelchat 2002). The orbitofrontal cortex is activated by the two major sensory components, gustatory and olfactory stimuli.

Obsessive-compulsive disorder

One study has shown people with obsessive-compulsive disorder (OCD) display significantly more disturbed eating attitudes and behaviour than healthy comparison subjects (Pigott *et al.* 1991). This may imply a pervasive obsessional nature that involves all attitudes and beliefs. People with OCD are likely to report differences in eating patterns, including carbohydrate snacking to improve mood and snacking when not hungry. There appears to be a high incidence of carbohydrate snacking among people with OCD, providing evidence that serotonin may be involved in this disorder (O'Rourke *et al.* 1994). As carbohydrate ingestion (in the absence of protein) enhances serotonin synthesis and a consequent short-term improvement in mood, it has been suggested that patients develop patterns of excessive carbohydrate snacking (Pigott *et al.* 1991).

One report observed compulsive hand-washing accompanied by fear of contamination as well as compulsive eating of food and non-food items as seen in Kluver-Bucy Syndrome (Tonkonogy and Barreira 1989). The MRI scan showed prominent atrophy in the caudate nuclei and frontal lobe while temporal lobes were spared. Neuroimaging techniques have previously shown increased metabolic activity in the caudate nucleus with decreased activity in frontal and basal ganglia connections (Fogel *et al.* 1996; Pigott *et al.* 1991). The basal ganglia provide complex patterning across a broad range of behaviours and mood states (Parker and Hadzi-Pavlovic 1996). Loss of frontal inhibition of these behaviours may release highly stereotyped eating behaviours, which are selective in nature.

Depression

People with depression may either gain or lose weight during an episode of depression. Evidence has suggested that "high restraint" people report increased ingestion and weight gain during depression, while "low restraint" people report weight loss (Frost *et al.* 1982). They propose that depression interferes with the self-control of high restraint people, leading them to eat more during depression.

Another depression study investigating eating behaviour showed a decrease in appetite and food intake, though a relative increase of carbohydrates, and particularly sugars (Kazes *et al.* 1994). They report an increase in this pattern in depressive times of seasonal affective disorder. During depression, they found reduced hunger and desire to eat, decreased taste sensation, reduced pleasure from eating, and higher satiety. People appeared to return to normal eating and taste sensations after the depression lifted.

Low levels of serotonergic activity seen in depression may be increased by carbohydrate ingestion, which is reinforcing and may lead to self-medicating with carbohydrates (Kazes *et al.* 1994; Pelchat 2002). Both frontal and temporal dysfunctions have been prominent in brain imaging of depression, together with the basal ganglia (Parker and Hadzi-Pavlovic 1996).

Psychosis

Extent of eating in psychosis can vary significantly from excessive overeating to poor oral intake. Svacina *et al.* (1998) described three psychotic patients with histories of large weight fluctuations, overeating and binge-eating episodes and eating up to ten meals per day. Overfeeding in psychotic patients is often induced by antipsychotic and antidepressant medications (Svacina *et al.* 1998). The extent of weight gain with antipsychotic medication can vary greatly and appears to be strongest with some second-generation (atypical) antipsychotics such as clozapine, olanzapine and risperidone (Zimmerman *et al.* 2003). Increased appetite is believed to be a mechanism, though interference with glucose metabolism has also been proposed (Zimmerman *et al.* 2003). People treated with dexfenfluramine, however, reduce the number of meals and snacks eaten, and tend to prefer protein intake to sugar and fat (Svacina *et al.* 1998).

Disordered eating in medical illness

Chronic medical illness may bring additional risk of disordered eating. This effect appears to be greatest in illnesses in which treatment imposes dietary restraint, such as diabetes and phenylketonuria (Rodin *et al.* 2002). Living with chronic diseases, which are treated with dietary management, may adversely affect eating attitudes and behaviours, hence increasing susceptibility to developing eating disorders. Adolescents with chronic disorders may be at higher risk of eating disorders than other adolescents (Walters 2001). It is believed that the desire to be thin and body dissatisfaction may be exacerbated by the physiological effects of medical conditions.

Also the factors common to adolescents with a variety of chronic illnesses (for example desire for autonomy and need for peer approval) may lead to increased disordered eating. The increased emphasis on somatic concerns, difficulties in identity development and need for peer acceptability may be contributing factors in the development of eating disorders (Neumark-Sztainer *et al.* 1996).

Mechanisms involved in disordered eating in medical illness are both specific such as tumours in the posterior fossa in children and non-specific such as cytokine inhibition of appetite in viral infections. Each illness may have specific and non-specific factors. Diabetes may disrupt appetite specifically through hyperglycemia or hypoglycemia or through non-specific malaise associated with poor control. Cystic fibrosis may have eating affected directly by pancreatic dysfunction or non-specifically by chronic secondary infection of lungs.

Cystic fibrosis

One study has shown no evidence of elevated levels of eating disorders in patients with cystic fibrosis (CF), and less concern about wanting to be thin or needing to diet (Raymond *et al.* 2000). Other studies, however, have shown higher eating disorders incidence in this population (Raymond *et al.* 2000). Like other young Western women, those with CF may wish to be thin and may also suffer from distorted body image (Walters 2001).

Pancreatic ducts are obstructed in patients with CF, leading to decreased pancreatic enzymes in the intestines and consequent poor digestion of foods and poor absorption of nutrients from the gut (Raymond *et al.* 2000). Secondary pancreatic damage may also lead to insulin insufficiency. Energy intakes are often compromised by poor appetite. Lack of enjoyment of eating, reluctance to attend mealtimes, preferring to drink rather than eat, eating snacks but not eating at mealtimes and attempting to negotiate foods eaten are also characteristics, which may be seen in children with CF (Aitken Duff *et al.* 2003). CF patients have been shown to take longer to eat a meal, to eat at a slower pace (increased dawdling) and to have more interactions with parents at mealtimes than controls (Stark *et al.* 1997). Altered digestion, absorption, appetite and lack of enjoyment in eating affect the CNS indirectly and non-specifically but also there is the risk of specific depletion of neurotransmitter substrates leading to behavioural and emotional changes.

Diabetes

In 2002 a large case-controlled study demonstrated that the prevalence of full syndrome and sub-threshold eating disorders among adolescents and young women with diabetes is twice as high as in their non-diabetic peers (Rodin *et al.* 2002). There appear to be inconsistent findings, however, regarding the incidence of eating disorders in diabetes.

Predictors of eating disorder in both healthy subjects and diabetes patients include body size, body image, adolescent age and female sex (Meltzer *et al.* 2001). Proposed aetiologies of eating disorders in diabetes include body dissatisfaction, wishing to lose weight because of insulin-related weight gain, feeling obsessed with food, feeling out of control and believing that diabetes is controlling one's life (Schwartz *et al.* 2002).

Presence of diabetes may heighten attention to weight gain, dietary restraint and food preoccupation (Neumark-Sztainer *et al.* 2002). Diabetes management may impose perceived dietary restraint, particularly those eating according to a predetermined meal plan, rather than in response to internal cues for hunger and satiety. Neglect of internal cues for hunger and satiety may contribute to dietary dysregulation in susceptible individuals, including in diabetes. Increased BMI may also heighten body image dissatisfaction, trigger a dieting cycle and consequently lead to binge eating and purging (Rodin *et al.* 2002). Schwartz *et al.* (2002) found adolescents with diabetes experience a lower sense of overall control and control over their body reporting more severe eating disorder symptoms. Parent–adolescent relationships can be challenged when a young person has diabetes, creating greater risk for engaging in health compromising behaviours including eating disorders.

Insulin omission or dose manipulation offers a unique form of purging to those with diabetes. Studies have shown this may occur in up to 40 per cent of young women with diabetes (Meltzer *et al.* 2001). Olmsted *et al.* (2002) have shown up to 38 per cent of women with type 1 diabetes admit to insulin omission for weight loss purposes and up to 60–80 per cent report binge eating in response to hypoglycaemic episodes.

Cancer

Ondansetron is a drug used for treatment of nausea and vomiting induced by serotonin release from gastric cells in response to radiation treatment and chemotherapeutic agents. Effects involve both central and peripheral actions.

Table 15.1 Typical symptom profile from a neurodevelopmental perspective

Disorder	Overeating	Food reduction	Vomiting	Altered food preference	Increased exercise	Pica	Body image disturbance	Weight phobia	Low BMI	High BMI	Authors
Classic eating disorders											
AN like syndromes	–	+	+/–	+	+	–	+	+	+	–	APA 2000
BN like syndromes	+	+	+	+	–	–	+	+	–	+	APA 2000
Neurodevelopmental disorders											
Deprivation syndromes	+	–	–	+	–	+	+	–	–	+	van der Kolk et al. 1994
Dementia	+	+	–	+	–	+	–	–	+	+	Fogel et al. 1996 Ikeda et al. 2002 Hope et al. 1989
Epilepsy	+	–	–	+	–	–	–	–	–	–	Mellanby et al. 1999 Tortora 1990
Head injury	+	–	–	–	–	–	–	–	–	+	Gillberg 1995 Strub et al. 1988 Capaldi 1996
Hypothalamic syndromes	+	–	–	–	–	+	–	–	–	+	Nunn et al. 1997
Kleine-Levin Syndrome	+	–	–	–	–	+	–	–	–	+	Lask et al. 2003 Strub et al. 1988
Kluver-Bucy Syndrome	+	–	–	–	–	+	–	–	–	+	Fogel et al. 1996 Varon et al. 2003 Mendez and Foti 1997

Disorder	Overeating	Food reduction	Vomiting	Altered food preference	Increased exercise	Pica	Body image disturbance	Weight phobia	Low BMI	High BMI	Authors
Prader-Willi Syndrome	+	–	–	–	–	+	–	–	–	+	Lask et al. 2003 Kohn et al. 2001 Dimitropoulos et al. 2000
Autistic spectrum	–	+	–	+	–	–	–	–	+	+	Williams et al. 2000 Cornish 2002
Psychiatric disorders											
Depression	+	+	–	+	–	–	–	–	+	+	Kazes et al. 1994
Schizophrenia/ psychosis	+	+	–	+	–	–	–	–	+	+	Svacina et al. 1998
OCD	–	+	–	+	–	–	–	–	–	–	O'Rourke et al. 1994
Opiate addiction	+	+	–	+	–	–	–	–	+	–	Kelley et al. 2002 Santrock 1996
Stimulant addiction	–	+	–	+	–	–	–	–	–	–	Sills and Vaccarino 1998 Santrock 1996
Medical illness											
Diabetes	+	+	–	+	–	–	+	+	–	+	Neumark-Sztainer et al. 2002 Meltzer et al. 2001 Olmsted et al. 2002
Cystic fibrosis	–	+	–	+	–	–	+	–	+	–	Aitken Duff et al. 2003
Oncology	–	+	+	+	–	–	–	–	+	–	Faris et al. 2000

Table 15.2 Implicated brain structures in disordered eating

Disorder	Frontal and/or temporal	Insula	Limbic system	Hypothalamus	Thalamus	Basal ganglia	Brainstem	Cerebellum	Neurotransmitters	Authors
Classic eating disorders										
AN-like syndromes	+ (frontal and temporal)	+	+	+	+	+	–	–	+ (noradrenaline)	Trummer et al. 2002 Swayze et al. 1996 Kingston et al. 1996 Urwin et al. 2002 Kaye et al. 1985 de Zwaan 2003 Connan et al. 2003 Halmi 2000
BN-like syndromes	+	–	+	+	–	–	–	–	+ (serotonin)	de Zwaan 2003 Halmi 2000 Stamatakis and Hetherington 2003 Hagan et al. 1998
Neurodevelopmental disorders										
Deprivation syndromes	+ (frontal and cingulate gyrus)	–	–	–	–			–	+	van der Kolk et al. 1994
Dementia	+ (frontal and temporal)	–	+	–	–			–	–	Mummery 2002 Ikeda et al. 2002
Epilepsy	+	–	+	–				–	–	Cullen et al. 1997 Mellanby et al. 1999

Disorder	Frontal and/or temporal	Insula	Limbic system	Hypothalamus	Thalamus	Basal ganglia	Brainstem	Cerebellum	Neurotransmitters	Authors
Head injury	+ (frontal)	–	+	–	–	–	–	–	–	Gillberg 1995 Strub et al. 1988 Nunn et al. 1997
Hypothalamic syndromes		–	+	+	–	–	+	–	–	
Kleine-Levin Syndrome	+ (frontal and temporal)	–	–	+	–	–	–	–	+ (serotonin)	Arias et al. 2002 Landtblom et al. 2002 Dauvilliers et al. 2002 Muller et al. 1998 Gillberg 1995
Kluver-Bucy Syndrome	+ (temporal)	–	+	–	–	–	–	–	–	Fogel et al. 1996 Varon et al. 2003 Mendez and Foti 1997 Lopez et al. 1995
Prader-Willi Syndrome	+ (frontal)	–	–	+	–	–	–	–	+ (serotonin)	Gillberg 1995 Dimitropoulos et al. 2000
Autistic spectrum	+ (frontal and temporal)	–	–	+	–	–	+	+	+ (serotonin)	Gillberg 1995 Daenen et al. 2002 Santrock 1996 Koves et al. 2002
Psychiatric disorders Depression	+ (prefrontal and hippocampal cortex in temporal lobes)	–	–	–	–	+ (basal ganglia)	–	–	+ (all monoamines)	Kazes et al. 1994

Table 15.2 (continued)

Disorder	Frontal and/or temporal	Insula	Limbic system	Hypothalamus	Thalamus	Basal ganglia	Brainstem	Cerebellum	Neurotransmitters	Authors
Schizophrenia/psychosis	+ (fronto-temporal)	–	–	–	–	–	–	–	(dopamine and glutamate)	Svacina et al. 1998 Carlsson et al. 2001 Parker and Hadzi-Pavlovic 1996
OCD	+ (orbitofrontal)	–	–	–	–	+ (basal ganglia connection with frontal lobes)	–	–	+ (serotonin)	O'Rourke et al. 1994 Tonkonogy and Barreira 1989 Fogel et al. 1996 Pigott et al. 1991
Opiate addiction	+ (nucleus accumbens)	–	+ (nucleus accumbens)	–	–	+ (nucleus accumbens)	–	– (endorphins)	(dopamine)	Soderpalm and Berridge 2000 Kurup and Kurup 2003
Stimulant addiction	+ (nucleus accumbens and orbitofrontal)	–	–	–	–	+ (nucleus accumbens)	–	–	(GABA) (dopamine noradrenaline serotonin)	Kelley et al. 2002 Wellman et al. 2002

The drug is a type 3 serotonin receptors (5-HT$_3$) antagonist, which blocks the activation of receptors on chemosensitive afferent vagal fibres in the gastric mucosa (Faris *et al.* 2000). They found that the use of ondansetron in BN patients led to significant improvement in bulimic symptoms, when compared to patients using placebo. Their findings indicate a normalization of physiological mechanisms controlling meal termination and satiation by a pharmacological correction of abnormal vagal neurotransmission. They proposed that in BN uncontrollable bingeing and vomiting might lead to compromised sensitivity and responsivity of the vagal satiety circuit or a self-induced dysregulation affecting neural systems.

Other medical problems

Children developing conditioned dysphagia after pharyngeal flap surgery for cleft palate have been reported in a high proportion of cases (Field *et al.* 2003). These authors suggest that many feeding problems are seen as the learned aversions due to aversive feeding experiences associated with medical conditions (Field *et al.* 2003).

Tables 15.1 and 15.2 summarize the findings from different diseases with respect to typical symptom profiles and implicated brain structures in disordered eating.

Normal brain function

Taste and gustatory sensation converge on the brain via the nucleus of the tractus solitarius in the brainstem. This is closely linked anatomically with normal vomiting mechanisms in the brainstem, which are mediated via 5HT and specifically 5-HT$_3$ receptors. This mechanism protects against poisoning in the natural environment. Regulations of hunger, thirst, satiety and meal size are strongly regulated within the hypothalamus which in turn has marked connectivity with limbic structures such as the amygdala. The amygdala is capable of single trial learning from aversive stimuli. Again, poisoning, or the association of traumatic events with eating or oral experiences, is likely to be mediated through these structures as in post-traumatic stress disorders. This highlights the role of contextual memory and therefore the role of the hippocampus, which is the central clearing-house for conscious memories. Both the amygdala and the hippocampus are in the temporal lobes and it is therefore not surprising that these are so often implicated in conditions affecting eating. Finally, the coordination and integration of all CNS information in terms of making sense and maintaining control is located within the frontal systems. How individuals integrate past and present, inner and outer reality and control basic drives such as hunger and thirst is finally arbitrated by the frontal systems. The reason that lesion studies tend to produce conflicting and confusing results is likely to reside in the high level of redundancy or backup in feeding mechanisms in humans. An examination of the central nervous mechanisms of eating suggests that the acquisition of food is so fundamental to survival that more than one level of dysfunction is needed for eating to be disrupted. Higher mechanisms related to meaning, control and context are likely to be much more significant in humans than lower animals. Structures involved with our latest evolutionary acquisition, the neocortex, such as the frontal lobes and the hippocampus, figure highly in almost all studies alongside older evolutionary structures such as the amygdala.

Conclusion

This chapter highlights the need for detailed analysis of many conditions in the light of both normal and abnormal brain function. At the present time numbers are small and samples may be quite unrepresentative. Findings are often contradictory or at best obscure as to their significance. However, it is now clear that there are key brain structures associated with particular eating difficulties and these structures have functional analogues in animal studies. The time has come to make a systematic study of the many eating disorders that co-occur with medical and psychiatric disorders and that emerge in the course of treatments.

References

Abu-Akel, A. (2003) "The neurochemical hypothesis of 'Theory of Mind' ", *Medical Hypotheses* 60, 382–6.

Aitken Duff, A.J., Wolfe, S.P., Dickson, C., Conway, S.P. and Brownlee, K.G. (2003) "Feeding behaviour problems in children with cystic fybrosis in the UK: prevalence and comparison with healthy controls", *Journal of Pediatric Gastroenterology and Nutrition* 36, 443–7.

Alberti, A., Pirrone, P., Elia, M., Waring, R.H. and Romano, C. (1999) "Sulphation deficit in 'low-functioning' autistic children: a pilot study", *Biological Psychiatry* 46, 420–4.

APA (Work Group on Eating Disorders) (2000) "Practice Guideline for the Treatment of Patients with Eating Disorders, revised", *American Journal of Psychiatry Supplement 1* 157, 1–39.

Arias, M., Crespo Iglesias, J.M., Perez, J., Requena-Caballero, I., Sesar-Ignacio, A. and Peleteiro-Fernandez, M. (2002) "Kleine-Levin Syndrome: contribution of brain SPECT in diagnosis", *Revista de Neurologia* 35, 531–3.

Capaldi, E.D. (1996) *Why We Eat What We Eat: The Psychology of Eating*, Washington, DC: American Psychological Association.

Carlsson, A., Waters, N., Holm-Waters, S., Tedroff, J., Nilsson, M. and Carlsson, M.L. (2001) "Interactions between monoamines, glutamate and GABA in schizophrenia: new evidence", *Annual Review of Pharmacology and Toxicology* 41, 237–60.

Connan, F., Campbell, I.C., Katzman, M., Lightman, S.L. and Treasure, J. (2003) "A neurodevelopmental model for Anorexia Nervosa", *Physiology and Behaviour* 79, 13–24.

Cornish, E. (2002) "Gluten and casein free diets in autism: a study of the effects of food choice and nutrition", *Journal of Human Nutrition and Dietetics* 15, 261–9.

Counts, D. (2001) "An adult with Prader-Willi Syndrome and Anorexia Nervosa: a case report", *International Journal of Eating Disorders* 30, 231–3.

Cullen, P., Abid, F., Patel, A., Coope, B. and Ballard, C.G. (1997) "Eating disorders in dementia", *International Journal of Geriatric Psychiatry* 12, 559–62.

Daenen, E., Wolterink, G., Gerrits, M.A.F.M. and van Ree, J.M. (2002) "The effects of neonatal lesions in the amygdala or ventral hippocampus on social behaviour later in life", *Behavioural Brain Research* 136, 571–82.

Dauvilliers, Y., Mayer, G., Lecendreux, M., Neidhart, E., Peraita-Adrados, R., Sonka, K., Billiard, M. and Tafti, M. (2002) "Kleine-Levin Syndrome: an autoimmune hypothesis based on clinical and genetic analysis", *Neurology* 59, 1739–45.

de Zwaan, M. (2003) "Basic neuroscience and scanning", in J. Treasure, U. Schmidt and E. van Furth (eds) *Handbook of Eating Disorders*, 2nd edn, Chichester: Wiley.

Dimitropoulos, A., Feurer, I.D., Roof, E., Stone, W., Butler, M.G., Sutcliffe, J. and Thompson, T. (2000) "Appetitive behaviour, compulsivity and neurochemistry in Prader-Willi Syndrome", *Mental Retardation and Developmental Disabilities Research Reviews* 6, 125–30.

Faris, P.L., Kim, S.W., Meller, W.H., Goodale, R.L., Oakman, S.A., Hofbauer, R.D., Marshall, A.M., Daughters, R.S., Banerjee-Stevens, D., Eckert, E.D. and Hartman, B.K. (2000) "Effect of decreasing afferent vagal activity with ondansetron on symptoms of bulimia nervosa: a randomised, double-blind trial", *Lancet* 355, 792–7.

Field, D., Garland, M. and Williams, K. (2003) "Correlates of specific childhood feeding problems", *Journal of Paediatric Child Health* 39, 299–304.

Fogel, B.S., Schiffer, R.B. and Rao, S.M. (1996) *Neuropsychiatry*, Sydney: Williams & Wilkins.

Frost, R., Goolkasian, G.A., Ely, R.J. and Blanchard, F.A. (1982) "Depression, restraint and eating behaviour", *Behaviour Research and Therapy* 20, 113–21.

Gillberg, C. (1995) *Clinical Child Neuropsychiatry*, Melbourne: Cambridge University Press.

Gillberg, C. and Svennerholm, L. (1987) "CSF monoamines in autistic syndromes and other pervasive developmental disorders of early childhood", *British Journal of Psychiatry* 151, 89–94.

Hagan, M.M., Castaneda, E., Sumaya, I.C., Fleming, S.M., Galloway, J. and Moss, D.E. (1998) "The effect of hypothalamic peptide yy on hippocampal acetylcholine release in vivo: implications for limbic function in binge eating behaviour", *Brain Research* 805, 20–8.

Halmi, K.A. (2000) "Eating disorders", in B.J. Sadock and V.A. Sadock (eds) *Kaplan and Sadock's Comprehensive Textbook of Psychiatry: Volume II*, 7th edn, London: Lippincott Williams & Wilkins.

Hope, R.A., Fairburn, C.G. and Goodwin, G.M. (1989) "Increased eating in dementia", *International Journal of Eating Disorders* 8, 111–15.

Ikeda, M., Brown, J., Holland, A.J., Fukuhara, R. and Hodges, J.R. (2002) "Changes in appetite, food preference and eating habits in frontotemporal dementia and

Alzheimer's Disease", *Journal of Neurology, Neurosurgery and Psychiatry* 73, 371–6.

Kaye, W.H., Jimerson, D.C., Lake, C.R. and Ebert, M.H. (1985) "Altered norepinephrine metabolism following long-term weight recovery in patients with anorexia nervosa", *Psychiatry Research* 14, 333–42.

Kazes, M., Danion, J.M., Grange, D., Pradignac, A., Simon, C., Burrus-Mehl, F., Schlienger, J.L. and Singe, L. (1994) "Eating behaviour and depression before and after antidepressant treatment: a prospective, naturalistic study", *Journal of Affective Disorders* 30, 193–207.

Kelley, A.E., Bakshi, V.P., Haber, S.N., Steininger, T.L., Will, M.J. and Zhang, M. (2002) "Opioid modulation of taste hedonics within the ventral striatum", *Physiology and Behaviour* 76, 365–77.

Kingston, K., Szmukler, G., Andrews, D., Tress, B. and Desmond, P. (1996) "Neuropsychological and structural brain changes in anorexia nervosa before and after refeeding", *Psychological Medicine* 26, 15–28.

Kohn, Y., Weizman, A. and Apter A. (2001) "Aggravation of food-related behaviour in an adolescent with Prader-Willi Syndrome treated with fluvoxamine and fluoxetine", *International Journal of Eating Disorders* 30, 113–17.

Koves, K., Kausz, M., Reser, D. and Horvath, K. (2002) "What may be the anatomical basis that secretin can improve the mental function in autism", *Regulatory Peptides* 109, 167–72.

Kurup, R.K. and Kurup, P.A. (2003) "Hypothalamic digoxin, hemispheric chemical dominance and eating behaviour", *International Journal of Neuroscience* 113, 1127–42.

Landtblom, A.M., Dige, N., Schwerdt, K., Safstrom, P. and Granerus, G. (2002) "A case of Kleine-Levin Syndrome examined with SPECT and neuropsychological testing", *Acta Neurologica Scandanavica* 105, 318–21.

Lask, B., Taylor, S. and Nunn, K.P. (2003) *Practical Child Psychiatry: The Clinician's Guide*, London: BMJ Books.

Lopez, O.L., Becker, J.T., Klunk, W. and DeKosky, S.T. (1995) "The nature of behavioural disorders in human Kluver-Bucy Syndrome", *Neuropsychiatry, Neuropsychology and Behavioural Neurology* 8, 215–21.

Mayer, G., Leonhard, E., Krieg, J. and Meier-Ewert, K. (1998) "Endocrinological and polysomnographic findings in Kleine-Levin Syndrome: no evidence for hypothalamic and circadian dysfunction", *Sleep* 21, 278–84.

Mellanby, J., Oliva, M., Peniket, A. and Nicholls, B. (1999) "The effect of experimental epilepsy induced by injection of tetanus toxin into the amygdala of the rat on eating behaviour and response to novelty", *Behavioural Brain Research* 100, 113–22.

Meltzer, L.J., Bennett-Johnson, S., Prine, J.M., Banks, R.A., Desrosiers, P.M. and Silverstein, J.H. (2001) "Disordered eating, body mass and glycemic control in adolescents with type 1 diabetes", *Diabetes Care* 24, 678–82.

Mendez, M.F. and Foti, D.J. (1997) "Lethal hyperoral behaviour from the Kluver-Bucy Syndrome", *Journal of Neurology, Neurosurgery and Psychiatry* 62, 293–4.

Montgomery, S.M., Bartley, M.J. and Wilkinson, R.G. (1997) "Family conflict and slow growth", *Archives of Disease in Childhood* 77, 326–30.

Mouridsen, S.E., Rich, B. and Isager, T. (2002) "Body Mass Index in male and female children with infantile autism", *International Journal of Research and Practice* 6, 197–205.

Muller, T., Kuhn, W., Bornke, C., Buttner, T. and Przuntek, H. (1998) "Kleine-Levin Syndrome and Parkinsonian Symptoms: a case report", *Journal of Neurological Sciences* 157, 214–16.

Mummery, C. (2002) "We are how we eat? The underlying neural substrates of eating behaviours", *Journal of Neurology, Neurosurgery and Psychiatry* 73, 358–9.

Neumark-Sztainer, D., Story, M., Toporoff, E., Cassuto, N., Resnick, M.D. and Blum, R.W. (1996) "Psychosocial predictors of binge eating and purging behaviours among adolescents with and without diabetes mellitus", *Journal of Adolescent Health* 19, 289–96.

Neumark-Sztainer, D., Patterson, J., Mellin, A., Ackard, D.M., Utter, J., Story, M. and Sockalosky, J. (2002) "Weight control practices and disordered eating behaviours among adolescent females and males with type 1 diabetes", *Diabetes Care*, 25, 1289–96.

Nunn, K., Ouvrier, R., Sprague, T., Docker, M. and Arbuckle, S. (1997) "Idiopathic hypothalamic dysfunction: a paraneoplastic syndrome?", *Journal of Child Neurology* 12, 6–12.

Olmsted, M.P., Daneman, D., Rydall, A.C., Lawson, M.L. and Rodin, G. (2002) "The effect of psychoeducation on disturbed eating attitudes and behaviour in young women with type 1 diabetes mellitus", *International Journal of Eating Disorders* 32, 230–9.

O'Rourke, D., Wurtman, J.J., Wurtman, R.J., Tsay, R., Gleason, R., Baer, L. and Jenike, M.A. (1994) "Aberrant snacking patterns and eating disorders in patients with obsessive-compulsive disorder", *Journal of Clinical Psychiatry* 55, 445–7.

Parker, G. and Hadzi-Pavlovic, D. (1996) *Melancholia: A Disorder of Movement and Mood, A Phenomenological and Neurological Review*, Cambridge: Cambridge University Press.

Pelchat, M.L. (2002) "Of human bondage: food craving, obsession, compulsion and addiction", *Physiology and Behaviour* 76, 347–52.

Pigott, T., Altemus, M., Rubenstein, C.S., Hill, J.L., Bihari, K., L'Heureux, F., Bernstein, S. and Murphy, D.L. (1991) "Symptoms of eating disorders in patients with obsessive-compulsive disorder", *American Journal of Psychiatry* 148, 1552–7.

Raymond, N.C., Chang, P., Crow, S.J., Mitchell, J.E., Dieperink, B.S., Beck, M.M., Crosby, R.D., Clawson, C.C. and Warwick, W.J. (2000) "Eating disorders in patients with cystic fibrosis", *Journal of Adolescence* 23, 359–63.

Rodin, G., Olmsted, M.P., Rydall, A.C., Maharaj, S.I., Colton, P.A., Jones, J.M., Biancucci, L.A. and Daneman, D. (2002) "Eating disorders in young women with type 1 diabetes mellitus", *Journal of Psychosomatic Research* 53, 943–9.

Santrock, J.W. (1996) *Psychology*, 4th edn, Madison, WI: Brown & Benchmark.

Schwartz, S., Weissberg-Benchell, J. and Perlmuter, L.C. (2002) "Personal control and disordered eating in female adolescents with type 1 diabetes", *Diabetes Care* 25, 1987–91.

Sills, T. and Vaccarino, F.J. (1998) "Individual differences in the feeding and locomotor stimulatory effects of acute and repeated morphine treatments", *Pharmacology, Biochemistry and Behaviour* 60, 293–303.

Soderpalm, A.H.V. and Berridge, K.C. (2000) "Food intake after diazepam, morphine or muscimol: microinjections in the nucleus accumbens shell", *Pharmacology, Biochemistry and Behaviour* 66, 429–34.

Stamatakis, E.A. and Hetherington, M.M. (2003) "Neuroimaging in eating disorders, review", *Nutritional Neuroscience* 6, 325–34.

Stark, L.J., Mulvihill, M.M., Jelalian, E., Bowen, A.M., Powers, S.W., Tao, S., Creveling, S., Passero, M.A., Harwood, I., Light, M., Lapey, A. and Howell, M.F. (1997) "Descriptive analysis of eating behaviour in schoolage children with cystic fibrosis and healthy control children", *Pediatrics* 99, 665–71.

Strub, R., Black, F.W. and Benson, D.F. (1988) *Neurobehavioural Disorders: A Clinical Approach*, Philadelphia, PA: Davis.

Svacina, S., Sonka, J. and Marek, J. (1998) "Dexfenfluramine in psychotic patients", *International Journal of Eating Disorders* 24, 335–8.

Swayze, V.W. II, Andersen, A., Arndt, S., Rajarethinam, R., Fleming, F., Sato, Y. and Andreasen, N.C. (1996) "Reversibility of brain tissue loss in anorexia nervosa assessed with a computerized talairach 3-D proportional grid", *Psychological Medicine* 26, 381–90.

Tonkonogy, J. and Barreira, P. (1989) "Obsessive-compulsive disorder and caudate-frontal lesion", *Neuropsychiatry, Neuropsychology and Behavioural Neurology* 2, 203–9.

Tortora, G.J. (1990) *Principles of Anatomy and Physiology*, New York: Harper & Row.

Trummer, M., Eustacchio, S., Unger, F., Tillich, M. and Flaschka, G. (2002) "Right hemispheric frontal lesions as a cause for Anorexia Nervosa: report of three cases", *Acta Neurochirurgica* 144, 797–801.

Urwin, R.E., Bennetts, B., Wilcken, B., Lampropoulos, B., Beumont, P., Clarke, S., Russell, J., Tanner, S. and Nunn, K.P. (2002) "Anorexia Nervosa (restrictive sub-type) is associated with a polymorphism in the novel norepinephrine transporter gene promoter polymorphic region", *Molecular Psychiatry* 7, 652–7.

van der Kolk, B.A., Bessel, A. and Fisler, R.E. (1994) "Childhood abuse and neglect and loss of self-regulation", *Bulletin of the Menninger Clinic* 58, 145–57.

Varon, D., Pritchard, P.B., Wagner, M.T. and Topping, K. (2003) "Transient Kluver-Bucy Syndrome following complex partial status epilepticus", *Epilepsy and Behaviour* 4, 348–51.

Walters, S. (2001) "Sex differences in weight perception and nutritional behaviour in adults with cystic fibrosis", *Journal of Human Nutrition and Dietetics* 14, 83–91.

Wellman, P., Ho, D., Cepeda-Benito, A., Bellinger, L. and Nation, J. (2002) "Cocaine-induced hypophagia and hyperlocomotion in rats are attenuated by prazosin", *European Journal of Pharmacology* 455, 117–26.

Williams, P.G., Dalrymple, N. and Neal, J. (2000) "Eating habits of children with autism", *Pediatric Nursing* 26, 259–67.

Young, J.K. (1975) "A possible neuroendrocrine basis of two clinical syndromes: Anorexia Nervosa and the Kleine-Levin Syndrome", *Physiological Psychology* 3, 322–30.

Zimmerman, U., Kraus, T., Himmerich, H., Schuld, A. and Pollmacher, T. (2003) "Epidemiology, implications and mechanisms underlying drug-induced weight gain in psychiatric patients", *Journal of Psychiatric Research* 37, 193–220.

Chapter 16

Psychological perspectives on atypical diagnoses in the eating disorders

Glenn Waller

Psychological frameworks and their relationship to diagnosis

> Medical science is fallible. What's diagnosis? A guess based on a very little knowledge and some indefinite clues that point in more than one direction . . . Doctors are just as much victims of preconceived ideas as anybody else.
>
> Agatha Christie, *Taken at the Flood* (1948)

This book was always going to be an odd one – in essence, a book about eating disorders that are not widely recognized as "true" eating disorders. However, the importance of such a venture is that our existing knowledge base is severely skewed. When we remove the "typical" adult cases (Anorexia Nervosa and Bulimia Nervosa) and what we know about them, we are left with a large proportion of our patient group but with only a tiny fraction of our clinical research and knowledge (e.g. Nielsen and Palmer 2003). Even that might be an underestimate of the knowledge gap. Only about half of our adult cases fit the two categories that we see as "typical" (e.g. Fairburn and Harrison 2003; Turner and Bryant-Waugh 2004). Indeed, the chapters in this book have pointed out that our concept of atypical cases might need to be expanded to encompass other groups, including younger individuals, athletes and those with some chronic physical complications (see Chapters 12, 13 and 14).

In contrast to this approach, I wish to argue that it is inadequate to extend the concept of "atypical" cases, because that makes the false assumption that there are truly "typical" cases. I will detail how the "atypical" cases are simply the product of our flawed diagnostic system, and that the fact that we have not developed (and never will do) a system that categorizes all cases gives us no excuse to marginalize those individuals. To explain why we have created atypical cases requires an understanding of the human drive to categorize, and hence why we have striven so hard to diagnose patients.

To diagnose or not to diagnose?

It seems reasonable to start by considering my own experiences and how they are linked to my prejudices in writing this chapter. Some years ago, I wrote an article considering the utility of diagnosis in the eating disorders (Waller 1993), concluding that diagnosis is unhelpful and could usefully be replaced by a system that focused on the function of the symptoms. As a young entrant to the world of clinical academia in the eating disorders, I lacked the foresight to understand that this would be an unpopular idea. While the editor informed me that the article had been accepted, he also told me that there would be a "reply" article, extolling the virtues of diagnosis in the eating disorders. My article came out, I felt embarrassed when I read it over (as usual), and then I waited for the reply article (which I knew would be devastating in its rapier-like precision). I am still waiting, though with less confidence as the years go by. The original article itself was a piece of juvenalia, which need not detain us. However, this experience illustrates for me the anxiety inherent in challenging an established system, however odd that system might be. Emotions can be very powerful in undermining cognitions.

The result is that many of the nosological developments since the early 1990s have failed to excite me. Is Binge Eating Disorder a distinct entity? How should one subtype AN and BN? Should we refocus diagnoses around purging behaviours? Other people have addressed these questions very well (for example, see Chapters 4 and 5), but none of these has escaped the problems that are inherent in assuming that diagnosis and sub-diagnosis matter. My view (and the view of many other clinicians) is that the multifactorial origins and manifestations of the eating disorders mean that subdividing patients into diagnoses can never be a successful exercise. Chapter 3 makes it very clear that the eating disorders do not meet criteria for a set of distinct syndromes. Nor is there any other immediately obvious way of recasting our definitions to be more inclusive. This is not to say that there is no value in identifying an eating disorder – simply that there is little real value in subdividing the eating disorders as we currently do. The move towards "transdiagnostic" work (Fairburn *et al.* 2003) makes sense to me, though many clinicians find it a new label rather than a new idea.

Reading through this book has emphasized for me the greatest peril of using diagnostic subgroups within the eating disorders – they distract us. In the early 1990, one rarely heard much about atypical eating disorders, eating disorder not otherwise specified, partial syndromes, subclinical cases and the like. They were the poor relatives who were not invited to the party for fear of causing embarrassment. They were mentioned in the work of pioneers like Russell and Bruch, but were often ignored thereafter. My own clinical work and that of my colleagues says that these cases have always been with us. I do not believe for a moment that since 1998 there has been a burgeoning of such eating patterns. However, as with most of the population, we have engaged in the practice of ignoring those things that do not fit our pre-existing beliefs. We have witnessed a wonderful human facility – the capacity to ignore the existence of a large "group" while knowing about (and offering treatment to) large numbers of the individuals who make up that group.

As with many "Road to Damascus" experiences (that little-known Bob Hope film . . .), the scales have now fallen from our eyes. A small number of highly significant studies (e.g. Turner and Bryant-Waugh 2004) have demonstrated that the number of "atypical" cases is probably as large as the number of "typical" cases (Fairburn and Harrison 2003). Splendid. Can we now give diagnosis the cold shoulder so that we can get on unfettered with the true work of treating patients? Of course we *can* – but whether we *will* is another question. Rather than the problem lying with patients who fail to read the necessary books and do not turn up with the correct cluster of symptoms, the true locus of the problem is in the heads of the clinicians and academics in this field. To understand the problems with abandoning rigid diagnoses, we need to understand the psychology of diagnosis. What psychological factors explain the drive to diagnose, and how can those factors explain our history of developing a diagnostic system that has successfully marginalized more than half of our patients?

Is there psychology in our diagnoses?

There is relatively little psychological content in diagnosis, and what psychology there is does not support the distinct diagnoses that exist on paper. The key psychological features are concerns about appearance and irrational fear of uncontrollable eating and weight gain. While these features are clearly key to understanding and treating most cases of AN and BN, they are not present in all such cases. In addition, they are present in most atypical cases. An alternative psychological perspective might be to attempt diagnosis using the presence or absence of compulsive and impulsive features (particularly behaviours) as means of personal and emotional control respectively. However, yet again, these features are rarely present in isolation, and lend themselves much more readily to a dimensional approach to understanding eating pathology.

The psychology of those who apply diagnoses

Human beings are not precise thinkers. As we know, we are prone to cognitive distortions that help us to simplify the world for easy understanding. What distortions are relevant to our use of diagnosis? The obvious culprits are stereotyping and black and white thinking. These patterns of thinking are often essential in the early stages of the development of a new construct (Spector and Kitsuse 1987), but the danger is that the relatively crude thinking of early claims-makers becomes engraved on tablets of stone in the heads of those who follow. I was pleased to see that several of the chapters in this book (e.g. Chapter 10) carried implicit and explicit questions about whether early ideas (e.g. the centrality of body image disturbance; the link to puberty) are as inviolable as we had thought. The danger of always believing the original ideas is that we can end up creating "atypical" cases by defining typicality too tightly to accommodate many real individuals.

Stereotyping

We need to take some of our own lessons from therapy. Human beings tend to like simplicity. We fail to process the true detail, and seek only those characteristics that confirm our existing beliefs. In other words, we use stereotypes – letting our schemas drive our information processing, rather than the available data (i.e. top-down versus bottom-up information processing). Thus, if the orthodoxy is that there are two clearly defined eating disorders, we will tend to label eating disordered individuals as belonging to one of the two camps if we possibly can. We will also tend to find it hard to see changes that take the individual into another diagnosis (as will often happen – e.g. Fairburn and Harrison 2003). Arkes and Harkness (1980) have shown how an early diagnosis makes us less likely to process contradictory evidence, while a late diagnosis makes us miss diagnosis-consistent information. If this looks like an unwinnable task, that might be because it is just that. One of my first rules is to doubt the diagnosis that has been provided in a referral letter, not because it will necessarily be wrong, but because it encourages me to be lazy and forget to focus on the patient.

Black and white thinking

While black and white thinking is clearly part of the stereotyping process, it has other consequences. First, it leads us to ignore dimensions in the eating disorders. For example, let us consider the scores of individual patients on a (hypothetical) dimensional measure of eating pathology. The proposed cut-off on this measure is, say, 20. Patients A, B and C score 19, 21 and 40 respectively. Would any clinician really agree that patients B and C are more alike than patients A and B? This is precisely what a categorical system encourages. Treasure and Collier (Chapter 8) advocate "dimensional categories". I remain to be convinced that this is the right concept, though it is more likely to be effective than the black and white dichotomies of diagnosis. Is there any real need to engage in categorization at all, beyond the relatively arbitrary guidelines that we develop regarding who is offered treatment?

Second, there is a rather defensive element to diagnosis, whereby we as clinicians seek to define ourselves as being in a different class from the unfortunate souls who present to us. To achieve this, we have to be able to find clear differences between ourselves and our patients. Black and white thinking is very helpful here. We feel more positive about our own eating and our alcohol intake because they are rarely as bad as those of our patients – except at Christmas, and our birthday maybe, and no one counts Saturdays, do they . . .? In our service, we hold large team meetings to reach decisions about what treatment to offer an individual who we have recently assessed. One of the delights of my week is to listen to a colleague describing what a patient eats in a typical binge, and observing the degree of disparity between team members when deciding if this is a true binge (and I do not exclude myself from the uncertainty engendered). Mercifully, Laurence *et al.* (2003) have shown that our team's lack of agreement is far from unique, and that it reflects human belief systems.

Third, I worry that there is a tendency to build artificial black and white barriers when deciding if individuals have "true" eating disorders. In my own team, we often have to remind ourselves that there is no reason why having other problems (such as a learning disability or psychosis) means that an eating disorder can be dismissed as "not our concern". To an extent, it seems to me that some workers in this field are keen to work with restrictive anorexics as the only "true" eating disordered patients. This approach seems to reflect the same aesthetic that permeates society – thin and restrictive is more virtuous than any other female form. If we cannot get past this particular form of black and white thinking, can we really expect to help our patients to do so?

Finally, we draw conclusions about the viability of treatment that are not justified by reference to the patient who is in front of us. Over the 15 years that I have worked in this field, I have been informed by experts about many limitations on our capacity to treat patients with the eating disorders. These include conclusions that: there is no point in trying to treat someone with a history of AN of longer than ten years; patients with eating disorders have a fundamental incapacity to understand emotions; patients with comorbid personality disorders cannot be treated for their eating disorder; and menstrual function will return once the individual gets to a set weight. Each of these clinicians' beliefs has been given with utter sincerity: each is wrong to a greater or lesser degree for a greater or lesser number of patients. (I am, of course, worried about how many pronouncements I have made that will be held up to justified ridicule in future years. Bob Dylan offered good advice when he reminded us: "Don't follow leaders", but then he went on to suggest that we should "Watch the parking meters", so discretion is advised.)

Prototypes

As clinicians, our human information processing frailties also manifest in the form of prototypical representations. Cognitive psychologists have long been able to demonstrate that we assume a "typical" form based on a composite derived from a set of individual cases, none of which exactly matches the prototype. The consequence of unacknowledged prototyping is that our mental typologies (of cases, outcomes of treatment, etc.) are not necessarily reflective of any single case. So what is it that we are treating when we gear up around the "typical" patient groups?

Fuzzy sets: a potential solution to the problem of differentiating the eating disorders?

A valuable cognitive construct here is the "fuzzy set". This might be the most useful tool that we can use in understanding the categorization of the eating disorders. The fuzzy set is a grouping that often makes intuitive sense, but around which it is difficult to draw clear boundaries. A common example is the human assumption that there is a clear differentiation between the animal and the plant kingdoms – an assumption that biologists and zoologists are less certain about. This lack of differentiation does not mean that we need to doubt the position of the central exemplars (e.g. there is no suggestion that a dog is not an animal) or the characteristics of those exemplars (e.g. the dependence on oxygen), but it does allow that the effort to create hard boundaries is unhelpful. We need no finer example than the efforts that have been made to define a binge. Bisaga and Walsh (Chapter 2) have shown how this definition has changed with increased efforts to ensure that patients are given a firm diagnosis, though the fuzzier the definition, the harder it is to say that a particular episode is a "true" binge.

Efforts to promote a transdiagnostic approach to the eating disorders (e.g. Fairburn *et al.* 2003; Waller 1993) are based on the implicit assumption that the easiest way of understanding the eating disorders is to think of them as a single fuzzy set. The core features can be described as eating concerns and the belief that eating must be rigidly controlled in order to avoid weight gain. There will be correlational and causal links to other features (e.g. body image disturbance, weight loss, bingeing, exercise, physical illness, age, impulsive behaviour, gender). It is clinically useful or necessary to be aware of and to respond to those features, but there is little clinical utility in placing individuals into subcategories on the basis of those features. They simply distract from the core pathology.

Thus, at a stroke, the "problem" of atypical eating disorders can be solved. If there is only one class of eating disorder (DSM-V Eating Disorder, defined by the core features outlined above) with a range of behavioural manifestations, then the only issue is defining the fuzzy boundary around all eating disorders. We appear to have a simple solution to a problem that was made more complex by the human drive to create subdivisions. Of course, the fuzziness of the overall boundary means that we still have to decide if we should be focusing on those who experience subjective eating distress or social isolation as a result of their eating problem. More importantly, is there any clear, coherent and objective reason why we do not include obesity as an eating disorder? Oh dear – things seem to have become complicated again, though for sociopolitical reasons, rather than clinical or scientific ones.

Who is diagnosis meant to benefit?

Of course, there is only the slimmest of possibilities that DSM-V will have a single category of eating disorders. If the existing proliferation continues, then we should expect more diagnoses, rather than fewer. Those diagnoses will be supported by even more convoluted diagnostic criteria, which utterly fail to be objective. Why should I be so pessimistic? The reason for this lies in who creates the diagnostic schemes, and who they are designed to serve. The key question is: who is diagnosis meant to benefit? The following is an unashamedly personal view.

The natural order of things

First, it can be argued that eating disorder diagnoses reflect natural clusters of behaviours and attitudes, rather than being for anyone's benefit. This phenomenological argument holds broadly true (though not entirely) for some behaviours. However, it can be argued that many such linkages are relatively trivial, in that they are relatively inevitable. For example, two of the key diagnostic criteria for AN are a sustained low weight and a sustained loss of menstrual function (see Appendix). It is hard to argue that these are independent. Similarly, diagnostic schemes assume that purging behaviours are unitary, when it is clear that they do not cluster in that way in the behaviour of real patients (e.g. Vaz et al. 2001). The other argument against the phenomenological view of existing diagnoses is that individuals do not remain in one category, as one would expect if there was such consistency. Indeed, they do not even move from one disorder to another in any consistent way (Fairburn and Harrison 2003).

The research perspective

There is little doubt that the scientific bent is towards creating categories. When I send an article to a journal, I do my best to have accurate diagnoses for each patient, because I know that this will be an issue that is raised by the reviewers and editors. Replicability is an important aspect of any scientific report, and it is hard to replicate an EDNOS group, due to its diversity. The danger is that we forget two key principles. First, as Lewis Carroll has reminded us, having a name for something does not mean that we understand it (or that it even exists). Second, the fact that we treat diagnosis as a given means that we do not focus on the more clinically important elements of the eating disorders. However, I am happy to note that there is significant but promising inconsistency in the way that clinical researchers use diagnosis, since they are rarely satisfied that simply moving the individual out of the "diagnosable" slot means that the individual has truly recovered.

The insurance perspective

There is no doubt that the concept of managed care has done a lot to rein in rising medical costs in some countries. However, it has become increasingly clear that the diagnostic labels used for such a system are not resulting in appropriate treatment for many of our patients. In many cases, the impression is of clinicians rebadging their work in order to be eligible to claim from an insurance company. Why should those of us who do not work in such a setting have to use diagnostic labels whose function is to allow an insurance company in another country to determine (often arbitrarily) how much they are prepared to spend on treatment?

The clinician's perspective

Some clinicians like diagnosis because it makes them feel that they know what they are dealing with. Unfortunately, there is little evidence that diagnoses are applied accurately. My own experience suggests that many clinicians do not have a clear idea of the difference between diagnostic categories and sub-categories (particularly where there is no need to generate diagnoses for insurance purposes). This is not necessarily ignorance or a lack of professional behaviour on the part of the clinicians. I believe that many of those clinicians do not give much attention to diagnostic criteria because those criteria simply do not matter in everyday clinical practice. In a similar vein, there is even less evidence that diagnosis has a particular impact on treatment. Most clinicians seem to have worked out that symptoms matter more than syndromes. Of course, there will always be a minority of clinicians who do not have any understanding of the eating disorders or of what will work in treatment. However, it is a profound error to assume that clinicians who are not worried about diagnosis are ignorant. Many are simply acknowledging (albeit often in an implicit way) the futility of the system.

One article in this field is that deserves far more attention than it has received is the work of Westen and Harnden-Fischer (2001). These authors have examined the subtyping of eating disorder cases that clinicians do intuitively (despite a diagnosis-based "managed care" culture). They have demonstrated that clinicians see three clusters of patients with eating disorders, which are personality-based rather than symptom-based – a "high-functioning perfectionist" group, a "constricted/overcontrolled" group and a "dysregulated/undercontrolled" group. It is clear that these clusters do not map onto existing diagnoses or treatment programmes. We need more work of this sort.

The carer's perspective

While some carers do not want to know about the patient's eating disorder, I find that many are keen to know the patient's diagnosis. In a way, this seems to validate their concerns about the patient. However, this is not going to be a sufficient explanation of why the eating disorder has developed or what can be done to help all those involved. It is also important to ensure that the carer is not left with the pessimistic view that no change is possible (as can happen when a diagnosis has been given and when black and white thinking comes into play), as this can impair the patient's progress.

The patient's perspective

Some patients have very negative reactions to diagnosis, experiencing being diagnosed as being pigeonholed rather than being understood. Others express confusion about diagnosis, having been in receipt of two or more distinct eating disorder diagnoses at successive assessments. A few patients are desperate to know their diagnosis (I often find that such patients are looking for an identity, and might be reluctant to let go of that identity once they have found it – the "pro-anorexia" websites seem to provide extreme examples). However, the majority of patients who I work with are not particularly concerned about their diagnosis. Their concerns are about whether I think they have an eating problem, and whether it merits help (as many believe that everybody else has a much more serious problem than they do, and that their own case for treatment is negligible).

Summary

Diagnostic groupings do not map onto phenomenology or onto clinician opinions. They do not reflect patient views very well, and are not always helpful for carers. They work for insurance companies and researchers. Is this really the function that we want DSM-V or ICD-11 to serve? Is it justifiable that we treat particular eating disorders as being "typical", and thus exclude the individuals who fall outside our self-defined remit? In case anyone is thinking about it, I can only conclude that the answer to both questions is a resounding "no".

Conclusion

This whole volume has demonstrated the importance of understanding those eating disordered patients who have come to be labelled as "atypical". My aim here has been to understand diagnosis, in order to explain how and why we have arrived at a situation where some eating disordered patients are seen as typical while many others are not. If diagnosis into "typical" categories has no external logic, then nor does the concept of atypical cases.

There are many reasons why we diagnose, none of which seem to be supported by a solid body of facts. Nor do our diagnoses reflect any coherent differentiating psychological factors in the eating disorders. Rather, the biggest drive behind our use of "typicality" seems to be the psychology of the person doing the diagnosis. The primary beneficiaries seem to be the medical insurance industry, the research community and a few lazy clinicians. Most notably, the transdiagnostic approach reflects the fact that our patients do not seem to derive any particular benefit from being defined as belonging to a specific "typical" group. However, paradoxically, our highly constrained knowledge base means that they are likely to suffer from *not* being typical.

The clearest solution to this problem would be to abandon our efforts to create subcategories, and to get used to working with core features of "eating disorders". This "fuzzy set" approach means that we can get on with the business of understanding the true complexity of the eating disorders, while still learning lessons that allow us to employ heuristics that mean that we can apply treatments that are likely to work across cases. We just need to ensure that we are focusing on eating and related pathology, rather than diagnoses. With such an approach, there would be no typical or atypical cases. After decades of trying to come up with a perfect diagnostic system (or even an adequate one), the time has surely come to try an approach with rational roots rather than irrational ones.

References

Arkes, H.R. and Harkness, A.R. (1980) "Effect of making a diagnosis on subsequent recognition of symptoms", *Journal of Experimental Psychology* 6, 568–75.

Christie, A. (1948) *Taken at the Flood*, London: Collins.

Fairburn, C.G. and Harrison, P.J. (2003) "Eating disorders", *Lancet* 361, 407–16.

Fairburn, C.G., Cooper, Z. and Shafran, R. (2003) "Cognitive behaviour therapy for eating disorders: a 'transdiagnostic' theory and treatment", *Behaviour Research and Therapy* 41, 509–28.

Laurence, B., Campbell, M., Neiderman, M. and Serpell, L. (2003) "Size really doesn't matter", *European Eating Disorders Review* 11, 397–404.

Nielsen, S. and Palmer, R. (2003) "Diagnosing eating disorders – AN, BN and the others", *Acta Psychiatrica Scandinavica* 108, 161–2.

Spector, M. and Kitsuse, J.I. (1987) *Constructing Social Problems*, New York: Aldine de Gruyter.

Turner, H. and Bryant-Waugh, R. (2004) "Eating disorder not otherwise specified (EDNOS): profiles of patients presenting at a community eating disorder service", *European Eating Disorders Review* 12, 18–26.

Vaz, F.J., Peñas, E.M., Ramos, M.I., Lopez-Ibor, J.J. and Guisado, J.A. (2001) "Subtype criteria for BN: short- versus long-term compensatory behaviours", *Eating Disorders* 9, 301–11.

Waller, G. (1993) "Why do we diagnose different types of eating disorder? Arguments for a change in research and clinical practice", *Eating Disorders Review* 1, 74–89.

Westen, D. and Harnden-Fischer, J. (2001) "Personality profiles in eating disorders: rethinking the distinction between axis I and axis II", *American Journal of Psychiatry* 158, 547–62.

Appendix

Current diagnostic criteria for the eating disorders

Diagnostic and Statistical Manual of Mental Disorders, 4th edn (DSM-IV, APA 1994)

Anorexia Nervosa

A   Refusal to maintain body weight at or above a minimal normal weight for age and height (e.g. weight loss leading to maintenance of body weight less than 85% of that expected; or failure to make expected weight gain during period of growth, leading to body weight less than 85 per cent of that expected).

B   Intense fear of gaining weight or becoming fat, even though underweight.

C   Disturbance in the way in which one's body weight or shape is experienced, undue influence of body weight or shape on self-evaluation, denial of the seriousness of the current low body weight.

D   In postmenarcheal females, amenorrhoea, i.e. the absence of at least three consecutive menstrual cycles. (A woman is considered to have amenorrhoea if her periods occur only following hormone administration, e.g. oestrogen.)

Specify type:

•   Restricting type: during the current episode of Anorexia Nervosa, the person has not regularly engaged in binge eating or purging behaviour (i.e. self-induced vomiting or the misuse of laxatives, diuretics or enemas)

•   Binge eating/purging type: during the current episode of Anorexia Nervosa, the person has regularly engaged in binge eating or purging behaviour (i.e. self-induced vomiting or misuse of laxatives, diuretics or enemas).

Bulimia Nervosa

A   Recurrent episodes of binge eating. An episode of binge eating is characterized by both of the following:

1   eating, in a discrete period of time (e.g. within any two-hour
period), an amount of food that is definitely larger than most
people would eat during a similar period of time and under similar
circumstances

2   a sense of lack of control over eating during the episode (e.g. a feeling
that one cannot stop eating or control what or how much one is
eating).

B   Recurrent inappropriate compensatory behaviour in order to prevent
weight gain, such as self-induced vomiting; misuse of laxatives, diuretics,
enemas or other medications; fasting; or excessive exercise.

C   The binge eating and inappropriate compensatory behaviours both occur,
on average, at least twice a week for three months.

D   Self-evaluation is unduly influenced by body shape and weight.

E   The disturbance does not occur exclusively during episodes of Anorexia
Nervosa.

Specify type:

•   Purging type: during the current episode of Bulimia Nervosa, the person
has regularly engaged in self-induced vomiting or the misuse of laxatives,
diuretics or enemas.

•   Non-purging type: during the current episode of Bulimia Nervosa, the
person has used other inappropriate compensatory behaviours, such as
fasting or excessive exercise, but has not engaged in self-induced vomiting
or the misuse of laxatives, diuretics or enemas.

Eating Disorder Not Otherwise Specified

The EDNOS category is for disorders of eating that do not meet the criteria
for any specific eating disorder. Examples include:

1   For females, all of the criteria for Anorexia Nervosa are met except that
the individual has regular menses.

2   All of the criteria for Anorexia Nervosa are met except that, despite
significant weight loss, the individual's current weight is in the normal
range.

3   All of the criteria for Bulimia Nervosa are met except that the binge
eating and inappropriate compensatory mechanisms occur at a frequency
of less than twice a week or for a duration of less than three months.

4   The regular use of inappropriate compensatory behaviour by an individual of normal body weight after eating small amounts of food (e.g.
self-induced vomiting after the consumption of two cookies).
5   Repeatedly chewing and spitting out, but not swallowing, large amounts
of food.
6   Binge eating disorder: recurrent episodes of binge eating in the absence of
the regular use of inappropriate compensatory behaviours characteristic
of Bulimia Nervosa.

Binge Eating Disorder (provisional criteria for research)

A   Recurrent episodes of binge eating. An episode of binge eating is characterized by both of the following:

1   eating, in a discrete period of time (e.g. within any two-hour period),
an amount of food that is definitely larger than most people would
eat in a similar period of time under similar circumstances
2   a sense of lack of control over eating during the episode (e.g. a feeling
that one cannot stop eating or control what or how much one is
eating).

B   The binge-eating episodes are associated with three (or more) of the
following:

1   eating much more rapidly than normal
2   eating until feeling uncomfortably full
3   eating large amounts of food when not feeling physically hungry
4   eating alone because of being embarrassed by how much one is eating
5   feeling disgusted with oneself, depressed, or very guilty after
overeating.

C   Marked distress regarding binge eating is present.
D   The binge eating occurs, on average, at least two days a week for six
months.
Note: The method of determining frequency differs from that used for
Bulimia Nervosa; future research should address whether the preferred
method of setting a frequency threshold is counting the number of days on
which binges occur or counting the number of episodes of binge eating.
E   The binge eating is not associated with the regular use of inappropriate
compensatory behaviors (e.g. purging, fasting, excessive exercise) and
does not occur exclusively during the course of Anorexia Nervosa or
Bulimia Nervosa.

American Psychiatric Association (1994) *Diagnostic and Statistical Manual
of Mental Disorders*, 4th edn (DSM-IV), Washington, DC: APA.

International Statistical Classification of Diseases and Related Health Problems, 10th rev (ICD-10, WHO 1992) (Clinical Descriptions and Diagnostic Guidelines)

F50.0 Anorexia Nervosa

For a definite diagnosis, all the following are required:

(a) Body weight is maintained at least 15 per cent below that expected (either lost or never achieved), or Quetelet's body mass index is 17.5 or less. Pre-pubertal patients may show failure to make the expected weight gain during the period of growth.

(b) The weight loss is self-induced by avoidance of "fattening foods" and one or more of the following: self-induced vomiting; self-induced purging; excessive exercise; use of appetite suppressants and/or diuretics.

(c) There is body image distortion in the form of a specific psychopathology whereby a dread of fatness persists as an intrusive, overvalued idea and the patient imposes a low weight threshold on himself or herself.

(d) A widespread endocrine disorder involving the hypothalamic–pituitary–gonadal axis is manifest in women as amenorrhoea and in men as a loss of sexual interest and potency. (An apparent exception is the persistence of vaginal bleeds in anorectic women who are receiving replacement hormonal therapy, most commonly taken as a contraceptive pill.) There may also be elevated levels of growth hormone, raised levels of cortisol, changes in the peripheral metabolism of the thyroid hormone, and abnormalities of insulin secretion.

(e) If onset is pre-pubertal, the sequence of pubertal event is delayed or even arrested (growth ceases; in girls the breasts do not develop and there is a primary amenorrhoea; in boys the genitals remain juvenile). With recovery, puberty is often completed normally, but the menarche is late.

F50.2 Bulimia Nervosa

For a definite diagnosis, all the following are required:

(a) There is a persistent preoccupation with eating, and an irresistible craving for food; the patient succumbs to episodes of overeating in which large amounts of food are consumed in short periods of time.

(b) The patient attempts to counteract the "fattening" effects of food by one or more of the following: self-induced vomiting; purgative abuse, alternating periods of starvation; use of drugs such as appetite suppressants, thyroid preparations or diuretics. When bulimia occurs in diabetic patients they may choose to neglect their insulin treatment.

(c) The psychopathology consists of morbid fear of fatness and the patient sets himself or herself a sharply defined weight threshold, well below the premorbid weight that constitutes the optimum or healthy weight in the opinion of the physician. There is often, but not always, a history of an earlier episode of Anorexia Nervosa, the interval ranging from a few months to several years. This earlier episode may have been fully expressed, or may have assumed a minor cryptic form with a moderate weight loss and/or a transient phase of amenorrhoea.

Includes: bulimia NOS
               hyperorexia nervosa.

Atypical Eating Disorders

F50.1 Atypical Anorexia Nervosa

This term should be used for those individuals in whom one or more of the key features of Anorexia Nervosa (F50.0), such as amenorrhoea or significant weight loss, is absent, but who otherwise present a fairly typical clinical picture. Such people are usually encountered in psychiatric liaison services in general hospitals or in primary care. Patients who have all the key symptoms but to only a mild degree may also be best described by this term. This term should not be used for eating disorders that resemble Anorexia Nervosa but that are due to known physical illness.

F50.3 Atypical Bulimia Nervosa

This term should be used for those individuals in whom one or more of the key features listed for Bulimia Nervosa (F50.2) is absent, but who otherwise present a fairly typical picture. Most commonly this applies to people with normal or even excessive weight but with typical periods of overeating followed by vomiting or purging. Partial syndromes together with depressive symptoms are not uncommon, but if the depressive symptoms justify a separate diagnosis of a depressive disorder two separate diagnoses should be made.
Includes: normal weight bulimia.

F50.4 Overeating associated with other psychological disturbances

Overeating that has led to obesity as a reaction to distressing events should be noted here. Bereavements, accidents, surgical operations and emotionally distressing events may be followed by a "reactive obesity", especially in individuals predisposed to weight gain.
Includes: psychogenic overeating.

F50.5 Vomiting associated with other psychological disturbances

Apart from the self-induced vomiting of Bulimia Nervosa, repeated vomiting may occur in dissociative disorders (F44.–), hypochondriacal disorder (F45.2) when vomiting may be one of several bodily symptoms, and in pregnancy when emotional factors may contribute to recurrent nausea and vomiting.
Includes: psychogenic hyperemesis gravidarum
            psychogenic vomiting.

F50.8 Other eating disorders

Includes: pica of non-organic origin in adults
            psychogenic loss of appetite.

F50.9 Eating disorder, unspecified

World Health Organization (1992) *ICD-10 Classification of Mental and Behavioural Disorders. Clinical Descriptions and Diagnostic Guidelines*, Geneva: WHO.

International Statistical Classification of Diseases and Related Health Problems, 10th rev (ICD-10, WHO 1993) (diagnostic criteria for research)

F50.0 Anorexia Nervosa

A   There is weight loss or, in children, a lack of weight gain, leading to a body weight at least 15 per cent below the normal or expected weight for age and height.
B   The weight loss is self-induced by avoidance of "fattening foods".
C   There is self-perception of being too fat, with an intrusive dread of fatness, which leads to a self-imposed low weight threshold.
D   A widespread endocrine disorder involving the hypothalamic–pituitary–gonadal axis is manifest in women as amenorrhoea and in men as a loss of sexual interest and potency. (An apparent exception is the persistence of vaginal bleeds in anorexic women who are on replacement hormonal therapy, most commonly taken as a contraceptive pill.)
E   The disorder does not meet criteria A and B for Bulimia Nervosa (F50.2).

Comments

The following features support the diagnosis, but are not essential elements: self-induced vomiting, self-induced purging, excessive exercise, and use of appetite suppressants and/or diuretics.

If onset is pre-pubertal, the sequence of pubertal events is delayed or even arrested (growth ceases; in girls the breasts do not develop and there is a primary amenorrhoea; in boys the genitals remain juvenile). With recovery, puberty is often completed normally, but the menarche is late.

F50.2 Bulimia Nervosa

A There are recurrent episodes of overeating (at least twice a week over a period of three months) in which large amounts of food are consumed in short periods of time.

B There is persistent preoccupation with eating, and a strong desire or sense of compulsion to eat (craving).

C The patient attempts to counteract the "fattening" effects of food by one or more of the following:

1   self-induced vomiting
2   self-induced purging
3   alternating periods of starvation
4   use of drugs such as appetite suppressants, thyroid preparations, or diuretics; when bulimia occurs in diabetic patients they may choose to neglect their insulin treatments.

D There is self-perception of being too fat, with an intrusive dread of fatness (usually leading to underweight).

Atypical Eating Disorders

F50.1 Atypical Anorexia Nervosa

Researchers studying atypical forms of Anorexia Nervosa are recommended to make their own decisions about the number and type of criteria to be fulfilled.

F50.3 Atypical Bulimia Nervosa

Researchers studying atypical forms of Bulimia Nervosa, such as those involving normal or excessive body weight, are recommended to make their own decisions about the number and type of criteria to be fulfilled.

F50.4 Overeating associated with other psychological disturbances

Researchers wishing to use this category are recommended to design their own criteria.

F50.5 Vomiting associated with other psychological disturbances

Researchers wishing to use this category are recommended to design their own criteria.

F50.8 Other eating disorders
F50.9 Eating disorder, unspecified

World Health Organization (1993) *ICD-10 Classification of Mental and Behavioural Disorders: Diagnostic Criteria for Research*, Geneva: WHO.

Index